THE LAST GUN

THE LAST GUN

How Changes in the Gun Industry Are Killing Americans and What It Will Take to Stop It

Tom Diaz

THE NEW PRESS

NEW YORK
LONDON

Requests for permission to reproduce selections from this book should be mailed to:
Permissions Department, The New Press, 38 Greene Street, New York, NY 10013.

Published in the United States by The New Press, New York, 2013
Distributed by Perseus Distribution

LIBRARY OF CONGRESS CATALOGING-IN-PUBLICATION DATA

Diaz, Tom.
    The last gun : how changes in the gun industry are killing Americans and
what it will take to stop it / Tom Diaz.
        pages   cm
    Includes bibliographical references.
    ISBN 978-1-59558-830-2 (hardcover : alk. paper) — ISBN 978-1-59558-841-8
(e-book)   1. Firearms industry and trade—United States.   2. Firearms—Law and
legislation—United States.   3. Gun control—United States.   I. Title.
    HD9744.F553U628   2013
    338.4'7683400973—dc23   2012047230

The New Press publishes books that promote and enrich public discussion and
understanding of the issues vital to our democracy and to a more equitable world.
These books are made possible by the enthusiasm of our readers; the support of a
committed group of donors, large and small; the collaboration of our many partners
in the independent media and the not-for-profit sector; booksellers, who often hand-
sell New Press books; librarians; and above all by our authors.

www.thenewpress.com

Composition by dix!
This book was set in Minion

Printed in the United States of America

10   9   8   7   6   5   4   3   2   1

With the deepest humility, I dedicate this book
to all of the sons, daughters, brothers, sisters, mothers,
fathers, aunts, uncles, grandparents, grandchildren, friends,
neighbors, companions, and passing strangers whose lives
have been needlessly cut short by gun violence in America,
and to the many times that who are our walking wounded,
mutilated in body and soul by guns, and to the many,
many more times the sum of all of that whose arms
and hearts ache day and night for the embrace
of their forever lost loved ones.

May a compassionate God have mercy on us all.

CONTENTS

ACKNOWLEDGMENTS

This book would not have been possible without the support of my former employer the Violence Policy Center. Executive director Josh Sugarmann did yeoman work in checking facts and offering substantive suggestions for the text. Marty Langley helped enormously in gathering data and assembling it into charts and tables. Kristen Rand's encyclopedic knowledge of federal law was invaluable.

The New Press and its fine staff are, of course, the keystone of this book. I thank editorial director Marc Favreau for giving me the opportunity to revisit this subject in depth.

Finally, I must thank my family. Writing is solitary work. Writing a book is monastic. They have paid the price.

THE LAST GUN

INTRODUCTION
A REIGN OF TERROR

In the four decades between 1969 and 2009, a total of 5,586 people were killed in terrorist attacks against the United States or its interests, according to a May 2011 report by a conservative Washington policy institute, the Heritage Foundation. This number includes those killed in the terror attacks within the United States on September 11, 2001.[1] By comparison, more than 30,000 people were killed by guns in the United States every single year between 1986 and 2010, with the exception of four years in which the number of deaths fell slightly below 30,000—1999, 2000, 2001, and 2004. In other words, the number of people killed *every year* in the United States by guns is about five times the grand total of Americans killed in terrorist attacks anywhere in the world since 1969.[2]

Here is another perspective. In 2010, five Americans were killed worldwide by terrorist attacks.[3] In the same year, fifty-five law enforcement officers were killed by guns in the United States—out of a total of fifty-six officers killed feloniously.[4] (The fifty-sixth officer was killed by a motor vehicle.) In plain words, more than ten times the number of law enforcement officers were killed by guns in the United States in 2010 than all of the Americans killed by terrorism anywhere in the world that year.

It gets even worse. Every year, more Americans are killed by guns in the United States than people *of all nationalities* are killed *worldwide* by terrorist attacks. Figure 1 compares the number of people killed worldwide in terrorist attacks in the six years 2005 through 2010 with the number of people killed by guns in the United States in the same years.

Figure 1. Worldwide Terrorism Deaths
and U.S. Gun Deaths, 2005–10

	2005	2006	2007	2008	2009	2010
Worldwide deaths in terrorist attacks	14,560	20,487	22,719	15,708	15,310	13,186
Gun deaths in the United States	30,694	30,896	31,224	31,593	31,347	31,672

Terrorism deaths, U.S. Department of State, *Country Reports on Terrorism, 2008* and *2010*; gun deaths, 2005–2010, Department of Health and Human Services, Centers for Disease Control and Prevention, WISQARS, "2001–2010, United States Firearm Deaths and Rates per 100,000."

America has engaged in a "War Against Terrorism" at tremendous social and financial cost since the so-called 9/11 attacks of September 11, 2001. As of March 2011, the wars in Afghanistan and Iraq, and a program called Operation Noble Eagle to enhance security at military bases, had cost American taxpayers $1.283 trillion.[5] In addition to the money spent on these wars, increased federal, state, and local costs for "homeland security" totaled more than $1 trillion over the decade between September 2001 and September 2011.[6] The scholars who compiled this number concluded in their 2011 book on the subject that "most enhanced homeland security expenditures since 9/11 fail a cost-benefit assessment, it seems, some spectacularly so, and it certainly appears that many billions of dollars have been misspent."[7] According to Ohio State University professor John Mueller, one of the authors of the homeland security cost study, an American's chances of being killed in an automobile accident are about one in 7,000 or 8,000 per year; of being a victim of homicide, about one in 22,000 per year; and of being killed by a terrorist, about one in 3.5 million per year.[8]

There is little sign that this "counterterrorism state unto

itself"—as the conservative *Washington Times* called it—is likely to wither away soon.[9] The Department of Homeland Security's budget request was $56.3 billion for fiscal year 2011, $57 billion for FY 2012, and $39.5 billion for FY2013.[10] In contrast, the combined budget request for the Centers for Disease Control and Prevention and the Agency for Toxic Substances and Disease Registry was $11.3 billion for FY2012 and $11.2 billion for FY2013.[11]

The specter of terrorism that drives these costs also has inspired infringements on civil liberties that at least some would have thought unthinkable before the attacks.[12] "The courts have been failing terribly," law professor Susan N. Herman, the president of the American Civil Liberties Union, told the *New York Times* in 2011. "The Fourth Amendment has been seriously diluted."[13] One of the features of the war on terror most salient to this book's subject has been what former attorney general John Ashcroft called "a new paradigm," which among other things added the "new priority . . . of prevention" of terrorism to the Justice Department's traditional focus on criminal prosecution.[14]

The questions compel themselves.

Why is there no equivalent "war" against gun violence, which takes and shatters the lives of more Americans than does terrorism by many, many times every single year?

Why, when other articles of the Bill of Rights—such as those involving searches, wiretaps, and preventive arrests—are "balanced" against the fear of terrorism, is the Second Amendment fiercely claimed to be "untouchable" by the gun lobby and by the politicians who hew to its line, and is slavishly protected by activist conservative judges? Why do even many who favor some form of gun control continue to focus on "illegal guns" and the prosecution of criminals instead of adding "a new paradigm" of prevention?

Given the lack of widespread public outcry for a reordering of our national priorities, Americans and their political leaders appear either to be ignorant of, or to have become inured to, the endless torrent of civilian gun violence in the United States. Why?

And finally, why has the subject of gun control become, even among influential "moderate" Democrats, the "third rail" of politics?

This book examines and answers those questions. It documents in detail each of the following factors that contribute to the unique position of the United States as the world's dark archetype of gun violence:

- Levels of gun death and injury that mark the United States as a frightening aberration among industrialized nations.
- Deliberate suppression of data regarding criminal use of firearms, gun trafficking, and the public health consequences of firearms in the United States.
- The almost universal failure of the American news media to report on, even to understand, the continuing hurricane of gun violence in America.
- Aggressive "hypermarketing" of increasingly lethal weapons by a faltering industry.
- Militarization of the civilian gun market as the driving force in that marketing.
- Indifference by policy makers who might be expected to lead on gun control, and widespread acquiescence by elected officials to the gun lobby's unrelenting legislative campaigns.

The intricate interweaving of these factors is aptly illustrated by an incident that occurred on Schriever Air Force Base in Colorado on November 21, 2011. On that date, at about ten o'clock in the morning, Airman First Class Nico Cruz Santos barricaded himself in a building, armed with his personal handgun.[15] The base, located near Colorado Springs, is home to the Fiftieth Space Wing, responsible for operating U.S. Department of Defense space satellites.[16]

Santos was serving in a squadron that "provides physical security, force protections measures and law enforcement services" to the wing.[17] He appears to have been a troubled person, reacting to his imminent discharge from the air force and possible imprisonment after having pleaded guilty in a civilian court to a charge of attempted sexual exploitation of a child.[18] Airman Santos surrendered without violence at about eight P.M.

The building in which Santos barricaded himself was a personnel processing center, a facility in which airmen are prepared for deployment. That fact brought immediately to mind the events of November 5, 2009, when U.S. Army Major Nidal M. Hasan is alleged to have gone on a rampage with his personal handgun in a similar deployment center at Fort Hood, Texas. Hasan left a total of thirteen dead and thirty-two wounded.[19] Major Hasan was subdued only after he was shot several times by police.

In the interval between the two events, and as a direct consequence of the Pentagon's reaction to Major Hasan's attack at Fort Hood, Congress imposed a significant restriction on the Department of Defense. Sandwiched between two sections of the defense authorization bill for fiscal year (FY) 2011, mandating public access to Pentagon reports and establishing criteria for determining the safety of nuclear weapons, was a new provision, Section 1062, "Prohibition on infringing on the individual right to lawfully acquire, possess, own, carry, and otherwise use privately owned firearms, ammunition, and other weapons."[20] As a result of that change in law, General Peter Chiarelli, the army's second-in-command, told the *Christian Science Monitor* in November 2011, "I am not allowed to ask a soldier who lives off post whether that soldier has a privately owned weapon."[21] The prohibition covers both members of the military and civilian employees of the Defense Department.

The massacre of which Major Nidal Hasan is accused generated a great deal of attention from the news media, policy makers, and politicians. However, most of this attention focused on two points: whether the mass shooting should be classified as a terrorist attack by "violent Islamist extremism,"[22] and where blame should be assigned within the nation's military and intelligence apparatuses for failure to anticipate and head off the rampage.[23]

Little media reporting and virtually no official scrutiny has been devoted to the singular implement with which Major Hasan is accused of mowing down forty-five of his comrades-in-arms within ten minutes. This was an FN Five-seveN, a 5.7mm high-capacity semiautomatic pistol manufactured by the Belgian armaments maker FN Herstal (FN).[24]

In one significant example, the U.S. Senate Committee on Homeland Security and Governmental Affairs issued a report purporting to address the "counterterrorism lessons" to be drawn from the Fort Hood matter. But the committee's report emphasized that it had not "examined . . . the facts of what happened during the attack."[25] The word *gun* or *firearm* appears nowhere in the committee's report, much less the make, model, and caliber of the efficient killing machine Major Hasan is accused of using. The committee described the incident itself in two sentences, as a "lone attacker" striding into the center, and "moments later," thirteen "employees" of the Defense Department "were dead and another 32 were wounded," all by some unnamed cause.[26] This is the remarkable equivalent of issuing a "lessons learned" report on the notorious 1995 bombing of the federal building in Oklahoma City without mentioning the truck bomb by which its principal perpetrator, Timothy McVeigh, carried out his attack, or presenting a lecture on the implications of the terrorist attacks of September 11, 2001, without addressing the use of commandeered jetliners as flying bombs. The omission is all the more remarkable because the committee chairman and co-author of the report, Senator Joseph I. Lieberman, had stated in a May 2010 hearing on terrorists and guns that "the only two terrorist attacks on America since 9/11 that have been carried out and taken American lives were with firearms."[27] He cited the Fort Hood shooting and the 2009 murder of an army recruiter in Little Rock, Arkansas, as the two attacks.

But according to testimony at a pretrial hearing, Major Hasan himself paid keen attention to selecting the weapon he used. He chose the FN Five-seveN pistol, and the accessories of laser aiming devices and high-capacity ammunition magazines, precisely because they suited his purpose of efficiently attacking a large number of people.[28] Thus, before buying the handgun on August 1, 2009, Hasan asked a salesman at the Guns Galore gun dealer in Killeen, Texas, for "the most high-tech gun" available. Another witness, Specialist William Gilbert, a soldier and self-described "gun aficionado" who was in the store when Major Hasan made his inquiry, testified that the accused also sought maximum ammunition magazine capacity. Specialist Gilbert further testified that he owned an FN Five-seveN himself, and that he had recommended that model to Major Hasan because it met the officer's stated specifications. "It's extremely lightweight and very, very, very accurate," said Specialist Gilbert. "It's easy to fire and has minimum recoil."[29] The soldier testified that he gave Major Hasan a forty-five-minute "full tactical demonstration" of the handgun's capabilities.[30] According to the manufacturer, those capabilities are considerable. "Five-seveN Tactical handguns and SS190 ball ammunition team up to defeat the enemy in all close combat situations in urban areas, jungle conditions, night missions, etc. and for any self-defense action."[31]

Specialist Gilbert and the salesman both noted that Major Hasan seemed to know nothing about handguns. The accused officer videotaped on his cell phone the salesman's demonstration of how to load and clean the weapon so that he could review these procedures later.

In the several months between his purchase of the handgun and the shootings at Fort Hood, Major Hasan also bought several extra ammunition magazines and magazine extenders that increased to thirty the number of rounds available to be fired in each loading of the gun, from the usual twenty.[32] He bought two expensive laser aiming devices, a green one for use in daylight and a red one for use at night. The major also bought hundreds of rounds of the 5.7×28mm ammunition the gun fires, including boxes of a variant specifically designed to penetrate body armor. According to testimony at the hearing, the line of ammunition in question had been ordered off the U.S. civilian market, but dealers were allowed to sell their existing stocks.[33]

Major Hasan was a frequent visitor to Stan's Outdoor Shooting Range, near Fort Hood, where he took a course to qualify for a concealed-carry permit. Witnesses said Major Hasan practiced at the range repeatedly. He specifically sought training in shooting at human targets from as far away as a hundred yards. Instructor John Coats testified that after one afternoon's tutelage, Major Hasan progressed from being an erratic shot to routinely hitting each target's head and chest. This is consistent with FN's boast that "the flat trajectory of the 5.7×28mm ammunition guarantees a high hit probability up to 200 m. Extremely low recoil results in quick and accurate firing."[34]

On the morning of November 5, 2009, Major Hasan allegedly put his high-tech weapon and training to use when he opened fire with his FN Five-seveN in a crowded waiting area near the entrance to Building 42003, a facility for processing soldiers being deployed. Ten minutes later, he lay paralyzed from the chest down, shot by police. When the bloodbath ended, twelve soldiers and one civilian had been shot dead. An additional thirty-one soldiers and one police officer were wounded. A number of other people were injured in the scramble to escape the methodical shooting. Army investigators found more than 200 spent 5.7mm rounds in and around Building 42003. So many rounds were fired that shell casings lodged in the tread of the shooter's boots, survivors testified, so that they could hear a clicking noise at every step he took. "You could hear the clack, clack, clack at the same time you could hear the bang, bang, bang of the guns," one testified.[35] Major Hasan had another 177 unfired rounds in high-capacity magazines when he was stopped.

Witnesses testified that the defendant reloaded often and effortlessly as he calmly walked though the building. One survivor, Specialist Logan Burnett, tried to rush the shooter when he saw an expended magazine fall from the pistol, but was shot in the head before he could reach the gunman. Another soldier contemplated also charging, but testified that the shooter reloaded magazines too quickly for him to act.[36]

Virtually none of the detailed testimony at Major Hasan's pretrial hearing has been reported in the news media. With the exception of newspapers in Texas and a handful of articles in other states, the details of Major Hassan's alleged massacre were not "newsworthy." And although mass shootings, cop-killings, and family annihilations have become virtually weekly events in the United States, their coverage by the news media is spotty. For all of the attention the Fort Hood affair generated in the media and particularly in the Congress, its toll of dead and injured was no greater than a number of civilian mass shootings involving handguns. These include the April 2009 shooting at the American Civic Association in Binghamton, New York (thirteen dead, four wounded), the April 2007 shooting at Virginia Tech in Blacksburg, Virginia (thirty-two dead, seventeen wounded), and the October 1991 shooting at Luby's Cafeteria in Killeen, Texas (twenty-three dead, twenty wounded). Many other civilian mass shootings have taken somewhat lesser tolls, such as the January 2011 shooting in Tucson, Arizona, in which U.S. Representative Gabrielle Giffords was gravely injured (six dead, thirteen wounded).[37]

Like the news media, the Department of Defense also appears to have missed the significance of the incredible level of firepower that was easily available to Major Hasan. After the Fort Hood shooting, Secretary of Defense Robert M. Gates appointed Togo D. West Jr., a former secretary of the army, and Admiral Vernon E. Clark, a former chief of naval operations, to conduct a review of the incident. The review focused primarily on how well the Defense Department was prepared to meet similar incidents in the future and how the department's policies might better deal with personnel like the alleged shooter. Aside from a single reference to an unnamed "gunman" having "opened fire," the report of the review neither described nor inquired into the means—the FN Five-seveN pistol, the high-capacity ammunition magazines, and the laser aiming devices—by which Major Hasan allegedly wreaked such great havoc in so short a time.[38] An appendix to the report, however, stated the finding that "the Department of Defense does not have a policy governing privately owned weapons," and recommended that the department "review the need for DoD privately owned weapons policy."[39]

Three months later, the Department of Defense announced its follow-up action on twenty-six of the seventy-nine recommendations of the independent review.[40] A detailed list accompanying Secretary Gates's action memorandum noted with respect to privately owned weapons that each of the individual armed services had developed its own policies and had delegated authority to base commanders to generate specific rules.[41] According to media reports, the commanders of some bases—including Fort Campbell, Kentucky; Fort Bliss, Texas; and Fort Riley, Kansas—required personnel living off post to register their personal firearms. In the case of Fort Riley, civilian dependents were also required to register their firearms.[42] The list attached to Secretary Gates's memorandum stated that the undersecretary of defense for intelligence was tasked to prepare department-wide guidance on personal guns, which would then be incorporated into the department's physical security regulations.[43]

These actions were sufficient to galvanize the National Rifle Association (NRA), the principal voice of the gun industry lobby.[44] One month after Secretary Gates's announcement, U.S. Senator Jim Inhofe introduced the "Service Member Second Amendment Protection Act of 2010," which was designed to forbid any action by the Defense Department that might affect personal weapons.[45] "Adding more gun ownership regulations on top of existing state and federal law does not address the problems associated with Hasan's case," Senator Inhofe stated in a press release. Referring to the proposed Defense Department regulations, he continued, "Political correctness and violating Constitutional rights dishonors those who lost their lives and is an extreme disservice to those who continue to serve their country." [46]

Senator Inhofe offered his bill as an amendment to the Defense Department's authorization bill for FY 2011. It was adopted by the Senate, and although no similar provision had been passed in the House version of the authorization bill, it was included in the legislation as enacted, and thus passed into law. [47] Chris W. Cox, executive director of the NRA's lobbying arm, the Institute for Legislative Action (ILA), took credit for the legislation, announcing in a "Political Report" on the matter that "your NRA has sought, and achieved, remedies to some of the worst abuses our service members have suffered, through legislation recently passed by the Congress and signed into law." [48]

The FN Five-seveN and the accessories chosen by Major Hasan are neither aberrant nor unusual products on the U.S. civilian gun market. They are, rather, typical examples of the military-style weapons that define that market today. There is no mystery in this militarization. It is simply a business strategy aimed at survival: boosting sales and improving the bottom line in a desperate and fading line of commerce. [49] The hard commercial fact is that military-style weapons sell in an increasingly narrowly focused civilian gun market. True sporting guns do not.

Like the tobacco industry, the gun lobby has gone to extreme lengths to draw a veil of secrecy over the facts surrounding its terrifying impact on American life. The tobacco industry successfully fought regulation for decades after its products were known to be pestilential. But a crack in the industry's wall of deceit and influence was opened through the process of discovery in private tort lawsuits. Putting aside compensation for the ravaging illnesses tobacco caused its victims, "litigation forced the industry to reveal its most intimate corporate strategies in the tobacco wars." [50] Discovery revealed that the tobacco industry "had not been dealing straightforwardly with the public but had been acting in deceptive ways to ease its customers' growing anxieties over the health charges." [51] This revealing light on the industry's darkest schemes helped accelerate tighter regulation—"perhaps the most significant change was the public recognition of the industry's extensive knowledge of the harms of its product, and its concerted efforts to obscure these facts through scientific disinformation and aggressive marketing."[52]

Knowing that the gun industry could only lose in any public forum in which information about the consequences of its products was freely available, the gun lobby's strategists marked well the tobacco industry's defeats in court. After tort litigation was brought against the industry by innocent victims of its lethal products and reckless marketing, the NRA succeeded in pushing though Congress the Protection of Lawful Commerce in Arms Act, which President George W. Bush signed into law in 2005.[53] This extraordinary federal law shields the gun industry against all but the most carefully and artfully crafted private lawsuits.

Another prong of the NRA's assault on freedom of information about the gun industry has been a series of so-called riders—prohibitory amendments attached to appropriations bills—that began in 2003 and have collectively come to be known as the Tiahrt amendments, after their perennial sponsor, former representative Todd Tiahrt of Kansas. These amendments have forbidden the federal Bureau of Alcohol, Tobacco, Firearms and Explosives (ATF) from releasing to the public useful information about gun trafficking and gun crimes. Although some information may be released to law enforcement agencies and ATF occasionally publishes its own limited summary reports, the agency's top officials have chosen to broadly interpret these prohibitions, virtually shutting down their responses to information requests from the general public and researchers.[54]

Section 1062 of Public Law 111–383 forbids the Department of Defense to "collect or record" any information about the private firearms of members of the military or its civilian employees, unless they relate to such arms on a defense facility proper, and further directs the department to destroy within ninety days of the date of its enactment any such records it may have previously assembled.

It was noted above that the word *gun* appears nowhere in the report of the U.S. Senate Committee on Homeland Security and Governmental Affairs regarding the shootings at Fort Hood. Like much of what goes on in Congress, the report's drafting was done behind closed doors, but some clue as to why the authors of the report chose not to mention Major Hasan's wondrously deadly weapon may be found in the words of one co-author, the committee's ranking Republican member, Senator Susan Collins, in her opening statement at the committee's hearing *Terrorists and Guns: The Nature of the Threat and Proposed Reforms.*

> For many Americans, including many Maine families, the right to own guns is part of their heritage and way of life. This right is protected by the Second Amendment.
>
> And so this Committee confronts a difficult issue today: how do we protect the constitutional right of Americans to bear arms, while preventing terrorists from using guns to carry out their murderous plans?[55]

One way to "protect the constitutional right" is simply to ignore the consequences of that right. This has increasingly been the choice of the nation's political leadership. In the words of Jim Kessler, vice president for policy at Third Way, a group distinguished both by its poll-driven policy proposals and its influence among moderate Democrats, "guns seem like the third rail."[56]

Although Congress and the White House are perfectly prepared to "balance" other constitutional rights in pursuit of the so-called war on terror, neither has even the slightest inclination to do so in the case of gun rights, notwithstanding the massively disproportionate harm guns inflict on Americans. In 2009, for example, when U.S. Attorney General Eric Holder had the temerity to suggest that Congress should reenact the expired federal assault weapons ban, then–Speaker of the House Nancy Pelosi swiftly squelched the idea. "Echoing the position often taken by advocates of gun rights," according to the *New York Times*, Pelosi observed, "On that score, I think we need to enforce the laws we have right now."[57] The issue is considered "toxic" to Democrats, according to many political observers.[58]

Staying clear of the third rail of gun control thus has become a political byword in Washington. If there was any debate at all on Senator Inhofe's amendment to the defense authorization bill, none of it appears in the public record. The proceedings both of the Senate Armed Services Committee and of the committee that reconciled the different versions of the House and Senate were closed to the public. No public statement in opposition was issued by any member of Congress nor by the Obama administration.

Thus, as the Fort Hood affair demonstrates, the gun lobby has successfully shut down information, intimidated any political opposition, and endangered all Americans by its reckless militarization of our public space. The consequences for public health and the safety of ordinary Americans are grim. We all are placed in danger by the gun lobby's actions and by the deafening silence in response from America's political leaders.

This book sets out to expose this shameful and entirely preventable record of inaction in the face of needless death and injury and to sound a sensible, fact-based call to action to end the needless bloodshed.

Chapters 1–3 mount a thorough inquiry into the numbing level of gun violence and its effects in America.

Chapters 4–6 explain the fundamental cause of that violence: a mercenary industry and a cynical gun lobby, working hand in hand to sell the last gun to the last buyer.

Chapters 7–9 counter the conventional wisdom that the pro-gun forces in America are too powerful to be broken. They ask, "What would happen if Americans decided to take on the industry and its powerful allies?" The chapters' answer is that the gun lobby can be defeated, and that well-framed, fact-driven solutions work to save lives.

1

OUR DAILY DEAD: GUN DEATH AND INJURY IN THE UNITED STATES

Nobody knows what happened within Michael E. Hance's interior life between 1978—his senior year of high school, when he was chosen Most Courteous because of his "consideration and good manners toward everyone"—and about eleven o'clock on the morning of Sunday, August 7, 2011, when he took deliberate aim with his recently-bought Hi-Point 45 caliber semiautomatic pistol and shot eleven-year-old Scott Dieter below the terrified boy's right eye.[1] Scott Dieter was the last of seven people whom Hance, armed with two handguns, calmly hunted down and shot to death in the archetypical white, middle-class suburb of Copley Township, Ohio.[2] An eighth victim, Rebecca Dieter, Hance's longtime girlfriend and Scott's aunt, was severely wounded; she was hospitalized but survived. A policeman shot Hance dead moments after he killed young Scott Dieter. The entire episode from first shot to last took less than ten minutes.[3]

"Unclear in all of this is the motive for these killings," Summit County Prosecuting Attorney Sherri Bevan Walsh noted in her report clearing the police officer of wrongdoing in shooting Hance.[4]

What is not "unclear" is that in spite of Hance's long-term and increasingly bizarre public behavior, his angry interactions with his neighbors, the judgment of several members of his family that he had severe mental illness, and a 2009 incident report by Akron police that concluded he was a "signal 43," or, as a police lieutenant later explained, "basically . . . crazy,"[5] Hance was easily and legally able to buy from a pawn shop the two handguns with which he fired more than twenty rounds at his fleeing family and neighbors.[6] In addition to the Hi-Point pistol, which he bought five days earlier from Sydmor's Jewelry, a pawn shop in neighboring Barberton, Hance used a .357 Magnum revolver that he bought in 2005 from the same store.[7] He also bought several ammunition "reloaders" that he carried with him.[8]

In the days between the time he bought the Hi-Point pistol and the morning that he unleashed his fury on his family and neighbors, Hance visited a local shooting range several times to familiarize himself with his new gun and practice shooting it.[9] Hi-Point asserts on its website that it "offers affordably-priced semi-automatic handguns in a range of the most popular calibers," and that its guns "are very popular with recreational target shooters, hunters, campers, law enforcement and anyone seeking an affordable, American-made firearm."[10]

Events like that Sunday morning in Copley Township have become quintessentially American. They are damning proof that modern guns not only kill people, they kill many people quickly. Variously called a "shooting spree,"[11] "shooting rampage,"[12] "mass shooting,"[13] "mass killing,"[14] and "mass murder,"[15] such carnage has become so common that a pattern of breathless but ultimately feckless ritual emerges from the news media's reporting.[16]

The ritual starts with a "breaking news" alert (that often misstates both the circumstances and the actual number of deaths and injuries).[17] "And, as we deliver the information to you, it is quite shocking," said a CNN news reader on the afternoon of the mass shooting at Virginia Tech, in which thirty-two victims were shot dead and seventeen wounded. "Because, when we first started reporting this, this morning, it was simply a shooting on campus. We didn't know if anyone had been injured."[18]

After police gain control of the shooting scene, high-ranking police officials and politicians give interviews and press conferences, ostensibly to assure their constituencies that the event in question was an aberration, the horror is now over, and the community is safe. Mayor Buddy Dyer, for example, told reporters after a mass shooting in an Orlando, Florida, office building, "The gunman has been apprehended so the community is safe." [19] Bill Campbell, then the mayor of Atlanta, "took an accustomed role Thursday after a shooting rampage left nine dead in two midtown office buildings, briefing the media and updating the city on the police's investigations in press conferences that were carried live nationally," the Associated Press reported, adding that "Campbell took the role usually handled by at best a chief of police and normally just a normal spokesperson." [20]

Other events at this stage include such ironic gestures as both houses of the U.S. Congress observing a "moment of silence" after news broke of the slaughter at Virginia Tech—as if the Congress has in recent years been anything *other* than silent on gun deaths, gun injuries, and gun control. [21] Perhaps even more bizarre was U.S. Representative J. Randy Forbes's pronouncement to CNN on the afternoon of the Virginia Tech shooting that "the state [of Virginia] has done a wonderful job in terms of dispatching plenty of police officers, state troopers and other people to make sure everyone is [sic] there can have a degree of safety and feel safe while they are on campus." [22] The presence of "plenty of police officers" after the gunman, Seung-Hui Cho, a student, had committed suicide, must have been small comfort to the thirty-two other dead and seventeen wounded he left in his wake. Not incidentally, Forbes is a hard-liner on "gun rights." He enjoys a coveted A rating from the NRA. In a press release announcing the gun lobby's endorsement of Forbes, the NRA's chief lobbyist, Chris W. Cox, praised "Forbes' unwavering commitment to preserving our Second Amendment rights." [23]

Even before the numbers of dead and injured are confirmed, the media scramble for "color" in column inches and broadcast time through interviews of neighbors, survivors, and random acquaintances of the shooter or his victims. This reportage invariably includes statements of surprise that a mass shooting could happen in the community involved. "Well, we of course all see things happen on the news and think that we live in a safe and quiet community and nothing like that certainly would ever happen here," a witness to a shooting in Binghamton, New York, told CNN after thirteen people were shot to death and four others wounded in a community center. "So everyone is shocked and amazed and still trying to grasp the whole import of it."[24]

There are also frequent observations that the shooter never seemed dangerous. "Mike was strange," a neighbor told a reporter about Hance, but added, "I wouldn't think he'd go to this extreme."[25] Judy Gren, described as a "longtime friend" of another mass shooter, Carey Hal Dyess, said he was "a very nice man, very kind. He loved animals. He helped you with anything you needed. We used to go horseback riding together." This "nice man" Dyess shot to death his ex-wife, her lawyer, and three of her friends, wounded another of her friends, and then shot himself to death.[26]

The next ritual station is a ponderous exploration of "why?" This inquiry typically ignores almost entirely the looming significance of the single objective fact that is common to all "shooting sprees"—the use of an easily available and almost always legally obtained gun, usually a handgun. Rather, the media pick speculatively through the mysterious lint of the shooter's alleged, possible, potential "motivation" or likely mental illness. "Fighter Pilot Murder Mystery; Did Elite Navy Pilot Snap?" ABC's *Good Morning America* asked after a navy pilot shot to death his roommate, the roommate's sister, and an acquaintance of the two, then shot himself to death.[27] What neither ABC in this case, nor other media in other cases, seriously address is whether the ubiquitous presence of guns makes a crucial difference in the outcome when someone like a highly trained, elite "Top Gun" pilot "snaps"—in this case, in a jealous rage.

In fact, much of this speculative reporting looks more like a puppet show than a newscast: badly informed television personalities voicing idiosyncratic theories through compliant talking-head guest experts. CNN network host Jane Velez-Mitchell, for example, just before pronouncing that guns are "a minuscule part of the problem," purportedly probed the cause of a mass shooting in Orlando with this fatuous question to an "expert" guest, "OK. I want to go right now to Alex Katehakis. She is an addiction specialist. She's also a sex specialist. Let's face it: a gun is a phallic symbol, Alex. What do you make about the fact that it's males primarily committing these kinds of, basically, revenge fantasies come to life with a squeeze of a trigger?" [28] According to the website of the Center for Healthy Sex in Los Angeles, of which Katehakis is the founder and clinical director, she "has extensive experience in working with a full spectrum of sexuality from sexual addiction to sex therapy, and problems of sexual desire and sexual dysfunction for individuals and couples. Alex has successfully facilitated the recovery of many sexually addicted individuals and assisted couples in revitalizing their sex lives." [29] There is no evidence that Katehakis has any expertise at all in the study of violence generally, much less gun violence. Notwithstanding Velez-Mitchell's peremptory assertion that "a gun is a phallic symbol," there is no reason to believe that she brings an informed view to the subject of mass shootings or gun violence prevention.

On the same CNN segment, former FBI agent Don Clark ventured to say cautiously, "I know some of my friends are going to beat me up about this, but I've been in law enforcement and the military. And I'm just tired of these guns." Velez-Mitchell firmly brushed Clark back in this exchange, which would be amusing if it were not so insidious:

VELEZ-MITCHELL: And let me tell you something. I agree with you 100 percent. From a psychological perspective, I'm not talking gun control. I'm talking psychology.

CLARK: No, neither am I.

VELEZ-MITCHELL: It takes an entire complicated situation, and it boils it down to one action. It takes a revenge fantasy in your head, and it makes it real. [30]

This exchange was not the first time former FBI agent Clark—who appears often in the CNN lineup as a utility expert on a range of subjects, including the custody of the late Anna Nicole Smith's body, hate crimes, and the proper investigation of repeat sex offenders[31]—had mentioned guns on CNN as a factor that just might possibly be relevant to mass shootings. The result of his earlier assertion (during an interview to discuss the Virginia Tech massacre) was strikingly similar in outcome. The flow of the dialogue—expert guest's tentative assertion, host's firm brush-back, subject dropped—provides telling insight into the self-censorship of the news media about the "hornet's nest" of gun control:

CLARK: And Tony, let's just go back even to the gun purchases. You know? And I don't want to get on that political hot potato about the guns . . .

[CNN host Tony] HARRIS: It is, you are right. It is.

CLARK: . . . but I want to say that there has to be a little bit more strenuous background investigations into people picking them up. Perhaps if there had been some opportunity to talk about the mental attitude of this—to search about the mental attitude of this person, maybe this person would not have been sold a weapon.

HARRIS: Yes. Boy, you've just stepped on the hornet's nest, and there they go.

CLARK: Yes.[32]

The exchange ended there, without further discussion of Clark's timidly advanced point.

In later stages of the ritual, 911 tapes are released and broadcast. It's possible that these grisly moments are broadcast not simply for their shock value. But one is then left with the curious proposition that the media's producers must think that the answer to the "puzzle" of why mass shootings happen might be found in the sound of terrified, frantic, and sometimes dying voices pleading for help.[33]

The sad final act of the mass shooting ritual is a public event or makeshift memorial involving candles and teddy bears, to show "support" for the victims and help "bring closure" to the survivors.[34] When CNN anchor Roland Martin asked Mayor Matthew Ryan of Binghamton, New York, to "give us a sense of the healing process in Binghamton tonight," the mayor's reply was typical. "Already churches around our city are having vigils. Tomorrow we're going to plan a big vigil for our city. This is a city that really comes together in time of crisis."[35]

Determinedly clutched throughout this ritual is the studied premise that the latest "gun rampage" is an aberration, something akin to the sudden appearance of a spaceship that spews death randomly for ten or fifteen minutes, and then just as suddenly disappears. But the cold fact is that mass shootings can no longer accurately be called aberrations in the United States. They are here, now, and everywhere—in our homes,[36] our schools,[37] our churches,[38] our places of work,[39] our shopping malls,[40] and even our military bases.[41]

This ritual of studied avoidance of this product of the gun industry and the so-called "gun culture" inspired the writer Dahlia Lithwick to pen this scathing paragraph for *Slate* magazine:

> It says so much about this country that we respond to Bernard Madoff with outrage and to mass shootings with teddy bears and candles. Frustrated columns are written and written and written and written. But we collectively refuse to connect one killing spree to the next or to accept that these events aren't random; like falling meteors from the sky. These events are the outgrowth of legal and policy choices we make every single day and the choices

we avoid making year after year. We're willing to roll the dice with our children and our neighbors—because we want to think it only happens to other people's children and other people's neighbors—on the principle that guns have nothing to do with gun deaths. The American debate about gun regulation begins and ends with a tacit agreement that the occasional massacre is the price we pay for freedom. No wonder teddy bears and candles are the only national gun policy we have.[42]

Unfortunately, even if mass shootings were aberrations, even if they suddenly stopped happening entirely, the toll of ordinary Americans killed and injured by guns every single day would remain staggering, a bloodletting inconceivable in any other developed country in the world. Firearms are the second leading cause of traumatic death related to a consumer product in the United States and are the second most frequent cause of death overall for Americans ages fifteen to twenty-four. Since 1960, more than 1.3 million Americans have died in firearm suicides, homicides, and unintentional injuries.[43]

More than 90 percent of American households own a car.[44] Fewer than a third of American households contain a gun.[45] Yet as motor vehicle–related deaths have gone down, firearm deaths have not. Gun fatalities exceeded motor vehicle fatalities in ten states in 2009.[46] And, as is explained in more detail in chapter 9, the nationwide trends of these two forms of death are on a track to intersect.

This gory march of our daily gun dead, however, is virtually invisible. It is invisible because it is grossly underreported in the news media, suppressed and distorted by the gun lobby, and poorly documented by the federal government and most state governments. The news media glide around the elephant-in-the-room of guns as the common denominator of mass shootings. But they flat-out ignore tens of thousands of other, more "routine" gun deaths and injuries every year in the shooting gallery that America has become.

As part of the research for this book, the author tracked shootings in the United States that were reported in the news media for the week of Monday, August 1, through Sunday, August 7, 2011. Two sources of comprehensive data were used: a Google alert for news stories that mentioned "shootings," and a similar alert through the commercial database Nexis.com. Several supplemental searches were made to track down shootings that were mentioned in stories originally captured, and to update the shootings that were found. The result was a list of fifty-two shooting incidents reported during that week. Appendix A contains a description of each of these shootings and the sources from which they were obtained. Figure 2 summarizes by category the seventy gun deaths and twenty-two nonfatal gun injuries that were reported in news media during this period.

This survey is by no means a complete inventory of shootings in the United States during the week in question. On the contrary, quite clearly it is not complete. It is offered only as a good-faith search effort, as exhaustive as possible, to document what Americans could have seen or heard about gun death and injury in the news media during that week. Many of these incidents were reported only in local media, so even the most assiduous newshound in any given place would not in the ordinary course of events have seen or heard about all of the shootings listed in appendix A.

That being said, how does this list compare to comprehensive national data collected by public health authorities documenting the level of gun violence in America? Figure 3 shows the number of gun deaths, gun injuries, and total people shot for the first nine years of the current century in the United States. (These are the latest years for which comprehensive national data on gun deaths and injuries was available at time of analysis. There is no real-time database of gun death and injury.)

Figure 2. Summary of Deaths and Injuries in Shooting Incidents in the United States, August 1–7, 2011

	Homicide	Homicide: ruled self-defense	Suicide (does not include suicides in murder-suicide)	Nonfatal injury (includes two persons who survived attempted murder-suicides)	Nonfatal injury inflicted in incident ruled self-defense	Murder-suicide	Unintentional death	Unintentional injury	Homicide as result of police shooting
Monday, August 1									
Tuesday, August 2			1			4			
Wednesday, August 3	4			1		2	1		1
Thursday, August 4	2		1	1		2			
Friday, August 5	7	1	1	4	1	6		1	1
Saturday, August 6	8		1	4		2			1
Sunday, August 7	13			8	1	9		1	1
Total for week	34	1	4	18	2	25	1	2	4

See appendix A for sources.

What emerges from this data is that the number of human beings killed and injured by guns in the United States during an average week is much greater than the number that an extraordinarily curious person could possibly find by diligently combing the news media. A total of 272,590 people were killed by guns between 2000 and 2008 inclusive. This is an average of 30,288 a year, for an average of 582 gun deaths a week in the United States. This is more than eight times the number of deaths that the survey found to have been reported in the news media during the first week of August 2011. An estimated total of 617,488 were injured by guns in the nine years but did not die, for an average of 1,319 gun injuries per week. This is just shy of sixty times as many gun injuries as were reported in the media during the week in question.

Clearly Americans live in a bubble, an information vacuum, unwittingly ignorant of the reality of the carnage howling around them. This virtual invisibility of firearms death and injury goes a long way toward explaining why Americans appear to be so complacent about gun violence. It sheds light on why the gun lobby

Figure 3. Gun Deaths, Injuries, and Total Shot in the United States, 2000–2008

Year	Death	Injuries	Total Shot
2000	28,663	75,685	104,348
2001	29,573	63,012	92,585
2002	30,242	58,841	89,083
2003	30,136	65,834	95,970
2004	29,569	64,389	93,958
2005	30,694	69,825	100,519
2006	30,896	71,417	102,313
2007	31,224	69,863	101,087
2008	31,593	78,622	110,215

Data on gun deaths and injuries is from the WISQARS database of the U.S. Centers for Disease Control and Prevention, National Center for Injury Prevention and Control.

can thumb its nose at gun violence, twist gun violence to its own ends by mischaracterizing its nature, and fob off folksy pabulum about guns on both the public and uninformed policy makers. It helps explain why politicians get away with avoiding the perceived "third rail" of gun control at the same time that their constituents are dying.

Philip J. Cook and Jens Ludwig, both of whom have devoted much of their professional lives to studying gun violence, have zeroed in on the fault line of fact-free policy making—the history of public health shows that people do indeed change their minds and move away from culturally taught beliefs when they learn key facts. Cook and Ludwig have explained that "we know that people's attitudes and behaviors about smoking and unprotected sex have changed dramatically over time. The changes have occurred, in part, in response to a growing body of epidemiological research about the health risks associated with each of these activities." [47]

The history of public health abounds with similar examples of factual investigations and resulting fact-based policies saving millions of human lives, flying in the face of what everybody thought they knew. In 1900, the *Washington Post* dismissed the idea that mosquitoes carried yellow fever—one of the most dreaded diseases of the era—as "silly and nonsensical rigmarole." [48] In 1900, the "culturally grounded understanding" of even the educated elite, including many in the medical professions, was that yellow fever was caused by dirt and filth. "I'm your friend, Gorgas, and I'm trying to set you right," Major General George W. Davis, governor of the Panama Canal Zone, advised Dr. William C. Gorgas, the surgeon general of the army whose eventually successful campaigns to control mosquitoes in Florida, Cuba, and Panama dramatically reduced malaria and yellow fever infections. "On the mosquito you are simply wild. All who agree with you are wild. Get the idea out of your head. Yellow fever, as we all know, is caused by filth." [49]

The news vacuum about the facts of gun death and injury is

a boon for the gun lobby. The absence of facts is precisely what makes it possible for many patently foolish perspectives on guns and gun control to survive in the United States. Among these perspectives, the most insidious is the one relentlessly promoted by the gun lobby, which not only deliberately exploits ignorance about the nature and extent of gun violence in America but also works vigorously to keep the facts about it sealed from view. At the other end of the spectrum, some "commonsense" solutions advanced by well-meaning advocates rest on the sands of an equal absence of relevant facts. The gun lobby, its facilitators, and their misguided "commonsense" ideas will be examined in detail in later chapters, but a brief overview of the gun lobby's propagandistic approach here may help put the problem of understanding gun violence in perspective.

The National Shooting Sports Foundation (NSSF) is "the trade association for the firearms industry." It sponsors the annual industry trade event, the Shooting, Hunting and Outdoor Trade Show, popularly known as the SHOT Show. NSSF defines its mission as "to promote, protect and preserve hunting and the shooting sports."[50] Blending a down-home style with corporate PR sensibilities, NSSF works hard at making guns seem a lot like bowling balls—harmless objects the whole family can enjoy in an atmosphere of glowing happy faces. In fact, the NSSF has made the claim that hunting is safer than bowling, a laughable proposition easily eviscerated:

> The NSSF makes no effort to evaluate the lethality or seriousness of different types of injuries in each activity it claims is less safe than hunting with firearms. A bullet to the chest and a sprained ankle are both counted as one injury in their statistics, and that's the basis of their claim that hunting with guns is safer than all but the least strenuous activities. According to a 2004 *Good Morning America* report, the International Hunter Education Association (IHEA) estimated that hunters were accidentally shooting

more than 1,000 people a year in the United States and Canada.[51]

Gun deaths and debilitating lifelong injuries simply don't exist in NSSF's glossy world, where assault rifles designed for war are transmogrified into "modern sporting rifles,"[52] poisonous environment-degrading lead ammunition becomes harmless "traditional ammunition,"[53] and shooting ranges are family-values venues—places where terrorists,[54] mass shooters, and assassins[55] never hone their shooting skills, but frolicking sport shooters have a "memorable and fun experience."[56]

When NSSF talks about guns killing and injuring people, it sticks to a script promoting the rosy view that "the firearms accident rate among all groups has dropped more than 60 percent during the last twenty-five years to a century-long low, with such accidents now comprising less than 1 percent of all fatal accidents nationwide."[57] But as Figure 4 graphically demonstrates about gun deaths in America, accidents are not the problem. Uninten-

Figure 4. Gun Fatalities in the United States, 1981–2010

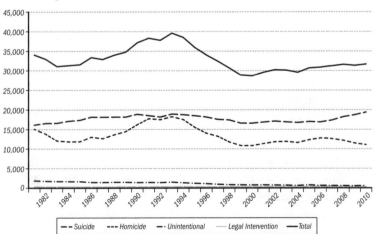

tional shootings have always comprised a tiny part of gun death and injury. The problem is people deliberately shooting other people and themselves.

The NRA—the gun industry's political front—takes a harder line. Its style combines a vehement "patriotic" meanness with a ruthless willingness to say or do anything to defeat even the most modest proposal to regulate guns. According to a well-informed former insider, this is largely cynical play-acting to whip up gun owners and raise funds by "the senior leadership and consultants of the NRA [who] have morphed the organization into this grand fundraising operation for the power and glory primarily of themselves." [58] The NRA's chief executive officer, Wayne LaPierre, reportedly "is making around a million dollars a year." [59] The NRA's specialty is "argument by assertion," an endless emission of statements it cannot prove and quite likely knows are false. LaPierre is often the orifice through which these assertions are vented. For example, the *St. Petersburg Times* in its *PolitiFact* fact-checking series found to be false LaPierre's assertion at the Conservative Political Action Conference in 2011 that "across the board, violent crime in jurisdictions that recognize the Right to Carry is lower than in areas that prevent it." [60]

One of the more spectacular examples of LaPierre's assertions is his claim that the Obama administration has a "secret plan" to "destroy the Second Amendment by 2016." In an article published in January 2012 in the Web edition of *America's 1st Freedom*—which the NRA calls its "pure news magazine"— LaPierre lets gun enthusiasts in on the conspiracy. Before getting into the thoroughly undocumented details, LaPierre makes a blatant fund-raising pitch by telling his readers that the best way that they can fight the evil Obama plan "is by carrying your new 2012 membership card . . . in your wallet as a symbol of your commitment—and by renewing or upgrading your NRA membership or making a contribution to defending freedom today." LaPierre then pulls out the stops on the NRA propaganda organ:

Think about it: Before moving into the White House, Barack Obama spent his *entire career* proudly, publicly advancing the most radical anti-gun positions you can imagine. . . . So what happened after they won the White House? Did Obama, Biden and the anti-gun extremists who soon filled the West Wing suddenly completely reverse their positions? No! In an act of pure political calculation, they plotted to keep their gun-ban objectives *concealed.*[61]

Get it? By not doing what the NRA spent millions of dollars during the 2008 campaign promising they would do if they won the election,[62] the Machiavellian geniuses in the Obama White House set up the American pro-gun voter for a cunning takedown of the Constitution in a second administration.

LaPierre cynically ignores the role of the NRA itself in suppressing any action on gun control. "With annual revenue of about $250 million," according to the *Washington Post*, "the group has for four decades been the strongest force shaping the nation's gun laws."[63] Had he cared to do so, LaPierre might have gotten a reality check from his co-worker, Chris W. Cox, the NRA's chief lobbyist. Cox bragged in an NRA political report—published both online and in print in parallel with LaPierre's screed—that, thanks to a "great deal of effort" by the NRA, "the most recent spending bill to pass the Congress and be signed by the president contained a dozen policy victories for gun owners."[64]

The NRA never lets the facts get in the way of its fund-raising stories. It ignores the truth of gun violence in America, spinning gun death and injury as a problem of criminal control, not gun control. It frames gun death and injury as the result of (too often coddled) rampaging violent criminals and not ordinary people owning guns. "When it comes to violent crime, NRA's 4 million members and America's 90 million gun owners stand for what works," LaPierre recently wrote, conveniently inflating his voice to speak for every gun owner in America. "Strong interdiction, swift arrest, tough prosecution and certain incarceration to re-move violent criminals from our society."[65] If ever there were occasion to recall the injunction of the biblical metaphor about focusing on a speck in another's eye while ignoring the beam in one's own, it may be found in the NRA's and the NSSF's hypo-critical propaganda about gun death and injury.[66]

But, as John Adams wrote, "Facts are stubborn things, and whatever may be our wishes, our inclinations, or the dictates of our passions, they cannot alter the state of facts and evi-dence."[67] And no matter what may be the greedy passions and self-interested wishes of the gun industry and its highly paid mouthpieces, one stubborn, bloody fact looms above all of their false assertions, impossible to avoid or erase: the United States stands alone in its high level of gun violence, a shocking contrast to other developed nations.

Two detailed cross-national comparisons of firearms deaths among comparable nations of the world—published in 1998 and 2011—arrived at similar conclusions. The 1998 study found that "the US is unique in several aspects. It has the highest overall fire-arm mortality rate, a high proportion of homicides that are the result of a firearm injury, and the highest proportion of suicides that are the result of a firearm injury."[68] The 2011 study reported that "the United States has a large relative firearm problem; fire-arm death rates in the US are more than seven times higher than they are in the other high-income countries. Firearm homicide rates are 19 times higher in the US compared with the other 22 countries in this analysis, firearm suicide rates, and unintentional firearm death rates are over five times higher. Of all the firearm deaths in these 23 high-income countries in 2003, 80% occurred in the United States."[69] This gun carnage is so, even though "our rates of crime and nonlethal violence are not exceptional."[70] In sum, a mugging or argument that goes wrong in Hamburg ends up with a few bruises. In Baltimore or a Denver suburb, it may likely end up with someone being shot.

As a consequence of all this, the United States also stands far

Figure 5. World Homicide Rates

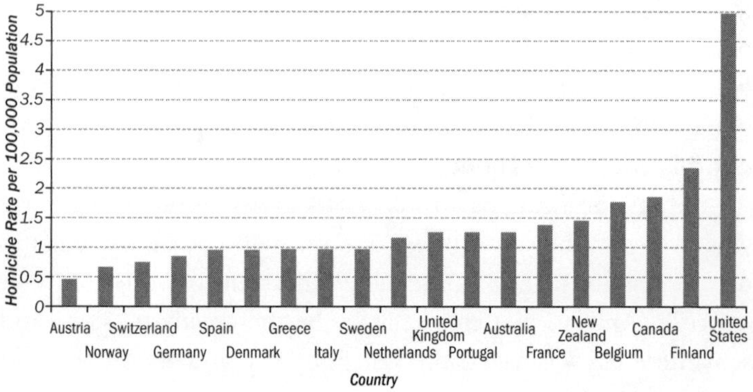

and away above other developed nations in its homicide rate, as illustrated in Figure 5.

How can this be? A closer look at the week of gun violence documented in figure 2 and appendix A provides some powerful clues. The first six deaths—in fact, the only gun deaths reported on the first two days—were suicides and murder-suicides.

On Monday, August 1, 2011, in Fort Huachuca, Arizona, a U.S. Army sergeant was found dead in his quarters of a gunshot wound. Base officials would not say whether he committed suicide. However, he had been arrested and escorted back to his quarters by military police the same day for bringing his personal handgun to the base's headquarters.[71]

The following day, Tuesday, August 2, in Lee, New Hampshire, Andrew Hubbard, twenty-seven, killed himself with a shotgun after being involved in a car crash. Neither driver was seriously injured in the head-on collision, but Hubbard grabbed a shotgun out of the back seat of his car, then fatally shot himself behind the premises of a nearby business.[72] In Hillsboro, Wisconsin, Joseph C. Satterlee, fifty-five, rammed his wife's car on a street with his own vehicle, climbed into her car, and shot her to death with his .357 Magnum revolver. He then shot himself to death. Satterlee fired a total of eight rounds from his six-shot revolver, pausing to reload it once. His wife, Anita K. Satterlee, had filed for divorce on June 20, 2011.[73] And in Kensington, Maryland, a quiet, upscale suburb of Washington, D.C., police officers found the bodies of Margaret F. Jensvold, fifty-four, and her son Ben Barnhard, thirteen, in their residence. Investigators concluded that Jensvold, a psychiatrist, had shot her son to death and then killed herself. The son had a number of special needs, and Jensvold was reportedly distressed that the local public school system would not pay for his attendance at a private school.[74]

These deaths aptly illustrate a fact that most Americans are surprised to learn. Most gun deaths are not homicides, but preventable suicides. Even in the case of homicide, the most common scenario is not—as the NRA prefers to imagine—a rampaging criminal, but an argument between two people who know each other.[75]

In this context, the human cost of the gun lobby's meddling in public policy becomes clear. For example, as is explained in the introduction, the NRA convinced Congress to forbid the armed services from collecting any information about personally owned guns among members of the military and its civilian employees. This law has had tragic yet entirely foreseeable effects. Between 2001 and 2008, 1,531 active-duty members of the military died from self-inflicted wounds.[76] (This number does not include suicides among former members of the military, which are also known to be numerous.) The military has not escaped the infection of suicide that accompanies the widespread availability of guns. But the new law has cut off an important avenue of suicide prevention among both active-duty and former military personnel.[77]

In the civilian context, "the empirical evidence linking suicide risk in the United States to the presence of firearms in the home is compelling."[78] The link is no less compelling among the military, serving and former alike. According to Dr. Elspeth Cameron Ritchie, who recently retired as a high-ranking army psychiatrist directly involved in the issue, "approximately 70 percent of Army and Pentagon suicides are by guns."[79] According to a study released in October 2011—ominously titled *Losing the Battle: The Challenge of Military Suicide*—48 percent of military suicides in 2010 were accomplished with privately owned weapons.[80] In spite of this, Dr. Ritchie noted, although the army is "committed to lowering the rate of suicide . . . there's a curious third rail that is seldom publicly discussed: the risks of suicide by firearm." She also notes that Army Post Exchanges—"basically government-owned Walmarts on major posts"—are increasingly selling guns and asks whether this is "sending the troops the right message."[81]

The media's reporting vacuum and the gun lobby's distortions have obscured another fact: the number of shootings in the United States is going up, not down.

The number of Americans killed by guns has remained fairly constant in the nine years for which complete data is available in the twenty-first century.[82] But the common focus on gun deaths as a marker to illustrate America's gun problem obscures an alarming trend. The number of persons who suffer nonfatal gunshot injuries—that is, who are shot but do not die—has risen over the same period. As graphically demonstrated by figure 6,

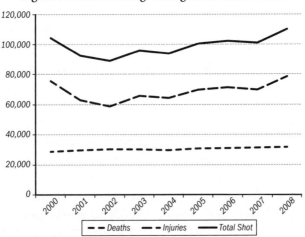

Figure 6. Total Shootings Rising in the United States

this means that more people are being shot by guns every year in the United States. In other words, America's gun problem is getting worse, not better. More guns means more shootings.

Figure 6 shows that between 2000 and 2008 a total of 617,488 people suffered nonfatal gunshot injuries in the United States. This averages about 68,610 persons per year. In 2008, however—a year in which gun deaths totaled 31,593, only slightly above the period's average—another 78,622 were shot but did not die, a figure markedly above the period's average. Most striking, the total number of people shot in 2008 totaled 110,215—the highest total recorded during the nine-year period.[83]

These civilian deaths and injuries may be put into further perspective by comparing them to the experience of the U.S. armed services during the same period. The total of U.S. active-duty military deaths, from all causes, in the years 2001 through 2008 was 12,390.[84] The total deaths caused by hostile action during the same eight years was 3,811, while the number of deaths from self-inflicted wounds among active duty military personnel was 1,531.[85]

Why have gun deaths remained fairly constant even though the total number of people shot is increasing? The answer is that improved emergency services and better medical care are saving lives that would otherwise be lost to guns.

The authors of a landmark study in 2002 on the relationship between murder and medicine concluded that advances in emergency services—including the 911 system and establishment of trauma centers—as well as better surgical techniques have suppressed the homicide rate. They concluded that "without these developments in medical technology there would have been between 45,000 and 70,000 homicides annually the past 5 years instead of an actual 15,000 to 20,000."[86]

That finding is confirmed by anecdotal observations from law enforcement officials and the medical community. "It would be fair to say gunshot wound victims, if they suffered the same injury 25 years earlier, their chances of survival would be much less," Major Pat Welsh of the Dayton, Ohio, police said in April 2011. "It's a credit to the advances in medical technology and procedures."[87] In Birmingham, Alabama, Dr. Loring Rue, chief of trauma care at the University of Alabama at Birmingham's Trauma Center, said in commenting on the fact that while the number of violent crimes was increasing in Birmingham, the number of resulting deaths was falling, "I am convinced that not just our hospital, but all those who provide trauma care in Birmingham, make a distinct contribution to keeping the murder rate lower."[88]

The bad news is that even nonfatal gunshot wounds often leave victims chronically damaged. "There have definitely been improvements in trauma care, and a remarkable job is being done in getting victims through life-threatening injuries, but we are still being left with injuries that drastically alter lives," according to Dr. Selwyn Rogers, director of a trauma center in Boston.[89]

The January 2011 shooting in Tucson, Arizona, in which U.S. Representative Gabrielle Giffords was gravely injured, is a well-known, if not singular, example. Fifty percent of all trauma deaths are secondary to traumatic brain injury such as Representative Giffords suffered, and gunshot wounds to the head caused 35 percent of these.[90] Gunshot wounds also account for about 15 percent of all spinal cord injuries in the United States.[91]

One question that remains unanswered is whether advances in care will outpace advances in gun lethality as the gun industry continues to militarize the civilian market with high-capacity semiautomatic pistols, assault rifles, and high-caliber sniper rifles.[92] "Many of the victims now have multiple gunshot wounds," then District of Columbia police chief Charles H. Ramsey observed in 2003. "The criminals also use high-caliber, high-powered weapons."[93] As the authors of the 2002 study trenchantly observed, "At some point in contesting the outcome of criminal assault to the body, weaponry may yet trump medicine."[94]

2

SUPREME NONSENSE AND DEADLY MYTHS

With the exception of one historic and widely reported event, Thursday, June 26, 2008, was a routine day in the universe of gun death and injury in the United States.[1]

The gunfire started well before sunrise.

At about one A.M., in Corpus Christi, Texas, a man angry about a stolen radio fired at least four shots into the air in front of a residence where he thought the culprit lived.[2] Around two A.M., twenty-five-year-old Manuel Davis was shot to death on a street corner in Cleveland, Ohio.[3] Half an hour later, at two thirty A.M. in Halsell, Alabama, Jimmy Tanks, a sixty-seven-year-old railroad retiree, heard noises outside his trailer home and grabbed his gun. The noise was a "repo man" in the process of repossessing Tanks's car.[4] Shots were fired and Tanks was killed. At just about the same time, in Muskegon, Michigan, a twenty-three-year-old woman and her boyfriend were wounded in what police described as a suicide attempt.[5] Less than an hour later, twenty-year-old Bernardino Hernandez allegedly opened fire on his ex-girlfriend in Elgin, Illinois, shooting her three times in the back—the two were reported to be in a dispute over custody of their baby.[6]

The shooting did not slack off with the sunrise. At about nine thirty A.M., a fourteen-year-old-boy in Gulfport, Florida, accidentally shot his friend in the arm with a .357 Magnum revolver, one of two handguns he had brought to the friend's home to show off.[7] Later in the morning, in Lebanon, Pennsylvania, Raymond Zegowitz, forty-three, shot to death his girlfriend,

Khrystina Bixa, twenty-three, then committed suicide with the gun. Neither of Bixa's children—three-year-old Christian and twenty-month-old David—were injured, although police could not say whether the children had seen the shootings.[8]

In Litchfield, Connecticut, Bruce Bochicchio, forty-three, was arrested and charged with threatening his wife and failing to surrender his guns after a restraining order had been issued against him for fighting with his son. Police seized eleven guns, including a rifle and two fully automatic submachine guns, from the family's home. In 2005, Bochicchio's brother, Michael, a retired state trooper, had shot his wife to death and wounded her lawyer in front of a courthouse, then killed himself. At the time of his arrest, Bruce Bochicchio and his wife, Christine, were caring for the orphaned children of his brother.[9] Later in the evening, Kenneth Anton Duckett, thirty-seven, walked into the observation area of the indoor pool at the Montclair, New Jersey, YMCA. He shot to death Monica Paul, thirty-one, in front of her eleven-year-old daughter, while her four-year-old son was swimming. Duckett, who was under a restraining order forbidding him from contact with Paul, fled the scene.[10]

Shortly after five thirty P.M. in Bridgeport, Connecticut, twenty-two-year-old Tamboria Raiford opened fire with a handgun from her front porch into a crowd of adults and children. April Barron, forty, was hit in the head by one of the bullets, but apparently survived her injury.[11] In Deerfield Beach, Florida, a bullet fired through the door hit three-year-old Salayah Buie in the leg while she was watching television with her family. Members of the family suspected that the shooting was in retaliation for an incident earlier in the day. They had notified the county sheriff's office that a pit bull had come into their yard and killed their cat.[12] Police arrested three teenagers in Rock Hill, South Carolina, after shots were fired from their car around six thirty P.M. The teens were chasing another car.[13]

The macabre dance continued into the night. In Hampton, Arkansas, a four-year-old boy found a loaded handgun in a living room cabinet at about eight thirty P.M. He shot his five-year-old sister in the head, killing her.[14] In Omaha, Nebraska, three separate shootings left seven people injured,[15] while in Hartford, Connecticut, a young man was shot and killed in a parking lot, and a teenage girl was shot in the face and seriously wounded in a separate incident.[16] Around eleven P.M., an armed standoff began in a trailer park in Tucson, Arizona, after police responded to a report of shots being fired and found one man dead outside a trailer. A SWAT team eventually entered the trailer and found two other people dead, one an apparent suicide.[17]

The day ended with the grisly discovery of a domestic murder-suicide. Just before midnight, police in Hattiesburg, Mississippi, found the bodies of Tracy Kennedy, sixty-six, and his wife, Judith, sixty-eight, inside their home. Both had gunshot wounds to the head. The county coroner concluded that Tracy Kennedy had shot his wife first and then committed suicide.[18]

These incidents are, of course, only a fraction of the gun violence that occurred that day. On average, slightly more than eighty people a day are killed by guns in America, and about twice as many are injured. So these anecdotes—gleaned from news reports of the day on Nexis.com—are just a glimpse of the real world of America's daily dead and mutilated, a blood-red flag seen faintly through the news media's gun-violence whiteout.

There was, however, no media whiteout at the U.S. Supreme Court in Washington, D.C.[19] The most dramatic incident of the day involving guns happened in the Court Chamber of that august body. There was a torrent of reportage about the majority opinion in the case of *District of Columbia v. Heller*,[20] delivered by Associate Justice Antonin Gregory Scalia.[21] Scalia delivered the opinion from an ideological ivory tower, far removed from the reality of gun violence in America.

It would be difficult to imagine a venue more remote than the Supreme Court from the trailer park in Alabama where Jimmy Tanks died defending his car with a gun, or the home in Lebanon, Pennsylvania, where Khrystina Bixa's boyfriend shot her to death.

The monumental bronze doors that guard the Supreme Court building at the top of the white marble steps on its West Front weigh six and a half tons. Oak doors open from a Great Hall into the Court Chamber, in which the nine justices of the Supreme Court sit when delivering their decrees. The courtroom "measures 82 by 91 feet and has a 44-foot ceiling. Its 24 columns are Old Convent Quarry Siena marble from Liguria, Italy; its walls and friezes are of Ivory Vein marble from Alicante, Spain; and its floor borders are Italian and African marble."[22] These royal appointments are appropriate to the nine justices who constitute the third branch of government, with as much power among them as Congress and the president. Seven of the nine are millionaires, one (Justice Thomas) may be a millionaire, while only one (Justice Kennedy) is definitely not.[23]

Scalia delivered his decree from the courtroom's wing-shaped mahogany bench in a grim, condescending, semimonotone.[24] As he droned on, he transported himself and the decision back to the eighteenth century—a disease-ridden world of powdered wigs, pockmarked faces, flea-bitten bodies, and ignorance of the basic principles of public health, disease, and injury prevention. It was a time when even educated leaders "knew" that regular baths promoted promiscuity and that many diseases were caused by foul smells or, as in the case of yellow fever, by immoral behavior.[25] It was from this dismal sump of smug ignorance that Scalia drew the wisdom he shared that day in 2008.

The Court's starkly divided (5–4) ruling turned on its head at least seventy years of settled Constitutional law. Hailed by ideological conservatives as an example of "originalism"[26]—a putative return to strict construction of the "original intent" of the Constitution's framers, as opposed to the judicial lawmaking liberal courts are accused of doing through their "loose construction" of the Constitution—*Heller* struck down the District of Columbia's long-standing ban on the private possession of handguns. "We hold that the District's ban on handgun possession in the home violates the Second Amendment, as does its prohibition against rendering any lawful firearm in the home operable for the purpose of immediate self-defense." [27]

"Our opinion is very lengthy," Scalia warned in his oral presentation. "This summary that I'm giving will state little more than the conclusions. If you want to check their validity against the dissent's contrary claims, you will have to read some 154 pages of opinions." [28] In a nation in which a serious contender for nomination as a candidate for the office of president derided the sitting president as a "snob" for promoting college education,[29] one might wonder how many of those affected by Scalia's decision would accept his challenge to read its arcane text. In fact, Scalia's opinion is so long that an eminent conservative judge quipped that its bulk would "perhaps just overwhelm the doubters." [30] Deep within this leviathan, Scalia wrote the following crucial paragraph:

> It is enough to note, as we have observed, that the American people have considered the handgun to be the quintessential self-defense weapon. There are many reasons that a citizen may prefer a handgun for home defense: It is easier to store in a location that is readily accessible in an emergency; it cannot easily be redirected or wrestled away by an attacker; it is easier to use for those without the upper-body strength to lift and aim a long gun; it can be pointed at a burglar with one hand while the other hand dials the police. Whatever the reason, handguns are the most popular weapon chosen by Americans for self-defense in the home, and a complete prohibition of their use is invalid.[31]

The statements in this paragraph are pivotal to the decision, in which the majority decided that the Second Amendment confers an "individual right"—as opposed to the long-standing rule that the right is a "collective right," intended to ensure the viability of state militias (and their successor, the National Guard). But as

Scalia acknowledged in his opinion in *Heller*, even an individual right is not limitless.[32] So where the Court drew the line limiting an individual's right was crucial to the modern gun industry. High-powered, high-capacity, military-derived handguns are a vital component of the gun industry's lifeblood. Scalia's portentous effusion provided a factual basis that ensured that the ruling in *Heller* would protect handguns, the most lethal implement of portable killing power ever invented. And yet every alleged fact in the paragraph is at best mischievous myth, at worst demonstrably false. It is significant that, in an opinion top-heavy with ponderous citations to legal authority, Scalia cited not a single source— not one—to support the assertions in this vital paragraph.

In truth, these words are no more than an example of what lawyers call ipse dixit—"a bare assertion resting on the authority of an individual."[33] Allen Rostron, a constitutional scholar and law professor, captured this in his critique of Scalia's opinion:

> Justice Scalia . . . is certainly entitled to whatever personal views he may have about the relative merits of handguns versus long guns for home defense purposes. But his reliance on that sort of nakedly personal assessment of a public policy issue, to resolve a crucial legal issue in a landmark decision on the Constitution's meaning, is startling. It looks very much like the sort of "judge-empowering" "interest-balancing" that he denounces the dissenters in *Heller* for endorsing.[34]

The criticism is more than ironic in Scalia's case. He blasted his colleagues for a decision in 2002, stating that "seldom has an opinion of this court rested so obviously upon nothing but the personal views of its members."[35] Unfortunately, Scalia's paragraph lies at the axis of a legal ruling that will cost millions of Americans their lives and millions more grave injuries. Its influence is like toxic waste thoughtlessly released into a water supply.

It was not the first time Scalia got his facts wrong in a rhapsody of enthusiasm for the make-believe world of gun rights. Praising a pro–gun rights book written by Joyce Lee Malcolm, then a history professor at Bentley University,[36] a business college in Massachusetts,[37] Scalia pronounced the book "excellent." He noted that the author was not a "member of the Michigan Militia, but an Englishwoman."[38] His point was apparently that an Englishwoman is more credible than an American member of a right-wing militia. Scalia was wrong on his facts, however. Malcolm is not an "Englishwoman." She is an American.[39]

Some might dismiss Professor Rostron's evaluation as sour grapes. Before he became a law professor, he was a senior staff attorney at the Brady Center to Prevent Gun Violence, a well-known gun-violence prevention organization. But it is hard to dismiss the caustic analyses of *Heller* by two federal appeals court judges—Richard A. Posner and J. Harvie Wilkinson III—both of whom were appointed to the bench by President Ronald Reagan and both of whom are highly regarded as conservative jurists. According to the *New York Times*, "Judge Wilkinson, who sits on the United States Court of Appeals for the Fourth Circuit, in Richmond, Va., was recently considered for a spot on the Supreme Court. Judge Posner, of the Seventh Circuit, in Chicago, is perhaps the most influential judge not on the Supreme Court."[40] CNN senior legal analyst Jeffrey Toobin[41] wrote of Posner in 2006, "A prolific scholar and perhaps the nation's best-known federal appeals-court judge, Posner wields singular authority from his chambers, in Chicago."[42] Perennial pro-gun activist John Lott, a virtual factory of much-criticized and regularly debunked pro-gun academic "studies," lauded Posner and Wilkinson as two of the three "outstanding" judges serving on federal courts of appeal in 2006.[43] The conservative magazine the *Weekly Standard* wrote that Wilkinson "long has been regarded as one of the most respected conservatives on the federal bench."[44]

Neither Posner nor Wilkinson can be dismissed as simpering liberal gun haters. Yet it is hard to decide which of these two conservatives jurists' scorn was more withering. The honor probably should go to Wilkinson, who, the *Weekly Standard* noted, "bestows upon Scalia's opinion the most scathing condemnation known to conservatives: comparison to *Roe v. Wade*."[45] The comparison has a special sting for Scalia, who was reported in 2005 to especially loathe two high-court cases: *Roe* and *Lawrence v. Texas*, a 2003 decision which declared unconstitutional a law forbidding homosexual sodomy.[46]

Writing in the *Virginia Law Review*, Judge Wilkinson pummeled the ruling in *Heller* as ultimately not "conservative" at all. "*Heller* represents a triumph for conservative lawyers. But it also represents a failure—the Court's failure to adhere to a conservative judicial methodology in reaching its decision. In fact, *Heller* encourages Americans to do what conservative jurists warned for years they should not do: by-pass the ballot and seek to press their political agenda in the courts."[47] Wilkinson dismissed Scalia's pontification as no more than a doppelgänger of Justice Harry Blackmun's 1973 decision in *Roe v. Wade*,[48] the ruling that declared a Constitutional right to abortion. "First, each represents a rejection of neutral principles that counseled restraint and deference to others regardless of the issues involved. Second, each represents an act of judicial aggrandizement: a transfer of power to judges from the political branches of government—and thus, ultimately, from the people themselves."[49]

Judge Posner was hardly more forgiving. He criticized Scalia's obstinately single-minded form of strict "originalist" interpretation as fakery. "Originalism without the interpretive theory that the Framers and the ratifiers of the Constitution expected the courts to use in construing constitutional provisions is faux originalism. True originalism licenses loose construction," Posner wrote.[50] This loose construction is "especially appropriate," the jurist noted, "for interpreting a constitutional provision ratified more than two centuries ago, dealing with a subject that has been transformed in the intervening period by social and technological change, including urbanization and a revolution in warfare and weaponry." Posner went on to observe acidly that "the Framers of the Bill of Rights could not have been thinking of the crime problem in the large crime-ridden metropolises of twenty-first-century America, and it is unlikely that they intended to freeze American government two centuries hence at their eighteenth-century level of understanding."[51]

Having scorned Scalia's "faux originalism," Judge Posner suggested that a motivation other than originalism might explain *Heller*:

> The true springs of the *Heller* decision must be sought elsewhere than in the majority's declared commitment to originalism. The idea behind the decision . . . may simply be that turnabout is fair play. Liberal judges have used loose construction to expand constitutional prohibitions beyond any reasonable construal of original meaning; and now it is the conservatives' turn. . . . It is possible that in both the gun control case and the campaign-finance cases the justices in the majority, rather than playing tit for tat, thought the laws they were invalidating very dumb, and in the case of the District of Columbia's ban on possession of pistols thought the law wimpish and paternalistic, like requiring bikers to wear helmets. . . . But judges are not supposed to invalidate laws merely because, as legislators, they would have voted against them.[52]

The most telling part of Posner's criticism raked over the ponderous, footnote-laden, pseudo-scholarly style of Scalia's writing. "The range of historical references in the majority opinion is breathtaking, but it is not evidence of disinterested historical inquiry. It is evidence of the ability of well-staffed courts to produce snow jobs." Judge Posner then went even further, declaring, "The statements that the majority opinion cited had little traction before *Heller*."[53]

Observing this intramural fracas, an editor of the libertarian magazine *Reason* observed, "Perhaps Scalia has changed his mind. Or perhaps . . . Scalia only selectively practices the judicial restraint he has long preached."[54]

In fact, it was no coincidence that the job of conjuring up a "snow job" on gun rights fell to Antonin Scalia and his law clerks. Scalia had his mind made up before the case arrived on the Court's docket. In 1997, eleven years before Scalia wrote his decision in *Heller*, he wrote—in the same book and footnote in which he praised Joyce Lee Malcolm, the "Englishwoman" who wasn't—exactly what he professed to discover in 2008. "It would also be strange to find in the midst of a catalog of the rights of *individuals* a provision securing *to the states* the right to maintain a designated 'Militia,'" Scalia wrote. "Dispassionate scholarship suggests quite strongly that the right of the people to keep and bear arms meant just that . . . there is no need to deceive ourselves as to what the original Second Amendment said and meant."[55]

Like the NRA, Scalia believes that the torrent of guns in America is not the real problem. "The attitude of people associating guns with nothing but crime, that is what has to be changed," Scalia said in 2006, during his keynote address before the National Wild Turkey Federation's annual convention at the Gaylord Opryland Hotel & Convention Center in Nashville, Tennessee. "I hope [hunting culture] can be preserved . . . the hunting culture, of course, begins with a culture that does not have a hostile attitude toward firearms."[56] The turkey hunters gave Scalia a rifle, which he valued at $600 in his 2006 annual financial disclosure report.[57]

Hailed by an adoring gun lobby as "the best friend gun-rights has up there,"[58] Justice Scalia has long been a gun enthusiast. He served on the junior varsity rifle team at Manhattan's Xavier High School, then a Jesuit military academy.[59] He is an avid turkey hunter,[60] who hunted ducks with former vice president Dick Cheney in 2004 and went on a similar venture in 2001 organized by the dean of the University of Kansas law school. He was criticized for not disqualifying himself from three separate cases, each of which arrived on the Supreme Court's docket shortly before or after one of his hunting outings—one involving Cheney and two in which the Kansas law school dean was a lead attorney.[61] Scalia has been continually dogged with criticisms about his indifference to the appearance of conflicts from early in his judicial career.[62] "Since World War II, I think it's fair to say, the extrajudicial conduct of only three justices have become significantly newsworthy in a harmful way: Fortas, Douglas, Scalia," Stephen Gillers, who teaches judicial ethics at New York University, told the *New York Times* in 2004.[63]

There is an even more direct conflict in Scalia's aggressive role in the *Heller* case. In 2007, the World Forum on the Future of Sport Shooting Activities (WFSA) gave Scalia its "Sport Shooting Ambassador Award," along with a solid silver reproduction of a sixteenth-century pistol with its powder flask.[64] He accepted the award and gave the keynote address in Nuremberg, Germany, at the forum's annual meeting—an international equivalent of NSSF's SHOT Show. WFSA, an international gun industry trade association, uses its annual ambassador award to improve the gun industry's image by "making public recognition of the social contribution made by some of the many public figures who have a longstanding interest in the shooting sports."[65]

There is an appearance of conflict within this appearance of conflict: Scalia was photographed at the meeting with Alan Gottlieb, who is head of the pro-gun Second Amendment Foundation.[66] At the very moment of the cozy Scalia-Gottlieb "grip and grin" photo, Gottlieb's foundation—using Alan Gura, the very lawyer who argued the *Heller* case before Scalia—was planning a lawsuit attacking Chicago's gun law. That suit was filed the day after the *Heller* decision and was eventually decided against Chicago by the Supreme Court.[67]

Ironically, Gottlieb happens to be a convicted felon (sent up on federal tax charges). When Gottlieb appeared on Fox News's *The O'Reilly Factor* to attack the animal rights group PETA's tax exemption, the organization's representative zinged the host and Gottlieb with her observation that "of your two guests tonight, there's only one convicted felon, and that's not me. Speaking of taxes, Alan Gottlieb went to federal prison for 10 months tax evasion. So that's what he knows about the tax laws."[68] Gottlieb, who has been described as "a mass-mailing wizard for far-right causes,"[69] and "one of the best people in the country on direct mail,"[70] was appearing on *The O'Reilly Factor* in his persona as president of the Center for the Defense of Free Enterprise, a group he co-founded to oppose environmental regulation.[71]

Fund-raising wizard Gottlieb reportedly advised followers of his technique that "a direct mail letter must appeal to three base emotions: Fear, Hate and Revenge," and must attack a "bogeyman" because "if you are not frightened, you won't send money."[72] Gottlieb has made a good living out of his network of foundations and businesses, which collectively gross millions.[73]

Scalia did not report the gift of the silver pistol and powder flask in his 2007 financial disclosure form, unlike the rifle he got from his turkey-hunting friends in 2006, which he did report.[74] No known public record of Scalia's keynote remarks exists. The fact of his award has been excised from WFSA's website.[75]

Scalia, however, continues to take seriously his duties as ambassador for the gun industry. After Justice Elena Kagan joined the Court, Scalia treated her to skeet-shooting lessons at his gun club, the Fairfax Rod & Gun Club.[76] The same suburban Virginia club has been active in a National Shooting Sports Foundation campaign to win friends and influence people in the news media by inviting journalists to "Media Weekends" and "Media Days" to enjoy free gun instruction, firearms-related gifts, and camaraderie with gun enthusiasts.[77] By way of interesting contrast, Scalia disqualified himself from a 2003 case involving the words "one nation, under God" in the Pledge of Allegiance. Although Scalia gave no reason, as is customary in such rare cases, he had been asked by one of the parties to step aside because of public remarks he had made about the specific case.[78]

All of this must be viewed in light of the fact that *Heller* was not a case that simply happened along in the natural course of

things. Scalia's pronouncement was the triumphant culmination of a well-funded campaign to overturn settled law, mounted
over several decades by a network of wealthy conservatives and
so-called libertarians—think tank scriveners funded by wealthy
conservatives—working in close concert with the gun lobby. As
pro-gun activist David Kopel crowed from a perch at the right-
wing magazine *Human Events*, "The human rights victory in today's Supreme Court decision in *District of Columbia v. Heller*
could never have happened without *Human Events* and the other
pillars of the conservative and libertarian movements."[79] And
Scalia's convicted felon friend Alan Gottlieb said—speaking of
the Chicago lawsuit that his organization ginned up to follow
on the heels of *Heller*—"We've had a very well-plotted-out legal
strategy for years, leading up to this."[80]

The "pillars" of the gun rights network that Kopel praised
have followed closely the strategy of the tobacco industry. This
includes "misrepresenting scientific evidence," "attempting to
directly influence government through the use of lobbying and
campaign contributions," and creating "a seemingly independent
organization [that] advantaged the tobacco industry by presenting its antiregulation agenda as an expression of popular will,
and allowed industry lobbyists access to policymakers who were
otherwise unwilling to work with them."[81] These shadowy ma-
nipulators of opinion and power vociferously attack any form
of government regulation, from guns to the environment. For
example, Ron Arnold, Gottlieb's sidekick at the Center for the
Defense of Free Enterprise and founder of the "Wise Use" movement, bragged, "Our goal is to destroy, to eradicate the environmental movement."[82] The same center, again employing Heller's
counsel, Alan Gura, has attacked the Michigan Liquor Control
Commission's regulation of beer labels.[83] It has also been active in
campaigns against the governmental rights of Native American
tribes.[84]

One result has been a proliferation of "think tanks," many
using patriotic sounding names, offering studies and reports

opposing government regulation. Among the better known of the gun lobby's friends in this web is The Heartland Institute, almost half of the funding for which comes from a single secret donor. Documents leaked from Heartland in 2012 revealed "how it sought to teach schoolchildren skepticism about global warming and planned other behind-the-scenes tactics using millions of dollars in donations from big corporate names."[85] This tactic of propagandizing children in the guise of education is used by the NRA in its notorious "Eddie Eagle" program, a marketing device pawned off as a "gun safety" program.[86] Heartland was also exposed in a 2010 book, *Merchants of Doubt*, as part of a "network of right-wing foundations, the corporations that fund them, and the journalists who echo their claims" that have "created a tremendous problem for American science."[87] The institute has "extensive, continuing programs to challenge climate science."[88]

But Heartland's role in the network of wealthy interests promoting a conservative agenda goes beyond spinning the debate over global warming. "The Second Amendment and gun control have long been of concern to Heartland and its researchers. In 1995, Heartland published The Heartland Institute policy study *Taking Aim at Gun Control* by Daniel Polsby." Heartland filed a "friend of the court" brief before the Supreme Court in *Heller*, and has filed other pro-gun briefs in other important cases, such as the attack on Chicago's gun laws.[89] David Boaz, executive vice-president of the pro-gun Cato Institute, was a keynote speaker at Heartland's 2011 Emerging Issues Forum.[90] Heartland's complex of extreme conservative issues is wide-ranging and interactive. Its president, Joseph Bast, challenged libertarians at the 2002 annual convention of the Libertarian Party of Illinois to support education vouchers, noting that "libertarians will get nowhere with their other issues—the drug war, taxes, property rights, and gun rights—if our children are indoctrinated in the government school system to think government is the answer to all our problems."[91] The institute's reports have been cited in the news and opinion media.[92]

It is not known whether Scalia has had more intimate contact with Heartland's web of influence beyond its amicus briefs. But it is known that he and Associate Justice Clarence Thomas have enjoyed the hospitality of Koch Industries owner Charles Koch—one of two brothers, each worth over $21.5 billion—who "coordinates the funding of the conservative infrastructure of front groups, political campaigns, think tanks, media outlets and other anti-government efforts through a twice annual meeting of wealthy right-wing donors."[93] When Koch sent out invitations for his 2011 retreat, he "highlighted past appearances at the gathering of 'notable leaders' like Justices Antonin Scalia and Clarence Thomas of the Supreme Court."[94] Some flavor of the tone of the Koch gatherings with respect to guns and gun control may be gathered from the reported remark of Fox News personality and retired New Jersey Superior Court judge Andrew P. Napolitano at the 2011 secret meeting that the Second Amendment was created to ensure "the right to shoot at the government if it is taken over by tyrants."[95]

Pro-gun former cable television star Glenn Beck and former Reagan attorney general Ed Meese are among those who have rubbed elbows at the billionaire Koch brothers' elite gatherings. And, yes, this Glenn Beck at a secret gathering of elites is the same Glenn Beck who warned his listeners, "This game is for keeps. This is who controls the United States of America and its destiny. Is it you? Or is it a group of elites?"[96] Beck has also ominously predicted gun violence as inevitable in the process of restoring freedom to America.[97]

Among other attendees at the Koch 2010 party were representatives of the Heritage Foundation, the American Enterprise Institute, and—quite naturally enough—the Cato Institute.[98] "Naturally" because billionaire Charles Koch founded the Cato Institute in 1974 as a Kansas nonprofit corporation under the original name of The Charles Koch Foundation, Inc., which was changed to Cato Institute in 1976. Edward H. Crane, the current president of the institute, was among three other original founders.[99] Since then, the Kochs have poured at least $30 million into Cato.[100]

The Cato connection goes directly to the *Heller* case, which was created and financed by Robert A. Levy, a Florida millionaire who is now chairman of Cato.

Surprising as it may seem—or not—the *Heller* case was not spontaneously generated by residents of the District of Columbia chafing for freedom from an oppressive gun law. On the day the *Heller* decision was announced, lead attorney Alan Gura claimed on CNN's *Glenn Beck* show that "about six years ago, six Washington, D.C., residents and a team of lawyers working independently decided it was time to challenge Washington, D.C.'s ban on handguns and other functional firearms in the home." [101]

That's not exactly the way it happened.

The lawyers and clients did not come together "independently." Levy—who lives in a four-thousand-square-foot condominium apartment in a gated luxury community in Florida and who has been described as "the Oz, the man behind the curtains" of *Heller*[102]—decided he wanted to take down the D.C. gun law. Levy used his money and influence to do just that. He and a friend, Clark M. Neily III, who works for a "libertarian" nonprofit law firm in Virginia, set about recruiting clients to sue the District of Columbia.[103] Levy told the *Washington Post* in 2007 that "with Cato's blessing," he paid for the entire lawsuit, from beginning to end, and refused other financial aid.[104] It should be noted, however, that Levy, Gura, Neily, and others who worked on the case subsequently won an award of just over $1.1 million in legal fees, to be paid by the taxpayers of the District of Columbia. The award was reduced by the deciding judge from the $3.1 million they had requested.[105]

Media profiles about the *Heller* case have tended to portray Levy as a sort of "aw, shucks" guy who just stepped in to help the poor people of the District of Columbia right an injustice. However, Levy has been an active operative at the Cato Institute since he joined its ranks in 1997, and he has authored numerous articles promoting Cato's antiregulatory line.[106] He is credited as the author of at least seventeen briefs filed with appellate courts.[107] Levy likes to point out that he was born in the District. In fact, he moved into the upscale Maryland suburb of Montgomery County as a young man and has not lived in the city itself for over forty years.[108]

Levy and Neily were both law clerks for Judge Royce C. Lamberth, now chief judge of the U.S. District Court for the District of Columbia.[109] When Levy decided to create his lawsuit, he called Neily, and the two started "recruiting a diverse group of plaintiffs." [110] In 2007, Levy described for the *Washington Post* how he and Neily spent months assembling the oppressed of the District.

> "We wanted gender diversity," he said. "We wanted racial diversity, economic diversity, age diversity." The plaintiffs had to be D.C. residents who believed fervently in gun rights and wanted loaded weapons in their homes for self-defense. And they had to be respectable.
>
> "No Looney Tunes," Levy said. "You know, you don't want the guy who just signed up for the militia. And no criminal records. You want law-abiding citizens."
>
> He and Neily worked the phones. "We called all our contacts in the legal community," Levy said. "We looked at the newspapers: Who was writing on the subject? Who was sending letters to the editor about gun laws?" They scoured the city. "Friends lead you to other friends, and you just keep talking and talking to people, until finally you have your clients." [111]

In sum, Scalia—known for his acerbic writing style and sarcastic wit[112]—was simply the sharp-tongued point of a well-funded ideological spear. This spear was aimed directly at the last of cases in which the Supreme Court had considered the meaning of the Second Amendment, *United States v. Miller*.[113]

The Supreme Court in *Miller*, decided in 1939, reaffirmed

what is known as the "collective rights" model of interpretation
of the Second Amendment. Simply put, the Second Amendment
"grants the people a collective right to an armed militia, as opposed to an individual right to keep and bear arms for one's own
purposes outside of, or even notwithstanding, government regulation." [114] It was not only the courts that uniformly accepted this
view of the Second Amendment. So did legal scholars. In fact,
from 1887 (when indexing began) until 1960, not a single law
review article advocated the "individual right" interpretation that
Scalia found in the Constitution. [115]

Thwarted by the uniform view of the courts against unrestrained individual access by anyone, anywhere, anytime, to guns
of any sort, the network of gun rights advocates turned their
focus to one of the most peculiar and little-known institutions
by which law is made in the United States—law review articles.
Astonishing as it may seem to most ordinary Americans, these
student-run journals supply an infinite variety of legalistic flakes
for lawyers, judges, and their clerks bent on producing "snow
jobs." By citing such articles as authority for their position on an
issue, the authors can cloak their naked manufacture of law—
or, as in Scalia's opinion, reversal of settled law—in an aura of
"scholarship."

Robert J. Spitzer, a professor of political science, examined
this phenomenon in the specific context of manufactured Second Amendment scholarship and observed:

> The discipline of law is unique among academic disciplines
> in that its professional journals are governed mostly by
> student-run law review boards, and with few exceptions,
> submissions are not subject to the process of peer review,
> or even faculty oversight. The consequences of these facts
> for law review content have been extensively discussed
> and debated within the law school community . . . law re-
> view student editors simply do not possess, and cannot be
> expected to possess, the knowledge and expertise of those

who have researched and published in a field . . . there is a proliferation, even a glut of law reviews—more than 800 by one count. Given such a huge publishing hole, these characteristics have increasingly produced a contrary editorial drive to publish articles for their distinctiveness rather than their scholarly soundness.[116]

It was into this "huge publishing hole" that pro-gun activists rushed, many of them former employees of or longtime collaborators with the NRA. "Contrarian positions get play," law professor Carl T. Bogus observed in another article on the same subject. Seeded in some cases by an NRA foundation that "began distributing large sums to friendly scholars" (one such scholar raked in $38,569.45 in 1991 and 1992 alone), a flurry of articles friendly to the individual rights view began to appear.[117] On the day after the decision was handed down, a Cato Institute blogger posted breathless "congrats to Eugene Volokh (of the Volokh Conspiracy blog) who had three of his law review articles cited in the majority opinion." The Russian-born Volokh is a relentlessly pro-gun blogger.[118]

Without descending into that thicket of argumentative "scholarship," one can assess the consequences in *Heller*, and thus for American gun violence, through the critical lens of Judge Posner's observation that Scalia was "engaged in what is derisively referred to—the derision is richly deserved—as 'law office history' ":

> [J]udges are advocates for whichever side of the case they have decided to vote for. The judge sends his law clerks scurrying to the library and to the Web for bits and pieces of historical documentation. When the clerks are the numerous and able clerks of Supreme Court justices, enjoying the assistance of the capable staffs of the Supreme Court library and the Library of Congress, and when dozens and sometimes hundreds of amicus curiae briefs have

been filed, many bulked out with the fruits of their authors' own law-office historiography, it is a simple matter, especially for a skillful rhetorician such as Scalia, to write a plausible historical defense of his position. . . . This is strikingly shown by the lengthy discussion of the history of interpretation of the Second Amendment. Scalia quotes a number of statements to the effect that the amendment guarantees a personal right to possess guns—but they are statements by lawyers or other advocates, including legislators and judges and law professors all tendentiously dabbling in history, rather than by disinterested historians: more law-office history, in other words.[119]

Heller was, then, a snow job produced from the flakes of dabblers in history, created and underwritten by a wealthy philosopher-king from the throne of his Florida condominium, with a cast of thousands from right-wing front groups, the NRA, the gun lobby, the gun industry, and paid-for scholars. Almost as disturbing as Scalia's ruling itself was its endorsement by some gun violence prevention advocates, who naively believed that the gun lobby would fold its tents and go away after their victory. One local activist enthused, "Actually, the Supreme Court's ruling last year was one of the best things to happen to the gun-control movement . . . that slippery-slope argument, that any new gun law is just another step towards taking all guns away, is dead." [120]

But that is not at all what *Heller* wrought. The decision has emboldened gun enthusiasts to attack gun control regulation all over America. One manufacturer, Beretta, donated a million dollars to the NRA for work on overturning gun control laws in the wake of *Heller*.[121] As of June 1, 2012, state and local governments were litigating forty-four significant civil lawsuits challenging various firearms laws under the Second Amendment. The lawsuits challenged a variety of gun control laws, including those regulating the carrying of concealed weapons, registration laws, bans on unsafe handguns and assault weapons, and safe-storage laws. There were also seven significant lawsuits pending against the federal government. Challenges have also been raised in a variety of criminal cases. These civil and criminal challenges have been largely unsuccessful at this writing, as even after *Heller* "courts have found that the Second Amendment is consistent with numerous federal and state criminal laws." [122] Nevertheless, the law after *Heller* is in flux, and some courts have ruled against strong gun laws. In March 2012, for example, a federal judge struck down a Maryland law requiring that persons wishing to carry a handgun outside their home must show "good and substantial reason." One of the lawyers in the case was Alan Gura—the same lawyer who brought down the District Of Columbia's gun law at Robert Levy's bidding, and who works closely with the gun advocate and anti-environmentalist Alan Gottlieb. [123]

Like Scalia in *Heller*, the gun lobby, its captive "gun press," and pro-gun policymakers aggressively tout "self-defense" as an important reason not only to allow but to encourage widespread ownership of firearms, and handguns in particular. This "common sense" argument appeals to the uninformed, not only as a reason to buy a handgun but also as a rationale for letting others own them. The argument actually turns the objective evidence on its head. Serious research by public health scholars—detailed in subsequent chapters—has demonstrated over and over that in virtually every civilian situation, the presence of firearms, particularly handguns, does not make people safer—it puts them in greater danger. David Hemenway, director of the Harvard Injury Control Research Center, has summarized this evidence:

> Within the United States, a wide array of empirical evidence indicates that more guns in a community lead to more homicide. Studies also indicate that a gun in the home increases the risk of murder for family members. Since a gun in the home tends to also increase the risk

of suicide and unintentional firearm injury, many public health practitioners emphasize the dangers of bringing a gun into the home, particularly if children are present.[124]

This is the core of the public health and safety approach to guns—an approach of which the eighteenth century was ignorant. It has saved millions of lives in other contexts, such as motor vehicle safety, disease, and consumer products. In this context, it is worth noting that a reviewer of one of Scalia's books observed that although in his opinion Scalia is brilliant, "he seems unaware of, or indifferent to, the real-world consequences of what he proposes."[125]

In contrast, the key question the public health and safety approach asks of any consumer product is *all* about real world consequences—what are the product's relative risks and benefits? If a product inflicts unreasonable harm, the inquiry then is whether the cause of harm is a defect in design or some factor inherent in the nature of the product. If the source of harm is a design defect, like a motor vehicle with a tendency to roll over on curves, it may be possible to correct the design. Some products, however, like highly toxic pesticides, are so inherently dangerous that no amount of design modification can make them reasonably safe. In such cases, the product may either be restricted to specific persons or banned outright.[126]

Unlike traditional "gun control" advocates who focus on criminal use of firearms, public health and safety experts look at physical *causes* of death and injury and seek ways to reduce the effects by modifying the physical causes. Thus, when people being hurled out of or through the windshields of cars was demonstrated to be a factor in motor-vehicle deaths and injuries, these experts advocated seatbelts and other restraints as effective means to reduce harm.

To such experts, the fact that an implement as lethal as a handgun has become ubiquitous and can be concealed and carried around becomes a significant risk factor. It plainly makes it much more likely that a human being will be killed or seriously injured in circumstances where, without the presence of a handgun, only bruised egos or minor injuries would occur. "A lighted match can certainly start a fire, but the potential for serious injury or death is much greater if you toss in a bucket of gasoline," wrote public health expert Dr. Arthur L. Kellermann. "Likewise, violence can certainly cause harm, but the potential for serious injury or death is increased when a firearm is involved." [127]

The public health and safety approach has become a well-established and highly effective way to reduce deaths and injuries from virtually every consumer product other than guns, including motor vehicles, toys, and power tools (among thousands of other products). But because the firearms industry is specifically exempted from the federal Consumer Product Safety Act, handguns have escaped the sort of close scrutiny to which every other consumer product in America is subject.

So what about Justice Scalia's homage to the handgun? In the absence of any citation, it is hard to know exactly whence he divined his statement that "the American people have considered the handgun to be the quintessential self-defense weapon." Surveys over time of households in five counties around Atlanta, Georgia, found that "a majority of respondents to all three surveys (55%) agreed with the statement 'A home with a gun is less secure than a home without a gun, because a gun can be involved in an accidental shooting, suicide or family homicide.' Among five home security measures, respondents rated a burglar alarm most effective and keeping a gun in the home least effective." [128]

The great majority of Americans do not own even a single gun, much less rely upon a handgun for "personal defense." An ongoing, long-term survey of gun ownership in America has found a "clear pattern" over the past several decades of a "persistent decline in household gun ownership." [129] From 1977 to 2010, the percentage of American households that reported having any guns in the home dropped more than 40 percent. In 2010, less than a third of American households reported having a gun in the home. In 2010, slightly more than one out of five Americans reported personally owning a gun.[130] Guns are "most likely to be owned by white men who live in a [*sic*] rural areas, those who are middle-aged or older, with a middle to higher income, who grew up with guns in the home and who live in the southern or midwestern regions of the country."[131] Moreover, fewer and fewer people are owning more and more guns. Gun owners reported an average of 6.9 guns per owner compared with 4.1 reported in 1994.[132] SAF's Alan Gottlieb—who used a loophole in federal law to restore his gun rights as a convicted felon—owns at least sixty guns.[133] In other words, the vast majority of Americans, who do not own or want guns, are put at risk every day so that a shrinking minority of "enthusiasts" can indulge their fascination with little killing machines. Quite literally, gun ownership is an aberration.

Moreover—putting aside the self-interested marketing hype of the gun industry—there is far from universal agreement, even among pro-gun experts, that the handgun is the "quintessential self-defense weapon" that Scalia imagined in his opinion would be used against a bogeyman burglar.

Duane Thomas, for example, wrote in his pro-handgun book that "the only thing handguns really have going for them as weapons is their small size."[134] Another pro-gun expert and author, Chris Bird, wrote in a manual intended for people who wish to carry a concealed handgun that the handgun "is the least-effective firearm for self defense." Unless one is at arm's length, he opined, "shotguns and rifles are much more effective." He also noted that the "handgun is the hardest firearm to shoot accurately."[135]

What is more likely than Justice Scalia's ipse dixit—and Robert Levy's kingly decree from a gated community in Florida to the citizenry of the District of Columbia—is that the American people understand quite well that a gun in the home increases the risk of homicide, suicide, and unintentional (accidental) injury.

The next chapter shows how the brunt of the gun industry's marketing falls particularly hard on women and children.

3

WOMEN AND CHILDREN LAST

James Ian Sherrill, thirty-five, stood weeping before Judge James M. Graves Jr. on August 16, 2010.

"If I could go back and redo it, I would take the beating," he sobbed.[1]

A resident of Fruitport Township, Michigan, Sherrill pleaded "no contest" a month earlier to a felony charge of assault with a dangerous weapon.[2] Now he stood at the court's bar, awaiting the judge's sentence. Sherrill plainly regretted his moment of reckless anger. That furious instant arrived on May 15, 2010, when he jerked his concealed 9mm handgun out of its holster, pointed the loaded gun at another soccer dad, and said, "If you don't back off, I'm gonna shoot you."[3] The threat in the parking lot of Fruitport's Pine Park—still crowded with children and other parents—was the climax of a series of verbal exchanges between the two men that began during a league match among six- to eight-year-old children.[4]

"I've been suicidal because of this," Sherrill said, making his tearful plea for leniency. He said he was on medication for panic attacks, and claimed that he had been scared ever since the incident, afraid to enter stores and restaurants.[5] Indeed, a single moment of armed anger had changed Sherrill's life forever.

Fruitport is yet another of the archetypical American small towns that clutter the map of gun violence in the United States. It lies on the eastern shore of Lake Michigan, about a third of the way up the western coast of Michigan, across the lake from Milwaukee. The vast Manistee National Forest sprawls off to the northeast, within which members of the West Michigan Volunteer Militia flop around and shoot guns in the brush from time to time, training for Armageddon "because a well-armed citizenry is the best Homeland Security and can better deter crime, invasion, terrorism or tyranny."[6] In 2000 the township had a population of about 12,500, 97 percent of whom are white, and a median family income of $54,634. Only 6.6 percent of the population were below the poverty line.[7] It was within this Michigan idyll that Sherrill built a solidly bourgeois life as a licensed counselor, a stay-at-home father with three young children, and a Cub Scout leader.[8] By his sentencing day, however, Sherrill's state counselor's license had been suspended.[9] His concealed-carry permit also would be permanently revoked the day after his sentencing.[10]

Amazing as it may seem to most Americans, Sherrill violated no law by simply bringing his hidden gun to a children's soccer match. He had a concealed-weapons permit for the handgun he had on his person that day, and the park was not posted as a "no carry" zone.[11] But after his arrest, he must certainly have pondered the same question that another family man, James Humphrey, forty-five, asked himself time and again after he shot a man to death in a moment of road rage following a night of drinking at bars. How does one go so quickly from "beloved family man with no criminal record" to violent criminal? "I've thought about it every day for the last 11 months," Humphrey said. "There is no answer for how you go from there to here."[12]

Actually, there is an answer. The presence of a gun in the midst of anger or other strong human emotion is a one-way ticket "from there to here."

Take Sherrill's case. Judge Graves concluded that he was "a basically decent person who overreacted" that day. "It's just very sad that human emotions get out of control in this way . . . from a children's game," he said. Sherrill's pulling his gun out was "greatly escalating the risk of potential harm and danger" with children nearby. He sentenced Sherrill to thirty days in the

Muskegon County Jail, less two days already served, and eighteen months of probation, plus costs and fees.[13] Putting aside his ruined life, Sherrill got off relatively easy. No one died or was injured.

But his intemperate act is a chilling example of what Brooke de Lench called "an endless series" of tales of angry parents out of control at youth events, of which "most go undocumented."[14] De Lench, the founder of MomsTeam.com, a website for parents, and a youth sports expert, cites a survey that "supports the view that the reports of misbehaving parents in the media are not isolated events."[15] Add a gun to the mix, and an argument goes from angry to deadly in seconds. A sports official in Lubbock, Texas—where angry parents had pulled guns at youth events three times within a decade—said, "It seems to be getting worse every year. Parents have become more and more abusive."[16]

In Roanoke, Virginia, Charles David Akers, thirty-six, was convicted of brandishing an AR-15 assault rifle at a girls' soccer match. According to witnesses, when his daughter did not make the soccer team, Akers became angry and made threatening remarks to the coach. He drove off, returned, pulled the assault rifle from his trunk, and made a sweeping motion around the field with the gun for several moments.[17] In Lubbock, Texas, Tye Burke, twenty-five, a concealed-carry weapons (CCW) permit holder, pulled his gun at a soccer game for seven- to eight-year-old girls. According to witnesses in news reports, Burke was yelling at the girls' team coach. The coach's husband confronted Burke, the two started arguing, and the husband shoved Burke. Burke then pulled out his pistol and aimed it at the husband's head. An off-duty prison guard tackled Burke and disarmed him.[18] A Lubbock grand jury declined to indict Burke.[19]

In Philadelphia, Wayne Derkotch, forty, also a CCW permit holder, got into a fistfight with his son's coach at a five- to six-year-olds football game. Witnesses said the fight started after Derkotch complained about his son not getting enough playing time. Derkotch pulled out his .357 Magnum revolver after the coach apparently got the better of him in the fight—he lost a tooth and his eye was swollen. A judge later acquitted him of criminal charges, ruling that he acted in self-defense.[20] In Memphis, Tennessee, yet another CCW permit holder, Nicholis Williams, twenty-nine, was accused of pointing his handgun at his ten-year-old son's baseball coach. Williams was reportedly annoyed because his son did not get as many times at bat as other children. After the game, the coach approached Williams in the parking lot and asked him not to curse in front of the kids. Williams told the coach to "shut the fuck up," pulled his gun out from under a car mat, loaded it, and pointed it at the coach. The coach disarmed Williams, who left the scene. Williams was later arrested and charged with aggravated assault. His CCW permit was suspended after the incident and had not been restored as of March 2012.[21]

The prospect of perturbed parents packing pistols at children's sports events understandably frightens other parents. "Everybody is worried about the safety of children," a Salem, Virginia, detective said after the Akers assault rifle incident. "If I were a parent, I'd be nervous."[22] The *Memphis Commercial Appeal* called the Williams incident "an alarming wake-up call about what can happen when emotions explode and a handgun is handy."[23]

In North Carolina, Carol Coulter, a member of the Ashe County Parks and Recreation Advisory Board, pointed out a classic problem with CCW vigilantism. "I've had ample opportunity to observe people in the stands at sporting events and it never ceases to amaze me how adults can act in such childish ways," she said. "I fear that by having access to a concealed weapon, in a thoughtless moment of rage a gun will be pulled and in response to that, others with concealed weapons will also pull their guns and perhaps if someone didn't see who pulled the gun first then you've got people pointing guns and they don't even know who they should be pointing at."[24] Coulter's concern is far from academic. On Long Island, New York, a federal Bureau of Alcohol, Tobacco, Firearms and Explosives (ATF) agent was unintentionally killed by a retired police officer who rushed up to the scene as the agent struggled with a robber outside a pharmacy. The retired officer shot the wrong man.[25] A related danger is stray shots hitting innocent bystanders. In May 2012 in Houston, Texas, a store customer and CCW holder pulled out his gun and exchanged gunfire with two armed robbers. The would-be defender accidentally shot and killed a twenty-six-year-old store clerk.[26]

But not everyone agrees that kids and guns don't mix. "Gun rights" activists—with the help of the NRA, the gun lobby, and blinkered judges—have relentlessly pushed back the boundaries of common sense to ensure their "right" to bring their guns to their children's Pee Wee Football, Little League baseball, and soccer—not to mention public parks, bars, churches, and schools. "The speed at which guns laws are being relaxed is increasing," said John Pierce, a co-founder of OpenCarry.org. "We're very happy about it."[27] An example of the kind of counterfactual wisdom propelling these victories can be found in the following harangue that enthusiasts of mixing guns, kids, and parks in Forsyth County, North Carolina, asked their supporters to send to officials who opposed lax gun-carry rules:

> Free Americans have the God-given right to bear arms EVERYWHERE.
>
> The evidence is clear: where these rights are restricted are [sic] dangerous.
>
> Where have mass-murders occurred? Where have child abductions, rapes and murders most often occurred? Claiming no reason for citizens to be lawfully armed in parks is wrong. Every American has personal responsibility for self-defense and the defense of family.
>
> Do you expect a 120 lb mother to defend herself and children against 250 lb criminals unarmed? If you believe that Forsyth County parks are immune to abductions/rapes/murders you are mistaken. It is not a matter of if, but when.[28]

To the denizens of this dark universe, a gun is an amulet that magically transforms the bearer into a righteous and invulnerable defender of all that is good, right, and holy, not a human being carrying a lethal weapon who is full of the emotions and chemicals that drive rage, fright, depression, anger, revenge, and jealousy. In the real world, that "120 lb mother" is much more likely to be shot and killed by her "250 lb" husband or boyfriend than ever to use a gun to defend herself from a criminal stranger.[29] Guns easily turn domestic violence into domestic homicide. A federal study on homicide among intimate partners found that female intimate partners are more likely to be murdered with a firearm than all other means combined, concluding that "the figures demonstrate the importance of reducing access to firearms in households affected by IPV [intimate partner violence]."[30]

The fact that a gun will more likely be used wrongly in a moment of rage, jealousy, depression, or mistaken perception than for some righteous purpose has been demonstrated from analysis of real-world data, collected decade after decade from the grim records of death and injury in America. Firearms are rarely used to kill criminals or stop crimes. Instead, they are all too often used to inflict harm on the very people they were intended to protect. According to the Federal Bureau of Investigation's Uniform Crime Reports, in 2009 there were only 261 justifiable homicides committed by private citizens. Of these, only 21 involved women killing men. Of those, only 13 involved firearms, with 10 of the 13 involving handguns.[31]

It is easier, and frankly more effective, for gun enthusiasts to spin fictional Fright Night tales than integrate such facts into their thinking. Supreme Court Justice Scalia pinned his statement on the utility of handguns in *Heller* largely to a familiar gun rights canard: "What if a burglar breaks into your home?" What Scalia did not write, and perhaps did not know, is that most household burglaries occur when no household member is in the home. A Justice Department study of household burglaries between 2003 and 2007 found that no one was home in 72.4 percent of household burglaries.[32] What's more, even when someone was at home and was a victim of violent crime, almost two thirds (65.1 percent) of the offenders were not strangers. Of those violent burglars who were not strangers, 31.1 percent were intimates or former intimates (girlfriends, boyfriends, or spouses), while 34 percent were either relatives or acquaintances of the victim.[33]

Another subject conspicuously absent from Justice Scalia's discussion is the danger that bullets fired from handguns present to one's innocent neighbors. According to a 2012 article in *Guns & Ammo* magazine, this risk of "overpenetration" is one that "has always been a concern when discussing the use of firearms in a dwelling." The article warns that the results of "exhaustive studies about what pistol and shotgun projectiles do when fired indoors" are "very interesting (and not in a good way)." Contrary to the uninformed belief of many gun enthusiasts that overpenetration is not an issue with handguns, "Such is not the case. Drywall sheets and hollow-core doors (which are what you'll find in the majority of homes and apartments in this country) offer almost no resistance to bullets. Unless brick or cinderblock was used somewhere in your construction, any pistol cartridge powerful enough to be thought of as suitable for self-defense is likely to fly completely through every wall in your abode."[34]

The point here is neither to deny the reality of burglary nor to diminish its trauma. The point is rather to ask: what is the better defense against burglary, to bring a gun into the home or to better secure one's residence? This is the balance that the gun industry and its advocates never consider.

One of the more vociferous advocates of the right to carry handguns anytime, anywhere was Meleanie Hain. The mother of three children, Hain lived in Lebanon, Pennsylvania.[35] If the seat of Lebanon County sounds familiar to the reader, it should. Lebanon is the town in which—on the morning the Supreme Court handed down the decision in *Heller* striking down the District of Columbia handgun law—Raymond Zegowitz shot to death his girlfriend Khrystina Bixa, then committed suicide.[36]

Meleanie Hain achieved a certain prominence as the "pistol-packin' soccer mama" and hero of the gun rights movement. Hain's firearms-rights flame flared up on September 11, 2008, when she wore a loaded Glock 26 semiautomatic pistol on her hip, openly displaying it at her five-year-old daughter's soccer game. Quite naturally, other parents were troubled. Controversy ensued. "What's the difference between a bulldog and a soccer mom?" a local newspaper writer scribbled. "In the case of Meleanie Hain, it's a loaded sidearm."[37]

Glock calls Hain's gun of choice for four- to five-year-olds' soccer games its "Baby" Glock, a "triumphant advance . . . specially developed for concealed carry . . . previously a domain of 5-round snub nose revolvers." The Austrian semiautomatic pistol maker boasts of the gun's "magazine capacity of 10 rounds as standard and [its] highly accurate firing characteristics."[38]

Settled in 1723 by German farmers, Lebanon County is described by its government website as a place where "residential, commercial and industrial development" is going on amid "its pastoral landscape, attractive farms and outstanding dairy and pork products, especially Lebanon Bologna."[39] But the pastoral landscape of Lebanon's rolling Pennsylvania Dutch country was not reassuring to Hain. A vegetarian and self-described "pseudo devotee" of the Hare Krishna sect,[40] she professed to have been haunted by fears for the safety of herself and her children. According to the *Philadelphia Inquirer*, Hain saw danger "lurking around every corner."[41]

In most accounts, Hain described the source of her vague but ubiquitous fear as a near-fatal automobile accident, which the *Inquirer* reported "destroyed her sense of security and convinced her that the worst can happen."[42] According to a newspaper brief, in April 2006 a van driven by Hain collided with a pickup truck. Hain, her two-year-old child, the driver of the truck, and his passenger were all taken to the hospital. Four days after the accident, Hain was described as in "fair" condition.[43] In another report by the *Patriot News* of Harrisburg, Pennsylvania, however, Hain is reported to have told a judge that she carried a gun "because her husband works in law enforcement."[44]

Whatever the reason, Hain decided that a gun was the answer to her fears. "I thought, 'What more can I do to ensure the safety of myself and my children,?" she told the *Inquirer*. "It's not a matter of being paranoid. People have smoke detectors and fire extinguishers in their homes. They're not paranoid; they're prepared."[45]

"Being prepared" for Hain first meant getting a permit to carry her gun concealed on her person. But at some point Hain decided to go beyond discreetly carrying her gun. She started packing it on her hip, in plain view, everywhere she went. "I don't really need anything extra in the way of the gun if I'm going to have to pull it out and I'm holding a baby and trying to shuttle two or three other kids," she said in a 2008 newspaper interview.[46]

Although Hain claimed she had worn the holstered gun openly without incident before, parents at Lebanon's Optimist Park on that September 11 noticed her wearing the gun and complained to Charlie Jones, a coach who was also the county's public defender.[47] "More than one parent was upset," Jones told the local newspaper.[48] In another interview, he said that he told Hain, "Kids are more in danger of falling off a piece of playground equipment or getting hit by a car in the parking lot than anybody coming and doing anything where you need a gun to defend yourself."[49]

The day after the incident, Hain got an e-mail from Nigel Foundling, director of the Lebanon soccer program. Foundling wrote that carrying guns to the games was against the soccer program's policy. "A responsible adult would realize that such behavior has no place at a soccer game," Foundling wrote. He told Hain that if she persisted in packing heat, she would be banned from the games, and that he would tell police about the incident. Within a few days, Hain got a letter from county sheriff Mike DeLeo, who had been contacted by another child's parent. DeLeo revoked Hain's concealed-carry permit, based on his assessment that her actions showed a lack of judgment.[50] The revocation of Hain's permit had the odd result that if Hain wished to continue to go about armed, she could do it only with her gun in plain sight, just as she had been doing. Such "open carry" is legal in most of Pennsylvania.

Hain was not inclined to back down. Because the soccer games were played on public property, she asserted, the league did not have the power to curtail her right to bear arms. She also appealed Sheriff DeLeo's suspension of her concealed-carry permit. The battle lines were drawn. Within a month, Hain won her license back. In a courtroom packed with Hain's supporters, Judge Robert J. Eby ordered her license returned but questioned her common sense. "What is the purpose [at] an event where 5-year-olds are playing soccer?" he asked. "To make other people afraid of you? Fear doesn't belong at a kids' soccer game. For protection? I absolutely hope we don't feel we need to be protected at a 5-year-old soccer game. . . . What if everyone came packing, so you'd have a visibly armed force on both sides?"[51]

"There's no question we all have rights under the Second Amendment," Judge Eby observed. "But with these rights come responsibilities. There are limitations on what rights you have, and there has to be a balancing . . . a balance between the rule of law and common sense."[52] The judge's lecture to Hain went on. "Society is replacing right versus wrong with legal versus illegal," he said. "They are not the same thing. They never were and it is my hope they never will be. There are times when someone's conduct may be perfectly legal, but it is still wrong."[53]

Eby's cautionary advice was like water off a duck's back. Hain promptly and publicly dismissed the judge's views as "only his opinion."[54] She intended to keep packing her gun wherever and whenever she wanted. As to his question about the purpose of it all? The headstrong Hain didn't need a purpose because "the Constitution has guaranteed me a right, and there is nothing more to say about it."[55] And what about the other parents? What if they wanted gun-free soccer games? Greg Rotz of Pennsylvania Open Carry, a group that loudly backed Hain, had a simple answer. "They don't have that right," he said.[56] As judges complied and politicians surrendered to the demands of Pennsylvania's gun toters, it looked as if Rotz was right. After consulting with lawyers, Tom Dougherty, the president of the Eastern Pennsylvania Youth Soccer Association, said, "We could put a rule in our books, but we can't enforce it. We're really kind of powerless." In this upside-down world of "gun rights," Sharon Gregg-Bolognese, the president of the Central Pennsylvania Youth Soccer League, began telling parents to abandon a game if they didn't feel safe. "We don't want kids at risk. Sometimes canceling the game is the only option," she said.[57]

Hain's case became a cause célèbre, sparking news reports nationally and as far away as Australia.[58] Not satisfied with her easy victory, Hain and her husband, Scott, hired Matthew Weisberg, a lawyer from Philadelphia, and sued Sheriff DeLeo, the Office of the Lebanon County Sheriff, and Lebanon County in federal court. The pair claimed that DeLeo and the local government had violated their civil rights. They asked for more than $1 million in damages to cover lost income from Hain's home baby-sitting service, which had gone from three clients to one in the wake of the controversy, "emotional distress," and attorneys' fees.[59]

Meleanie Hain now began to be painted as victim rather than provocateur. "She has been stigmatized unfairly," said Weisberg,[60] whose website says his law practice concentrates on "Consumer Fraud and Financial Injury based litigation, Mortgage Foreclosure, Professional Negligence (including Legal Malpractice) and Civil Rights."[61] Parents who didn't like Hain's packing to five-year-olds' soccer games, Weisberg told the press, should have transferred their children to another team, rather than force Hain to "bear the result of their disapproval."[62]

"I am a victim of Sheriff [Michael] DeLeo's," Hain claimed. "I am a victim of those in society as a direct result of his actions as well. The way people look at me sometimes when I am out running errands, I feel as if I am wearing a scarlet letter, and really, it's a Glock 26."[63]

The appearance of Scott Hain's name on the lawsuit was an anomaly. He had lain low throughout most of the drama. "My husband has been supportive all along," Meleanie Hain wrote in an e-mail answering questions from the *Harrisburg Patriot News* in December 2008. "He has just kept himself out of the public eye because of the sensitive nature of his employment."[64] When the *Philadelphia Inquirer* interviewed Meleanie Hain for a profile, it reported that "her husband, who taught her to shoot, works in law enforcement but stays out of the fray, fearing it will cost him his job. She won't say where he works and in fact, he sat in his car while a reporter and photographer were in his house with Hain."[65] Scott Hain's mysterious employment was as a state probation officer in neighboring Berks County. A former prison guard, he also worked part time for Lebanon County Central Booking.[66]

Sometime within the next six months, Meleanie told her lawyer that she and Scott were having marital problems and said Scott should be dropped from the lawsuit. She later told Weisberg that she was going to get a protective order against her husband. Neither of these things happened—Scott's name stayed on the lawsuit and Meleanie never got a protective order.[67]

Nevertheless, clearly all was not well in the Hain household, "on their leafy street of neat 1½-story brick homes."[68] The couple had reportedly been fighting, and on Tuesday, October 6, 2009, Scott Hain left the home.[69] He returned the following day. According to a neighbor, at about three thirty P.M. on Wednesday, "He was mowing his lawn, and the dog was outside. There was nothing out of the ordinary. He didn't seem strange at all."[70]

At about six twenty P.M., Meleanie was chatting on a webcam with an unidentified male, who was said by police to be a mutual friend of the Hains. The friend turned away from his computer for a moment. He heard a gunshot and a scream, and turned back. "The person saw Scott Hain standing over the location he had previously seen Meleanie Hain and pulling the trigger several times on a handgun," the Lebanon police chief told a press conference.[71] The friend called 911. At the same time, the Hains' three children—ages two, six, and ten—ran from the house screaming, "Daddy shot Mommy!"[72]

Lebanon police, complete with SWAT team, responded and took positions surrounding the deathly quiet house. When repeated attempts to contact Scott failed, police went in. Meleanie was lying in the kitchen, Scott in an upstairs room. Shortly after eight thirty P.M., Lebanon County coroner Dr. Jeffrey Yocum pronounced them both dead.[73] After conducting autopsies, Yocum pronounced the shootings a case of murder-suicide. Scott had pumped six rounds into Meleanie with a handgun found in his pocket, then gone upstairs and killed himself with a shotgun.[74]

Meleanie's "Baby" Glock 26 was found, fully loaded, in a backpack hanging on a hook on the back of the house's front door. Several other handguns, a shotgun, two rifles, and several hundred rounds of ammunition were also found in the Hain residence.[75]

"It's a Shakespearean, ironic tragedy," Matthew Weisberg observed. "The first irony is she was killed by a gun. The second irony is, she was fighting for the right to defend herself by carrying a gun, and she could not defend herself."[76]

Shakespearean, Greek, or Wagnerian, the tragedy went far beyond the ironic murder of a gun rights champion. My colleague, Josh Sugarmann, observed:

As an advocate who debated gun control supporters, Hain was well aware of the facts presented in opposition to her views. Yet she parried them as irrelevant to her world, in the same way that the concerns of her fellow Pennsylvania soccer moms were dismissed as the intellectual flotsam of the anti-gun mind. To this mindset, gun homicides, unintentional deaths and suicides were events that happened to other people who lacked the temperament, training or personal fortitude to own a gun. In essence, Hain, like many of her fellow pro-gun advocates, lacked an ability to think in the abstract: Her gun experience was positive and whatever negative effects others felt from firearms, the gun, and gun owners like herself, were never to blame.[77]

Meleanie Hain's story was not—indeed still is not—over. Like a legal zombie, the lawsuit she and Scott filed lurched forward. Matthew Weisberg continued to press the case on behalf of their children until Chief Judge Yvette Kane of the United States District Court for the Middle District of Pennsylvania drove a stake through the lawsuit's heart, dismissing all of its claims.[78] Pro-gun groups in the Middle Atlantic area still hold "memorial shoots" and "memorial dinners" to honor Hain's memory and ostensibly to raise money for her children.[79]

As dramatic as Hain's story may be, it was anything but exceptional. Meleanie Hain simply wrote large and in relatively slow motion what public health scholars already know. Guns in the home are much more likely to be used against occupants of that home—especially women—than against invaders from the outside. While two-thirds of women who own guns acquired them "primarily for protection against crime," the results of a California analysis show that "purchasing a handgun provides no protection against homicide among women and is associated with an increase in their risk for intimate partner homicide."[80] A 2003 study about the risks of firearms in the home found that females living with a gun in the home were nearly three times more likely to be murdered than females with no gun in the home.[81] There is more. Another study reports that women who were murdered were more likely, not less likely, to have purchased a handgun in the three years prior to their deaths, again invalidating the idea that a handgun has a protective effect against homicide.[82]

Meleanie Hain's saga fits precisely into this grim reality. In 2009—the year in which her husband shot her to death—1,818 females were murdered by males in single victim/single offender incidents that were submitted to the FBI for its Supplementary Homicide Report. Examination of that data dispels many of the myths regarding the nature of lethal violence against females:

- For homicides in which the victim-to-offender relationship could be identified, 93 percent of female victims (1,579 out of 1,693) were murdered by a male they knew.
- Nearly fourteen times as many females were murdered by a male they knew (1,579 victims) as were killed by male strangers (114 victims).
- For victims who knew their offenders, 63 percent (989) of female homicide victims were wives or intimate acquaintances of their killers.
- There were 296 women shot and killed by either their husband or intimate acquaintance during the course of an argument.
- Nationwide, for homicides in which the weapon could be determined (1,654), more female homicides were committed with firearms (52 percent) than with any other weapon. Knives and other cutting instruments accounted for 22 percent of all female murders, bodily force 13 percent, and murder by blunt object 7 percent. Of the homicides committed with firearms, 69 percent were committed with handguns.[83]

In the context of the year, Hain's murder was thus clearly not exceptional. Nor was it exceptional that Scott Hain then took his own life. The event fit the national pattern for murder-suicide. The most prevalent type of murder-suicide is between two intimate partners, the man killing his wife or girlfriend. Such events are commonly the result of a breakdown in the relationship.[84]

Unfortunately, no national database or tracking system exists to systematically document the toll in death and injury of murder-suicide in the United States. But starting in 2002, the

Violence Policy Center (VPC) began collecting and analyzing news reports of murder-suicides in order to more fully understand the human costs. Since then it has published a series of studies titled *American Roulette: Murder-Suicide in the United States*. Medical studies estimate that between 1,000 and 1,500 deaths per year in the United States are the result of murder-suicide. All of the VPC's reported analyses support this estimate. All major murder-suicide studies in the United States completed since 1950 have shown that firearms are by far the most common method of committing homicide, with the offender choosing the firearm for suicide as well. Estimates of firearms being used range from 80 percent to 94 percent of cases.

Studies analyzing murder-suicide, including those of the VPC, have found that most perpetrators of murder-suicide are male—more than 90 percent in recent studies of the United States. A study that looked only at murder-suicides involving couples noted that more than 90 percent were perpetrated by men. This is consistent with homicides in general, of which 89 percent are committed by males. However, most homicides involve male victims killed by male offenders (65 percent), whereas a male victim being specifically targeted by a male offender in a murder-suicide is relatively rare.

What about the microcosm of bucolic Lebanon County? The record there also demonstrates just how toxic guns are to families in America. A review of news stories reporting the autopsy findings of Dr. Jeffrey Yocum—the Lebanon County coroner—reveals a deadly contour remarkably similar to that of the nation as a whole. In addition to the Hain (2009) and Bixa (2008) murder-suicides, Dr. Yocum conducted autopsies in a 2005 murder-suicide at a chicken processing plant, in which a common-law husband shot his wife to death with a small handgun.[85] In 2010 there was another murder-suicide, when a thirty-five-year-old woman shot to death her thirty-nine-year-old boyfriend and then killed herself with the gun.[86] In 2011, a thirty-three-year-old mother was shot to death by her husband, who briefly took the couple's ten-year-old daughter hostage before state troopers subdued him.[87]

As of March 2012, there were no reports of any shooting in self-defense at soccer fields or anywhere else in Lebanon County.

But there were plenty of other shootings in Lebanon County, demonstrating the toxicity of the American domestic arms race. Dr. Slocum's annual report to the county commissioners details another scourge: suicide by gun. Over the five years from 2007 through 2011, the percentage of all suicides in Lebanon County committed by gun has rocketed from 45 percent in 2007 to 64 percent in 2011.[88] This data is shown in table form in figure 7 and graphically in figure 8.

Figure 7. Suicides in Lebanon County, Pennsylvania, 2007–2011

	All Suicides	Suicide by Gun	Percent Suicide by Gun
2007	11	5	45
2008	19	9	47
2009	12	7	58
2010	13	8	62
2011	14	9	64

"Suicides Up by 1 in 2011," *Lebanon Daily News*, Feb. 3, 2012; "Coroner Reports on 2010 Deaths," *Lebanon Daily News*, Feb. 27, 2011; letter dated Jan. 18, 2010, from Jeffrey A. Yocum, coroner, to Lebanon County commissioners, summarizing coroner's cases for 2009, in files of Violence Policy Center; "Coroner: County Suicides Up in 2008," *Lebanon Daily News*, Jan. 23, 2009; "Report Profiles '07 Coroner Cases," *Lebanon Daily News*, Feb. 1, 2008.

In spite of all of this evidence, the gun lobby continues to pitch its deadly products to women. The reason is simple. "When it comes to buying strength, women are no longer a niche market," *Shooting Industry*, the premier gun trade magazine, advised its readers in 2009.[89] The industry and a network of "shooting sports" groups see women as a key to profiting from the sale of firearms and related products to the whole family. "If you teach

Figure 8. Gun Suicides in Lebanon County, Pennsylvania, 2007–2011

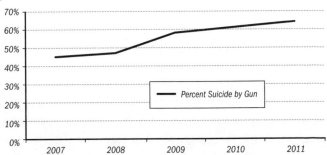

a man to hunt, he goes hunting. If you teach a woman to hunt, the entire family goes hunting," said the director of an Alabama program oriented toward women.[90]

The "effort to get more women shooting is a collaborative effort for all within the firearms industry."[91] Trade associations, manufacturers, the "gun press," and local gun dealers and shooting clubs are locked into a nationwide daisy chain to get a gun in every woman's hand in America. "We believe that a meaningful percentage of recent firearm sales are being made to first time gun purchasers, particularly women," the Freedom Group, a consolidated group of firearm manufacturers assembled by Cerberus Capital Management, stated in its annual report for fiscal year 2011.[92]

The NRA has a full clip of interlocking programs it aims at women.[93] The NSSF, which has women in the sights of its own programs, collegially reinforces the NRA's pitch. For example, NSSF's website boosts the NRA's "Women's Wilderness Escape" program. "Launched in 2008," the NSSF blurb gushes, "this eight-day camp is led by some of the nation's most experienced instructors and is dedicated to introducing women, ages 18 and older, regardless of experience level, to the countless forms of outdoor recreation awaiting them, all of which relate directly or indirectly to our shooting and hunting traditions."[94]

Gun manufacturers have their own lures for women.

A number—including Taurus, Charter Arms, and Smith & Wesson—make handguns in pink colors. According to one gun dealer, this hits women right where their dollars are. "Women get all excited about pink guns, even if they don't buy one," he said. "Women will come in and buy a Beretta pink visor. They might not even have a gun; they just think the visor is cool." [95] Glock— the maker of Meleanie Hain's "Baby" Glock 26—sponsored a "GLOCK Girl Shootout, the first ever ladies only match," in Reevesville, South Carolina. Not coincidentally, Lisa Marie Judy, whose "vision" the GLOCK Girl Shootout was, is also the owner of B.E.L.T. Training, where the event was held in 2011. [96] "Just because I am a girl, it doesn't mean I can't Rock out with my GLOCK out!" Judy was quoted as saying in a Glock media release. [97]

Gun dealers and shooting ranges also sponsor special "ladies days" and classes, billed as introductory training, but actually designed to generate buying traffic. [98] "Work with a local range and hold an introductory event," *Shooting Industry* advises gun stores. "NSSF's First Shots program is specifically designed to build customer traffic at shooting ranges. That traffic will transfer to your store when those participants need equipment." [99] Apparel and accessories for women have also become an important follow-on market for the gun industry. "The growth is with women," Shelah Zmigrosky, owner of Foxy Huntress, told *Shooting Industry*. "Men have their toys and clothes, and now women want their own." [100] A website devoted to women's shooting accessories is called GunGoddess.com. "Move over boring black and olive drab green, because the shooting range is about to get a lot more colorful! At GunGoddess.com you'll find ladies' shooting accessories, apparel and gifts in fun, feminine fabrics and colors." [101] *Shooting Industry* has another idea, suggesting that "dealers have a new venue for offering women's hunting clothing that doesn't take up one bit of their sales floor—the Camp Wild Girls Home Hunting Party." [102]

The gun industry's obsession with women has another,

seamier side. While on the one hand the industry is trying to lure women as customers, often arguing that guns are empowering, on the other a number of its denizens exploit women as cheese-cake. Unabashed examples abound, some distributed on the floor of the NSSF's annual SHOT Show extravaganza. Ads in *Shotgun News*—a widely circulated national gun advertising tabloid—regularly feature women in provocative dress and poses. In the June 1, 2012, edition, for example, the importer American Tactical Imports posted an ad for its FX45 Thunderbolt semiautomatic pistol. The ad features a buxom young woman clad in a brassiere, midriff bare, holding a pistol in each hand. The tagline reads, "Enhanced For Your Pleasure."[103] In the same edition, a full-page ad for European American Armory Corporation (EAA) displays another young woman with a bare midriff and cocked hips, clad in tightly fitting clothes and holding a Baikal shotgun. Below the woman appears the phrase, "XOXO Candy!" and to the side, the logo "See It All."[104] EAA also sells pinup calendars, displaying guns and women in titillating poses, for current and past years, from its Internet website.[105]

In spite of the industry's strenuous efforts to promote guns and its intermittent revival every few years of the entirely specious canard that gun sales to women are soaring, the hard fact is that female personal gun ownership remains relatively rare. It fluctuates within a narrow range, with no recent signs of increase. In 2010, only one out of ten American females reported personally owning a gun. Female personal gun ownership peaked at 14.3 percent in 1982. In 2010, the female personal gun ownership rate was 9.9 percent.[106]

The industry just as cynically targets children as its future consumers. It has ginned up "youth-oriented" campaigns for girls, similar to those for women but aimed at a younger demographic. The first "National Take Your Daughters to the Range Day," for example, was scheduled to be held on June 9, 2012. "This event will be an opportunity for gun ranges throughout the nation to introduce many young women to a sport that may just become a life-long hobby, or even a profession," one promoter claimed in a leadup to the event. "Boys learn to shoot in Scouts or with their Dads," Lynne Finch, National Take Your Daughters to The Range Day co-founder and firearms instructor, was quoted as saying. "Often, the girls are left behind because shooting isn't 'girly.' Well, we can, and do shoot, and well." [107]

The National Shooting Sports Foundation, U.S. Sportsmen's Alliance, National Wild Turkey Federation, Congressional Sportsmen's Foundation, and the National Rifle Association sponsor a program called Families Afield: An Initiative for the Future of Hunting. [108] The reason for this national "initiative" (marketing campaign) is simple. The number of kids who are drawn into hunting has been shrinking dramatically for years. Hunting is one of the prime ways that long-term future buyers are introduced to guns. Fewer young hunters equals fewer future gun buyers. [109]

The gun industry coalition attempting to reverse this trend has manufactured a nationwide lobbying campaign to pressure state legislatures to lower the legal hunting age. "Studies show that children's interests and leisure time are set by age 12. We wanted to get to them before soccer, hockey and other organized sports," a Michigan Department of Natural Resources employee explained about the purpose of the younger-hunter programs. [110]

It is no surprise that the gun industry's goal is to lower safety standards to the cellar in pursuit of profits. "Our goal is to have all fifty states in the least restrictive category," a Families Afield report stated. [111] The "least restrictive" category means states that have "regulations or laws that 1) permit youth hunting largely at the parents' discretion and 2) hunter education requirements that largely permit youth participation before passing hunter education tests. None of these states have a minimum hunting age." [112]

Can this feverish marketing of guns to kids be good in the long run for America's children? The answer is clearly no. This book has already described several stories of children who were killed or maimed by guns in America. One of them was the four-year-old boy in Hampton, Arkansas, who found a loaded hand-gun in a living room cabinet and shot his five-year-old sister to death on the day the Supreme Court handed down its wisdom in *Heller*.[113] The tide of tragedy continues without ebb.

On March 14, 2012, a traveling family stopped for gas near Tacoma, Washington. The father put his pistol under the seat and got out to pump gas. The mother went inside the station. A three-year-old boy in the car climbed out of his child seat, found the gun, and shot himself to death. "It is incredible in light of the other ones," said Tacoma police officer Naveed Benjamin. "You would think people would take more care, not less."[114]

The "other ones" to whom Officer Benjamin referred were two other children who had been shot within a month's time in Washington State. On February 22, 2012, an unidentified nine-year-old "75-pound boy with the buzz cut and blue eyes" brought a loaded 45 caliber semiautomatic pistol in a backpack to his third-grade class in Bremerton, Washington. When he dropped the pack on his desk, the gun fired. A bullet struck eight-year-old Amina Kocer-Bowman near her spine, causing serious in-juries. As of March 2012, she had undergone five surgeries and remained in serious condition. The boy had taken the gun from the home of his mother and her boyfriend.[115]

The third shooting gives the lie to the gun enthusiasts' tired argument that such tragedies happen only to people who lack, in Josh Sugarmann's words, "the temperament, training or personal fortitude to own a gun."[116] On March 10, 2012, seven-year-old Jenna Carlile, the daughter of a Marysville, Washington, police officer, was playing with her three younger siblings in the fam-ily's silver Volkswagen van. The parents were nearby. Jenna's younger brother found a loaded gun in the glove compartment and accidentally shot her in the torso. She died of her injury the next day.[117]

It was not the first time the child of a law enforcement officer—a class of persons society presumes to have the proper training and temperament to be trusted with guns—was killed in Washington State by a sibling. Neighbors of Clark County Sheriff Sergeant Craig Randall complained for fourteen years about the lax handling of guns around the family home and about incidents involving some of the six Randall children and guns. Among other things, Sergeant Randall kept his semiautomatic pistol at home and unlocked. On January 13, 2003, ten-year-old Emilee Joy Randall, the youngest of the children and only daughter, whom the family called Princess, was shot in the head and killed by her older brother, Matthew. Her brother, who was already on probation for a gun-related conviction, had picked up his father's gun from a bedroom dresser.[118]

Sadly, these few anecdotes from a single state reflect the national data. A 2002 study at the Harvard School of Public Health found that "children 5–14 years old were more likely to die from unintentional firearm injuries, suicides and homicides if they lived in states (or regions) with more rather than fewer guns." Other types of violence against children—specifically nonfirearm homicides and nonfirearm suicides—were "not significantly associated with the availability of guns."[119] The relationship between more guns and shattered children's lives was true regardless of state-level poverty, education, and urbanization. The study's authors concluded that "where there are more guns children are not protected from becoming, but are rather much more likely to become, victims of lethal violence."[120]

The gun lobby does not let the lives of children get in the way of its resolute opposition to even the most tepid laws or regulations restricting access to guns. In Washington, State Senator Adam Kline sponsored legislation to simply require owners to have trigger locks and safes for their guns. "The NRA gets up in arms and says, 'Oh my God, this is the end of the Second Amendment. This is total violation of everything that Western civilization stands for.' The fact is it would've saved this girl's health and it would save the lives of kids," Kline said, referring to the shooting of Amina Kocer-Bowman.[121]

It may be that gun enthusiasts believe, as the gun industry and its front groups cynically pretend, that by mixing kids and guns they are continuing a historical ethic of self-reliance and promoting traditional values. If that is so, they are blind to the consequences, which are thrown into high relief by looking at the rest of the world.

> In contrast, children in other industrialized nations are not dying from guns. Compared with children 5–14 years old in other industrialized nations, the firearm-related homicide rate in the United States is 17 times higher, the firearm related suicide rate 10 times higher, and the unintentional firearm-related death rate 9 times higher. Overall, before a child in the United States reaches 15 years of age, he or she is 5 times more likely than a child in the rest of the industrialized world to be murdered, 2 times as likely to commit suicide and 12 times more likely to die a firearm-related death.[122]

The obvious question is, why is the gun industry doing this to America, and especially to its women and children? The next section answers that question, going beyond the motivation of mere greed to explain the method behind the industry's dark madness.

4

TWO TALES OF A CITY

Murfreesboro, Tennessee—another all-American town—lies 745 miles southwest of Lebanon, Pennsylvania, where gun rights activist Meleanie Hain was shot to death.[1] The seat of Rutherford County, Murfreesboro is in the exact center of Tennessee,[2] about 30 miles from Nashville. A comparison of the lives of two of Murfreesboro's famous sons casts into relief the choice America faces. Save lives by using proven public health and safety methods? Or knuckle under to the gun industry's aggressive marketing of militarized death under the false flags of Constitutional "right" and faux patriotism? The choice is no less stark than that.

Rutherford County, like Lebanon County, has its share of routine gun violence inflicted by otherwise law-abiding citizens on themselves and each other. The day-to-day shooting is pretty much like the shooting elsewhere in America.[3] As in other places, suicide and murder-suicide are prominent. A recent cross-state study—controlled for poverty, unemployment, urbanization, mental illness, and drug and alcohol dependence—found that "in states with more guns there were substantially more suicides because there were more firearms suicides."[4] About 63 percent of the suicide deaths reported in Tennessee in 2010 involved firearms.[5] The overall suicide rate in the state has increased significantly in recent years. In 2008, the rate rose by 14.6 percent.[6]

As tragic as the needless deaths in Rutherford County are, they are not extraordinary. Identical stories occur every day, all over America. But in recent years, Murfreesboro and Rutherford

County have grappled with another species of gun violence, fed by the deliberate design and marketing decisions that the magnates of the gun business have made—and continue to make—to keep their industry alive.

In 2012, this plague touched the upscale community of Amber Glen, described by a local real estate broker as a long established Murfreesboro neighborhood "of beautiful manicured lawns and well-maintained homes." Prices asked for homes listed on another broker's website in March 2012 ranged from $129,900 to $250,000.[7] The ethnicity of the neighborhood elementary school's children is 66 percent white, 21 percent black, 9 percent Asian–Pacific Islander, and 5 percent Hispanic.[8]

At about five ten P.M. on Presidents' Day, February 20, 2012, gunfire broke out on the elementary school's basketball court. Fourteen-year-old Taylor Schulz fell, shot twice in the leg. As many as a dozen children were playing on the school grounds at the time. Schulz required multiple surgeries. Two fifteen-year-old boys were arrested and charged with the shooting. Three other youths and one adult were charged with conspiracy.[9] The accounts of witnesses and the accused youths agree that the conflict involved rivalry over a girl. The conspirators allegedly arrived at the school armed with two pistols taken from a parent's gun cabinet. The cabinet was locked, according to police, but the youths knew where the keys were. Rude gestures and words were exchanged. Shots were fired.[10]

What made this shooting stand out was that even in quiet, upscale Amber Glen the gunfire ignited alarm about criminal gangs.[11] It now appears that there was no gang connection. But fear and concern that the shooting might be related to gangs was not fanciful; Murfreesboro and Rutherford County have both suffered a burst of gang-related gun violence in recent years. Perspective about its causes and the choices America faces can be found in the contrast between the lives and work of two of Murfreesboro's honored sons.

The first, Dr. Robert Sanders, "Dr. Seat Belt," devoted his

life to protecting children. When Dr. Sanders died in 2006, the *Nashville Tennessean* praised his life and accomplishments. "He fought ... for Tennessee citizens, particularly Tennessee's children," the paper's editors eulogized. "This state is deeply in his debt." [12] Dr. Sanders's life is a model of the comprehensive, fact-based public health and safety approach that could dramatically reduce gun death and injury in the United States.

Dr. Sanders was born in Tennessee. After completing his medical education, he went to work in 1966 as the Rutherford County Health Department's chief physician, in 1969 became its chief health official, and in 1983 took on the additional job of county medical examiner. [13] Rutherford County had a strong public health tradition going back to a decade before the Great Depression of the 1930s, when "Murfreesboro and its rural surroundings were the beneficiaries of an amazing infusion of finances and training" for public health. [14]

Dr. Sanders brought two elements to this public health–conscious environment. The first was the compassion of a gifted man who had seen and "detested the horribleness of car crashes and what they did to unrestrained babies and young children." [15] The second was that during his postgraduate study in Sweden, he saw seat belts that a safety-conscious doctor had designed and installed by himself in his car. "Dr. Sanders was impressed with this doctor's innovative idea, and that's when his interest in seat belts and safety devices began." [16]

In October 1974 Dr. Sanders was impressed by a speech about hazards to children by the public safety advocate Ralph Nader at the American Academy of Pediatrics meeting in San Francisco. [17] At the time, only a few countries had any laws requiring seat belts in motor vehicles. There were no laws anywhere in the world mandating restraints for children, even though unsuccessful attempts to pass such laws had been made in at least thirty states. Dr. Sanders took on the issue of protecting children in motor vehicle crashes. [18]

He and a handful of allies promoted a bill in the Tennessee

legislature requiring use of child restraints. One of the early surprises was how many people—even within the medical community—opposed the legislation. The arguments against child safety restraints were remarkably similar to those stubbornly clung to by gun enthusiasts today. The strongest opposition was that requiring seat belts invaded individual liberties. Some parents with bigger families objected to the cost of car seats.[19] The bill did not reach the floor of the legislature in 1976, the first year it was introduced.[20]

Dr. Sanders did not give up. He and his wife enlisted an "army of pediatricians" for a grassroots lobbying effort. In 1977, the bill was passed into law. It became effective in January 1978. Tennessee was the first state in the union to require children under four years of age to ride in a car seat. By 1985, every state and the District of Columbia had similar laws.[21]

Those who sought passage of child safety laws in other states had to overcome the same ill-informed polemics that Dr. Sanders had faced in Tennessee. The New York Times, for example, quoted State Representative James S. ("Trooper Jim") Foster of Florida arguing in 1982 against a proposed child seat law. "We've got people out there with three or four young 'uns," Foster said. "You're going to hear them squalling and carrying on something terrible. You don't do that to a biddy young 'uns."[22] Foster, who ironically was formerly a public relations safety officer with the Florida Highway Patrol, and a country singer,[23] also argued the same year against a proposed seventy-two-hour "cooling-off" period on handgun sales.[24]

The Tennessee child-restraint law had dramatic results. A study published in the Journal of the American Medical Association in 1984 found that the law had been "a remarkable success."[25] Six years after it went into effect, motor vehicle fatalities among children younger than four years had been cut in half. The children who died were "almost exclusively . . . transported without benefit of child restraint devices." Not a single child younger than four years old traveling in a child-restraint device died in a motor vehicle accident in Tennessee during 1982 and 1983. In contrast, seventeen such children who were not restrained died.[26]

Researchers, however, noted a tragic problem stemming from the conventional wisdom that inspired what was known as the "babes in arms" exemption in the original bill. They noted, "A particularly troublesome aspect of the child restraint question is the sentiment that the best place for a baby to travel is in its mother's arms. Proponents of this view have not been easily swayed by studies that have shown that no human can successfully hold on to even a 4.5-kg [9.92-pound] child under the stress of the decelerative forces involved in a 30-mph crash, and that the adult holding the child usually becomes a huge blunt object that crushes the baby against the dashboard."[27] One article reported that children who were in their mothers' arms in vehicle accidents in 1982 and 1983 "suffered injuries and death at a rate approaching that of entirely unrestrained children."[28] In short, parents who were either ignorant of the facts or thought they knew better than the experts were killing their own children. The exemption, which came to be known as the child-crusher exemption, was removed from the law in 1981.

This sad waste of young life is the precise analog of the gun enthusiasts' devotion to the myth that a gun in the home protects the family, in the face of study after study showing otherwise. A recent cross-state study, for one example, found that "compared to children in states with low gun ownership, children in states with high gun ownership were more than twice as likely to be murdered with a gun, fourteen times more likely to commit suicide with a gun, and ten times more likely to die in an unintentional shooting."[29]

The child-restraint law not only saved the lives of children; it saved Tennessee taxpayers money that would have been spent on medical care. According to researchers, "the use of child restraint devices saved $2 million in Tennessee in 1982 and 1983 alone." The savings in these direct costs of medical care would have been $8.4 million if all children who traveled in the state had been in child-restraint devices. "Many of these costs are borne directly by the taxpayers through Medicaid and other government-supported health care programs; another portion is paid indirectly by the public through higher insurance premiums."[30]

The same medical cost shifting occurs with gun injuries. The cost of medical care for gun violence victims in the United States is about $4 billion per year. National data reported in 2001 show that government programs pay for about 49 percent of this amount, 18 percent is covered by private insurance, and 33 percent is paid by all other sources.[31] It should be noted that direct medical costs are only part of the burden America bears because of guns. The overall economic cost—including health care, disability, unemployment, and other intangibles—is about $100 billion per year.[32]

Dr. Sanders accepted no commissions from car seat manufacturers, and scrupulously avoided profiting from his activism.[33] The National Highway Traffic Safety Administration (NHTSA) estimates that from 1975 through 2009, child restraints saved 9,310 lives.[34]

Dr. Robert Sanders's life stands as a model for selfless service devoted to public health and safety. Its antipode is that of another of Murfreesboro's widely-known sons, Ronnie Gene Barrett. In 1982, at about the same time that Trooper Jim Foster was trying unsuccessfully to save "biddy young 'uns" from child-restraint laws in Florida, Ronnie Barrett began work on an invention that would make him rich, powerful, and famous—at least among gun enthusiasts. It was an extremely accurate sniper rifle that fires a massive bullet with such force that it blasts through an inch of steel at a thousand yards.

A measure of the man—and of his self-estimation—may be found under the pontifical rubric "Meet the Maker" on the Barrett Firearms Manufacturing, Inc., website.

You can't share the history of Barrett without talking about Ronnie. It all started in 1982 when he created the world's first shoulder-fired .50 caliber rifle. Thousands of rifles later, the company that bears his name has become a revered icon in the world of firearms manufacturing.[35]

A self-described dyslexic with attention deficit disorder,[36] Barrett never went to college.[37] He never served in military uniform, so far as has been publicly reported, although he does claim to have served for an unspecified period of time and place as a reserve deputy.[38] A lifelong gun enthusiast and Second Amendment fundamentalist, now on the board of the NRA, he became a commercial photographer by trade, getting his start shooting weddings.[39]

According to the company's buttery hagiography, the idea for Barrett's deadly invention came to him in 1982 while he was taking pictures on a Tennessee river for another gun company. The photos were of a river patrol boat armed with two Browning 50 caliber machine guns. "Barrett was wowed by the amazing Browning Ma Deuce. He wondered to himself if the incredible .50-caliber cartridge could be fired from a rifle; maybe one operated from the shooter's shoulder. He decided to find out. With no manufacturing or engineering experience, Barrett drew a three-dimensional sketch of his idea for a .50-caliber, semiautomatic rifle to show how it should function."[40]

The Browning 50 caliber heavy machine gun was developed by John Browning in 1918 at the end of World War I.[41] After several modifications, the standard M2 machine gun became known as the Ma Deuce. Big, heavy, and usually mounted on a tripod, it is still relied on by the U.S. military and armed forces all over the world.[42] "Employed as an anti-personnel and anti-aircraft weapon, it is highly effective against light armored vehicles, low flying aircraft, and small boats," according to the U.S. Army.[43] Barrett proposed to put the 50 caliber's massive firepower and unequalled range into a rifle that could be fired by one person from the shoulder.

Barrett's 1987 patent called his invention an anti-armor gun. He described the .50 BMG rifle in his patent claim as a "shoulder-fireable, armor-penetrating gun." Barrett related the genius of his invention as follows:

> The recoil and weight of the Browning M-2 heavy-barrel machine gun (50 cal.), belt-fed, make it unsuitable for firing from the shoulder. The bolt-fed sniper rifle of smaller weight and caliber will not penetrate armored targets. The bolts of guns of a caliber that will penetrate armored targets are often broken by recoil because of excessive strain on the lock lugs. Thus, there is a need for a light-weight, shoulder-fireable, armor-penetrating gun that can stand up to heavy duty use. After extended investigation I have come up with just such a gun.[44]

Barrett calls his antiarmor rifle an "adult toy" when he talks to the news media. "It's a target rifle. It's a toy. It's a high-end adult recreational toy," he said on the *60 Minutes* television program in 2005.[45] "It's like, what does a 55-year-old man do with a Corvette?," Barrett told the Associated Press in the same year. "You drive it around and enjoy it." He also boasted in the same interview that his customers included doctors, lawyers, moviemakers, and actors. "I know all the current actors who are Barrett rifle shooters, some Academy Award-winning people. But they don't publicize it. They love to play with them and have fun. Shooting is very fun."[46]

The 50 caliber antiarmor sniper rifle is not a toy at all, but a deadly serious weapon of war, the most powerful gun available to ordinary civilians in America. Quite unlike the car seats for children that Dr. Sanders promoted to save lives, Ronnie Barrett's sniper rifle has taken countless lives in war and criminal violence all over the world. Regulated by federal law only to the same extent as an ordinary hunting rifle, Barrett's 50 caliber antiarmor sniper rifle is the archetype of the gun industry's ruthless militarization of the civilian gun market. It has spawned dozens of imitators. But, according to the company, "Barrett dominates this market and enjoys customer allegiance approaching a cult following."[47] With the exception of a few states, including California, these armor-piercing, long-range killing machines are legally and easily available throughout the entire country.

Its lethality cannot be exaggerated. "The .50 BMG is infinitely more powerful than any other shoulder-fired rifle on the planet," enthuses a 2004 book aimed at civilian fans. "The point to be made here is that no matter how you measure energy and stopping power, the .50 BMG is well off the charts. It is far more powerful than any other rifle cartridge known according to any measuring system yet devised."[48]

"A bullet of such size and weight traveling at well over Mach 2 can be called a missile in the modern context without a high-altitude flight of fancy," the same book exclaims. The author notes the extraordinary range of the 50 caliber round in comparison to the 30–06, one of the 30 caliber rounds common in hunting rifles. "The trajectory of the two rounds is similar out to the limits of the 30–06's stability, but when the 30-caliber bullet is ready to call it a day and dive for the dirt, the .50 is still charging along with more than enough authority to cut a man in half and keep on going."[49] Another enthusiastic reviewer of the Barrett 50 caliber antiarmor sniper rifle's accuracy and power reported firing match-grade armor-piercing ammunition "against 1-inch-thick armor steel at 300 meters distance. Not only did the rounds penetrate with enough behind-armor effect to be lethal, but the three-round group we fired could be covered with the palm of the hand. Two rounds were actually touching."[50]

According to the U.S. Army, the rifle's effective range is five times that 300-meter distance. A U.S. Army News Service article summarized the capabilities of the Barrett ".50-caliber long range sniper rifle"—called the M-107 in Army nomenclature—as follows:

The M-107 enables Army snipers to accurately engage personnel and material [sic] targets out to a distance of

1,500 to 2,000 meters respectively. . . . The weapon is designed to effectively engage and defeat materiel targets at extended ranges including parked aircraft, computers, intelligence sites, radar sites, ammunition, petroleum, oil and lubricant sites, various lightly armored targets and command, control and communications. In a counter-sniper role, the system offers longer stand-off ranges and increased terminal effects against snipers using smaller-caliber weapons.[51]

One need only consider the civilian equivalents of such military targets to understand the concern that many security experts have about the unrestricted sale of long-range antiarmor sniper rifles to civilians. The Violence Policy Center has published a number of monographs detailing the rifle's capabilities, its proponents' often specious claims, its use by criminals and terrorists, and the concerns of security experts going back at least as far as a classified report written for the U.S. Secret Service.[52]

In 1985, the deputy assistant director of the Office of Protective Operations, U.S. Secret Service, wrote a research paper for the faculty of the National War College of the National Defense University titled "Large Caliber Sniper Threat to U.S. National Command Authority Figures." The "National Command Authority" refers to the president and the secretary of defense.[53] After reviewing developments in the marketing of these antiarmor rifles and their use in earlier terror attacks and assassinations, the author concluded that such "large caliber long range weapons pose a significant threat for U.S. National Command Authority figures if used by terrorists or other assailants."[54] His report then summarized the specific threats that 50 caliber antiarmor rifles present to agencies charged with security, such as the Secret Service:

The weapons are capable of defeating light armor of the type used in limousines, aircraft, ballistic shields, etc.

When so used modern ammunition makes them highly effective.

The weapons are more accurate than shoulder fired antitank rockets and, if used against aircraft, immune to electronic counter measures. They are man portable and easily concealed.

Large caliber long range weapons can be employed effectively from places of concealment outside the scope of normal security measures against personnel, aircraft, lightly armored vehicles and buildings. They thus pose a threat in environments generally thought secure.[55]

Recent developments have made the domestic threat from anti-armor sniper rifles much more serious than those envisioned by the Secret Service in 1985. In a 2007 report prepared for the U.S. Department of Homeland Security on terrorist use of conventional weapons, the RAND Corporation included sniper rifles and recently evolved technology supporting snipers among what it called "game changing weapons." In the hands of terrorists, such weapons "would force the defender to dramatically alter its behavior."[56] The report noted that "in recent years, considerable advances have been made in sniper technology that have changed the requirements for effective use of sniper tactics." These advances include small ballistic computers to correct for wind and temperature, platforms that allow a rifle to be fired by remote control, improved scopes and other optics, and night vision devices.[57] This technology "has made it so that advanced rifle marksmanship skills are no longer necessary in sniping."[58] It has also extended the effective range of sniping rifles to a mile or more, and made the impact on the target more devastating.[59]

The result is that terrorists can now "carry out line-of-sight attacks or assassinations that would previously not have been possible, either because of their lack of skill and training or because the security perimeter around a very important person

(VIP) target would be on the lookout for attacks from a shorter range."[60] The report warns that "since such sniping systems are now widely available, it appears that the Secret Service will be forced to expand its secured perimeter to deny line of sight out to beyond 2 km."[61]

It must also be noted that although the Secret Service can expand security perimeters, other potential targets—such as government officials at other levels, media and entertainment celebrities, noted figures in business and industry, and law enforcement officers—do not enjoy such protection. Nor are most of them protected in vehicles as heavily armored as presidential limousines and helicopters. The gun industry and its technology is thus making these other potential targets increasingly vulnerable to deadly attack from long range by 50 caliber antiarmor sniper rifles.

Ronnie Barrett has scoffed at this reality for two decades. "This is not something a drug lord or a bank robber is going to want to use," he told the *New York Times* in 1992.[62] On February 27, 1992, less than two months after Barrett's smug pronouncement to the newspaper, a Wells Fargo armored delivery truck was attacked in a "military-style operation" in Chamblee, Georgia, by several men using a smoke grenade and a Barrett 50 caliber antiarmor sniper rifle.[63] Barrett's antiarmor sniper rifle has had a dark side almost from the moment it came into production. A sinister brigade of crackpots, terrorists, and violent criminals lust after it for the same reasons the world's armies do. And because the gun is virtually unregulated and freely sold on the U.S. civilian market, these evil forces easily obtain Barrett's antiarmor rifle in quantity. "You just have to have a credit card and clear record, and you can go buy as many as you want. No questions asked," Florin Krasniqi, a gunrunner who smuggled Barrett sniper rifles to Kosovo, said in 2005. "Most of [*sic*] non-Americans [buying guns for him] were surprised at how easy it is to get a gun in heartland America. Most of the dealers in Montana and Wyoming don't even ask you a question. It's just like a grocery store."[64]

Figure 9. Known Sales of 50 Caliber Antiarmor Sniper
Rifles to Terrorists, Criminals, and Fringe Groups

Group	Number
Kosovo Liberation Army	At least 140
Gun Trafficking to Mexico	At least 37
Osama bin Laden Organization	25
Church Universal and Triumphant	10
Branch Davidians (David Koresh)	2
Irish Republican Army	2

Traffic to Mexico, federal indictments, and other court documents in the files of the
Violence Policy Center; Kosovo Liberation Army, "Clear and Present Danger: National
Security Experts Warn About the Danger of Unrestricted Sales of 50 Caliber Anti-
Armor Rifles to Civilians," July 2005, and sources cited therein; all others, Vio-
lence Policy Center, *Voting from the Rooftops: How the Gun Industry Armed Osama bin
Laden, Other Foreign and Domestic Terrorists, and Common Criminals with 50 Caliber
Sniper Rifles* (Washington, DC: Violence Policy Center, 2001) and sources cited therein.

Osama bin Laden's Al Qaeda acquired at least twenty-five
Barrett 50 caliber sniper rifles in the late 1980s. The transaction
came to light during the federal trial in New York of terrorists
charged with bombing American embassies in Africa. A government witness, Essam al Ridi, testified that he had shipped twenty-
five Barrett 50 caliber sniper rifles to Al Qaeda. The testimony is
ambiguous as to the exact date of the transaction, but it appears
to have been in either 1988 or 1989. When VPC reported this fact
in a 2001 report, Ronnie Barrett heatedly retorted that the sales
were part of a secret CIA program to supply mujahideen rebels
fighting the Soviet occupiers in Afghanistan. The VPC then interviewed several former CIA officials who had managed the mujahideen supply program. They confirmed that some Barrett rifles
had indeed been supplied through the CIA's clandestine program
to Afghan rebels through Pakistan. But these former officials ve-
hemently denied that any CIA-sponsored money or supplies went
to bin Laden, including specifically any Barrett antiarmor sniper
rifles. Other evidence supported the CIA officials' denials.[65] It was

clear that bin Laden had obtained his Barrett 50 caliber antiarmor sniper rifles through some other channel.

In 2005 Ronnie Barrett came clean. After describing the VPC allegation, the *Nashville Tennessean* reported, "Barrett doesn't dispute that sale took place, but says a congressman bought the rifles to supply the fighters, rather than he or the gun industry selling them directly."[66]

Although the news report does not identify the congressman in question, the most likely candidate is the late former U.S. Representative Charlie Wilson from Texas. Wilson was the subject of a 2003 book by George Crile, *Charlie Wilson's War: The Extraordinary Story of the Largest Covert Operation in History*, and a 2007 film derived from the book. Wilson was described by Crile in an interview as a man who "had to pistol-whip the CIA into the biggest war they ever fought."[67] Barrett and Wilson became close friends. According to the *Murfreesboro Post*, "Barrett still has the personal letter from Charlie Wilson, dated September 22, 1987, ordering the purchase of the Barrett rifles."[68]

At about the same time, an official of the Church Universal and Triumphant, a Montana cult, was buying Barrett antiarmor sniper rifles in bulk. The official pled guilty to buying seven of them under a false name. According to the Government Accountability Office (GAO), the group bought a total of ten Barrett rifles.[69] Federal law enforcement investigators said that the official—the chief of the cult's security unit, the "Cosmic Honor Guard"—was "basically buying weapons and paramilitary supplies to outfit a 200-man army."[70] The Barrett rifles seized from the Montana sect were later shipped to Miami and used as bait by federal agents, who arrested a suspected Irish Republican Army (IRA) terrorist shopping for weapons. The suspect, who was collared while trying to stuff a five-foot Stinger antiaircraft missile into his car, specifically requested Barrett 50 caliber antiarmor sniper rifles from federal agents posing as arms dealers.[71] In the 1990s, at least two Barrett 50 caliber sniper rifles were acquired in the United States by the IRA, whose snipers murdered a total of eleven soldiers and policemen in five years.[72]

The phenomenon of the militarized criminal is not a fantasy of some future American dystopia. It is here now. The Violence Policy Center keeps tabs on news media reports of 50 caliber sniper rifles linked to criminal activity in the United States. As of June 2012, it had documented more than three dozen incidents of such criminal use or possession of the antiarmor sniper rifles since 1989.[73] One of the better known of this growing list of criminal incidents in the United States is the use of Barrett 50 caliber antiarmor sniper rifles by members of David Koresh's Branch Davidian cult at their compound near Waco, Texas, in 1993. The Davidians' arsenal included two Barrett 50 caliber sniper rifles and armor-piercing ammunition. The weapons' ability to penetrate "any tactical vehicle in the FBI's inventory" prompted the agency to request military armored vehicles "to give FBI personnel adequate protection from the 50 caliber rifles" and other more powerful weapons the Branch Davidians might have had. Cult members did in fact fire the 50 caliber sniper rifles at federal agents during the initial gun battle on February 28, 1993.[74]

The biggest civilian buyer of Barrett's rifles in bulk, so far as is publicly known, was the gunrunner Florin Krasniqi. He bought at least one hundred and probably several hundred 50 caliber antiarmor sniper rifles in the United States and shipped them to the Kosovo Liberation Army (KLA) over a period of several years, beginning in 1998. Krasniqi created a network of straw buyers among his compatriots. He declined to say on camera on *60 Minutes* in 2005 how many of these rifles he and his comrades bought and shipped to Kosovo. But Stacy Sullivan—who documented Krasniqi's activities in her book, *Be Not Afraid, for You Have Sons in America*—told *60 Minutes* in the same program that she believes Krasniqi probably shipped "a couple hundred." This estimate by Sullivan, who covered the Balkans for *Newsweek* magazine and spent five years researching her book with the cooperation of Krasniqi, is buttressed by a 1999 Congressional staff report, *Suspect Organizations and Individuals Possessing Long-Range Fifty Caliber Sniper Weapons*, that reported a KLA claim that it had 140 Barrett 50 caliber antiarmor sniper rifles at the time.[75]

Examination of the most recent gun trafficking involving Ronnie Barrett's antiarmor sniper rifle brings us straight back to the 2012 schoolyard shooting in Murfreesboro's tranquil Amber Glen community.

Federal agents have been investigating the smuggling of 50 caliber antiarmor sniper rifles to Mexico for use by drug cartels since at least 1999.[76] An ongoing Violence Policy Center analysis of federal indictments and other documents filed in U.S. courts in connection with criminal gun trafficking cases found that between February 2006 and September 2012, at least twenty-nine 50 caliber antiarmor sniper rifles destined for Mexico were seized by U.S. law enforcement officials. Of these, nineteen were Barrett rifles.[77] By definition, this count includes only cases in which the guns were discovered and seized before they got to Mexico. It does not include guns successfully smuggled. Nevertheless, these seized rifles are representative of the huge flow of guns from the U.S. civilian market to criminal organizations in Mexico and elsewhere in Latin America.

This is a marriage made in hell.

Guns from the wide-open U.S. civilian market directly empower these ruthless cartels—who produce and ship illegal drugs to the United States—to wage merciless paramilitary war among themselves and against the governments of Mexico and, increasingly, Central America. In the past, Mexican drug trafficking organizations (DTOs) have used guns to establish and maintain control of drug trafficking routes and entry points into the United States. In recent years, however, these organizations have demanded more sophisticated and more powerful arms and have used them to confront not only each other but the Mexican government and civil society. According to a 2010 report on fire-arms trafficking to Mexico:

> While DTOs still use firearms to establish control over drug trafficking routes leading to the United States, in the last few years they more regularly use firearms in open combat with rival DTOs, Mexican authorities, and the public. Such open confrontations with the Mexican state indicate a move "into a sphere that is typically inhabited by groups with a much more overt political stance, such as terrorists, guerrillas or paramilitaries." Mexican DTOs are also demanding more sophisticated firearms and larger quantities of arms and ammunition.[78]

The vast majority of the firearms seized in Mexico between 2007 and 2011 and traced by the federal Bureau of Alcohol, Tobacco, Firearms and Explosives (ATF) came from the United States, according to ATF trace data released in April 2012. According to ATF, "Trace information shows that between calendar years 2007 and 2011 the Government of Mexico recovered and submitted more than 99,000 firearms to ATF for tracing. Of those firearms more than 68,000 were U.S.-sourced. . . . Law enforcement in Mexico now report that certain types of rifles, such as the AK and AR variants with detachable magazines, are used more fre-quently to commit violent crime by drug trafficking organiza-tions." ATF also released trace data showing that 99 percent of the guns traced in Canada during this period came from the United States as well as data on U.S. guns recovered in the Caribbean.[79]

It is difficult to exaggerate the harm that this traffic in guns is doing, both to Mexico and to the United States. An investigation into sales from just one gun store in Houston, Texas—Carter's Country gun store—revealed that twenty-three buyers had pur-chased 339 guns worth $366,450 in a fifteen-month period. These were mostly AR-15 semiautomatic rifles, FN Herstal 5.7mm rifles and pistols, and Beretta pistols. One or more of these guns were later found at crime scenes in Mexico where police had been murdered, judicial personnel had been executed, the military had been fired on, or a businessman had been kidnapped and murdered. A total of eighteen Mexican law enforcement officers and civilians were killed with these guns, from a single U.S. gun store.[80]

The 50 caliber rifles among the guns smuggled from the United States also play a prominent role in this tragic bloodbath. In Ciudad Juárez, for example, gunmen used a 50 caliber rifle to murder the head of local police operations. In Tijuana in October 2008, a Mexican Special Forces soldier was shot in the head as his unit entered a drug lord's neighborhood. After a two-hour standoff, police found a Barrett 50 caliber antiarmor sniper rifle, along with four other rifles. U.S. District Court documents show that the guns were bought in Las Vegas.[81]

How does all of this relate to Murfreesboro's gun violence problem? The Mexican criminal organizations are not a local phenomenon whose violent power and noxious influence is restricted to Mexico. They are transnational criminal organizations (TCOs). In other words, their criminal structure and operations reach across borders, into the United States, Canada, Latin America, Africa, and Europe.[82] "Mexican-based TCOs and their associates dominate the supply and wholesale distribution of most illicit drugs in the United States. These organizations control much of the production, transportation, and wholesale distribution of illicit drugs destined for and in the United States."[83]

The tentacles of the Mexican TCOs reach all the way into communities like Murfreesboro through criminal gangs. "Criminal gangs—that is street, prison, and outlaw motorcycle gangs—remain in control of most of the retail distribution of drugs throughout much of the United States, particularly in major and midsize cities. Gangs vary in size and in sophistication from loose coalitions to highly structured multinational enterprises, but they form the bedrock of retail drug distribution in the United States."[84]

The national economic impact of this international web is estimated to total $193,096,930,000, with the majority share attributable to lost productivity.[85] But it has a more violent effect. It begins when the drug trafficking organizations "regularly employ lethal force to protect their drug shipments in Mexico and while crossing the US-Mexico border."[86] It continues down to the street level in communities all over America, and every indication is that it is going to get worse. "Gang members are acquiring high-powered, military-style weapons and equipment, resulting in potentially lethal encounters with law enforcement officers, rival gang members, and innocent bystanders. Law enforcement officials in several regions nationwide report gang members in their jurisdiction are armed with military-style weapons, such as high-caliber semiautomatic rifles, semiautomatic variants of AK-47 assault rifles, grenades, and body armor."[87]

The FBI warns that this trend is ominous. "Gang members armed with high-powered weapons and knowledge and expertise acquired from employment in law enforcement, corrections, or the military may pose an increasing nationwide threat, as they employ these tactics and weapons against law enforcement officials, rival gang members, and civilians."[88]

In sum, the wide-open U.S. civilian market in military-style weapons, like the Barrett 50 caliber antiarmor sniper rifle and others of its ilk, directly contribute to the power of the international criminal drug organizations. This evil has inevitably seeped down into towns like Murfreesboro. By 2007, the Murfreesboro police had identified a hundred gang members in the city. Carter Smith, who began investigating gangs as a U.S. Army Criminal Investigation Division agent and helped form the Tennessee Gang Investigators Association, told the local newspaper that some gang members migrated to smaller cities like Murfreesboro, Smyrna, and La Vergne after they were pushed out of nearby Nashville. "They don't play by the same rules the rest of society does," Smith said. "They don't care if something is illegal. If they need something, they find a way to get it even if it means killing you or someone else." [89]

Someone else did get killed in Murfreesboro when a gang war erupted in late 2007 over distribution of cocaine, marijuana, and methamphetamines. On November 14, 2007, Moss James Dixon, sixty-six, an innocent bystander, was shot to death when gangsters shot up a West Main Street apartment. Murders and retaliatory killing continued through 2008. In October 2009, a sixty-four-count federal indictment was handed up, charging gang members in Nashville and Murfreesboro with racketeering, including several charges of murder, drug trafficking, and various violent acts. [90]

Although local authorities pronounced the problem abated with the indictment, the Murfreesboro Police Department nonetheless was reported in January 2012 to have found use for a federal grant to strengthen its new gang unit, increase antigang education in schools, and track gang activities. [91] It was against all of this background—the arming of Mexican drug traffickers, the increasing militarization of gangs, and local gang wars—that the anxious reaction to the shooting of fourteen-year-old Taylor Schulz on Presidents' Day, just one month later, must be judged.

As the gun industry is pushed more and more into the position of attempting to defend the indefensible—the recklessly unrestricted sale of militarized weapons—it has fallen back on the plaintive plea that its civilian sales are necessary to support manufacture for the armed forces. "If it weren't for the civilian sales, I wouldn't be here. There's a lot of defense contractors that would not be here," Ronnie G. Barrett told *60 Minutes*. [92] He went on to say that he "would never have been in business" if he could not sell to civilians. [93]

Barrett's story in 2005 was different from what he told the ATF in 1984. Records from Barrett's federal firearms license file indicate that he told the ATF back then that his intention was to market his newly designed 50 caliber antiarmor sniper rifle primarily to the military and law enforcement. Thus, the written report of the ATF agent who delivered Barrett's first federal firearms manufacturer's license to the company in 1984 states:

> Mr. Barrett said that this is a sniper-type weapon, and he intends to try to market it to the U.S. military or police departments prior to considering sales to the public. He said that it will be quite expensive and probably of interest only to collectors. He said that the number manufactured will be limited unless a large military sale is possible.[94]

Moreover, Barrett has claimed that he was losing money selling to civilians and was $1.5 million in debt until he made his first big military sale, to the Swedish army in 1989.[95]

Proposals to regulate 50 caliber antiarmor sniper rifles are part of a struggle between good and evil, in Barrett's view.[96] "When you have governments disarming citizens, you have catastrophe on your hands," Barrett told a reporter.[97]

The gun situation in America is not the inevitable corollary of a free society. The Harvard public health professor David Hemenway, for example, compared the U.S. record with those of the three other developed "frontier" nations where English is spoken: Canada, Australia, and New Zealand. Hemenway points out that, although the four countries are similar in per capita incomes, cultures, histories, and rates of violent and property crimes, "What distinguishes the United States is its high rate of lethal violence." The difference, he concluded, is that these other countries "do a much better job of regulating their guns."[98] Like the tobacco industry before it, the American gun industry and its lobby have successfully employed political intimidation, the crassest form of flag-waving propaganda, and mass-marketing techniques appealing to fear and loathing to prevent being called to account for the public health disaster it has inflicted on America and to avoid meaningful regulation.

What drives the gun industry is, perhaps surprisingly, not success but failure. The civilian firearms industry in the United States has been in decline for several decades. Although it has from time to time enjoyed brief peaks in sales, it has been essentially stagnant. For example, demand for firearms apparently increased beginning in 2008 because of fears that "high unemployment would lead to an increase in crime" and that the administration of President Barack Obama would "clamp down" on gun ownership by regulating assault weapons. But demand fell back as neither of these happened.[99] Unlike many other consumer product industries, the gun industry has failed to keep up with population growth. Between 1980 and 2000, the U.S. population grew from 226,545,805 to 281,421,906—a 24 percent increase.[100] Over the same period, total domestic small arms production fell from 5,645,117 to 3,763,345—a 33 percent decrease.[101]

In short, as America has gotten bigger, the gun industry has gotten smaller. But like a snake in its death throes, the gun industry has also become more dangerous. This trend began in the mid-1980s, when China began dumping semiautomatic AK-47 and SKS assault rifles on the last great civilian market, the United States. Militarization gathered steam through the 1990s, and is now hurtling through America. As a recent article in an industry publication observed, "If you're a company with a strong line of high-capacity pistols and AR-style rifles, you're doing land office business. If you're heavily dependent on hunting, you are hurting."[102]

The gun industry today feverishly designs, manufactures, imports, and sells firearms in the civilian market that are to all intents and purposes the same as military arms. It then bombards its target market with the message that civilian consumers—just like real soldiers—can easily and legally own the firepower of militarized weapons. The industry has done this through three major types of firearms: high-capacity handguns like the FN Five-seveN used by Major Hasan, assault rifles and pistols like the AK-47 clones that are flooding in from the factories of Eastern

Europe, and sniper rifles like the Barrett 50 caliber antiarmor rifle.

One last story from Murfreesboro serves as a bridge to further discussion of the industry's effect on America in the next chapter.

In March 2009, Stephen Summers, a fifty-one-year-old Murfreesboro man, was showing his wife, Evy Elaine Summers, fifty-three, how to clean and disassemble his Glock pistol. Summers, the holder of a concealed handgun carry permit, and his wife were watching television at the same time. "Mr. Summers advised that he and his wife were watching 'Cher' on television and must have been distracted," a Murfreesboro police officer reported. "Mr. Summers cocked the Glock and it went off and struck Mrs. Summers in her right wrist, left breast and (traveled) out her left tricep." Police checked Summers's story with his hospitalized wife. "She advised that her husband . . . racked the slide and the gun went off," police reported.[103]

The report naturally generated wry criticism, including the sarcastic observation that "one of those highly trained, absolutely responsible, law-abiding citizens who are licensed to carry handguns in Tennessee almost killed his wife with his Glock," and the incident was "more proof of how much safer Tennessee has become since our elected officials, in their infinite wisdom, decided to let a couple hundred thousand Barney Fifes walk around with loaded handguns."[104]

This, however, is precisely what advocates of allowing the unrestricted carrying of handguns argue: that more guns in circulation make us all safer. The next chapter examines this rationale and links it to a long-standing gun industry marketing and legislative campaign to sell more—and more powerful—handguns.

5

THE THIRD WAVE:
BEYOND THE GUNSHINE STATE

When it comes to lax gun laws and frequent gun violence, Florida is an epidemic in itself.[1] Editorialists, op-ed writers, and journalists in the state's own newspapers regularly mock it as the "Gunshine State."[2] The sarcastic phrase is a verbal play on Florida's official nickname, "The Sunshine State," adopted by the state legislature in 1970.[3] The mockery is well earned. The state's compliant legislature has been used for several decades as a Petri dish by the gun-mad scientists of the NRA's lobbying arm, the Institute for Legislative Action (ILA).[4]

The NRA's person on the spot in Florida is Marion Hammer.[5] Starting as an NRA volunteer lobbyist in 1975, Hammer rose to become the first female NRA president. But Hammer told the *Washington Post* in 1987 that she was "certainly not" a feminist and scoffed at such women's initiatives as equal pay for equal work. "That's their fault," she said. "No one ever gave me special favors." She also told the newspaper that her personal arsenal consisted of fourteen handguns, six rifles, two shotguns, and three muzzle-loading rifles.[6] Currently an NRA board member, Hammer has been the executive director of the Unified Sportsmen of Florida (USF) for more than thirty years.[7] "Organized in 1976, with the assistance of the National Rifle Association," according to a membership application, USF is "affiliated with NRA as the Florida Legislative affiliate." Hammer herself "did business" with the NRA in the amount of $122,000 in 2011, according to the NRA. The exact nature of the business was not specified.[8]

Throughout her career, Hammer has been portrayed as something of a cross between a chain-smoking bulldog and a steely-eyed, uncompromising drill sergeant.[9] "Generally, the NRA brings out the redneck good ol' boys with the gun racks, but when you scratch Marion, she's no different," Harry Johnston, a former Florida State Senate president, said in 1987. "She's a good ol' boy in a skirt."[10] For decades, this "good ol' boy in a skirt" has lashed Florida's legislators—Democrat and Republican, urban and rural alike—into impotent compliance while she rams the most bizarre and deadly "gun rights" laws imaginable through the halls of Florida's capitol in Tallahassee.

Some have shrugged and concluded that Florida's inert citizenry gets the kind of weak gun laws it deserves.[11] But these virulent ideas—from Florida's pioneering "shall issue" concealed-carry-permit law to the misshapen monster twins of its "castle doctrine" and "stand your ground" laws—have been injected into the veins of scores of other state legislatures all over the country. The NRA, packaging its poison in the back rooms of a slick and well-funded network of right-wing legislators known as ALEC, the American Legislative Exchange Council, has already pushed two great waves of ill-advised and poorly considered legislation into American life. The first was a nationwide weakening of state concealed-carry laws; the second, a combination of the "shoot first" castle doctrine and the "shoot anywhere" stand-your-ground laws.[12]

It's interesting that many rank-and-file police organizations sat out these waves of legislation. Some endorsed them. But a third wave—a mutated form of "self-defense" with law enforcement officers in the crosshairs—may be building. The idea is to grant citizens the right to shoot first, even at a police officer, if they conclude that the officer's intrusion into their lives is unconstitutional. The disastrous potential of this "shoot cops" third wave has got the attention, and the opposition, of at least one otherwise gun-friendly police organization, the Grand Lodge of the Fraternal Order of Police.[13] "Shoot first" may have been OK, even a good thing, when ordinary citizens were being put at risk. But it seems not to be such a good idea when cops are endangered.

The case of concealed-carry-permit holder Humberto Delgado Jr. is an instructive parable about this infectious gun madness. Delgado was pushing a shopping cart full of guns down Nebraska Avenue in the Sulphur Springs neighborhood of Tampa, Florida, at about ten o'clock on the night of August 19, 2009. A few minutes later, he used one of his guns to pistol-whip Tampa police corporal Michael Roberts, then shot him to death.

Just about everyone who came into serious contact over any length of time with Humberto Delgado—including the judge who sentenced him to death on February 10, 2012—concluded that he had serious mental illness. The question Circuit Judge Emmett Lamar Battles addressed at the time of Delgado's sentencing was not whether he was seriously mentally ill. That was evident. The question was whether Delgado was legally insane.

Florida law presumes everyone to be sane. The burden is on a defendant to prove otherwise. The applicable statute required Delgado to show not only that at the time of his offense he had "a mental infirmity, disease, or defect." He also had to show that either he "did not know what he ... was doing or its consequences" or that although he "knew what he ... was doing and its consequences," he did not know that what he was doing "was wrong." [14] Judge Battles ruled against Delgado. "The court is reasonably convinced that the defendant was under the influence of an extreme mental or emotional disturbance at the time he killed Cpl. Roberts," he wrote in his sentencing order. "The court is reasonably convinced that the defendant's ability to conform his conduct to the requirements of the law was impaired, albeit not substantially." [15]

Humberto Delgado was born in St. Croix in the U.S. Virgin Islands. He was a police officer there from April 1996 to October 2000. [16] During this period, according to his family and mental health professionals who examined him after his arrest, Delgado began to develop a lifelong complex of paranoid delusions. More specifically, he became convinced that a woman in the Virgin Islands had tried to poison him and that she had influenced a cult of Masons to get him.[17] The Masons, he believed, were harassing him, threatening him, and interfering with his work.[18] His life spiraled downward after he left the police force. He worked for a while in an oil refinery, but his paranoia—he thought it was the Masons at work against him—ruined that job. His family ticked off some of the manifestations he displayed. "He made his wife and children sleep on the floor because there were demons outside, people in trees and eyes peering through the windows. He wore gloves, walked with a cane and said he was Abel from the Old Testament. He said his kids had goat legs that needed to be cut off." [19]

Somehow, Delgado managed to enlist in the United States Army and served between September 2004 and December 2005.[20] Private First Class Delgado was a petroleum supply specialist, fueling aircraft and vehicles. He was stationed at Fort Lee, near Petersburg, Virginia, and at Fort Bragg in Fayetteville, North Carolina.[21] But his illness caught up with him at Fort Bragg, home of the Eighty-second Airborne Division. According to an army doctor, Delgado started carrying a pellet gun, a hammer, and a flashlight for self-defense. He thought the rapper 50 Cent was out to get him. Diagnosed by an army psychiatrist as "bipolar with psychotic issues," Delgado was medically discharged from the Army in December 2005.[22] After his discharge, Delgado had trouble finding a job. His girlfriend in North Carolina, the mother of one of his children, told detectives that she kicked him out.[23]

It was sometime around then that Delgado apparently decided to acquire guns. In November 2006, he was issued a concealed-handgun permit in Cumberland County,[24] where Fayetteville and Fort Bragg are located. Sometime later, probably in 2008, he bought at least four guns from Guns Plus, at 1503 North Bragg Boulevard in Spring Lake, near Fort Bragg.[25] The nature of Guns Plus is described in the following review, posted on the North Carolina Gun Owners website:

It's well stocked with both handguns and rifles, although most of it leans toward military style guns. Based on that, if you're looking for pure hunting stuff, you might be better off going somewhere else, but if you are looking for high-speed, low-drag Soldier of Fortune stuff, this is the place to go. Guns Plus definitely caters to the Ft Bragg community, with a hint toward the Black-Ops wannabes (you know the type). Like previously mentioned, they do carry virtually everything you will need to go out and fight the war on terror single-handedly.[26]

This "high-speed, low-drag Soldier of Fortune stuff" is exactly what sustains the gun industry's dimming fortunes today. "The modern sporting rifle . . . platform continues to provide dealers with strong sales, even as the buying frenzy of a couple of years ago has quieted," *Shooting Industry* reported in March 2012. The magazine highlighted the strong role that follow-up accessories also play in the assault weapon market. "Manufacturers are introducing new models of the rifle, along with a seemingly endless number of add-ons and accessories. There are magazines and loaders, lights and lasers, slings, multi-rail hand-guards, conversion kits, bipods and rests—the list goes on and on." One manufacturer's representative told the magazine, "The AR platform is like Legos for grown men."[27]

On the night of August 19, 2009, Humberto Delgado was well stocked with the guns he thought he would need to fight his personal terror. He had in his possession a Kel-Tec PLR-16, a Glock Model 17 semiautomatic 9mm pistol, a Taurus Millennium 45 caliber semiautomatic pistol, and a 22 caliber revolver of uncertain make and model.[28] The Kel-Tec PLR-16, manufactured in Cocoa, Florida, has been mistakenly identified in some reports as an assault rifle.[29] It is actually an assault pistol. Designed to accept the high-capacity magazines of the AR-15 and M-16 assault rifles, it combines the power of a rifle with the concealability of a handgun. As the NRA's *American Rifleman* magazine put it in its review of the gun, "You can enjoy all of the head-turning flash and hoorah of a magnum revolver, but with modest recoil similar to that of a 9mm pistol." [30]

Delgado had drifted south from North Carolina to live with an uncle in the town of Oldsmar, located about fifteen miles west of Tampa. But his family said he refused to accept the fact that he was mentally ill and had stopped taking his medication because it made him "feel like a zombie." [31] His uncle had thrown him out of the house. Delgado had thus been homeless, probably for about a week. [32] Disheveled, his hair a tangled mass of unkempt dreadlocks, he had cleaned out most of a storage locker he rented, put the contents in his shopping cart, and walked all day from Oldsmar to Tampa. Among the items in the cart was a laptop computer. Mental health experts for the defense testified that lack of food and sleep made Delgado delusional by the time he got to Tampa. [33]

Corporal Mike Roberts spotted Delgado pushing his shopping cart down Nebraska Avenue. It was an area where there had recently been a rash of burglaries. At 9:58 P.M., Corporal Roberts radioed two cryptic phrases to the police dispatcher. "Lincoln 61," he said. "Signal 80." The first was his personal identifier, the second signaled his intent to conduct a "field interrogation." There was relative silence after that, except for a brief, inaudible transmission three minutes and forty seconds later. The dispatcher interpreted that transmission as a sign of distress. Other units were dispatched to the scene, where Corporal Roberts was found, lying on his back. [34] He had been shot once. Although he was wearing body armor, the powerful 45 caliber slug had ripped through his shoulder, into his chest, and perforated his heart and lungs. [35] At 10:50 P.M., less than an hour after he had signaled his intention to question Humberto Delgado Jr., Corporal Michael Roberts was pronounced dead at Tampa General Hospital. [36]

The field interrogation had gone terribly wrong, terribly fast. The exact sequence is unknowable, but it appears that at some point within those few minutes, Corporal Roberts may have looked into Delgado's backpack and asked him about the laptop computer. Delgado tried to run away and Roberts fired a non-lethal, ordinarily disabling Taser gun at him. At least one of the barbed electrodes the gun fires became entangled in Delgado's dreadlocks instead of anchoring in his flesh. Rather than falling immobilized to the ground, Delgado turned around, and the two men fought. Delgado got the upper hand, pistol-whipped Roberts into unconsciousness, and then shot the officer with Delgado's Taurus Millennium 45 caliber semiautomatic pistol.[37]

Responding police officers found Delgado hiding nearby. During a struggle with them, Delgado shouted, "Don't hurt me," "I'm sorry," "I'm crazy," and "I'm one of you."[38] The next day, investigators opened Delgado's storage locker. Among other things, they found a 22 caliber semiautomatic rifle with a scope and laser sight, and a *Shooter's Bible*, a popular source for gun enthusiasts, a combination gun catalog and reference book.[39]

There is a final thread to this tragic story. A record was made of Delgado's statements while he was in a holding cell. Among them were these: "He deserved it. . . . It was self defense. . . . I was scared and I ran when he discovered my guns. . . . He f— violated my rights by going through my bag. . . . He shouldn't have went through my s—."[40]

Later, Delgado had a conversation with a defense psychiatrist, Dr. Michael Scott Maher. "He told me that the police officer searched through his backpack without asking permission," Dr. Maher said. "Mr. Delgado was afraid that the police officer would misunderstand and react to the fact that he had a laptop computer . . . and guns." According to the doctor, Delgado reacted with fear and paranoia. "This was confirmation that the officer was after him. He was going to get him. He was going to kill him. He was going to do bad things to him. There was no way out of this situation."[41]

As crazy as it may seem, Delgado's addled expressions of fear and assertion of his rights are precisely the elements of the rhetorical foundation upon which gun rights activists now are building a third wave of dangerous gun laws, this one aimed directly at cops. To understand why it may well succeed, one needs to understand the first two waves of gun laws pushed by the NRA, the role of Marion Hammer, and the logic that propelled the gun industry's arguments.

The NRA's first wave gutted laws restricting the concealed carry of guns (and in some states, other weapons, such as blackjacks and knives). Until 1987, Florida, like most states at the time, had a discretionary system for issuing licenses to carry concealed guns, commonly referred to as "may-issue" licensing. Under a "may-issue" system, authorities such as a county sheriff, judge, or local police official have discretion as to whom they grant a license to walk around with a gun tucked out of sight. Such discretionary systems lessen the chance that a mentally disturbed person like Humberto Delgado will get a concealed-carry license. Applicants are generally required to show a good reason for carrying a concealed weapon and to pass a thorough background check.[42]

Marion Hammer and the NRA were determined to change that. They wanted a system known as "shall-issue" licensing, under which authorities have no discretion. The state must issue a concealed-carry license to any applicant who meets a few specific, minimal criteria. These include being a citizen or resident alien and not having a felony record—or having had one's civil rights restored after a felony conviction. Perfunctory training, or a substitute for training, such as military or law enforcement service, may be required.

The difference between the two points of view about the advisability of handing out gun licenses on demand was aptly summed up by the *Miami Herald* in 1987. "Pro-handgun people divide the world into two kinds of human beings: law-abiding citizens and criminals. Anti-handgun people think it consists of many kinds: law-abiding citizens, criminals, mental patients, angry husbands, drug addicts, housewives, disgruntled former employees and so on."[43]

The NRA's gun mill had tried to loosen the concealed-carry law in Florida before 1987, but had repeatedly failed. In 1985, the legislature passed such a bill, but Governor Bob Graham vetoed it. In 1986, similar legislation was bottled up in committee. To make matters worse from Marion Hammer's point of view, populous urban counties in the southern part of the state had imposed waiting periods on would-be handgun buyers. Two of the counties did so after their residents voted in local referenda for "cooling off" periods.[44]

That would change in 1987. Robert "Bob" Martinez, a Republican, had been elected governor. State Representative Ron Johnson, a Democrat, introduced another shall-issue bill. Johnson was the kind of man who during a newspaper interview would prop his feet up and cough "a gooey wad of Levi Garrett chewing tobacco into a yellow cup. He does not excuse himself for that."[45] Hammer and the NRA "spent thousands of hours and tens of thousands of NRA dollars" to finally ram their change in law and common sense through the legislature. It also helped that police groups in the state, who had opposed earlier legislation, "pulled the old switcheroo," as the *Miami Herald* described their action, and endorsed the NRA's bills. "If you see a freight train coming," the cops' chief lobbyist explained, "do you stand in front of it? Or do you stand aside and grab ahold of it and try to ride it to glory?"[46]

When the final vote came, Hammer was sitting in the gallery behind bulletproof glass, making sure there were no defectors. Governor Martinez signed the bill into law the day before a delegation from South Florida—the Broward County commissioner, the Palm Beach County commissioner, and a Dade County gun-control activist—had an appointment with him to urge him to veto it.[47]

At the same time, the Florida legislature attempted to preempt the subject of gun regulation, wiping out the ability of counties and cities to issue sensible regulations. Local waiting periods and other laws and ordinances were intended to be erased, overriding the expressed will of local voters. However, some localities persisted in regulating guns, such as forbidding their carry in public buildings and parks and on beaches, and requiring trigger locks.[48] The NRA and some citizens filed lawsuits to stop the local regulation, which according to Hammer was a case of "gun haters" flouting state law.[49] In 2011, the legislature complied with NRA demands that the law be tightened, and enacted a sweeping measure that imposed the penalties of fines and removal from office on any local officials who dared regulate guns.[50] In the wake of the new law, cities and counties gave up and effectively abandoned gun regulation.[51] "We just want local public officials, elected and otherwise, to quit violating the state law and stop trampling the rights of Florida's law-abiding gun-owners," Hammer wrote in an e-mail supporting passage of the law.[52] Regarding concealed carry in particular, the Florida law states that the legislature "finds it necessary to occupy the field of regulation of the bearing of concealed weapons or firearms for self-defense to ensure that no honest, law-abiding person who qualifies under the provisions of this section is subjectively or arbitrarily denied his or her rights."[53]

Such cant about self-defense rights, and its obtuse division between "honest, law-abiding" people and criminals is typical of the gun lobby's close-minded arguments. In 1987, Hammer dismissed concerns about the risks of vigilantes killing innocent people—such as would allegedly happen in the notorious Trayvon Martin case in 2012—or being shot with their own guns as "hysterical, emotional. If an individual is responsible for protecting himself and his family, he's entitled to have the proper tools." In a similar vein, the NRA ran "huge" newspaper ads in Florida, one of which portrayed "a blurred face menacingly encased in a stocking cap and, in bold black type, the question: 'SHOULD YOU SHOOT A RAPIST BEFORE HE CUTS YOUR THROAT?'"[54]

But this equivalent of sticking one's fingers in one's ears and shouting rude noises does not change the reality about the consequences of pumping guns into public spaces, a reality that was apparent within months in Florida. It turned out that in its frenzy to pass the shall-issue package, the legislature had inadvertently made the open carrying of guns legal. This caused an uproar. Another legislative battle ensued under the watchful eye of Marion Hammer and the NRA. The *Washington Post* provided a picturesque glimpse of the Gunshine State's shooting scenery in 1987:

> In just the days in which the legislature debated closing the open-carrying loophole, a Miami jitney driver was killed by a passenger who argued over a 75-cent fare, a 17-year-old Miamian was severely wounded walking to school by a shot meant for another man, a purse snatcher opened fire at 11 a.m. on a crowded street before police shot him, and a man walked into a suburban restaurant with a gun in his waistband, fought with another customer and shot him to death. In rural Marion County, an 8-year-old was shot in the head by a 10-year-old friend showing off his parents' pistol. And a 5-year-old was shot dead as his father tried to grab the gun his child had taken from the car.[55]

This week of gun carnage was merely the precursor of years to come. The NRA's argument in favor of relaxed concealed-weapons laws rested on three articles of faith: criminals do not apply for concealed-carry licenses, criminals do not receive concealed-carry licenses, and concealed-carry-license holders do not commit crimes. Yet a 1995 review of records obtained by the VPC from the Florida Division of Licensing and the state's Board of Executive Clemency revealed that hundreds of criminals, convicted of crimes ranging from firearm violations to kidnapping and aggravated rape, applied for concealed-carry licenses in Florida, criminals did succeed in getting concealed-carry licenses, and concealed-carry-license holders in Florida did have licenses revoked or suspended for various crimes, including firearm and drug violations.[56]

The following year, 1996, Tanya Metaksa, then executive director of the NRA's Institute for Legislative Action, stuck her rhetorical fingers in her ears and, in another of the NRA's trademark arguments by false assertion, told a press conference in Dallas that people who got concealed-carry licenses were "law-abiding, upstanding community leaders." According to Metaksa, "These citizens don't commit violent crimes."[57] Mounting objective evidence proves otherwise. The VPC has tracked non-self-defense deaths since May 2007 involving private citizens legally allowed to carry handguns. As of June 29, 2012, VPC's Concealed Carry Killer project found that a total of 462 people had died in such non-self-defense incidents.[58] Of these victims, fourteen were law enforcement officers, like Corporal Michael Roberts in Tampa. Since this data is derived from media reports, the only national source of information available, the actual number of concealed-carry killers is likely far higher. And as the reader has seen in earlier chapters, many concealed-carry permit holders commit crimes of armed aggression short of murder. Moreover, directly contrary to Metaksa's bland assertions about the good character of permit holders, criminal gang leaders "have learned how to structure their crews so that at least one of them can be legally armed. One member of a crew will have a concealed weapons permit, allowing them to be armed."[59]

These cautionary facts were swept aside as Florida became a national incubator of gun death and injury. Relaxed concealed-carry laws swept over America's legislatures. The real force behind this wave was not a citizenry clamoring to lawfully pack heat. It was the gun industry, a force that has never been deterred by the mayhem its products wreak on others. This was evident in Florida within months of the concealed-carry law's passage. Praising Marion Hammer as "a real American," John Katon, the owner of the Tamiami Gun Shop, enthused in 1987 that first-time buyers prompted by the new law had boosted his gun sales "an overwhelming 50 percent."[60] The NRA's Tanya Metaksa was even more blunt in 1996. "The gun industry should send me a basket of fruit—our efforts have created a new market."[61]

The gift of a new market was exactly what the industry needed. "As more states pass concealed-carry legislation, we'll see an increase in handgun sales," Michael Saporito, of RSR Wholesale Guns, said the year before, when industry reports were gloomy about slumping sales.[62] In 1996, Massad Ayoob, a pro-gun writer who specializes in advising dealers on the subject of selling lethal force in the form of handguns, waxed enthusiastic about the gun industry's gift. "A high point for gun dealers, as well as those who believe in freedom and safety," wrote Ayoob, "was 1995's record number of states passing favorable concealed handgun carry legislation. Persons enabled to carry a concealed weapon in public for the first time are willing to splurge to get the right blend of discretion with speed and power. (Some have been known to buy a new gun just to celebrate the permit!)"[63]

The only problem was that the bloodred NRA tide had not yet washed over every state. Greg Griffeth, owner of the Sportsman Den gun shop in Shelby, Ohio, complained to *Shooting Industry* in 2002 that Ohio's lack of a concealed-carry law was holding back his sales of semiautomatic pistols. Griffeth explained, "Smith & Wesson, Taurus and Ruger comprise about 80 percent of my handgun sales, mostly in revolvers. If we could get a CCW law through our state government, our semi-autos would take off."[64] Not to worry. The NRA lobbying machine was on the case. In 2004, pistol sales could "take off" in Ohio after the state's new concealed-carry permit law went into effect. By then, *Shooting Industry* triumphantly crowed, "Self-defense products have been and continue to be the heart of the weapons market. Self-defense sells."[65]

Ayoob pointed out another important profit center for gun shops, derived directly from concealed-carry laws. "Remember, too, the first-time gun carrier is a walking cluster of ancillary sales: inside the waistband holster for maximum concealment, outside the belt high-ride scabbard for waistbands too tight for IWB ("inside the waistband"), fanny pack, spare magazines or speedloaders, a secure firearm storage unit, and of course, the best premium-grade defensive ammo money can buy."[66] In fact, many experts advise that gun shops can make more money from the sale of accessories to "walking clusters" than from guns. "Accessories are where you make your profit," advised gun store owner Mike Goschinski in 2003. "If you're selling handguns but not selling accessories, you're doing a lot of work for nothing."[67]

"Customers who spend several hundred (or, in some cases several thousand) dollars on a handgun are usually willing to drop 40 or 50 extra bucks to buy something extra for their 'new baby.' . . . Now's the perfect time to cash in," *Shooting Industry* suggested to retailers.[68] By 2003, Ayoob noted a marked change in gun enthusiast garb. "For generations, retail firearm dealers have found hunting clothes and other outdoor garb to be a profitable sideline," he wrote. "Today's gun clothing has been augmented by garments expressly designed to discreetly conceal defensive handguns."[69] In 2006 the same monothematic writer suggested that "many of your customers may not realize their 'wardrobe of firearms' should include a 'winter ensemble.' If that's the case, do them a favor by bringing it to their attention. And, since you are their 'gun-wear store,' you'll be helping your bottom line, also."[70]

Another profitable sideline for gun store owners was mandated by the relaxed concealed-carry laws the NRA husbanded through compliant state legislatures. This was the requirement for training by—no surprise here—NRA-certified instructors. In Roseburg, Oregon, Curly Jensen, a certified NRA instructor and owner of the Gunner's Club gun shop, offered such classes and told *Shooting Industry* in 1996 that "a high percentage of those taking the classes buy a handgun, or at least ammunition and accessories, like holsters."[71] As usual, Ayoob had advice on the subject. "Firearm training is something your customers want and need, even if you or your staff don't have the time or the facilities," he wrote. "Likely, there are competent trainers within driving distance of your store. They'll do the training and be happy to pay a commission to you for the referrals or give your customers a discount."[72]

An idea of how much fresh blood concealed-carry laws have pumped into the anemic gun industry is demonstrated by Florida's experience. Before the new law, 16,000 Floridians were reported to have concealed-carry licenses.[73] As of August 31, 2012, Florida had dispensed 1,151,537 gun licenses, of which 963,349 were run-of-the-mill concealed-carry licenses. The remainder were for various specialized occupations, such as private investigators.[74] Add to this growth the increased sales in all of the forty-one states that as of February 2012 have shall-issue laws similar to Florida's, and it's clear that the NRA's gift to the gun industry was a big one, a gift that keeps on giving profits to the industry while taking innocent lives.

If this boom from the NRA's concealed-carry push made gun retailers happy, gun manufacturers and importers were tickled pink. Designing and marketing new lines of small but powerful "pocket rockets" in high calibers for the new concealed-carry market boosted manufacturers as well. This factor explains why the industry has never thrown its weight behind the "open-carry" movement. Just about any gun will do for open carry. A handgun can be stuck into a waistband or shoved into a holster. A long gun can be slung over the shoulder. No special gun size or design is required for carrying a gun openly, no accessories are needed, and no specialized clothing need be worn. Thus, open carry offers few new, if any, profitable marketing ploys to tempt Ayoob's "walking cluster" gun buyer.

A Brazilian handgun manufacturer, Taurus, was one of those who caught the new wave. (Many foreign gun manufacturers export to the United States guns that they cannot legally sell to civilians in their own countries.) Taurus "began seriously pursuing the U.S. firearms market in 1982" and within two years "had established a beachhead in the American market."[75] In 1998 the company announced its Millennium handgun series, "notable for its extremely compact size that almost literally fits in the palm of one's hand."[76] Two years later, *Shooting Industry*'s self-promotional "Academy of Excellence" gave Taurus its Manufacturer of the Year Award.[77] And in 2001 the company's 45 caliber Millennium model "joined the family . . . a signal achievement of firearm design and engineering, placing 10 man stopping rounds of .45 ACP into a pistol that is more compact than most 9mm handguns."[78]

In 2009, Humberto Delgado shot Corporal Michael Roberts to death with a single shot from a Taurus "signal achievement of firearm design and engineering." Corporal Roberts, however, was not the first police officer to have been shot to death in the United States by a palm-sized 45 caliber Taurus Millennium with its "10 man stopping rounds."

At about 1:30 P.M. on September 23, 2008—less than a year before Corporal Roberts was killed in Tampa—a Philadelphia police officer, Patrick McDonald, pulled over a car with a broken taillight. One of the occupants, twenty-seven-year-old Daniel Giddings, jumped out and ran. Giddings had a 45 caliber Taurus Millennium in his waistband. He had been released from prison about a month earlier and was already wanted for violating his parole and assaulting police officers. McDonald gave chase, caught Giddings, and the two men fought. In the course of their struggle, they exchanged gunfire. Like Corporal Roberts, Officer McDonald was killed by a powerful 45 caliber round fired from a Taurus Millennium handgun. Just as in the case of Roberts, the huge 45 caliber slug blasted through McDonald's shoulder and pierced his heart.[79]

Connecting the dots between weakened concealed-carry laws that have pumped millions of handguns into the United States and the resulting death and injury was not something that NRA executives Marion Hammer, Tanya Metaksa, and Wayne LaPierre; handgun manufacturers and importers; or anybody else in the gun lobby were likely to do. They would continue to divide the complex human world into "law-abiding citizens" inside their smugly righteous walls and "criminals" outside.

But there was a cloud over this Happy Valley and its neat division between law-abiding good guys and criminally violent bad guys. That cloud was raining on the gun market's growth potential. As previous chapters have documented, most people in America just aren't interested in having a gun around the home, much less inside (or outside) their waistbands. The gun lobby's challenge has been to persuade more and more Americans that they need to carry a gun in order to be safe. But there were also legal flies in the gun industry's marketing ointment, its dream of bringing back to modern streets the mythical gunslinging ways of the Old West.

Putting aside the moral questions inherent in going about armed—daring and perhaps hoping for violence to happen—there are long-standing, wisely developed limitations in law on killing other people, even in self-defense. Over the centuries since the Middle Ages, the English common law upon which American law is based has recognized that one has the right to defend oneself, including killing another in extreme cases. But the interests of a civil society have required that one asserting self-defense prove that a *reasonable* person would have feared death or serious bodily injury in the circumstances at issue. The common law has also required that—even in the face of such a reasonably perceived threat—one must avoid violence if possible. For this reason, the general rule has been that "one should first try to disengage or retreat, if attacked, which was often a prerequisite for a claim of self-defense."[80] This rule "places a priority on human life. It also reflects the notion that a person would rather retreat than kill their attacker and have to live with the consequences or, worse, accidentally kill an innocent bystander."[81]

An exception to this general duty to retreat—when one is *attacked* in one's own home—has been long recognized. In 1914 Benjamin Cardozo, then a judge on the New York State Court of Appeals and later an associate justice of the U.S. Supreme Court,[82] stated this exception in *People v. Tomlins*, an often quoted New York case in which a man killed his own son during a domestic altercation. "It is not now, and never has been the law that a man assailed in his own dwelling, is bound to retreat. If assailed there, he may stand his ground, and resist the attack. He is under no duty to take to the fields and the highways, a fugitive from his own home."[83] This exception has historically been known as the castle doctrine, referring to a statement by Sir Edward Coke, an English jurist in the seventeenth century, that "a man's home is his castle."[84] Even this castle doctrine, however, was not without limit. Judge Cardozo also noted in the classic case on the subject, "A man who is himself the aggressor or who needlessly resumes the fight, gains no immunity because he kills in his own dwelling."[85]

In 2004, a legal advice column in the *Miami Herald* summed up the Florida law of armed self-defense, both in the home and elsewhere, as it stood at the time. The law then was consistent with the traditional common law.

> With reference to when a person is justified in the use of deadly force, Florida Statute Chapter 776 permits it "only if he or she reasonably believes that such force is necessary to prevent imminent death or great bodily harm to himself or herself or another or to prevent the imminent commission of a forcible felony."
>
> Usually a person is required to retreat in the face of threatened violence and avoid confrontation if possible, including when in their car. And they may not use lethal force after a crime has been completed or the criminal has surrendered. But the "retreat rule" gives way to the "castle doctrine" when one is attacked within their own home or place of business and allows the use of deadly force, if necessary.[86]

The pivotal points here were the requirement of the defendant to prove reasonable fear, the duty to retreat and avoid violence if possible, and the precondition of being actually attacked in one's home before the castle doctrine's right to stand one's ground applied. Even today, after decades of Florida's lawmakers weakening gun-control laws, Florida licensing authorities ironically—one might fairly say hypocritically—urge caution on their website:

> Applying for a license to carry a concealed weapon or firearm for self-defense is a right of law-abiding Floridians. However, you must remember that a license to carry a weapon or firearm concealed on your person does not authorize you to use that weapon. Use of a concealed weapon or firearm is regulated by other provisions of Florida law.[87]

Those other provisions of Florida law as they existed in 2004 were exactly what the industry's "gun rights" alliance set out to gut. Hammer and her allies appropriated the language of the tightly drawn and sensible exceptions to the general common-law duty to avoid violence—the traditional castle doctrine and its limited permission to stand one's ground when attacked in the home—and distorted it into ideological slogans. Turning the law on its head, they twisted the terms *castle doctrine* and *stand your ground* from carefully crafted restrictions on lethal violence into mindless rhetorical banners that encourage carrying guns and using them to shoot people. Hammer once again badgered the Florida legislature into lowering the gun violence bar as a way into expanded handgun markets.

She did it by inventing a problem that did not exist.

According to Marion Hammer and her minions, law-abiding citizens who shot bad guys were being hounded by prosecutors and charged with criminal offenses while felons walked free. "Florida licenses law-abiding people to carry concealed firearms when they're out on the streets for lawful self-protection, but the courts have been taking away their right to protect themselves by imposing a duty to retreat," Hammer claimed in 2005. "So if a rapist tries to drag a woman into an alley, under current case law, and jury instructions that a judge gives a jury, that woman is supposed to try to pull away and run and could be chased down and stabbed in the back or shot in the back."[88]

The fact that neither Hammer nor anyone else could cite a single case in which such a prosecution had ever happened to any self-defender anywhere in Florida did nothing to deter the next wave of laws hatched in the Florida gun violence incubator.[89] The mutant forms of the venerable castle doctrine and stand-your-ground laws written into the Personal Protection Bill Florida enacted in 2005 bore little resemblance to the common-law originals. The new law eliminated the duty to retreat to avoid violence. It also:

- Replaced the common law "reasonable person" standard with a "presumption of reasonableness" or "presumption of fear" in many instances. This shifted the burden of proof to prosecutors, who are required to prove a negative.
- Extended the right to deadly self-defense from the old castle doctrine to areas outside the home. If a person's actions are covered by the "presumption of reasonableness," that person can legally use deadly force anywhere that he or she has a right to be.
- Broadened the circumstances in which one can legally respond with deadly force to include those in which only property is threatened and the threat is not imminent. This was a significant change from the common-law standard that only an imminent threat to a person justified deadly force.
- Provided blanket civil and criminal immunity for a person using force as defined and permitted by the new law.[90]

The *Palm Beach Post* summed up the proposed new Florida law in 2005, as bills made their way through the Florida House and Senate:

The bills eliminate the "attack" requirement. They presume that if someone is illegally entering your home, that person has the intent to cause death or bodily harm. The current law requires that intent to be proved. The bills also would extend the Castle Doctrine to an attached porch or someone's vehicle, and to a lesser extent to a situation in public where someone fears for his or her life. But the bills do not extend the right to use force to shooting a police officer who has identified himself as such.[91]

Marion Hammer's reading was more expansive. "The bill removes the duty to retreat if you're outside your home or in a public place," she explained. "It only allows you to stand your ground and meet force with force, if you reasonably believe that force is necessary to defend yourself against death or great bodily harm."[92] State Senator Steve Geller, a Democrat from Hallandale Beach, argued against the bills. "We never said . . . that the street is your castle," he said. "I don't think you ought to be able to kill people that are walking toward you on the street because of this subjective belief that you're worried that they may get in a fight with you."[93] But in a masterpiece of circular reasoning, Wayne LaPierre, the NRA's executive vice president, told the *New York Times* that the new law sent a good message to Florida's good citizens. "If they make a decision to save their lives in the split second they are being attacked, the law is on their side," he said. "Good people make good decisions. That's why they're good people. If you're going to empower someone, empower the crime victim."[94]

The new law twisted the common-law castle doctrine into a "shoot anywhere" rule—not only did one not have to retreat to avoid attack inside one's home, one no longer had to retreat from anywhere one had a right to be outside the home. And by legislatively decreeing the presumption of reasonable fear, the law turned the right to stand one's ground inside the home into the right to "shoot first" virtually anywhere. The clear legal terminology of the common law was reduced to vague rhetorical slogans cast about by "gun rights" advocates. "Castle doctrine" and "stand your ground" came to mean virtually the same thing: the "right" of "good people" to shoot first anywhere they happened to be.

Florida's prosecutors were alarmed. The Palm Beach County State Attorney's Office pointed to a high-profile 2003 case in which a teenager had been shot and killed by a homeowner while playing a door-knocking prank with friends on his sixteenth birthday. The homeowner heard the teenager trying to tie a fishing line to the door knocker, got his 40 caliber handgun, and shot the youth to death—in the back. The homeowner pleaded guilty to a charge of manslaughter and was sentenced to spend fifty-two weekends in the Palm Beach County Jail and ten years of probation. "If this bill were in effect back then, that case would not be prosecuted," a spokesman for the local state attorney said prophetically.[95]

Hammer brushed such warnings aside and lashed Florida's lawmakers into line. This time, she had the help of Democrats who were trying to align themselves with Republican values. "While perhaps [the bill] may go a little too far, it sends a message that Democrats believe in those same core values," Democrat Representative Will Kendrick, a co-sponsor of the House version of the bill, said. "The majority of Democrats have gotten away from basic principles. They've realized they were way out in left field. I think some of them voted for this one in an attempt to get back to a balance." Another Democrat, Representative Richard Machek, explained that he was in favor of the home and vehicle portions of the bill but opposed the part that allowed standing one's ground in the streets. "You don't have an option," Machek said. "The problem was, if I was voting against it, I was voting against protecting yourself in your home. I hope I did the right thing." Representative Dan Gelber said simply, "The NRA is a very powerful lobby and a lot of members don't want to cross it." Even State Senator Steven Geller, a Democrat who led the charge against the bills, ended up voting for them.[96] "Voting against the Castle Doctrine, which is wildly popular and which does make sense . . . would be seen as, 'Those Democrats are soft in [*sic*] crime,'" he said.[97]

Newspapers and other observers outside the daisy chain of "gun rights" lobbyists and compliant legislators were disgusted. The *Bradenton Herald*, for example, raked those who caved in to Hammer and supported the new law. It was "another case of overreach by the National Rifle Association, and another example of cowardice by lawmakers who put political ambition ahead of public safety," the paper editorialized. "Afraid of being labeled soft on guns, most legislators gave the NRA a pass in ramrodding the bill through the Republican-controlled Legislature. Most law enforcement agencies remained neutral, also aware of the power of the gun lobby."[98]

One of the bills' Republican sponsors piously denied that the matter had anything to do with gun sales, claiming that he didn't even own a gun himself. "But what I want is for the criminal to know that every single door he breaks in, those people may have a firearm and they absolutely have the right to protect themselves," he said. "I'm not trying to sell guns, I'm trying to empower the freedom of our people."[99] Two months later, *Shooting Industry* had a more sanguine view of the impact of the new law on the gun industry's prospects.

> Self-defense is an important segment of the industry's market—and it continues to grow. . . . Most recently, Florida grabbed the attention of the nation when Gov. Jeb Bush signed into law a measure that allows citizens to use deadly force outside of their homes "if he or she reasonably believes it is necessary to do so to prevent death or great bodily harm." There also has been an upsurge in self-defense related sales in recent years as more citizens throughout the nation "take more responsibility for their own safety." That has translated into increased

development and production of self-defense firearms and related products—and increased sales for gun dealers.[100]

The NRA took its new present for the gun industry on the road. Executive Vice President Wayne LaPierre told the *Washington Post* that the new Florida law was merely the "first step of a multi-state strategy." Giving Hammer credit for conceiving the new law, LaPierre promised to use the model of the concealed-carry wave to push the new shoot-first-anywhere wave. "There's a big tail-wind we have, moving from state legislature to state legislature," he said. "The South, the Midwest, everything they call 'flyover land,' . . . we can pass this law in that state."[101] He told the *New York Times* that the NRA planned to introduce the new law in every state. "We will start with red and move to blue," he said. "In terms of passing it, it is downhill rather than uphill because of all the public support."[102]

What LaPierre did not mention was that "all the public support" was to be generated by the American Legislative Exchange Council (ALEC), a secretive network of conservative state legislators who often overrode public opinion and prosecutorial judgment against the law. "ALEC is essentially a corporate bill factory," Anna Scholl, executive director of a Virginia advocacy group said in 2012. "ALEC writes model legislation that is designed to increase corporate bottom lines, and then they turn around and hand it off to state legislators to take it home and introduce it."[103] The NRA is one of ALEC's funders, among others including organizations linked to the Koch brothers. At a secret August 2005 meeting in Grapevine, Texas, Hammer asked ALEC's "Criminal Justice Task Force" to adopt the Florida castle-doctrine bill as an ALEC model bill. In September 2005, the bill was adopted by ALEC's National Board of Directors. State legislators linked to ALEC then set about introducing this cookie-cutter bill.[104]

Like the concealed-carry relaxation, Florida's new law swept over other states. State after state fell into line, as sponsoring legislators pretended to find flaws in state laws of self-defense, then introduced ALEC's legislative cookie as the remedy. In 2006, for example, Arizona governor Janet Napolitano—the very politician who would later oversee the spending of trillions of dollars on "homeland security" and the "war on terror"—signed a bill into law over the objections of state prosecutors. "She believes in the fundamental right of self-defense," her spokesperson said. "And the law still requires the defendant to be in imminent peril of death or serious physical injury." [105] By 2007, *Shooting Industry*—in an article headlined "Self-Defense Unleashed! No Season on Sales, No Limit on Profits!"—could tell gun dealers, "If you're not cashing in on self-defense sales, it's like running a bait-and-tackle shop—and not selling hooks and sinkers!" [106]

When ALEC's role became known in 2012, after an estimated thirty-two states had passed some or all of its model law, a number of its corporate sponsors—including Coca-Cola, PepsiCo, and Kraft Foods—bailed out of the organization. The notorious Trayvon Martin case suddenly made being associated with the right-wing legislative string-pullers toxic. [107]

But the awful damage had already been done, just as had been predicted by the law's critics. "The bill . . . would define self-defense so broadly as to impose few restraints on individual behavior in the heat of an argument," the *South Florida Sun-Sentinel* warned while the law was being considered in Florida. "It would give Floridians the impression that they have a quick-trigger right to violence in many situations that have not resulted in violence in the past." [108]

Florida's law now says a person "has no duty to retreat and has the right to stand his or her ground and meet force with force, including deadly force if he or she reasonably believes it is necessary to do so to prevent death or great bodily harm." And although Hammer and other advocates claim that the new law was simply a technical expansion of the old common-law castle doctrine, the Association of Prosecuting Attorneys, a national group, says otherwise: that it bars the prosecution of criminals. "It's almost like we now have to prove a negative—that a person was not acting in self-defense, often on the basis of only one witness, the shooter," Steven A. Jansen, the group's vice president, told the *Washington Post* in 2012. Justifiable homicides by civilians have tripled in Florida since the new law was passed, from an average of twelve per year to an average of thirty-six per year.[109]

John F. Timoney, Miami's police chief, warned about specific scenarios at the time the law was passed. "Whether it's trick-or-treaters or kids playing in the yard of someone who doesn't want them there or some drunk guy stumbling into the wrong house," Chief Timoney said, "you're encouraging people to possibly use deadly physical force where it shouldn't be used."[110] The chief was exactly right about stumbling drunks and deadly force—at least two such instances occurred in 2008. In April, an honor law school student in Alabama was killed, and in October a college student in Florida was seriously wounded when, after a night of drinking, each accidentally entered an apartment that looked "identical" to his own but was in fact the wrong place. In both instances, the new "model" law insulated the shooters from prosecution.[111] In a similar incident in 2009, a homeowner stepped outside of his house after a drunken youth twice mistook the house for the one hosting a party he had stumbled away from. The homeowner shot the youth in the chest and seriously wounded him, but he, too, was insulated from accountability by the Florida law.[112]

The novelist Carl Hiaasen, a columnist for the *Miami Herald*, was also right. "Every gang-banger in the state should write a thank-you note to the NRA," he wrote in 2005. "For years, street thugs have tried without much luck to use self-defense as an excuse for their bloody shootouts. Now it's right there in the statute books: If you get fired at, dawg, you can fire back. Better yet, the law is so purposefully slack that if you even imagine you're going to be fired at, you can pull out your legally purchased AK-47 and open up."[113] So let it be written, so let it be done. In 2010, a Florida circuit judge ruled that the law insulated two defendants facing murder charges in the case of man who was shot to death with an AK-47. The incident involved a running street battle between affiliates of rival gangs. "What this means, as illustrated by this case, is that two individuals, or even groups, can square off in a middle of a public street, exchange gunfire, and both be absolved from criminal liability if they were reasonably acting in self defense," the judge wrote. "It is very much like the Wild West. Maybe that is not what was intended, but that seems to be the effect of the language used."[114]

Farther west, in Pasadena, Texas, a sixty-one-year-old retiree named Joe Horn saw two burglars breaking into a neighbor's home in November 2007. The exchange between Horn and a 911 dispatcher, as reported in the *New York Times*, raised a red flag about the troubling prospect of vigilantism under the new laws—one private citizen acting on his own as police officer, prosecutor, judge, jury, and executioner:

> In a low, calm and steady voice, he [Horn] said he saw the men breaking in and asked: "I've got a shotgun; do you want me to stop them?"
>
> The Pasadena emergency operator responded: "Nope. Don't do that. Ain't no property worth shooting somebody over, O.K.?"
>
> Mr. Horn said: "But hurry up, man. Catch these guys will you? Cause, I ain't going to let them go."
>
> Mr. Horn then said he would get his shotgun.
>
> The operator said, "No, no." But Mr. Horn said: "I can't take a chance of getting killed over this, O.K.? I'm going to shoot."
>
> The operator told him not to go out with a gun because officers would be arriving.
>
> "O.K.," Mr. Horn said. "But I have a right to protect myself too, sir," adding, "The laws have been changed in this country since September the first, and you know it."
>
> The operator said, "You're going to get yourself shot."

But Mr. Horn replied, "You want to make a bet? I'm going to kill them."

Moments later he said, "Well here it goes, buddy. You hear the shotgun clicking and I'm going."

Then he said: "Move, you're dead."

There were two quick explosions, then a third, and the 911 call ended.

"I had no choice," Mr. Horn said when he called 911 back. "They came in the front yard with me, man."

The two men, both undocumented aliens, were found in neighboring yards, both shot dead.[115] A grand jury later declined to indict Horn.

Joe Horn's chilling dialogue with the 911 operator was echoed less than five years later, this time in Florida. And this time, the body lying on the grass was not an undocumented alien or burglar. It was an innocent teenager.

On the evening of Sunday, February 26, 2012, Trayvon Martin, a seventeen-year-old high school junior, walked to a nearby 7-Eleven store from the home where he was staying with his father. The home was in a racially mixed gated community in Sanford, Florida. The young man bought some iced tea and candy and started walking back in the rain.

At 7:11 P.M., George Zimmerman, a resident of the neighborhood and the "neighborhood watch volunteer," spotted Martin. Zimmerman, armed with a Kel-Tec 9mm pistol, called the police, as he had often done in the past. "Hey, we've had some break-ins in my neighborhood, and there's a real suspicious guy," he told the 911 operator. "This guy looks like he's up to no good, or he's on drugs or something. It's raining, and he's just walking around looking about."

At about the same time, Martin noticed that he was being followed. It happened that he was talking on the phone with his girlfriend, who advised him to run. He did. At 7:13, Zimmerman told the police operator, "S—, he's running."

A beeping sound is heard at this point on the 911 tape. Zimmerman had opened the door of his vehicle. He went after Trayvon Martin on foot.

"Are you following him?" the operator asked Zimmerman.

"Yeah," he replied.

"OK, we don't need you to do that," the operator said, an eerie echo of the admonition given to Joe Horn in Texas.

Zimmerman spent a few more minutes on the phone. First he gave the operator directions about where he would meet a police officer. Then he seemed to change his mind.

"Actually, could you have him call me, and I'll tell him where I'm at?" he said.

At 7:15, four minutes after the call began, he hung up.

What happened next is a classic case of the only survivor to a shooting death claiming self-defense. What is known for sure is that within a few more minutes, George Zimmerman shot Trayvon Martin to death. Zimmerman claimed that he had acted in self-defense.[116] The Sanford Police Department agreed. Sanford police chief Bill Lee claimed that his detectives did not have enough evidence to arrest Zimmerman in the face of his claim that he acted in self-defense. "Until we can establish probable cause to dispute that, we don't have the grounds to arrest him," the chief said.[117]

The case caused a national outcry.

Pummeled by civil rights activists, the news media, gun violence prevention groups, and politicians outraged by the pass seemingly given Zimmerman, Governor Rick Scott, a Republican, appointed a special prosecutor, State Attorney Angela Corey of Jacksonville, to take over the investigation and decide whether charges were warranted. The governor also said he would convene a panel to review the law.[118] But Democratic critics complained that he was dragging his feet.[119] The Civil Rights Division of the U.S. Department of Justice and the FBI jointly opened a separate criminal investigation into possible violations of federal civil rights law.[120]

On April 11, 2012, Corey announced that, after a "thorough review" of the evidence, the state had concluded that the new law, often called the stand-your-ground law, did not apply to Zimmerman's case. "If Stand Your Ground becomes an issue, we fight it," Corey said.[121] Zimmerman was charged with second-degree murder, an offense that carries a maximum sentence of life in prison in Florida.[122] In a succinct affidavit filed to support the charges, investigators stated that Zimmerman "profiled" Martin, who was "unarmed and was not committing a crime."[123]

He turned himself in the same day.[124] In August 2012, Zimmerman's lawyer announced that he intended to use the stand-your-ground defense. Accordingly, a trial-like hearing was to be scheduled to determine whether Zimmerman's assertion is valid. If a judge rules that the law's defense applies to Zimmerman, the second-degree murder charge will be thrown out.[125] At this writing, no hearing had been scheduled and Zimmerman's case was still pending.

Marion Hammer still says the shoot-first law is just fine. "This law is not about one incident," Hammer told the *Palm Beach Post* after the Martin shooting. "It's about protecting the right of law-abiding people to protect themselves when they are attacked."[126] But other voices in the state disagreed. "The divergent interpretations by justice officials in the Martin case raise the haunting specter of justice denied in other 'stand your ground' cases," the *Orlando Sentinel* declared. "If those who uphold the law can't consistently judge self-defense, how are citizens supposed to know?"[127]

It is precisely that question—the instant judgment of ordinary citizens in the heat of the moment—that leads back to the "shoot cops" law, an extreme expansion of the castle doctrine, passed by the Indiana legislature in 2012.

The context in which the "shoot cops" law was passed in Indiana is the radical right-wing view that law enforcement is, or is rapidly becoming, the conveniently visible face of the enemy, the state. Guns can and ought to be used to fight back against this "police state." An article in *The New American*, a John Birch Society magazine,[128] distilled this view in criticizing the *Heller* decision for not going far enough to ensure gun rights. "In isolation, an individual's right to possess firearms for the purpose of self defense in his own home can only minimally deter rogue public officials from attempting to impose a police state on this country. Without thoroughgoing organization, sufficient arms, and legal authority for collective action, Americans cannot expect to deter, let alone to resist, large-scale para-militarized police forces and other instruments of oppression."[129]

The question of whether homeowners can resist police entry erupted in Indiana on November 18, 2007, when Mary Barnes called Evansville police and complained that her husband, Richard, was throwing things around their apartment. When responding officers arrived, they found Richard Barnes in the parking lot. A heated verbal confrontation ensued. When Richard Barnes went back into the apartment, a police officer attempted to follow him. Barnes shoved the officer against the wall and was subdued after a struggle and his being shot with a Taser.[130]

In his defense against charges of assault against a police officer, Barnes claimed that, because the officers had neither a warrant nor his permission to enter the apartment, his resistance was immunized by the old common-law castle doctrine. The case ended up in the Indiana Supreme Court, which sided with the police in a May 2011 decision. The court acknowledged that, under the ancient doctrine, one indeed could resist unlawful authority. But it pointed out that because of the combination of protections against arbitrary police action in modern law and the danger of violence escalating, "a majority of states have abolished the right via statutes in the 1940s and judicial opinions in the 1960s."[131]

> We believe . . . that a right to resist an unlawful police entry into a home is against public policy and is incompatible with modern Fourth Amendment jurisprudence.

Nowadays, an aggrieved arrestee has means unavailable at common law for redress against unlawful police action. . . . We also find that allowing resistance unnecessarily escalates the level of violence and therefore the risk of injuries to all parties involved without preventing the arrest—as evident by the facts of this instant case. . . . In these situations, we find it unwise to allow a homeowner to adjudge the legality of police conduct in the heat of the moment. As we decline to recognize a right to resist unlawful police entry into a home, we decline to recognize a right to batter a police officer as a part of that resistance.[132]

The court's ruling ignited protests from libertarians and the right wing, notwithstanding the fact that, as the court took pains to point out, the decision was well within the mainstream of American common law.[133] A legislative reversal was introduced.

"Our forefathers fought for a right to live freely without fear of unwarranted intrusion by an oppressive government," stormed State Senator Mike Young. "Certainly times have changed since then, but this right is among the most basic we have and should not be tampered with in any way."[134] State Representative Mike Speedy agreed. A legislative reversal was necessary, he said, to prevent "the coercive power of government. . . . We can't kid ourselves—it is as powerful as ever, and without undoing the *Barnes* decision, it has crept into our home in a way that is wildly unpopular in our communities."[135] One voter, a fan of the bill, showed up at a legislative hearing wearing a medieval knight's costume, apparently a symbolic reference to the castle doctrine.[136]

Opponents warned that the bill would have unintended consequences. Representative Craig Fry cautioned that "it's too late after somebody dies for a jury to sort it out. Somebody's going to die, whether it's a police officer or an individual who thinks a police officer is entering their home unlawfully. People are going to die."[137] Steuben County Sheriff Tim Troyer said methamphetamine abuse had already caused a spike in violence toward his officers. "You interject that substance with that mindset that they have a pass now to resist law enforcement and I fear a genuine problem for our communities," he said. David Powell, executive director of the Indiana Prosecuting Attorneys Council, said the law would prevent prosecution of a person who attacked an undercover police officer trying to make an arrest. "In their mind, they did not know this individual was a police officer, and if they hurt that police officer, their lawyer in court is going to say, 'He's undercover, he was out on the street and I didn't know he was a police officer,' " Powell said. "So we give that person who could have . . . battered and injured a police officer . . . a pass with this bill." [138]

Nevertheless, the bill passed, and Governor Mitch Daniels signed it into law. [139] The State of Indiana issued a statement. "We do not live in a police state; we live in a free society." [140]

The history of the toxic mix of Florida's laws, the NRA, and ALEC shows it was a short legislative step from "shoot first at home" to "shoot first anywhere." It has yet to be seen whether a similar third wave will add "shoot cops at home" and "shoot cops anywhere" to this volatile brew of "gun rights." If it does, a future Humberto Delgado Jr. will have a ready defense. And a cop who doesn't ask permission to go through a backpack or who enters a home to protect a wife being battered will run the risk of being shot first.

6

AS CLOSE AS YOU CAN GET
WITHOUT ENLISTING

On July 20, 2012, twenty-four-year-old James Eagan Holmes bought a ticket for the midnight premiere of the Batman movie *The Dark Knight Rises*, playing at the Century Aurora 16 complex at Aurora Town Center in Aurora, Colorado.[1] Holmes entered the theater, then exited through an emergency door, which he propped open. He reentered the theater about fifteen minutes into the movie.[2]

When he returned, Holmes was dressed in black and was wearing the gear of a Special Weapons and Tactics (SWAT)[3] team member—ballistic helmet and vest, throat and groin protectors, black tactical gloves, and a gas mask.[4] He was also armed as if he were a one-man SWAT team, with a .223 Smith & Wesson M&P15 (an AR-15-type assault rifle), a 40 caliber Glock semiautomatic pistol, and a shotgun. Another 40 caliber Glock pistol was found later in his car.[5] He had fitted his Smith & Wesson assault rifle with a drum magazine, which was capable of holding one hundred rounds of ammunition in a single loading. After tossing some sort of incendiary or smoke device into the theater, Holmes allegedly opened fire on the theater's patrons. Within minutes, twelve people were killed and fifty-eight wounded, several grievously.[6]

Survivors said Holmes was calm and methodical. "Every few seconds, it was just boom, boom, boom. He would reload and shoot, and anyone who would try to leave would just get killed," said one. "It almost seemed like fun to him."[7] Holmes was "as calm as can be," another said. "He was trying to shoot as many people as he could." [8]

Shooting as many people as one can is precisely the purpose of the design upon which the Smith & Wesson M&P15 assault rifle is based. Derived from the U.S. military's M-16 assault rifle, it is one of a devil's armory of weapons that the gun industry designs for war but aggressively markets to civilians in America. In 2003, four-star General Wesley Clark—a West Point graduate and a man intimately familiar with assault weaponry—said, "I have grown up with guns all my life, but people who like assault weapons . . . should join the United States Army, we have them." [9] The gun industry has turned General Clark's pithy advice inside out. It perversely promotes sales of military-style guns—assault weapons and high-capacity semiautomatic pistols—by touting the fact that civilians can legally buy virtually the same guns adopted by armed services and police agencies. Advertising, catalogs, and promotional articles in the gun enthusiast media directly link the weapons used by military and law enforcement agencies to the fantasies of potential customers in the civilian market. The marketing message is anything but subtle. Why join the army when you can stay at home and outfit yourself for combat, just like a real soldier?

FN Herstal USA's 2010 catalog, for example, touts the company's SCAR 16S assault rifle as "the semi-auto only version of the U.S. Special Operations Command's newest service rifle." According to the catalog's text, owning the gun is "as close as you can get without enlisting." [10] To promote its armor-piercing handgun in the U.S. civilian market, FN likewise emphasizes its military cachet. (This is the model that Major Nidal M. Hasan allegedly used in the November 2009 mass shooting at Fort Hood, Texas, discussed in detail in the introduction.) An ad in the FNH USA 2008 catalog contains a picture of what appear to be troops in the field in the top half and the Five-seveN 5.7mm armor-piercing handgun in the bottom half. The phrase "Built for them" is superimposed over the picture of the troops, and "Built for you" over the handgun. Accompanying text states, "Today FN provides 70% of the small arms used by U.S. Military Forces around the globe. FN is the name you can trust. JUST LIKE THEY DO." (Capitals in original.)[11] Similarly, a Springfield Armory ad for its M1A rifle in the May 2010 edition of the NRA's *American Rifleman* invokes a militaristic vision in the phrase, "Any mission, any condition, any foe, at any range."[12]

In addition to direct links to military images in product promotion, the industry also relies heavily on "patriotic" and "heroic" imagery to identify ownership of military-style weapons with grand themes of patriotism and homeland defense. For example, the top half of a Beretta ad for its Px4 Storm semiautomatic pistol displays in the background a soldier in field dress, holding a handgun. Text superimposed over the soldier states, "Sweltering heat. Howling wind. Sand that fouls every moving part. This is where we perfected our firearms." Another section of text next to an illustration of the pistol reads, "You won't find a more inhospitable place than Iraq. Beretta has been there since day one, on active duty with the U.S. Military. . . . And now, Beretta brings its experience in field-proven sidearms to the Px4 Storm. Whether you're protecting home or homeland, you need proven reliability in a firearm."[13]

Executives of several gun companies have quite openly discussed their strategies to leverage military and law enforcement sales to profit in the larger commercial market. After an intense competition, Beretta, an Italian gun manufacturer, won a Defense Department contract in 1985 to replace the military's existing sidearm, the Colt Model 1911 .45ACP pistol. In 1993, the top executive of Beretta U.S.A. Corp. told the *Baltimore Sun* that the military contract was "part of a carefully planned strategy dating back to 1980." The company's plan was to use the military contract to make Beretta a household name in the United States. It could then move into the larger law enforcement and commercial markets. To help get the contract, the company sold its pistols to the military at close to production cost.[14] The Austrian entrepreneur

Gaston Glock had a similar objective when he founded his handgun manufacturing company, won an Austrian army competition
in 1982, opened a U.S. subsidiary, and then went after the American law enforcement market. "In marketing terms, we assumed
that, by pursuing the law enforcement market, we would then receive the benefits of 'after sales' in the commercial market," Glock
told *Advertising Age* in 1995.[15] A full-page ad on the inside cover of
the 2011 edition of a Glock infotainment magazine, *Glock Annual
11*, features a photograph of two men dressed in SWAT team gear
and posed as if entering a room through a doorway. The nearer of
the two is thrusting a Glock 40 caliber pistol forward.[16]

The history of the M&P15 model assault rifle that James Eagan Holmes used during his shooting spree in the Aurora theater is bound intimately to this business of military and police
marketing cachet. In early 2006, Smith & Wesson announced
that it had begun shipping its new line of "tactical rifles." The
terms *tactical rifles* and *modern sporting rifles* are two of the most
prominent gun-industry euphemisms for semiautomatic assault
rifles. The M&P15 was the first true long gun made by Smith &
Wesson, which had long been known as a manufacturer of handguns only. The rifle was designed and produced because Smith &
Wesson found itself in a marketing corner. Military-style semiautomatic assault rifles had become essential to profit in the U.S.
civilian gun market, but Smith & Wesson did not make rifles. It
had, however, successfully marketed a line of "Military & Police"
semiautomatic handguns to military, police, and civilian customers. Smith & Wesson's executives decided to introduce their own
line of assault rifles, label them with the established M&P brand,
and heavily pitch them to civilians. "We believe the features of
these tactical rifles make them strong contenders in the military and law enforcement markets," said Michael Golden, Smith
& Wesson's president and CEO. "We also believe that our M&P
rifle series fills a tremendous gap in the marketplace by delivering
high-quality, feature-rich tactical rifles that will be readily available in commercial channels."[17]

The money rolled into Smith & Wesson's coffers according to plan. On July 20, 2009—exactly three years to the day before the Aurora mass murder—Golden stated in an interview that a "category that has been extremely hot is tactical rifles, AR style tactical rifles." On a June 2009 investors conference call, Golden enthused that "tactical rifles were up almost 200% versus the same period the year before. We have increased our capacity on that rifle." The company was doing so well with its assault rifles that it decided to introduce a new variant in 22 caliber, because that ammunition is much cheaper than the military-style ammunition used in the M&P15. "We have an M&P15 that shoots .223 ammo that sells extremely well," Golden said. "We have just launched an AR-style rifle that shoots 22 caliber rounds that we think will be extremely popular because of the price of ammo." [18]

Public reports of another gun company, Freedom Group Inc., underscore the vital role that military-style weapons play in today's commercial gun market. A conglomerate, the Freedom Group boasts that its structure includes thirteen widely recognized brands of guns, ammunition, and related products. [19] It claims to hold "the #1 commercial market position across all of our major firearms categories in the United States and the #2 commercial market position for ammunition in the United States, the largest firearms and ammunition market in the world." [20] Freedom Group also asserts that it is "the only major U.S. manufacturer of both firearms and ammunition, which provides a significant competitive advantage and supports our market leadership position." [21]

A Freedom Group quarterly report stated that "the adoption of the modern sporting rifle has led to increased long-term growth in the long gun market while attracting a younger generation of shooters," and that the company is "experiencing strong demand for modern sporting firearms and handguns." [22] In another report, the group noted the importance of the fact that assault rifle demand has grown, "especially with a younger demographic of users and those who like to customize or upgrade their firearms." [23]

Customizing and upgrading are gun industry jargon for the profitable aftermarket of hardware accessories that can be fitted onto assault weapons, like scopes, bipods, lasers, forward pistol grips, flash hiders and high-capacity ammunition magazines.

Until recently, the Freedom Group's stable of manufacturers produced only rifles and no handguns, the converse of Smith & Wesson's market situation. To fill the gap, in January 2012 it acquired the handgun manufacturer Para USA Inc., which was originally a Canadian company.[24]

With studied banality, the company recently observed that "the continued economic uncertainty and the 2012 presidential election is likely to continue to spur both firearms and ammunition sales. Additionally, returning military are likely to purchase firearms for recreational use and to maintain training."[25] The company's report did not explain what sort of "training" would be necessary for returning military to "maintain." That line of thinking, however, will almost certainly be used by the gun industry to justify its sale of military style weapons to the civilian market. Making and selling assault weapons becomes more than a sordid way to make money. It's elevated to the level of a patriotic act—helping to keep America's heroes trained for war.

Training for another eventuality—a "Zombie Apocalypse"—has also proved profitable for the gun industry. Although dressed in the thin outer garments of spoof and fun, so-called "zombie shoots" are at their core a clever appeal to gun enthusiasts who believe that they must prepare for social disorder and government breakdown or tyranny. According to *Shotgun News*, "the younger set is all about zombie shooting, and a whole industry has sprung up to supply the undead in target form."[26] Zombie shoots are organized shooting events that feature three-dimensional humanoid targets, filled with paintballs or other inserts that "bleed" when hit by bullets. One company, Zombie Industries, specializes in designing and making such zombie targets. DPMS, a leading maker of AR-15-type assault rifles in the United States and a star in the Freedom Group's constellation, sponsors an annual zombie shoot it calls Outbreak: Omega. The company claims that its event is "the world's premier recreational zombie shoot."[27]

At its most superficial level, the zombie shoot craze is simply an example of the industry's aggressive and exploitative marketing. "We have found that what may have worked in the past with the Baby Boomer generation, doesn't seem to be working well with the X, Y and Millennium generations," Rex Gore, president and CEO of Black Wing Shooting Center in Delaware, Ohio, told *Shooting Industry* magazine in January 2012. "We have hired some younger people to work in our operation, asking them to help us understand what excites and motivates the younger age groups. Then, we are developing shooting activities focused toward that demographic, like bachelor parties, zombie shoots, full-auto shoots and other fast-paced activities."[28]

At a deeper level, however, zombie shoots are thinly disguised events to train for shooting other people in numbers large and small. *Shotgun News* discussed the phenomenon in its July 20, 2012, issue—published on the very day of James Eagan Holmes's murderous rampage in Aurora. "A crackhead or a meth addict isn't a great deal different from a post-apocalyptic zombie," the industry tabloid newspaper observed, blandly exposing the true mentality underlying the "sport" of zombie shoots. The article noted approvingly that Zombie Industries "has developed special training targets that illustrate the vital organs. These allow shooters to engage the targets at angles rather than strictly head-on. There's also a psychological dimension; shooting a 3D target is a lot closer to shooting an enemy than is firing on a flat paper target. If the target 'bleeds,' well, that's just an added dimension of realism."[29]

The ease of acquiring military-style firepower in the U.S. civilian market has—as noted in chapter 4—generated a massive market for smuggling guns to Mexico, Canada, and other countries in the Western Hemisphere. An online resource maintained by the Violence Policy Center (VPC) contains indictments and other documents related to federal gun-trafficking prosecutions filed since 2006, primarily in the southwest United States. The documents detail specific information, such as the make, model, caliber, manufacturer, and retail source of firearms seized in criminal trafficking cases. These resources confirm that military-style semiautomatic firearms readily available on the U.S. civilian gun market are highly sought after by international gun traffickers; they also describe the methods, such as "straw purchases," that are commonly employed to obtain weapons in the United States to smuggle to Mexico and other Latin American countries. Categories of guns cataloged on the site, Cross-Border Gun Trafficking, include assault rifles, assault pistols, 50 caliber sniper rifles, body-armor-penetrating handguns, standard pistols and revolvers, as well as other firearm types. As of September 2012, of the 4,454 guns detailed on the site, 2,278 were assault rifles (primarily AK-47 and AR-15 variants), 255 were assault pistols (almost all AK-47 pistol variants), 29 were 50 caliber sniper rifles, and 373 were body-armor-penetrating handguns (all of which were FN Five-seveN pistols, known as the *mata policía*, or "cop killer," in Mexico).[30]

Unfortunately, U.S. law enforcement officers are finding themselves increasingly in the sights of military-style guns, wielded by criminals, the mentally deranged, and radical extremists. A VPC study published in 2010, based on reports of assault weapons in the news over a two-year span—between March 1, 2005, and February 28, 2007—made clear that assault weapons are frequently used in crime and confiscated from criminals. Moreover, it demonstrated that the number of incidents in which law enforcement officers were reported to have been confronted with assault weapons rose dramatically in the two-year period monitored. More than one out of four assault-weapons incidents in the study involved police. Those incidents are likely to involve shots being fired, with injuries to law enforcement personnel, gunmen, and bystanders. Shots were fired from assault weapons (other than police weapons) in three out of every four reported incidents involving police.[31]

One example of the impact of assault weapons on police occurred in April 2009 in the Stanton Heights area of Pittsburgh, Pennsylvania, a "close-knit, family oriented and pet friendly neighborhood" that "appeals to those looking for a quiet and relaxed way of life."[32] Many Pittsburgh police and fire service officers live in Stanton Heights.[33] In April 2009, Eric G. Kelly was among them. A fourteen-year veteran of the Pittsburgh Bureau of Police, Kelly had changed the police zone in which he worked in January. He wanted to be closer to his home, where he lived with his wife and three daughters.[34] His new policing area included Stanton Heights.[35]

Another family lived on Fairfield Street, several blocks away from Officer Kelly. Three generations of the family that lived in this small ranch-style house had immersed themselves in the great American gun culture. The youngest, Richard Jr., held a concealed-carry permit from Allegheny County.[36] He was an outspoken advocate for permits. In 2008 he posted on the website of the Pennsylvania Firearms Owners Association, "I want all the guys that deserve them to have their licenses without fear of cracking a fart and the county sheriff smelling it. Ya dig?"[37]

Richard's grandfather, the late Charles Scott, was a "deadbeat alcoholic who beat his wife and other family members." Unemployed for the most part, he drank up to two cases of beer a day and kept a cache of guns in the house.[38] He liked to walk around with a handgun stuffed into his belt and was known for uttering racial slurs.[39] Scott was a man given to rage. He beat his wife and daughter. He deliberately shot a family kitten to death, fired through the ceiling and roof of his house, and pointed his guns at other family members.[40] During one domestic argument, he shot two telephones that his wife tried to use to call for help. When she began studying to get a GED (General Educational Development) diploma,[41] he shot up her textbooks because he was against the idea.[42]

It is perhaps not surprising that Charles's daughter, Margaret, took up drinking at an early age and (unsuccessfully) attempted suicide at least three times, including shooting herself with a shot-gun.[43] Her marriage to Richard Poplawski produced the future concealed-carry-permit holder Richard Jr. The elder Poplawski left the home when his son was about three years old. Richard Poplawski Jr. was left largely to the care of his grandparents.[44]

The younger Poplawski followed the cycle of guns, violence, hatred, and failure. (All references to Poplawski hereafter are to the son, Richard Jr.) Said to have been bright and likable as a child, Poplawski spiraled down into anger and bitterness. By 2009, when he was twenty-two, he had already enlisted in the U.S. Marine Corps and lasted only three weeks. He had also tried dental school, computers, and a string of other jobs. He failed at them all. He went to Florida for a while, came back, and ended up living at home with his mother. The two had loud and bitter arguments. Within the last year, Richard had acquired two pit bull puppies from an animal rescue center.[45] On the morning of Saturday, April 4, 2009, the action of one of the two dogs set off an explosion of violence that stunned Pittsburgh.

On Friday night, April 3, Officer Kelly worked the 11:00 P.M. to 7:00 A.M. shift.[46] Richard Poplawski partied with friends,[47] came home late, and surfed the Web. Among the sites he visited Saturday morning between 3:30 A.M. and 5:00 A.M. was the web-site of the white supremacist organization Stormfront.[48]

Poplawski left markers of his disintegrating identity and festering hatred on the Internet beginning in high school. According to Mark Pitcavage, director of the Anti-Defamation League's investigative research department, Poplawski's first Internet writings were about smoking marijuana and making dope pipes, which Poplawski said his mother was "cool with." He first appeared on white supremacist sites in 2007, when he scribbled about his hatred of minorities and a government collapse that was supposedly coming. Poplawski believed that the federal government was building concentration camps for dissenters and that under President Obama's leadership it was planning to suspend the Constitution, declare martial law, and confiscate

Americans' firearms.[49] "If a total collapse is what it takes to wake our brethren and guarantee future generations of white children walk this continent, if that is what it takes to restore our freedoms and recapture our land: let it begin this very second and not a moment later," he wrote in March 2009.[50] In 2007, Poplawski explained his hatred for blacks on the Stormfront hate site. "I attribute it, in part, to my solid upbringing . . . my mother made it clear that it would be frowned upon (to say the least, she actually told me she would bust me with a frying pan) to bring home a non-white girlfriend long before I had started thinking about bringing home any girls period, lol." [51]

Poplawski also posted several hundred times on the website of the Pennsylvania Firearm Owners Association, beginning in December 2007. Most of his posts there—made under the name of "RWhiteman"—discussed concealed-weapons permits, police arrests and gun confiscations he believed were illegal, and buying and selling guns.[52] In an early post, Poplawski made a twisted allusion to Dr. Martin Luther King Jr.'s "I Have a Dream Speech," in which King said, "I have a dream that my four little children will one day live in a nation where they will not be judged by the color of their skin but by the content of their character." [53] In December 2007, Poplawski wrote, "I can only hope I would be judged not on the make of my firearm, but on the content of my character." [54] In the same year, he posted this statement about police:

> I dont [sic] care to bend at all from harassment from the police If I'm doing nothing more than exercising a right. If that means pissing a cop or two off, then so be it, if they are so ignorant as to try to trample my rights or inconvenience me in any way for no reason. I mean Im [sic] not talking about DISRESPECTING any cops, just not bending for them in fear as so many people do.[55]

Poplawski discussed his private "hit list" on a white supremacist Internet radio program he co-hosted sometime in the weeks before April 4, 2009. The list included a Pittsburgh police officer, a black, a Jew, his ex-girlfriend, her parents, and neighbors' pets.[56] "You have an individual who is, by any stretch of the imagination, a total failure in life with very deep feelings of inadequacy and filled with tons of hatred," Louis B. Schlesinger, professor of forensic psychology at John Jay College of Criminal Justice told the *Pittsburgh Tribune-Review* in 2011. "This guy had a mind-set that was anti-government and conspiratorial. He had organizations like these white supremacist groups telling him that it wasn't him. It was foreigners, minorities and the government causing his problems."[57]

In addition to getting his concealed-carry permit—he encouraged Eddie Perkovic, his hate radio co-host, to get one too[58]—Poplawski bought body armor (popularly called a bulletproof vest) from a friend.[59] He built up an arsenal at home. His guns included a .380 semiautomatic pistol, a 22 caliber rifle, a .357 Magnum handgun, a shotgun, and an AK-47 semiautomatic assault rifle. He had more than a thousand rounds of ammunition, better than nine hundred rounds of it for his AK-47.[60] "Hand everybody an AK and a sidearm," Poplawski wrote on a Penguin hockey team fan website in December 2008. "Everybody. And see how long these mass murdering spree's [*sic*] last, if anybody even dares to attempt them."[61]

Poplawski bought at least three of his guns from Braverman Arms Co., a gun shop on Penn Avenue in Wilkinsburg, a borough in Allegheny County next to Pittsburgh.[62] Wilkinsburg had its moment of national attention in 2000, when Ronald Taylor, thirty-nine, a black man, went on a racially motivated shooting spree. Taylor shot to death three white men and wounded two others. Investigators found lists and notes in Taylor's apartment that denounced whites, Jews, Asians, Italians, police, and the news media.[63] The gun Taylor used also was traced back to Braverman Arms Co.[64]

Of all his guns, Poplawski most loved his AK-47 assault rifle. On December 8, 2008, Poplawski posted a comment on

Stormfront's website, in response to a question posed there, "If You Could Have Just One Weapon—SHTF [shit hits the fan], What Would It Be?" His answer was, "I guess I'd have to say my AK. Which is nice because it doesn't have to fall from the sky—its [*sic*] in a case within arms [*sic*] reach."[65] His friend and co-host Petrovic told the *Pittsburgh Post-Gazette* that Poplawski "always said that if someone tried to take his weapons away he would do what his forefathers told him to do and defend himself."[66]

This is where matters stood early on the morning of Saturday, April 4.

Sometime before seven A.M., Richard's mother, Margaret, awoke and found that one of the dogs had urinated on the floor. She woke Richard and confronted him about the dog.[67] After their argument, she called 911 at 7:03 A.M. and asked that the police come and remove Poplawski.[68] A police dispatcher sent the call out at 7:05 A.M. as a domestic disturbance.[69]

Officer Kelly's shift was over. Officially off duty, he picked up his oldest daughter, Tameka, twenty-two. She also worked the night shift, as a nursing assistant at a health care facility.[70] They were in his personal vehicle, only minutes from their home.

Richard Poplawski later told police that his mother was "extremely stupid" to call the police, knowing how well armed he was. Immediately after the call, he prepared himself for battle. He went into his bedroom, put on his ballistic vest, and grabbed his 12-gauge shotgun. "You're not going to do this," his mother said to Richard. But his mind was made up. He later told a police detective that he thought in his head at that moment, "Come on with it."[71]

Pittsburgh police officers Paul J. Sciullo II and Stephen J. Mayhle arrived at the Poplawski house at 7:11 A.M., eight minutes after Margaret's call to 911. She met them at the door, let them in, and said, "Come and take his ass."[72] Walking out of his bedroom with his shotgun, Poplawski saw Sciullo standing in the front doorway.[73]

"The police arrived much quicker than I expected," he later

said in a statement to police. "I was caught off guard. This led to a snap decision to shoot. [I] just believed police were going to kill me."[74] He fired a single shot from the hip at Officer Sciullo, who was struck and immediately went down in the threshold.[75]

"What the hell have you done?" Margaret yelled at Richard before fleeing to the basement.[76]

As Officer Mayhle entered the house, Poplawski tried to shoot him, too. But his shotgun jammed. "Code 3! Code 3! Officer down! Officers are being shot at!" Mayhle shouted into his radio.[77]

A furious gun battle ensued between the two men, raging through much of the house. A trail of 40 caliber casings fired from Mayhle's service pistol indicated that the officer chased Poplawski from the living room, through the kitchen, into the dining room, and then into a hallway, where the trail stopped.[78] That is when, it appears, Poplawski grabbed his AK-47 and started firing at Mayhle. The officer had fired eight 40 caliber rounds from his gun as he chased Poplawski. Two of his bullets struck Poplawski, one in the chest, near his heart. But Poplawski's ballistic vest stopped that bullet. Another bullet struck Poplawski in the leg. Mayhle then tried to run out of the house, but was struck down by bullets from Poplawski's assault rifle. Twenty-eight spent AK-47 casings were found just in the living room. Some of the bullets from those casings ripped through Mayhle's ballistic vest.[79] Poplawski went outside and shot both officers again multiple times as they lay on the ground.[80]

At 7:15 A.M., just a few blocks away, Officer Kelly and his daughter heard the sounds of gunfire as they pulled up to their house. Kelly told his daughter to run into the house. "I was shook up," she later testified. "He told me to just go in the house, lock the door. He'll be fine." She watched her father speed away. "She was banging on the door," his wife, Marena Kelly recalled. "She was saying, 'Daddy went down there.'"[81]

Meanwhile, Poplawski had holed up in his mother's bedroom. He saw Kelly drive up in his white SUV and opened fire on him immediately with his AK-47 assault rifle.[82] Kelly was hit by rounds from Poplawski's AK-47 three times before he could get out of his vehicle. The rounds easily punched through the car's metal and into Kelly's body. He was hit at least three more times by AK rounds outside the SUV, one of which was fatal, striking his right kidney, liver, and lung.[83]

Other officers responded to the scene, and a gun battle began. It lasted for two and a half hours. A detective testified that hundreds of rounds were fired from the guns Poplawski used that day—a 12-gauge shotgun, .357 Magnum revolver, and 7.62 mm AK-47 assault rifle.[84] "Bullets were whizzing and pinging everywhere," Sergeant James Kohnen said. "It was a meat grinder. We were totally outgunned—pistols against assault rifles."[85] A SWAT officer later testified, "We began to run low on ammo because we were sustaining so much fire." He said each officer carried 125 rounds of ammunition into the fight.[86] Margaret Poplawski was seen during the violent standoff, pacing in both the garage and the driveway, smoking cigarettes.[87]

Richard was eventually engaged in conversation by a police negotiator. "This is really an unfortunate occurrence, sir," Poplawski said at one point. Later he assured the negotiator, "You know, I'm a good kid, officer." He also moaned, swore, and spewed racial epithets.[88] "Boy, getting shot is really painful," he complained.[89] At one point during the battle, Poplawski considered suicide, he later told police. But he decided against it. Prison wouldn't be so bad, he concluded.[90] Eventually, he was worn down by his own wounds. "I need medical attention. It's really painful. I'm [expletive] shot. I'm in pain. I'm dizzy," he said. "Get in here and get me some medication attention."[91]

Margaret Poplawski ran out to the police at 10:36 A.M.[92] Less than ten minutes later, her son surrendered.[93] Richard Poplawski Jr. was convicted of three counts of murder and numerous other offenses. He was sentenced to death for the murders, and an additional 85 to 190 years were added for his other crimes.[94]

The gun lobby and its enthusiasts obstinately deny the lessons taught by Poplawski's tale. As chapter 5 discussed and this case demonstrates, concealed-carry-permit holders are not by definition community leaders. A larger question is raised by the murderous actions of Richard Poplawski and James Eagan Holmes. What is there about the civilian semiautomatic assault rifle that enables a single man to kill three armed police officers in less than fifteen minutes and then hold off a huge responding force, including SWAT officers, for almost three hours? Or to murder twelve people and wound another fifty-eight in a few minutes? Why on earth are machines so efficient at killing people so freely available in the United States?

The answers are these. Assault weapons were designed to do in war precisely what Holmes did in a movie theater and Poplawski did in his quiet Pittsburgh neighborhood—kill or wound large numbers of people within short to medium distances. And the gun industry, hand in hand with the NRA, the NSSF, and other members of the gun lobby, has aggressively marketed assault weapons to help keep its foundering fortunes afloat.[95]

Semiautomatic assault weapons are civilian versions of automatic military assault rifles, such as the AK-47 and the M-16. The civilian guns look the same as their military brethren because they function identically, except for one feature: military assault rifles are machine guns. A machine gun fires continuously as long as its trigger is held back—until it runs out of ammunition. Civilian assault rifles, in contrast, are semiautomatic weapons. The trigger of a semiautomatic weapon must be pulled back separately for each round fired. Because federal law has banned the sale of new machine guns to private persons since 1986 and heavily regulates sales to civilians of older model machine guns, the availability of military assault weapons for the civilian market is limited.

The distinctive look of assault weapons like Poplawski's AK-47 is not merely cosmetic, as the gun industry and its lobby often argue. The assault weapon's physical appearance is the result of design following function. All assault weapons—military and civilian alike—incorporate specific features that were designed to provide a specific combat function. That function is laying down a high volume of fire over a wide killing zone, also known as "hosing down" an area. Civilian assault weapons keep the specific design features that make this deadly spray-firing easy. The most important of these design features are:

- High-capacity detachable ammunition magazines (often called "clips") that may hold more than a hundred rounds of ammunition.[96] According to gun expert Chuck Taylor, "This allows the high volume of fire critical to the 'storm gun' concept."[97] A gun that held the three to five rounds of a traditional hunting rifle or the six rounds of a classic revolver would have to be reloaded many times to discharge as many bullets as are available in a single high-capacity magazine.
- A rear pistol grip (handle), including so-called "thumb-hole stocks" and extended ammunition magazines that function like pistol grips.
- A forward grip or barrel shroud. Forward grips (located under the barrel or the forward stock) "give a shooter greater control over a weapon during recoil," according to gun expert Duncan Long.[98] The front and rear grips allow the shooter to hold the gun in a manner that is convenient for either spray-firing from the hip or more controlled aiming from the shoulder. Forward grips and barrel shrouds also make it possible to hold the gun with the non-trigger hand, even though the barrel gets extremely hot from firing multiple rounds. In the case of assault pistols, the forward grip is often an ammunition magazine or a barrel shroud (a heat-dissipating vented tube surrounding the gun barrel).

Military assault rifles usually feature what is known as "selective fire"—the ability to change, with the flick of a small lever, from semiautomatic fire to fully automatic fire. Is this selective ability to use automatic fire an essential feature of a "real" assault weapon? The answer is, "absolutely not." But that hasn't kept the gun industry from using this line of argument to pretend that civilian assault weapons simply don't exist. For example, in June 2010, Tom Givens, a gun writer who also runs a gun training range (complete with gun shop) in Memphis, Tennessee, told the *Commercial Appeal* that the AR-15 is not an assault rifle because it is semiautomatic.[99] This red herring began to be raised by the gun lobby only after civilian assault weapons were widely criticized. The criticism understandably arose after mass murderers and drug traffickers began to "hose down" America's streets and schoolyards with civilian assault weapons. The argument is entirely semantic. By limiting the definition of assault weapon to machine guns, the gun industry and its friends hope to define the problem away. But fully automatic fire has little to do with the killing power of assault weapons. As pro–assault weapons expert Duncan Long wrote in his 1986 publication, *Assault Pistols, Rifles and Submachine Guns*, "The next problem arises if you make a semiauto-only model of one of these selective-fire rifles. According to the purists, an assault rifle has to be selective fire. Yet, if you think about it, it's a little hard to accept the idea that firearms with extended magazines, pistol grip stock, etc. cease to be assault rifles by changing a bit of metal." [100]

Long's point is well taken, because military and civilian experts (including an NRA magazine) agree that semiautomatic fire is actually more—not less—likely to hit the target than is automatic fire and is thus more deadly.[101] In fact, Long wrote about the semiautomatic UZI in another book, "One plus of the semiauto version is that it has a greater potential accuracy." [102] In any case, an NRA magazine reported that a person of moderate skill—like Richard Poplawski—can fire a semiautomatic assault weapon at an extremely fast rate of fire.[103]

The history of assault weapons confirms Long's view that the fundamental design of the assault weapon has little to do with automatic fire and everything to do with high capacity and ease of firing. The German army developed the first assault rifle during World War II. The STG 44 (*Sturmgewehr*, or "storm gun") was the "father of all assault rifles. . . . After the war it was examined and dissected by almost every major gunmaking nation and led, in one way and another, to the present-day 5.56mm assault rifles." [104] The Soviet Army's AK-47 was derived from the STG-44 shortly after the war. [105]

After studying over three million casualty reports from three wars, the U.S. Army's Operations Research Office (ORO) found that, "in the overall picture, aimed fire did not seem to have any more important role in creating casualties than randomly fired shots. Marksmanship was not as important as volume. . . . From this data, ORO concluded that what the Army needed was a low recoil weapon firing a number of small projectiles. . . . The [Armalite] AR-15 was chosen as the best small caliber weapon and it was adopted as the M16." [106] One gun expert put the army's reasoning into plain words. "The studies showed that . . . in spite of the huge amounts of money spent by the military services in training combat infantrymen to be marksmen, few were capable of firing effectively beyond ranges of 200 to 300 meters in the heat of battle. 'Spray and pray' would come to be the practice on the future battlefields of Vietnam." [107] More recently, in September 2009, a gun industry observer summed up the assault rifle's design concept. "From the minute you get your first modern, AR-style rifle, the first thing that you notice is the fact that it truly is one of the most ergonomic long guns you'll ever put to your shoulder. Makes sense, it was designed to take young men, many of whom had never fired a gun of any sort before, and quickly make them capable of running the rifle—effectively—in the most extreme duress, armed combat." [108]

Why are these weapons of war on America's streets? Simply to make money for the gun industry. In the 1980s, foreign manufacturers began dumping semiautomatic versions of the Soviet-designed AK-47 military assault rifle onto the U.S. civilian firearms market. Colt Industries, a domestic manufacturer, marketed the AR-15, the semiautomatic version of the M16, the standard U.S. military infantry rifle. When Colt's basic patent expired, other gun makers jumped into the civilian market.

Assault weapons have become hot items on the civilian market for a variety of reasons. For manufacturers, assault weapons originally helped counter the mid-1980s decline in handgun sales. Criminals—especially drug traffickers—were drawn to assault weapons' massive firepower, useful for fighting police and competing traffickers. Survivalists—who envisioned themselves fending off a horde of desperate neighbors from within their bomb shelters—loved the combat features of high ammunition capacity and antipersonnel striking power of assault weapons. Right-wing paramilitary extremists made these easily purchased firearms their gun of choice. And for gun enthusiast fans of popular entertainment, semiautomatic assault weapons offered the look and feel of the "real thing."

Since the 1980s, the gun industry has aggressively used as selling points the military character of semiautomatic assault weapons and the lethality of their distinctive designs.[109] Poplawski's murderous attack amply demonstrates that these civilian semiautomatic assault weapons, like their military counterparts, are every bit as deadly as the gun industry promises. Examples of the use of assault weapons against law enforcement officers by extremists and criminals continue to abound, as fatal attacks on police officers have grown to alarming numbers. FBI data for 2011 reported that seventy-two officers were killed by criminal suspects in 2011—a 25 percent increase from 2010 and a 75 percent increase from the forty-one reported killed in 2008. The year 2011 was the first one in which more officers were killed by suspects than in car accidents, and the total was the highest in nearly two decades (not including officers murdered in the 2001 terrorist attacks and the 1995 Oklahoma City bombing).[110] Guns were used in sixty-three of the seventy-two murders. Forty-nine of the victims were wearing body armor.[111]

One bloody instance of this escalating carnage began on

May 20, 2010, in West Memphis, Arkansas, when police officer Thomas "Bill" Evans stopped a van driven by Jerry Kane, forty-five, of Forest, Ohio, along I-40. Soon afterward, Sergeant Brandon Paudert arrived to back up Evans. Within minutes, Kane's son, Joseph Kane, seventeen, jumped out of the van and shot both officers with an AK-47 assault rifle. Sergeant Paudert was shot fourteen times, including three times in the head. Officer Evans was shot eight times in the chest, back, and arms.[112]

About ninety minutes after Paudert and Evans were slain, two more law enforcement officers were critically wounded when they spotted and cornered the Kanes' van in a Walmart parking lot. A blazing fifteen-minute shootout with law enforcement officers ensued, and both Kanes were killed.[113]

The Kanes were members of the so-called sovereign citizens movement. Among the members' beliefs are that the United States is under martial law and they are entitled to use armed force to resist police. As of February 2012, members of the movement had killed six police officers since 2000. In what the *Los Angeles Times* described as a "notable shift in policy," federal agencies have begun intensively monitoring the movement.[114] No amount of "monitoring," however, has kept assault weapons out of the hands of these violent radicals.

"Brandon and Bill had no chance against an AK-47," Sergeant Paudert's father, West Memphis Police Chief Bob Paudert, said. "They were completely outgunned. We are dealing with people who rant and rave about killing. They want government officials dead. We had a 16-year-old better armed than the police."[115] (It was later learned that Joseph Kane was actually seventeen years old.)

A chillingly similar ambush occurred on August 16, 2012, in Louisiana, leaving two sheriff's deputies dead and two wounded. The chain of events began early in the morning in a parking lot at an oil refinery. The refinery had hired off-duty deputy sheriffs to direct traffic. St. John Sheriff's Deputy Michael Boyington was sitting in his car when someone opened fire on him with an assault weapon. Boyington, who was hit several times but survived his wounds, was able to radio in a description of the car from which the shots were fired. Subsequent investigation led three other deputies to a trailer park. While they were interviewing two men, a third emerged from a trailer and began shooting with an assault weapon. Deputies Brandon Nielsen and Jeremy Triche were killed. Deputy Jason Triche was wounded.[116] Seven people were arrested in connection with the incident.[117] Authorities in Tennessee had previously linked the apparent patriarch of the group to the sovereign citizens movement.[118]

Common criminals also find themselves well armed to resist police, thanks to the gun industry's reckless and relentless marketing of military-style weapons. In 2009, only months after Poplawski killed the three Pittsburgh officers with his AK-47, a police officer in a Pittsburgh suburb also was murdered with an assault rifle. Penn Hills police officer Michael Crawshaw, thirty-two, was the first to respond to a 911 call in which dispatchers heard gunshots. Crawshaw was advised to wait in his patrol car until backup arrived. According to a police detective's testimony, Ronald Robinson, thirty-two, later confessed to the crime. Robinson had shot to death another man in the house over a drug debt. Officer Crawshaw saw Robinson leaving and ordered him to stop. Robinson opened fire with his MAK 90 Sporter, a cheap and popular AK variant. Crawshaw was hit in the head and killed.[119]

It was just such attacks that led many law enforcement agencies in the late 1980s to demand that the federal government take action to stringently control or ban semiautomatic assault weapons. But the history of attempts to regulate assault weapons since then has been one of political compromise, poor law writing, and, as a result, ultimate failure. The health and safety of law enforcement and the public has been continually trumped by gun industry and NRA muscle. Presidents George H.W. Bush and Bill Clinton both attempted to restrict the import of assault weapons by exercising executive power under a federal statute that limits the import of firearms to those that are "generally recognized

as particularly suitable for or readily adaptable to sporting purposes." The administrations of later presidents, George W. Bush
and Barack Obama, however, allowed these restrictions to effectively lapse.

Congress has done no better. In 1994, President William J.
Clinton signed into law the 1994 federal assault weapons "ban."
The 1994 law, however, was deeply flawed.[120] At the outset, the
law, forged out of a political rather than a technical compromise, exempted millions of semiautomatic assault weapons by
"grandfathering" all such firearms legally owned as of the date
of enactment. For the trade in these guns, it was as if the law
had never been passed. They continued to be bought and sold,
many at gun shows where no questions are asked of prospective
buyers in nominally "private" sales.[121] Moreover, most of the design characteristics by which new production or imports were
to be defined as banned assault weapons were simply a laundry
list of superficial cosmetic features that had nothing to do with
the weapons' most deadly functional features. The gun industry
quickly and easily evaded the 1994 law by making slight, cosmetic
changes to the supposedly banned firearms. Gun manufacturers
and importers soon openly boasted of the ease with which they
could circumvent the ban. By the time the 1994 law expired by its
sunset provision in 2004, there were actually many more types
and models of assault weapons legally on the civilian market than
before the law was passed.[122]

For all practical purposes, the federal government has abandoned its attempts to regulate commerce in assault weapons into
and within the United States. As a result, an unknown but certainly substantial number of foreign assault weapons poured into
the United States during the Bush administration and continues
to pour in under the Obama administration. These guns, primarily AK-type designs, are in addition to the enormous number of
AR-type assault weapons manufactured domestically. "With the
number of companies making those particular black rifles today,
it's tough to keep up them [sic]," a gun industry insider wrote

low-capacity rifles. It is not merely incidental that, as the Freedom Group noted, there is a tremendous after-market in accessories for these assault rifles.

Unfortunately for the NSSF and the industry, some within their own ranks apparently never got the rebranding memo. They continue to call semiautomatic assault rifles exactly what they are—assault rifles—and even write lurid prose promoting the most dangerous features of these guns. For example, the August 2010 edition of *Gun World* magazine headlined "Ruger's Mini-14 Tactical Rifle" as " 'Combat Customized' from the Factory." [128]

Among other outbursts of naked candor in this enthusiastic article were these verbatim gems: "Ruger's Mini-14 Tactical Rifle is a version of the well established Mini-14 incorporating many of the assault rifle features that end users have being [*sic*] applying themselves for decades, this time straight from the factory," according to the article. "Being seen over the years as a sort of 'poor man's assault rifle' the Mini-14 has spawned a huge array of after-market parts that may be applied to make it more 'assault rifle-y.' Recently Sturm, Ruger & Co. finally decided to get into the act themselves by producing their Mini-14 Tactical Rifles." [129] This spasm of honesty is typical of the "wink and nod" game that the gun industry plays when it talks to itself and to its hard-core consumers: call them what you will—"black rifles," "tactical rifles," or "modern sporting rifles"—semiautomatic assault weapons are plainly and simply military-style assault weapons.

A rapidly emerging and particularly deadly variant in the gun industry's marketing program has been the sale of civilian assault pistols. Not since the late 1980s and early 1990s—the height of the domestic drug wars—has there been such a wide selection of assault pistols available for sale in the United States. During that period, UZI pistols, MAC-10s, and TEC-9s were the prominent assault pistols seen on television and movie screens as well as displayed on gun store counters. Today, more assault pistol makes and models are available than ever before for civilian sale in the United States. They range from models that were named under the now-expired federal assault weapons ban (such as the UZI pistol, MAC-10, and Calico) to newer models, such as AK-47 and AR-15 pistols. As a 2011 article published in *Handguns* magazine titled "AR Pistols: The Hugely Popular Rifle Platform Makes a Pretty Cool Handgun as Well" noted, "There's no doubt in the last few years that AR pistols have become extremely popular."[130]

This increase in the quantity of makes and models has been matched by an increase in the quality of their lethality. The earlier generation of assault pistols were primarily high-capacity military-style pistols in 9mm or 45 caliber. The most popular models today are derived from assault rifles and thus have the penetrating power of an assault rifle in the concealable form of a pistol. Whereas the most commonly worn levels of police body armor would be able to protect the wearer from a 9mm or 45 caliber handgun round, the .223 or 7.62 assault rifle rounds would be far more likely to penetrate. As one poster on Survivalist Boards.com wrote about the Draco AK-47 pistol, "It can penetrate body armor and holds 30+ rounds. . . . I figure this is a lot of firepower in a legal and small package."[131] After detailing the pistol's military pedigree and suitability as a PDW (personal defense weapon), *Tactical Weapons* magazine approvingly noted that the "result is a 5.5 pound pistol with an overall length of 20.5 inches that offers full rifle power in a very compact package— A desirable combination for many!"[132] As noted earlier, it's clear that AK-47 pistols are a "weapon of choice" of illegal gun traffickers who purchase firearms in the United States and then smuggle them into Mexico.[133]

A related design and marketing innovation has been the sale to civilians of "vest busters," handguns specifically designed to penetrate body armor. The FN Five-seveN—known as the "cop killer" in Mexico—is a virtual poster child for this aspect of the militarization trend. The 5.7x28mm round it fires was specifically designed to defeat body armor on the modern battlefield. Given its use by Major Nidal Hasan at Fort Hood, it's ironic that this handgun was designed for use by counterterrorism teams.

FN clearly recognized the danger of the genie it was releasing when it introduced the Five-seveN. The company originally claimed that it would restrict the sale of its new armor-piercing ammunition and pistol. A company spokesman told the *Sunday Times* (London) in 1996 that the pistol was "too potent" for normal police duties and was designed for antiterrorist and hostage-rescue operations.[134]

The gun industry press, which invariably fawns over any new gun at its debut, played along with FN's righteous fiction. The NRA's *American Rifleman* claimed in 1999, "Law enforcement and military markets are the target groups of FN's new FiveseveN pistol," and told its readers, "Don't expect to see this cartridge sold over the counter in the United States. In this incarnation, it is strictly a law enforcement or military round."[135] Similarly, *American Handgunner* magazine assured the public in 2000, "For reasons that will become obvious, neither the gun nor the ammunition will ever be sold to civilians or even to individual officers."[136]

In fact, however, greed overcame caution, and both the gun and its ammunition are easily, legally, and widely available in the United States.

The gun industry's campaigns to sell death-dealing military firepower is in large degree enabled by the stranglehold it has on official sources of information and data about the consequences. The vacuum of reliable data enables the industry and its lobby to manufacture phony "facts" to suit its case—and successfully peddle its specious assertions to ill-informed politicians, policy-makers, and news media. The next chapter explores the terrain of this Alice-in-Wonderland world.

7

TOP SECRET: AMERICA'S GUNS

"We're at Desert Hills Shooting Club near Boulder City, and Paul Barrett steps up with a Glock 17," reported the *Las Vegas Sun* in January 2012. "He fires the 9mm semi-automatic pistol 18 times in about five seconds and hits the target every time."[1]

An assistant managing editor and senior feature writer at *Bloomberg Businessweek*, Barrett writes "cover articles on subjects that range from the energy industry to the gun business."[2] He was in Las Vegas during NSSF's annual SHOT Show in 2012 to promote his new book about the Austrian gunmaker Glock and its high-capacity semiautomatic pistol design, which Barrett calls "America's gun."[3] Careful to maintain the appearance of journalistic neutrality, Barrett's book won a friendly reception both from gun enthusiasts, who are one of the most defensively critical audiences in the world, and from some gun control advocates.[4]

"The Glock became to handguns what Google became to Internet searches," Barrett told the *Atlanta Journal Constitution*. "It's a Glock world."[5]

If Glock's pistols are collectively "America's gun" in a "Glock world," Barrett's firepower demonstration graphically illustrated why Glocks have had a special appeal to mass murderers in the United States. At Barrett's reported recreational amateur's firing rate of roughly 3.6 bullets per second, a Glock pistol can pump out 33 bullets (from a legal and commonly available Glock high-capacity magazine) in less than 10 seconds.[6] Easily reloaded by dropping the expended magazine with a simple push of a button and shoving a new magazine into the grip, the Glock has turned

tranquil scenes all over America into screaming, bloody, human abattoirs. Figure 10 lists some of the more notorious examples of mass shooting incidents in the United States in which the shooter chose to use a Glock pistol.

Figure 10. Examples of Mass Shootings with Glocks in the United States

Mass Shooting Incident	Casualties	Firearm(s)
Safeway parking lot Tucson, Arizona January 8, 2011 Shooter: Jared Loughner	6 dead, 13 wounded	Glock 19 pistol
Virginia Tech Blacksburg, Virginia April 16, 2007 Shooter: Seung-Hui Cho	33 dead (including shooter), 17 wounded	Glock 19 pistol, Walther P22 pistol
Xerox Office Building Honolulu, Hawaii November 2, 1999 Shooter: Byran Uyesugi	7 dead	Glock 17 9mm pistol
Thurston High School Springfield, Oregon May 21, 1998 Shooter: Kip Kinkel	4 dead, 22 wounded	Glock 9mm pistol, .22 Sturm Ruger rifle, .22 Sturm Ruger pistol
Connecticut State Lottery Headquarters Newington, Connecticut March 6, 1998 Shooter: Matthew Beck	5 dead (including shooter)	Glock 9mm pistol
Luby's Cafeteria Killeen, Texas October 16, 1991 Shooter: George Hennard	24 dead (including shooter), 20 wounded	Glock 9mm pistol, Sturm Ruger P-89 9mm pistol

Violence Policy Center, "The Glock Pistol: A Favorite of Mass Shooters," July 2011, www.vpc.org/fact_sht/GlockBackgrounderJuly2011.pdf.

The examples in figure 10 were extracted by VPC from news reports. Flawed and incomplete as media reports may be, they are often the only available source about the details of gun violence in America.

Given the pestilential effect guns have on America, it is little short of incredible that the gun industry and its relentless lobby have succeeded in preventing the federal government from collecting, organizing, analyzing, and—most of all—releasing detailed data about guns and gun death, injury, and crime in America. What data exists is scattered over several different federal agencies in collections that are more often than not inconsistent, incomplete, and incompatible with each other. Information that might shed light on, for example, what makes and models of guns are used in crimes, and how frequently, is locked up tight. Laws slipped through Congress by lawmakers friendly to the gun industry's agenda bar the release of data—even to members of Congress—that was once freely available and routinely released to the public.

The sluggish bureaucracy at ATF takes the laws a step further by spinning timid rationales to avoid releasing information. No wonder. ATF's executive ranks have been brazenly infiltrated by the gun industry. In 2006, *Shooting Industry* gleefully reported—under the headline "Our Man at ATF"—that "John Badowski, a five-plus-year veteran of the National Shooting Sports Foundation staff, is now the Firearms Industry Technical Adviser at ATF."[7] During his tenure at NSSF, Badowski helped start the National Association of Firearm Retailers to "provide federal firearms licensees with a unified voice in regulatory and legislative affairs."[8] He also promoted the NSSF's "Retailer University," which offered gun dealers such courses as Developing a Place to Shoot, and Winning Sales Techniques for Your Staff."[9] In 2003 the "university" announced a course titled Dealing with the Media. Badowski described the curriculum to *Shooting Industry*. "Let's say a firearm has been used inappropriately and the retailer gets a phone call from a news director who says, 'Hey, we're on

the way over with a news crew for an interview. What do you do? This is high-powered training about how to deal with the media in an adverse situation." [10]

The gun industry may have learned how to "deal with the media," but it nevertheless keeps its business as secret as possible. The greater part of the industry is privately held, foreign based, or both. The few public companies—Ruger and Smith & Wesson—stick to what they are required to file by the Securities and Exchange Commission, which regulates public trading in stocks. The rest of what is known about the business of guns in America must be meticulously panned out of a steady stream of hyperbolic promotional releases, the occasional memoir by an insider,[11] and intra-industry business publications. Is the gun industry booming or failing? Are women buying more or fewer guns? The industry can—and does—put the rosiest public spin on such questions to conceal its declining fortunes and validate in the American psyche the goodness of guns.

This desert of information is no accident. By choking off detailed data about the effects of its products, the gun industry can promote its fantasy world of good gun owners and bad criminals, a world in which the social utility of guns outweighs the harm they do.

Take Glock, for but one example among many. According to Paul Barrett, "Glock . . . is not a particular villain within the fraternity of firearms." [12] Perhaps, perhaps not. Given the information lockdown, it is impossible to quantify the comparative villainy of Glock handguns and any other make. The comparison would, in any case, miss the point. Whether Glock or Taurus or Ruger or Smith & Wesson is the most evil is irrelevant. The point is that their products do tremendous, unnecessary harm to tens of thousands of innocent Americans every year.

Figure 10 illustrates the use of Glock guns in mass shootings in the United States. But what about Glock's role in the everyday carnage documented throughout this book? How often are Glocks—or any other manufacturer's guns—used in the crimes, murders, domestic suicides, shooting rampages, rage shootings, and other instances of violence that take so many lives and inflict so many injuries in the United States every year? These are questions the answers to which the gun industry very much does not want you to know.

One might think that ATF would be the logical place to go for an answer about the use of guns in crime (putting aside the typical delay of a year or two from collection to release of government data on any subject). After all, one of ATF's principal law enforcement support functions is tracing the origin of guns recovered at crime scenes and matching guns with the ballistic traces left on fired bullets and casings. The ATF says its National Tracing Center (NTC) is the nation's only crime-gun tracing facility. "As such, the NTC provides critical information that helps domestic and international law enforcement agencies solve firearms crimes, detect firearms trafficking and identify trends with respect to intrastate, interstate and international movement of crime guns."[13] Here is how ATF recently described the process:

> Firearms tracing is the systematic tracking of the movement of a firearm from its first sale by a manufacturer or importer through the distribution chain in an attempt to identify the first retail purchaser in order to provide investigative leads for criminal investigations. After the firearm is recovered and the identifiers are forwarded to the NTC, ATF contacts the manufacturer or importer to ascertain the sale or transfer of the firearm. ATF will attempt to contact all ensuing Federal firearms licensees (wholesale/retail) in the distribution chain until a purchaser is identified or the trace process cannot continue due to a lack of accurate or incomplete information on the trace request or in the Federal firearms licensee's records.[14]

There is no question that ATF has an enormous database documenting in detail—by make, model, caliber, origin, etc.—these "crime guns." The NTC traced over 295,000 guns in calendar year 2007; in 2008, over 288,000 guns; in 2009, over 354,000 guns; in 2010, over 285,000 guns; and in 2011, over 319,000 guns.[15] That's a million and a half crime-gun traces in just five years.

One might think that the massive cost of gun crimes would inspire the release of this entire valuable database, rather than the sparse summary data ATF releases from time to time. According to a 2012 report by the Police Executive Research Forum, a nonprofit police research organization,[16] in 2010 alone the cost of gun crime in America—gun murder, armed robbery, and aggravated assault—was almost $58 billion: $57,926,815,000 to be exact (using the most conservative of the three most recent studies of such costs).[17]

One would, however, be mistaken in that thought.

There is no chance under present law—known as the Tiahrt Amendment—and federal government policy that the ATF data will be released in any form that is of serious use to the general public, public policy analysts, or much of anybody else, for that matter. Combined with a federal law barring most civil lawsuits against the gun industry, the dearth of information is an essential part of the industry's strategy to insulate itself from liability for the consequences of its products, a civil liability that almost every other consumer product in America bears.

In addition to protecting itself from lawsuits, the gun industry and its advocates are also aware that when the broader public debate about guns and gun violence is fact based, they lose. When Americans get a glimpse of the truth, they are appalled. For example, the VPC's continuing research on fatal, nondefensive shootings involving private persons legally allowed to carry concealed handguns in public revealed in May 2012 that within a single state, Michigan, over a single year (July 1, 2010, to June 30, 2011), permit holders took thirty-eight lives, by either killing others or committing suicide.[18] "Michigan is one of the few states that releases any data about non-self-defense deaths associated with concealed handgun permit holders," VPC's legislative director Kristen Rand noted in releasing the data. "If we could obtain similar data for every state that issues concealed handgun permits, the numbers would be staggering. The public deserves to know the truth." [19]

Congress has even required ATF to state—in the few reports that it does release from its gun-trace data—that the traces are not a "random sample" and "are not chosen for purposes of determining which types, makes or models of firearms are used for illicit purposes." [20] What Congress does not acknowledge and does not require ATF to state is that there is no other source of data, random or not, that comes near to matching the value of the millions of crime-gun histories in the ATF trace data. Only ATF has such extensive records of traces of guns associated with crimes in the United States. And in any case, ATF does not "choose" the guns it traces—the trace requests come to ATF from law enforcement agencies.

As one commentator has noted, "a flawed representation is better than no representation at all." [21] If Congress truly wanted better sources of analytical data than ATF crime-gun trace data, it would take a different tack. It would mandate the creation and funding of a comprehensive data gathering and analysis system that would provide a complete, detailed, and freely accessible national picture of guns and gun violence, integrating law enforcement and public health data sources. Such a fact-based resource—with great granularity at national and local levels of experience—would provide such information as: the number and rate of murder-suicides, the characteristics of the perpetrators and their victims, and the kinds (type, model, caliber, and manufacturer) of guns they use; the number and kind of gun crimes committed by concealed-carry-permit holders and other private persons legally allowed to carry concealed guns, as well as the kind of guns they used; the number and types of gun crimes by type, model, caliber, and manufacturer (and importer, in the case of imported guns); the use of high-capacity magazines in gun crimes; and the means by which persons using guns in crime obtained their guns.

The collection and analysis of data about the public health factors in gun death and injury have also been suppressed by the gun industry and the NRA. For ten years—from 1986 to 1996—the Centers for Disease Control and Prevention (CDC) sponsored groundbreaking peer-reviewed studies of the public health effects of guns in the United States.[22] The agency's gun violence research agenda was a relatively small part of its overall program of research into the causes of deaths and injuries and ways to reduce them. The NRA, however, launched an aggressive program—aided by a small group of conservative doctors—to shut down the CDC's research effort.[23] The NRA's objective was initially to eliminate entirely the CDC's National Center for Injury Prevention and Control, thus intending to sacrifice all injury prevention research on the altar of "gun rights." When they were unable to wipe out the agency, the gun lobby enlisted a Republican U.S. representative from Arkansas, Jay Dickey, to help it push through Congress an amendment that cut $2.6 million from the injury prevention center's budget. That was roughly the same amount that had been spent the year before on its gun research programs.[24] "It's really simple with me," Dickey told the *New York Times* in 2011. "We have the right to bear arms because of the threat of government taking over the freedoms that we have." The NRA's success not only cut off funding. It cast a deep chill over the CDC's willingness to sponsor research into the causes of gun violence and the best ways to prevent it. "We've been stopped from answering the basic questions," Mark Rosenberg, the former director of the injury prevention center, told the *Times* for the same 2011 article.[25]

But following the 2012 Aurora massacre, former representative Dickey and Rosenberg joined forces to argue in favor of resuming the kind of government research that Dickey had helped cut off. "Now a body of knowledge makes it clear that an event such as the mass shooting in Aurora, Colo., was not a 'senseless' occurrence as random as a hurricane or earthquake but, rather, has underlying causes that can be understood and used to prevent similar mass shootings," the two wrote in an opinion piece published by the *Washington Post*. "Firearm injuries will continue to claim far too many lives at home, at school, at work and at the movies until we start asking and answering the hard questions," they observed.[26]

Media reports provide a glimpse of the gun violence that Congress has chosen to hide from the American people. Appendix B, for example, is a compilation of incidents involving Glock handguns that were reported in the media between May 1, 2011, and April 30, 2012, extracted from searches of the Nexis .com commercial database. Glock seemed a fair choice for this snapshot, given its iconic nature. "It's not the romantic idea of a gun," according to Paul Barrett, the Glock chronicler. "It's the essence of a gun."[27]

As shown in chapter 1, the news media underreport gun incidents in general. In addition, media reports of gun incidents often do not specify the make or model of the gun used. For these reasons, this compilation without a doubt understates reality. Nevertheless, appendix B illustrates the magnitude of the harm that Glock's handguns routinely inflict on ordinary Americans. The reported incidents include the familiar categories of gun violence: murder-suicides, rage killings, criminal trafficking, children killing themselves or killing other children, unintentional mayhem, and so on. A few incidents deserve a closer look because they illustrate how ATF collects gun crime data and how much that data could contribute to an informed public.

One of the more tragic of these examples is the horrific murder of Skyla Whitaker, eleven, and Taylor Paschal-Placker, thirteen, on Sunday afternoon, June 8, 2008, near the small town of Weleetka, Oklahoma.

Skyla and Taylor were inseparable friends. Taylor was "a big-hearted girl who rescued turtles crawling in the middle of the road and wanted to become a forensic scientist." Skyla was "the carefree adventurer—the girl who walked barefoot almost everywhere and rode her bicycle down dirt roads." Taylor was the only girl in the sixth grade class, Skyla the only girl in the fifth.[28]

The girls often spent weekends at each other's homes.[29] That Sunday at about five P.M., Skyla and Taylor went for a walk—as they often did—down a deserted dirt road toward the Bad Creek bridge. The bridge is "a popular place for teens to gather and shoot guns."[30] A few minutes later, Taylor's grandfather called her to tell the girls to come home. When she did not answer her cell phone, he went looking for the two. He found both girls lying side by side in a ditch, shot dead.[31] An autopsy found that Skyla was shot eight times and Taylor five. Both were shot in the legs, torso, neck, and base of the skull. Both were shot with guns of two different calibers. Both were apparently facing the shooter.[32]

There was little for investigators to go on. Authorities suspected that the shooter was probably a local, given the remote rural location, even though residents were horrified by the thought. "Everybody wants it to be a monster because they don't want to believe it could happen in their town," an Oklahoma City detective said of such cases. "But monsters come in all shapes and sizes. It's not like a Disney movie where you can see the villain right away."[33] Investigators doubted that a stranger would wander into the remote area.[34]

They also considered the possibility that, given the two types of guns used, there had been two shooters.[35] One of the guns the girls had been shot with was a 22 caliber, and some of these comparatively small bullets, less than a quarter of an inch in diameter, were recovered in the autopsy. But what would turn out to be most important clue were five shell casings found at the scene, fired from another gun. The shells were in 40 Smith & Wesson caliber. They were manufactured by Winchester. The casings were sent for analysis to the Oklahoma State Bureau of Investigation (OSBI) Forensic Science Center in Edmond, Oklahoma.[36]

Microscopic but highly individual tool marks are left on the working parts of guns during their manufacture, "analogous to the fingerprints of the firearm."[37] By comparing under magnification the microscopic marks on the shell casings found on the crime scene, an OSBI firearms criminalist was able to determine that they had all been fired from the same gun, and that it had been a Glock 40 caliber pistol.[38]

The 40 caliber round was developed by Smith & Wesson and Winchester and introduced at NSSF's 1990 SHOT Show. The plan was that Smith & Wesson would make the guns and Winchester would manufacture the ammunition in the new caliber. The .40 Smith & Wesson round was the "perfect compromise," according to the gun writer and entrepreneur Massad Ayoob, between those who wanted more rounds in their pistols' ammunition magazines and those who wanted bigger bullets. The existing "wondernine" 9mm pistol typically held about sixteen rounds. Although the .45 ACP bullet was much bigger and thus capable of inflicting more damage, its size demanded bigger magazines and thus bigger grips for pistols chambered in it. The 40 caliber was developed as a compromise. Glock quickly followed Smith & Wesson into the market with a pistol chambered in the new round.[39]

Heavily marketed to law enforcement by Glock, the new round became widely favored for its "stopping power" among law enforcement agencies and civilians.[40] A trainer at the Georgia Peace Officers Standards and Training Center told the *Atlanta Journal-Constitution* in 2004 that the "heavier bullet" used in the 40 caliber "tends to penetrate deeper . . . into the body to impact the organs deep in the body. This whole thing is about terminal ballistics."[41]

Agents took pictures of people as they left the girls' funeral and confiscated the funeral service registry.[42] Investigators also released a drawing of a "person of interest" in the case.[43] But the investigation stalled. The OSBI originally assigned about a dozen agents to the case. Three months later, that number had dropped to four as leads dwindled.[44] OSBI case agent Kurt Titsworth continued to follow up clues as they came in. In January 2010, for example, he learned that a man named Kevin Joe Sweat had bought a 40 caliber Glock in the fall of 2007. Titsworth interviewed Sweat, who said that he had sold the gun in 2007 and did not know the serial number.[45] Authorities later said that there was no reason at that time to connect Sweat to the murders.[46] He was just one more of a score of people who owned Glock 40 caliber pistols in and around bucolic Okfuskee County.

That is where matters remained until August 15, 2011, more than three years after the Weleetka shootings, when Kevin Joe Sweat was arrested and charged with the capital murder of Ashley Taylor, his girlfriend. Ashley and Kevin left the town of Okmulgee, near Weleetka, on July 17, supposedly headed for Louisiana to get married. When they did not return, Ashley's mother reported her missing. Kevin was tracked down and gave several different explanations to Agent Titsworth, who was investigating the woman's disappearance. Eventually, the investigation led to the property of Kevin Sweat's father near Weleetka, and the charred remains of a bonfire. In the ashes, investigators found burned clothing, bits of eyeglasses consistent with those of Ashley, and human remains believed to be hers.[47]

Soon after, agents returned to the elder Sweat's property and searched an area where, he had told OSBI agents, Kevin sometimes shot his gun. A number of 40 caliber shell casings were found in the dirt. Forensic examination revealed that they had been fired from the same gun as the shells found at the site of the 2008 murder of Skyla and Taylor.[48]

On September 13, 2011, Titsworth interviewed Kevin Sweat, who was already in custody on the charge of murdering his girlfriend. Sweat confessed to the murders of Skyla and Taylor, according to the affidavit filed in support of charges against him.

Sweat pulled over on the side of the road and saw "two monsters" come at him. Sweat then "panicked." Sweat grabbed his Glock .40 caliber handgun from between the seats of his car. Sweat then "shot the monsters" with the Glock handgun. Sweat then grabbed a ".22 caliber" gun from the glove box and "shot the monsters" with the .22 caliber gun. Sweat then got into his car and left. Sweat told Titsworth that he shot the "monsters" with the Glock .40 caliber handgun that he had purchased in 2007 while living in Henryetta, OK.[49]

A question of proof still remained. Agents had evidence connecting the shell casings on the crime scene to the casings on the elder Sweat's property. Were those casings fired from the very Glock 40 caliber pistol that Kevin Sweat had admitted buying and claimed that he had sold? If investigators had the gun, they could cycle a round through the chamber and compare the marks on the shell casing to the ones they already had. By then, OSBI had obtained the serial number of the gun from the dealer who sold it to Sweat—EKG463US.[50]

But they could not find the gun itself. OSBI asked the FBI to run a crime-gun trace request through ATF, using the gun's serial number. That trace turned up an interesting history, and a one-in-a-million piece of physical evidence that sealed the case tight.

The FBI reported that the ATF trace revealed that the Glock pistol had originally been sold to the Baltimore Police Department sometime around 2005. The Baltimore police sent the gun back to Glock shortly thereafter, one of a batch of defective pistols. Glock refurbished the guns, and one from Baltimore ended up in the Oklahoma gun store where Kevin Joe Sweat bought it in the fall of 2007. But there was more. It turned out that the Baltimore police test-fire all guns before they are distributed to officers and keep the sample casings on file.[51] The police department had a shell casing from the 40 caliber Glock with serial number EKG463US. On October 5, 2011, an OSBI agent picked up the shell casing from the Baltimore Police Department. The next day, an OSBI technician matched the casing to the shells recovered at the crime scene and on the Sweat property near Weleetka.[52]

As of this writing, the gun itself has not been found.

There are millions of similar tracing reports in ATF's records. It was reported in 2007 that every day ATF agents from six ATF regional gun-tracing centers "use a combination of science and shoe-leather detective work to track hundreds of firearms from crime scenes."[53] This data documents the links among millions and millions of guns like Kevin Sweat's 40 caliber Glock and crimes like Sweat's murder of Skyla and Taylor. "Every gun has a story to tell," William G. McMahon, the special agent in charge of the ATF's New York field office told the Associated Press in 2007.[54] Aggregating this data in summary or "wholesale" form—i.e., cutting it free from the details of specific criminal investigations—would provide a picture over time of the types, makes, models, calibers, and origin of guns used in crime in America.

The gun industry's makeshift rationale for not releasing this data to the public is that it might compromise criminal investigations and endanger undercover operations. But Bradley A. Buckles, who was the director of ATF at the time the first of the Tiahrt restrictions was passed in 2003, told the *Washington Post* in 2010 that ATF did not ask for the amendment—for that or for any other reason. "It just showed up," he said. "I always assumed the NRA did it."[55]

He was right, of course. The NRA did do it, on behalf of the gun industry. The makeshift law-enforcement-protection argument was and is a cynical cover story. Tiahrt slipped his amendment into an appropriations bill, ensuring that it would be considered without any sort of hearing. When the Republican chairman of the relevant appropriations subcommittee objected, Tiahrt assured his colleagues that the NRA had reviewed the language. "I wanted to make sure I was fulfilling the needs of my friends who are firearms dealers," Tiahrt said. NRA officials "were helpful in making sure I had my bases covered."[56]

The "needs" of Tiahrt's friends in the gun business were simple. They wanted insulation from lawsuits that were seeking to hold the industry responsible for deliberately polluting

communities all over America with increasingly deadly militarized guns. The Tiahrt Amendment was very specifically and precisely aimed at cutting off these lawsuits.

One notable such suit was *City of Chicago v. Beretta U.S.A.
Corp.*, in which the City of Chicago filed a civil suit in Illinois
state court against firearms manufacturers, distributors, and
dealers. The city alleged that these defendants created and maintained "a public nuisance in the city by intentionally marketing
firearms to city residents and others likely to use or possess the
weapons in the city, where essentially possession of any firearm
except long-barrel rifles and shotguns is illegal." [57]

Chicago's case was based on the defendants' distribution practices. In order to show the irresponsible pattern of those practices, the city submitted a Freedom of Information Act request
to ATF, seeking trace data. Although ATF had often provided
such information in the past, it refused to comply fully with the
city's request. Chicago then filed suit against ATF in federal district court to force the agency to provide the requested information. The city won against ATF both in the district court and the
court of appeals. Then, while an appeal was pending in the U.S.
Supreme Court, the NRA and Representative Tiahrt worked behind the scenes to save the gun industry. Acting in the legislative
equivalent of the dead of night, Tiahrt introduced what is known
in Congress-speak as a rider, an amendment to the Consolidated
Appropriations Act of 2003. Professor Colin Miller described the
result in a law review article. "By appending the rider to the appropriations bill, he was able to prevent it from being scrutinized
in a congressional committee and subjected to a floor debate. Indeed, the only opposition to the rider came after the rider was
already appended to the appropriations bill. In a floor statement,
Senator Richard Durbin of Illinois lamented that the rider was
'slipped in the bill' and contended that it was a response to *City
of Chicago*." [58]

It was as crass and as simple as that.

What about the argument that withholding even summary,

abstracted ATF data is necessary to protect law enforcement? In 2002, this assertion was all but laughed out of court by the U.S. Court of Appeals for the Seventh Circuit, in a caustic opinion written by Judge William Joseph Bauer, who was appointed to the district court by Richard Nixon and the court of appeals by Gerald Ford.[59] Judge Bauer wrote on behalf of a three-judge panel in the Chicago case against ATF that "in all its affidavits, documents and testimony, ATF could not identify a single concrete law enforcement proceeding that could be endangered by the release of this information."[60] The judge wrote:

> For example, they testified that if an individual pieced any withheld information together with what has already been disclosed, that individual might deduce that a particular investigation is underway. However, ATF concedes that it is not aware of a single instance in which information has been pieced together in this type of scenario. ATF's witnesses also testified that release of this data might threaten the safety of law enforcement agents, result in witness intimidation, or otherwise interfere with an ongoing investigation. Again, ATF's witnesses failed to testify as to any specific instances in which disclosing the type of records requested did result in interference with any proceeding or investigation. ATF's hypothetical scenarios do not convince us that disclosing the requested records puts the integrity of any possible enforcement proceedings at risk. . . . Conversely, the City had several witnesses at the evidentiary hearing in the district court who testified that the release of this data was unlikely to compromise any police investigations. . . . Thus, it is highly improbable that any revelation of this information could endanger an investigation. . . . In sum, ATF's arguments that the premature release of this data might interfere with investigations, threaten the safety of law enforcement officers, result in the intimidation of witnesses,

or inform a criminal that law enforcement is on his trail are based solely on speculation. Nothing the agency submitted is based on an actual pending or reasonably anticipated enforcement proceeding.[61]

It's no wonder ATF officials could do no more than parrot the industry's line. If one thinks about it, the argument is absurd on its face. What is really at issue in the bigger picture of the Tiahrt amendments are not the active case files of specific ongoing investigations but summaries of data from millions of transactions. One might as well argue that the Census Bureau should not release its detailed population tables because of the fantastically speculative premise that somewhere, someone, somehow, might figure out a way to "piece together" the data and find out something personal about somebody else somewhere.

Moreover, most of the actual criminal investigations underlying the statistical data are not even being conducted by ATF itself, but by other agencies who request a trace, as did the OSBI. "ATF itself is not and does not plan to conduct any relevant investigations," the appeals court stated. "It does not track the status of investigations surrounding traced weapons, and law enforcement agencies do not inform ATF of the status of any investigation surrounding any traced weapon."[62]

A useful analogy is the matter of the Justice Department's annual reports on foreign intelligence surveillance requests, one of the most secretive and sensitive areas of government investigation. Although the number of cases is much smaller, the principle is the same. The Justice Department's National Security Division keeps a highly classified database of all applications for court orders authorizing electronic surveillance or physical searches under the Foreign Intelligence Surveillance Act (FISA). In layperson's terms, these are court-approved wiretaps and physical searches that are so sensitive they are approved in secret by a special court. The investigations underlying the requests involve such subjects as terrorism and spying on the United States by other countries.

Access to the database, much less to the actual investigative files, is restricted to persons with a special top-secret clearance who have a "need to know" the information.[63] And yet every year the Justice Department publishes a statistical summary of these extremely sensitive applications, apparently unconcerned that a terrorist or foreign spy might "piece together" the fact that the FBI might be listening in on their particular plot.[64]

The Seventh Circuit's scathing dismissal of ATF's manufactured claims was by implication also damning to the Fraternal Order of Police, the nation's largest rank-and-file police union. FOP had submitted a friend of the court brief supporting ATF's argument. Its tenuous argument was described, and dismissed, by one legal commentator thusly:

> The Fraternal Order of Police described the following scenario: If a criminal gains access to trace data as soon as it is posted, he "learns that a specific firearm is the subject of an ongoing investigation." The criminal is "tipped off" and able to alter his behavior. This argument assumes: that data released pertain to current investigations, that the most sensitive fields of the trace database are released, that those fields are made publicly available, and that the criminal actually learns of the data and realizes that the "specific firearm" subject to the investigation is a firearm with which he is involved. Any number of protective restrictions can eliminate the already tenuous likelihood that a criminal will learn that his exact gun is under investigation.[65]

Why, one might reasonably ask, would a police union want to align itself with such a transparently feeble argument, especially when scores of police chiefs support repeal of the Tiahrt restrictions? Often in Washington, when one lifts a rock, one finds curious things beneath it.

Under this particular rock is a man named James O. Pasco Jr.

Jim Pasco, as he is usually known, is executive director of the
FOP. He is based in an office on Capitol Hill in Washington, D.C.
Pasco has been described by the *Washington Post* as "a product
of the capital's revolving door culture" and a person who is said
by people who know him to be "a charming operator whose motives can be opaque."[66] He was ATF's chief lobbyist in the middle
1990s, retired, and went to work for FOP. But in addition to being
the FOP's man in Washington, Pasco also runs his own lobbying
business—Jim Pasco and Associates—using the same address,
phone number, and e-mail as his FOP contact numbers.[67]

Although several newspapers have noticed a congruence between some of FOP's positions on legislation and those of some
of Pasco's clients, he is modest about his influence at FOP. "I
don't make the policy here," Pasco told *USA Today* in 1998.[68] His
protestation was in the context of the newspaper's having discovered that at the same time Pasco was soliciting law enforcement
groups on behalf of FOP to warn that a proposed tobacco regulation bill would create a black market in cigarettes, he was also
employed in his private lobbying business by the cigarette manufacturer Philip Morris. "We're not doing this for Philip Morris,"
Pasco explained. "Obviously, I'm concerned. I don't want it to be
construed that I have a conflict."[69] Nevertheless, letters from four
police groups were posted on the website of the tobacco companies. The letters and pictures of police officers were also featured
in a full-page ad in national newspapers. The ad asked, "If the
police are afraid of tobacco legislation . . . How safe can it be?"[70]

In 2010, the *Washington Post* observed that as a police union,
"the FOP primarily focuses on traditional labor issues," but it had
also "frequently weighed in on gun-related issues during Pasco's
tenure."[71] For example, in April 2007 the FOP "became pivotal to
the debate on the Tiahrt Amendment" when a coalition of city
mayors sought to repeal the Tiahrt restrictions to allow them to
investigate trafficking into their communities. Notwithstanding the appeals court's rebuke of the flimsy argument, "Pasco

joined National Rifle Association lobbyists to talk to members of Congress, telling them that the release of the data compromised undercover investigations."[72] The value to the NRA and the gun industry of the cover that Pasco and the FOP have given to the Tiahrt amendments cannot be overestimated.

An op-ed piece opposing the mayors appeared in the *Wichita Eagle* under the byline of FOP president Chuck Canterbury, Pasco's boss. Canterbury resurrected the chimera of the supposed danger of releasing details of active cases, writing that "officers in the field who are actually working illegal gun cases know that releasing sensitive information about pending cases can jeopardize the integrity of an investigation or even place the lives of undercover officers in danger."[73] More recently, the NRA's chief lobbyist reported that "NRA and the nation's largest police group, the Fraternal Order of Police, have worked together on numerous issues, and thanks to the leadership of FOP National President Chuck Canterbury our working relationship is now stronger than ever."[74]

Pasco went even further than Canterbury in his criticism of the mayors' efforts to hold the gun industry accountable. "This is like mayoral vigilantism," he told the Associated Press in May 2007. "It's not their law to enforce. They go out like a bull in a china shop and wander around outside their jurisdictions trying to make civil cases. It's absurd."[75]

The same month, NSSF gave a $100,000 check to the FOP for its memorial to fallen police officers. According to the *Washington Post*, "Pasco said there was no connection between the donation and the FOP's positions."[76]

That may be. But here's another curious and related fact under this particular rock. Jim Pasco is also a principal in another lobbying group called CornerStone Associates.[77] CornerStone Associates states on its website that it is "a lean integration of professionals with complementary expertise," whose "government affairs consulting" can help its clients "navigate using strong relationships in both the Executive and Legislative branches of Government." [78] And, according to CornerStone Associates' client list, the National Shooting Sports Foundation is one of its clients. [79]

Todd Tiahrt is no longer in Congress. He was defeated in a primary race for the Republican senatorial nomination in 2010. It may not have helped his cause that his hometown newspaper, the *Wichita Eagle*, endorsed his opponent. The paper noted that Tiahrt "can be too ideological, relying on GOP talking points and marching orders." [80]

Tiahrt's legacy lives on, however.

As a presidential candidate, Barack Obama promised in 2008 that he would repeal the Tiahrt Amendment. He has done no such thing. Local law enforcement agencies have been allowed some greater access to the ATF's data concerning local matters. But a great deal more of its national trace data remains locked away from police, from mayors, and from the public. [81]

8

PAPER TIGER

"You would get a far better understanding if you approached us as if you were approaching one of the great religions of the world," the NRA's executive vice president J. Warren Cassidy told *Time* magazine in 1990.[1] "Like any religion, the NRA has its gods, commandments and hierarchy," Josh Sugarmann wrote in his 1992 book about the NRA. "The faith is passed down by the leadership to the laity, and, like all good fundamentalists, both are unswayed by the complexities of modern life."[2]

Once lost to the NRA, Mitt Romney was found in 2012. He came home to Wayne. "What a job Wayne LaPierre just did," Romney said at the NRA's annual convention, praising its chief executive officer and executive vice president. "What an extraordinary man. I owe him a great debt of gratitude."[3]

Romney did not explain why he owed LaPierre his gratitude. It was no doubt because of Wayne's power to absolve Romney of his sins. In 1994, when Romney was running against Senator Edward Kennedy, he supported the assault weapons ban pending in the 1994 crime bill. A "campaign source" told the *Boston Herald* that "there was a lot of soul-searching" before the decision to support the legislation.[4] A few days later, the candidate himself made a stronger assertion. "There's been no wavering [on the assault ban]," Romney said. "I studied it and made a decision."[5] Two months later, Romney said that he also supported the new Brady law, imposing background checks on gun purchasers. "I think it will have a positive effect," Romney said.[6] He publicly rejected help from the NRA, citing his support for the assault weapons ban and the Brady law. "That's not going to make me the hero of the NRA," he said. "I don't line up with a lot of special interest groups."[7]

Kennedy beat Romney, but the latter was later elected governor of Massachusetts, serving from 2003 to 2007. As governor, Romney continued to advance a legacy of strong gun regulation that, in 2009, rewarded the people of Massachusetts with the lowest per capita gun death rate in the nation. In 2000, the state's attorney general had begun enforcing what have been described as "the strictest and most comprehensive handgun safety laws in the nation, banning all gun makers and dealers doing business in the state from selling handguns that do not have tamper-proof serial numbers, trigger locks and safety devices enabling a user to know whether the gun is loaded."[8] In 2003, Governor Romney raised gun license fees from $25 to $100.[9] In 2004, he signed the state's revised assault weapon ban, amended to remain in effect after the demise of the sunsetting federal law.[10] "I believe the people should have the right to bear arms, but I don't believe that we have to have assault weapons as part of our personal arsenal," Romney said on Fox News.[11]

The strong gun controls that Romney supported and expanded have worked to save lives in Massachusetts. An April 2012 analysis by the Violence Policy Center of 2009 national data (the most recent then available) demonstrated that states like Massachusetts with low gun ownership rates and strong gun laws also have the lowest rates of gun death.[12] Household gun ownership in Massachusetts stood at 12.8 percent, and its gun death rate was 3.14 per 100,000—the lowest in the nation. By comparison, household gun ownership was at 45.6 percent in Louisiana, which had the highest gun death rate in the nation at 18.03 per 100,000.[13]

Romney clearly would be entitled to take credit for saving lives through his sensible gun control policy. Mulling his presidential prospects, however, Romney apparently decided that politics and ideology trump public health and saving lives. He concluded that—contrary to his earlier assertion—he actually did need to "line up" with the NRA. He got a "sheep dip"[14] by going hunting with Rob Keck, "an outdoor television host, renowned hunter and conservationist."[15] Keck endorsed Romney and boosted his credentials as a sportsman to news media at the NRA convention.[16] Romney said in his NRA speech exactly what he needed to say to get right with Wayne.

> This administration's attack on freedom extends even to rights explicitly guaranteed by the Constitution. The right to bear arms is so plainly stated, so unambiguous that liberals have a hard time challenging it directly. Instead they've been employing every imaginable ruse and ploy to restrict it and to defeat it. . . . And if we're going to safeguard our 2nd Amendment it's time to elect a president who will defend the rights President Obama ignores or minimizes and I will protect the 2nd Amendment rights of the American people.[17]

But the NRA's religion is about more than guns. At its core, it's about culture—socioeconomics; race; ethnicity; the modern politics of an old doctrine, Manifest Destiny; and Anglo-Saxon singularity. Romney deliberately touched this broader and deeper theology. "We will not just select the president who will guide us," he said of the coming 2012 election. "We will also choose between two distinct paths and destinies for the nation."[18] This language of "paths and destinies" is dogma. The NRA's savage religion of conflict and the gun industry's technique of marketing military firepower share a common cultural source, summed up by James William Gibson in his 1994 book *Warrior Dreams*.[19] Gibson traced this source to the shock of American defeat in Vietnam, and the tumult of other societal change in its wake:

> During the 1960s, the civil rights and ethnic pride movements won many victories in their challenges to racial

oppression. Also, during the 1970s and 1980s, the United States experienced massive waves of immigration from Mexico, Central America, Vietnam, Cambodia, Korea, and Taiwan. Whites, no longer secure in their power abroad, also lost their unquestionable dominance at home; for the first time, many began to feel that they too were just another hyphenated ethnic group, the Anglo-Americans.[20]

Three years later, Charlton Heston, first vice president of the NRA, evoked exactly this resentment before the right-wing Free Congress Foundation at its twentieth anniversary gala. In his speech, given December 7, 1997—"Pearl Harbor Day"—Heston spoke at length about those who were collectively the "victim of the cultural war."[21]

> Heaven help the God-fearing, law-abiding, Caucasian, middle class, Protestant, or—even worse—Evangelical Christian, Midwest, or Southern, or—even worse—rural, apparently straight, or—even worse—admittedly heterosexual, gun-owning or—even worse—NRA-card-carrying, average working stiff, or—even worse—male working stiff, because not only don't you count, you're a downright obstacle to social progress.[22]

Gibson's articulation and Heston's evocation raise a question: what could be done to prevent America from taking this new path? For some of those frightened or angered by this change, the answer lies in a call to arms. That call has become the explosive gospel of the American right wing, with which the NRA has closely allied itself.[23] "When you're in the NRA, the problem is never extreme moderation," said Richard Feldman, a former NRA political operative.[24] Constantly hinting at armed resistance to government, the NRA and the gun industry exploit the warrior fantasy that Gibson described in his book:

American men—lacking confidence in the government and the economy, troubled by the changing relations between the sexes, uncertain of their identity or their future—began to *dream*, to fantasize about the powers and features of another kind of man who would retake and reorder the world. And the hero of all these dreams was the paramilitary warrior. . . . Terrorists and drug dealers are blasted into oblivion. Illegal aliens inside the United States and the hordes of non-whites in the Third World are returned by force to their proper place. Women are revealed as dangerous temptresses who have to be mastered, avoided, or terminated.[25]

Few better examples of this warrior dream exist than that of American neo-Nazi Jason Todd ("J.T.") Ready. A former Marine discharged for bad conduct, Ready led the "U.S. Border Guard," an anti-immigrant paramilitary group. "This is a white, European homeland," Ready said at a National Socialist Movement rally in October 2009. "That's how it should be preserved if we want to keep it clean, safe, and pure."[26] Ready's ragtag group patrolled the desert south of Phoenix, Arizona. They carried assault rifles and wore military-style battle dress and body armor. "We're not going to sit around and wait for the government anymore," Ready said in a July 2010 interview with the Associated Press. "This is what our Founding Fathers did."[27]

On May 3, 2012, J.T. Ready shot four people to death—his forty-seven-year-old girlfriend, her fifteen-month-old grand-daughter, her twenty-three-year-old daughter, and a twenty-four-year-old fellow "Border Guard." He then shot himself to death. Investigators, who found military ordnance in the home, called it a case of domestic violence.[28] Violence it was. But to dismiss it as only domestic misses the significance of the new warriors like Ready, who get their gospel from the NRA and their tools from the gun industry. The same trumpets Ready heard were sounded in Heston's speech to the Free Congress Foundation.

> They [Caucasian "victims"] prefer the America they
> built—where you could pray without feeling naive, love
> without being kinky, sing without profanity, be white
> without feeling guilty, own a gun without shame, and
> raise your hand without apology. They are the critical
> masses who find themselves under siege and long for you
> to get some guts, stand on principle and lead them to vic-
> tory in this cultural war.[29]

This sense of victimhood and the violent metaphor of a war between cultures echoed in Mitt Romney's act of contrition before
the NRA. "There was a time not so long ago when each of us
could walk a little taller, stand a little straighter because we had
a gift that no one else in the world shared. We were Americans,"
Romney said, later adding, "Let's take back our nation and defend our freedoms."[30]

The NRA's faithful need no one to fill in the blanks of from
whom and how the country should be taken back. Speaking at the
2009 Conservative Political Action Conference (CPAC), Wayne
LaPierre told cheering attendees that "our Founding Fathers understood that the guys with the guns make the rules."[31] Marion
Hammer, the NRA's Florida advocate, put it more bluntly. "There
are a number of atrocities at the hands of our government, if
people want to be honest and they don't put on blinders," she told
the *Washington Post* in 2000. "If our government were to use mass
destruction against our populace, the Army would start to desert.
And that's where your privately owned small arms would come
into play. You don't realize these guns preserve our freedom."[32]
NRA board member Ted Nugent hinted at violence several times
in remarks at the 2012 NRA convention. "Because it isn't the enemy that ruined America," he said. "It's good people who bent
over and let the enemy in. If the coyote's in your living room,
pissing on your couch, it's not the coyote's fault. It's your fault for
not shooting him."[33]

The Obama reelection apparatus jumped on Romney's

repentant speech. But it focused not so much on Romney's bowing to the NRA as on Obama's equal devotion to the Second Amendment. "The president's record makes clear that he supports and respects the Second Amendment, and we'll fight back against any attempts to mislead voters," the campaign press secretary said.[34]

Any political mechanic in the mood to sneer at Mitt Romney's pilgrimage ought first to review the history of other candidates. William Jefferson (Bill) Clinton's record is a good example. Bill Clinton scrambled to win the NRA's endorsement in 1982. He was trying to win back the Arkansas state house, which he lost in 1980 after serving one term as governor.[35] When his opponent published parts of Clinton's answers to the NRA's candidate questionnaire, Clinton claimed that his true position had been misstated in his answers to the questionnaire.[36] He insisted that he was a strong opponent of gun control,[37] and telephoned the NRA to give new answers, blaming the wrong answers on his staff.[38] Clinton wrote a letter to the NRA in which he stated, "I am against any legislation or regulation on gun control that goes beyond the current law, and am in support of the NRA position on gun control."[39]

Clinton tacked differently near the end of his tenure as governor of Arkansas, as he readied his run for the White House. He twice vetoed a "preemption" bill—an NRA national priority[40]— that would have barred cities and counties in Arkansas from passing local gun control laws.[41] These 1989 and 1991 vetoes were 180 degrees opposite to Clinton's earlier declaration to the NRA. Explaining his unacceptable answer to the original questionnaire, he told the NRA in 1982, "Based on lengthy conversations between my staff and yours, I was under the impression that NRA opposed preemption of local firearms laws by state acts. I am now advised that NRA favors state preemption and, therefore, my answer to [the preemption question] should read 'yes.' "[42]

Clinton waffled as he pursued the presidency. In 1991, shortly after his second veto of the preemption bill, Governor Clinton said he supported an early version of the Brady Bill, which proposed both a waiting period and a background check before a person could buy a handgun. But he said he favored the system of on-the-spot instant checks that was demanded by the NRA in exchange for having any checks at all—a system that was by definition inconsistent with a waiting period. "I think the NRA is right about that," Clinton said. "I think it's a good thing to try to make the records as subject as possible to instantaneous check." [43]

Candidate Clinton was also equivocal on semiautomatic assault weapons. [44] When he vetoed the first state gun law preemption bill in 1989, he said assault weapons and guns in schools were potential local problems and said, "The state should not take away the capacity of local communities to act as they see fit, should such a danger occur." [45] In February 1991, however, he avoided aligning himself with an effort at the National Governors' Association winter meeting to pass a resolution calling for a national ban on assault weapons. Clinton expressed doubt that a ban could be passed in Arkansas. "All states won't do it, so its got to be the feds who do it," the governor was quoted as saying. "If you're asking me what I'll do, I don't know what I'm going to do. I'm going to wait. I'm just going to be open and see what happens." [46] In August 1991—during the week in which he formed his presidential campaign exploratory committee—Clinton "dodged questions about his stand on assault weapons," according to the *Washington Post*. [47] The governor said, "I'd have to see what the options are." [48] Scarcely three years later, however, President Clinton decided to take up the gun control movement's cause and lobbied Congress aggressively in favor of a federal assault weapons ban that had become part of his administration's comprehensive anticrime bill. [49]

The point here is neither to criticize Bill Clinton nor to expose his varied stands on gun control as political dirty laundry. It is rather to show by example that politicians are rarely natural gun control advocates, and they are not always reliable allies. Moreover, and perhaps most damaging, their default impulse is to blame the NRA for their failure to create a coherent, effective national program against gun violence. Unfortunately, too many advocates have bought into this excuse.

"The NRA is buying votes with blood money!" emcee Rosie O'Donnell shouted at the "Million Mom March" rally on Mother's Day 2000. "We have had enough! Enough of the NRA and their tactics. Enough of the stranglehold the NRA has on Congress and in the Senate."[50]

But there is a great and growing body of analytical evidence that "the myth of the fearsomely potent NRA . . . is just that—a myth."[51] For example, an exhaustive 2004 study—conducted with the cooperation of the NRA itself—found that the conventional wisdom (started by Bill Clinton) that the NRA cost Democrats control of the House of Representatives in 1994 is simply not true.[52] "When the impact of organized interest groups on election outcomes is closely examined . . . the systematic evidence routinely fails to support claims like Clinton's."[53] Other independent studies have found the same thing. A study published in 2012 declared, "Despite what the NRA has long claimed, it neither delivered Congress to the Republican party in 1994 nor delivered the White House to George W. Bush in 2000."[54]

It also turns out upon objective examination that "while the NRA spends a good deal of money in total, that money is spread over so many races—well over 200 House races alone every election—that it has little more than symbolic effect. . . . [It] may be enough to keep the volunteers in donuts, but it won't swing any races."[55]

And the NRA's vaunted endorsements and "grass roots" power? The NRA brags, talks tough, and threatens. But the electoral successes it claims are in fact those of the broader coalition to which it has attached itself. "The NRA's influence . . . seems to interact with the party trend that is evident in any particular election year."[56] In other words, like the remora, or suckerfish, which attaches itself to a shark for scraps of food, the NRA simply gets the benefits of its association with a much larger right-wing coalition. Like the remora, it neither causes harm nor contributes significant value.[57] The NRA's bloviating might be of incidental benefit, but it doesn't make or break elections. The NRA rides the trend. It declares victory in good elections and the coming apocalypse in bad ones. "The NRA has virtually no impact on congressional elections," the latest study concludes. "The NRA endorsement, so coveted by so many politicians, is almost mean-ingless. Nor does the money the organization spends have any demonstrable impact on the outcome of races. In short, when it comes to elections, the NRA is a paper tiger."[58]

If the NRA is a paper tiger, politicians in Washington are trembling pussycats. This political surrender—and the NRA's ex-ploitation of it to puff up its credibility—can be traced to three interwoven trends. The first is the influence of poll-driven, "tri-angulating" political operatives searching for a "third way" to evade taking hard stands on core principle. The second is the re-visionist history of the political impact of gun control legislation, expounded by Bill Clinton and adopted as gospel by "moderate" politicians and the political mechanics they employ. The third is the rise of what media critic Tom Rosenstiel has described as "synthetic" journalism that is "shallowing out our understanding of American politics."[59]

Scholars of political science describe one of the core dynam-ics of power in Washington as the "iron triangle"—special in-terests, the career bureaucracy, and Congress.[60] There ought to be added now another geometric figure, the "golden triangle" of commercial public opinion pollsters, well-paid professional po-litical consultants, and career politicians. Interacting with these artful technicians, ambitious political "candidates are using polls to select their voters and to fashion their policy choices," with the overall effect of "distorting the process of democratic account-ability and responsiveness." In order to "avoid the risk of electoral punishment, they turn to polls to craft appealing campaign mes-sages and to microtarget voters," according to Lawrence R. Jacobs and Robert Y. Shapiro, professors of political science.[61]

Recent trends in the news business have made the media not only receptive to, but eager for, the golden triangle's output of polls and artfully spun candidate and issue narratives. One of these influences has been the vastly expanded universe of the "information revolution."

> The explosion in outlets has not meant more reporters doing original shoe-leather reporting. Instead, more people are involved in taking material that is secondhand and repackaging it. This greater reliance on secondhand material inevitably has two consequences. First, it means that the reporting news organization is less likely to have independently verified the information. Second, the understanding of the reporting news organization is usually more superficial. They did not do the work themselves, discovering its nuances and limitations. Rather than conducting the work, usually the reporter or editor is paring down, summarizing, or rewriting a news agency account.[62]

Other factors include staff cuts and the demands of a twenty-four-hour news culture in which there is "more news time to fill than there is news to fill it," so that "there is more appetite for the latest poll, the latest anything." Finally, the reduced news staffs "tend to be less experienced" and thus have a "shallower grasp" of issues they report on.[63] In this environment, "Values, political philosophy, life experience, authentic belief, and all the other motivations behind political action are devalued in the coverage because they are harder to report, harder to identify, harder to measure."[64]

The politics of guns and gun control combine the worst of these influences. If "the best way to think about public opinion and its relationship to politics and policymaking is that the American public is typically short on facts, but often long on judgment,"[65] gun control compounds the problem by orders of magnitude.

The inflated myth of the NRA's invincibility began in the late summer of 1994, when the Clinton administration badly needed a win in Congress. The President's health care proposal was stuck on a reef. Other plans, like welfare reform, were foundering. On top of all this, the White House was hit by a court-ordered change in the special counsel conducting a criminal investigation into the Whitewater affair, ensuring that it would drag on at least through the 1994 election.[66] Democrats were "clinging to the passage of a crime bill as their only evidence of late that a Democratic majority in Congress can accomplish something of lasting significance," observed the *New York Times*.[67]

The omnibus crime bill on which Democrats now hung their hopes was a wallowing $30 billion tub. "With the bulk of a Tolstoy novel, this 960-page monster includes something for everyone," the *National Journal* reported.[68] "The law includes a sprawling array of programs, many of them untested, that taken together have little overall coherence," reported the *New York Times*. "It reflects the ideological divisions that had stymied Congressional efforts to enact a crime bill for years as well as the pet projects of legislators whose votes were needed to pass it at last."[69] On the eve of the final vote in the House of Representatives, the bill's cargo included the assault weapons ban, a revived federal death penalty, and grants to help local governments hire a hundred thousand police officers. It was also packed with federal funds for crime prevention programs.

The original youth-programs amendment to the crime bill, introduced by Senator Chris Dodd, a Democrat, called for $1 billion of funding for one program.[70] By the time the Senate passed its version of the bill, the package had grown to $3.8 billion and a dozen programs. The House version ballooned up to $6.6 billion and even more programs. The funding topped out at $7 billion and twenty-eight programs after the House and Senate reconciled their bills in conference.[71] These programs came to be lumped under the phrase "midnight basketball," an image charged with social and racial subtext.

Passage of the reconciled conference crime bill was predicted to be "an easy win for Clinton and a certain campaign trophy for Democrats."[72] But on August 11, 1994, the conference report suffered a surprise in the House. Republicans and recalcitrant Democrats voted down a procedural rule that would have brought the bill to the House floor for a final vote.[73] Such "special rules," issued by the House Rules Committee, specify the length of debate on substantive bills and detail other procedural matters.[74] When such a rule is defeated, consideration of the underlying bill halts until a revised or new rule is approved.[75]

"Democrats were so stunned at their loss that they could hardly explain their gross miscalculation," reported the *New York Times*.[76] President Clinton was described as "very nearly sputtering with shock and anger."[77]

What had gone wrong?

According to contemporary post mortems, the bloated prevention programs, which had grown from $1 billion to $7 billion, were the fulcrum that gave the bill's opponents—who had a wide variety of motives, including opposition from the left to a federal death penalty provision—the leverage to bring it to a halt. Certainly, the NRA was doing all it could to rip the assault weapons ban out of the bill. But the ban had so much public support that President Clinton insisted that it stay in the crime bill during the next two weeks of frantic negotiation to resuscitate it.[78]

The *Washington Post* reported that the bill's opponents "have turned the debate over the final version of the crime bill into a debate on the merits of the prevention programs, which they denounce as 'social welfare' and 'pork.' "[79] The *New York Times* saw the same dynamic. "The bill was much ridiculed for spending money on dance programs, arts and crafts, midnight basketball leagues and programs to promote self-esteem," it reported.[80] A lengthy analysis in the *New Yorker* traced the roots of the rout to radio rants by the right-wing commentator Rush Limbaugh, who "had been hammering away at the crime bill—not as much on its anti-gun provisions as on the social programs it contained."[81]

Limbaugh and other talk-radio hosts "plainly struck a chord and excited an antipathy toward the crime bill." [82] As a result, casting a vote against the bill lost the sting of its being seen as soft on crime by conservative voters. House minority whip Newt Gingrich asked conservative polling consultant Frank Luntz for a read on public opinion. Luntz's poll confirmed the wisdom of attacking the prevention programs. Those polled, he wrote, "are far more concerned that convicted criminals remain behind bars than teenagers in inner cities learn to ball-room dance and slam dunk from the foul line by the pale moonlight." Luntz advised Republican members, "If you want to oppose this legislation, you should." [83]

Two weeks later, Democrats got their crime bill, slightly pared down. The bill included the assault weapons ban. [84] The president signed the bill into law on September 13, 1994. [85] Republicans, however, were conspicuous by their absence from the signing ceremony. [86] Newt Gingrich and his party's strategists had gained a valuable insight into the public mood.

On September 27, he and more than three hundred Republican lawmakers and candidates stood on the steps of the Capitol and announced their commitment to a ten-point Contract with America. [87] They said they would run a campaign focused on its promises, and would implement the contract's laundry list if they regained the majority in Congress. Frank Luntz had "market tested the message like a breakfast cereal." [88] The Republican "contract" promised a tougher "anti-crime package," the "Taking Back Our Streets Act." [89] But significantly, the legislation did not propose repeal of the assault weapons ban or the Brady law. [90]

The NRA was reported to have spent about $4 million in the 1994 midterm campaign, including a battery of television ads in which Charlton Heston attacked specific Democrats who had voted for the Brady and assault weapons bills. [91] The NRA's funds went "overwhelmingly to support Republican congressional candidates,"[92] evidencing its embryonic "culture war" alliance with the right wing.[93]

Democrats woke up to disaster the morning of Wednesday, November 9, 1994. Riding "a tidal wave of voter discontent," Republicans had taken control of the Congress, winning their first majority in the Senate since 1986, and their first in the House since 1954.[94] For the first time since Abraham Lincoln was president, a sitting Speaker of the House, Thomas S. Foley, was rejected by voters in his own district.[95] But virtually no one—including President Clinton—blamed the sweeping Democratic loss on the assault-weapons ban or even gun control in general. Clinton accepted some of the blame, saying his agenda of change had not moved fast enough. But "he drew the line on any turning back against gun control and the banning of assault weapons, two pieces of legislation he was able to get through Congress this year."[96]

The *New York Times* opined that morning that it was "easy to see why the Democrats got whacked."[97] Adding to "the sour national attitude toward politics generally and the rebellion against incumbents in particular," the *Times* wrote, "failure of governance must be laid at the feet of the retiring Senate majority leader, George Mitchell; the embattled Speaker, Thomas Foley, and a leadership team that placed loyalty to them above cooperation with the White House or public demands for Congressional and campaign finance reform."[98] The *Boston Globe* reported that "throughout the nation, voters complained about a bickering Congress, bloated government and what one described as 'a cream puff' president who had made many hopeful promises but had produced little."[99]

As for Speaker Foley, opinion in his home state of Washington noted the NRA's turn against him but cited a laundry list of miscues and reasons for voter anger that eclipsed the gun issue. "The NRA was not the only friend turned foe," wrote one local newspaper columnist. "Foley's humiliating defeat came from a combination of factors," including, among others, "the hubris of an insulated, overconfident incumbent presiding over a hated, 'Imperial Congress,' " and "a cavalier campaign effort in a year of a heavily organized anti-government and Christian Coalition turnout." [100] Foley's pollster, Celinda Lake, summed up the election. "I think the voters are really mad," said Lake. "And because we're in charge, they're really mad at us. They said they wanted a change [in 1992], and they don't think they got it." [101]

If the Republicans thought that the 1994 election was won by the NRA, they showed little evidence of it. They planned instead "to reopen this year's angry debate over federal funding for crime-prevention measures in hopes of getting rid of midnight basketball and other programs aimed at crime prevention." [102] Not only was repeal of the ban not in the legislation proposed in the Contract with America, but even after their convincing win, the GOP leadership squashed proposals to repeal the law. The NRA soon was reported to be angry because "the Republican strategy is to steer clear of the assault-weapons ban in the first part of the session and pass measures showcasing the GOP's resolve to change the way Congress does business." [103] By July 1995—following the bombing by Timothy McVeigh of the Alfred P. Murrah Federal Building in Oklahoma City—the subject of repealing the ban was completely off the Senate calendar. [104] In October the conservative *Weekly Standard* reported that "some conservatives are getting tired of the National Rifle Association." [105]

But in January 1995, President Clinton sat down with reporters and editors of the *Cleveland Plain Dealer*. During a long interview, Clinton planted the seed of a narrative that has grown into conventional political wisdom purporting to explain the humiliating 1994 defeat. The deletion of a single sentence in subsequent media reporting completely distorted what Clinton said, not to mention savaging the truth.

According to the *Plain Dealer* transcript, this is what Clinton said, the crucial sentence italicized for emphasis by this writer:

The fights that I fought, bloody though they were, cost a lot. The fight for the assault-weapons ban cost 20 members their seat in Congress. The NRA is the reason the Republicans control the House. I can't believe nobody has written that story, but it is—partly because our guys didn't know how to fight them—the NRA. *If they had all done what Bob Kerrey did, almost all of them would have survived.*[106]

But this is how the *Plain Dealer* reported the conversation in its news report the next day (the transcript ran inside the paper):

President Clinton yesterday said the historic Republican takeover of the House was made possible because the National Rifle Association targeted Democrats who supported his crime bill.

"The fights I fought . . . cost a lot—the fight for the assault-weapons ban cost 20 members their seats in Congress," the president said in an interview with *Plain Dealer* reporters and editors. "The NRA is the reason the Republicans control the House."[107]

Cutting out the last sentence of the President's quote clearly transformed the NRA from an entity that could have been beaten "if they had all done what Bob Kerrey did" into an invincible juggernaut, the single reason "the Republicans control the House." Tanya Metaksa, the NRA's chief lobbyist, was delighted to accept the credit. "For once the president and I agree," she was quoted by the *Plain Dealer* in its story with Clinton's truncated quote.[108]

Reporters and editors across the nation commenced "paring down, summarizing, or rewriting."[109] The president's salient reference to Kerrey's tough stance immediately disappeared down the media memory hole. Eventually the myth won the imprimatur of the *New York Times* in an article following the 1999 mass shooting at Columbine High School in Littleton, Colorado.

Reciting almost verbatim the *Plain Dealer* version, the paper reported as fact, "after he forced a ban on assault weapons through Congress, the Democrats lost control of the House and Mr. Clinton ascribed the loss to the gun lobby's campaign against those Democrats who had supported the ban." [110]

But the *Plain Dealer* itself had questioned Clinton's blame-the-NRA version of the loss almost as soon as it was uttered. The paper cited political analysts who scoffed at the idea. "Just because the president says it doesn't make it so" the paper reported. "And plenty of political observers around the country say Clinton's explanation is at best a gross overstatement. At worst, it is a convenient self-delusion." One of those who disagreed with Clinton was Stuart Rothenberg, an independent political analyst. [111] "Anyone with a 'D' behind their name had a big problem in November, whether the issue was guns, abortion or NAFTA," he said. "All the elements of the Republican coalition worked together to crank out the Republican vote, while the Democratic interest groups, whether pro-choice, pro-gun control or women's groups, did a poor job cranking out the Democratic vote." [112] Roger Stone—a self-described "GOP hitman" [113]—agreed. "The last election was not about gun control, but a repudiation of Bill and Hillary and their policies," Stone told the newspaper. "To scapegoat the NRA is self-delusional. But I guess you can't expect him to say, 'Well, they are repudiating me and my wife.'" [114]

So, what was it that Bob Kerrey did in 1994 that others did not? The Nebraska senator was one of those specially targeted by Charlton Heston's NRA television broadside. But rather than running away from the NRA, Kerrey ran straight at it:

> Kerrey grabbed his shotgun and headed out to a target range to film an aggressive response ad. After plucking a clay pigeon from the sky with a shotgun blast, Kerrey turns to the camera and says that he supports the right to bear arms and that hunters are entitled to a good weapon. But

then Kerrey hands off his shotgun, picks up an AK-47 and recalls his service as a Navy Seal commando during the Vietnam War, when he lost his right leg below the knee.

"Twenty-five years ago, in the war in Vietnam, people hunted me," Kerrey says. "They needed a good weapon, like this AK-47. But you don't need one of these to hunt birds." [115]

More recent in-depth analysis has confirmed the contemporary understanding that the election was about something much broader than guns.

The best way to understand 1994 is in terms of partisanship, not in terms of the specifics of the gun issue, or any other one issue. To the extent a vote in favor of the crime bill made a difference to a Democratic incumbent's election prospects, it was as one of a group of indicators—on issues like health care, gays in the military, and taxes—of whether the candidate was with or against his party in a year when that party did poorly in Republican areas. All these factors combined to create a wave election in which issues could not be separated from party. And if there was any single issue that did the most damage to Democrats that year, it was more likely the failed attempt at health care reform, according to post-election polling by Stanley Greenberg, Clinton's pollster at the time. [116]

Bill Clinton certainly did not believe that the NRA was omnipotent or that the assault weapons ban was a "third rail" during his successful 1996 reelection campaign. In July 1995, his campaign rolled out television ads touting his passage of the crime bill, including specifically the assault weapons ban and a measure to fund expanding local police forces. "The President is determined not to let the N.R.A. and their supporters on the Hill roll back the assault weapons ban, or his commitment to 100,000 cops," a White House official told the *New York Times*. Deputy White House press secretary Ginny Terzano said the assault-weapons ban was one of the president's "major achievements" and "he wanted his important message taken directly to the American people, that we must not roll back the progress." [117]

The advertisements were the work of prominent members of Clinton's golden triangle—consultants Bob Squier and Dick Morris.[118] Among other things, Morris became noted during Clinton's 1996 reelection campaign for his "poll-driven, pragmatist's notion of 'triangulation,' a nautically inspired gambit, meaning that to get from point A to point B, Clinton may have to tack first to point C. Ideological consistency can be cast overboard." [119]

Others thought that the triangulation strategy did not go far enough. One of them was Al From, the president of the "centrist" Democratic Leadership Council (DLC), who urged Clinton to break with liberals and their "old orthodoxies and old arrangements." [120] The DLC wanted—through such policies as embracing the death penalty and welfare reform—to " 'inoculate' Democrats against charges that they ignored middle-class values." At about the time of Clinton's reelection campaign, From and others began developing a strategy they called the third way, supposedly divining new policy positions. "Triangulation is fine, but not enough," From told the *New Republic* in 1996. "It goes halfway. . . . I believe we can develop an ideology for the dominant party." [121]

From's "third way" would eventually uncoil in the form of the Third Way think tank in Washington. Along the way, the idea would throw gun control under the bus in the wake of Al Gore's 2000 defeat. Democratic political mechanics fixated on the excuse that gun control was the party's problem. "A lot of people—[former DNC Chairman Terry] McAuliffe, Daschle, [former House Minority Leader Dick] Gephardt—were going around saying that guns had been the key. . . . There was a lot of talk about how

Democrats should avoid the issue entirely," Matt Bennett, vice president for public affairs at Third Way, explained in 2007.[122]

But blaming defeat on guns was as uninformed and self-serving in 2000 as it was in 1994. "For the NRA to argue that this single issue swung these states into the Bush column is revisionist history at its worst," pollster Celinda Lake wrote in 2003.[123] A more recent analysis explained the popular error in detail:

> When one looks for actual evidence that the gun issue cost Gore more votes than it gained him, one comes up empty. Few scholars have performed a quantitative analysis of the role of guns in the vote of 2000, though one study examining a range of policy issues determined that the gun issue gave Gore a small advantage on election day. The argument from those who believe that the gun issue was decisive and worked against Gore usually amounts to little more than the fact that Gore lost some states where there are many pro-gun voters. This argument presumes that there were no areas in which Gore's position on guns *helped* him win a state he might otherwise have lost. But Gore won swing states like Pennsylvania, Michigan, Minnesota and Iowa largely on his strength among urban and suburban voters, who are more likely to support restrictions on guns.
>
> If there is one state the proponents of the theory that guns delivered the White House to George Bush inevitably point to, it is Gore's home state of Tennessee. After all, if Gore lost his home state, it must have had something to do with his position on guns. . . . Yet there are other more compelling explanations for the outcome in Tennessee, the simplest of which is a partisan one. Tennessee was in the midst of a larger trend in the South, where the state was growing more and more Republican over time. . . . Gore's problem in Tennessee wasn't the gun issue, it was

something much simpler: he needed more Democrats in a state that was trending Republican.[124]

Nevertheless, the easy "conventional wisdom" about guns being the reason for Gore's loss in 2000 grew, inspiring the political commentator Jules Witcover to observe that "the question now is whether this perception will make lambs out of previous anti-gun Democratic lions in Congress."[125] Waiting to shepherd any Democratic gun control lambs was Matt Bennett (quoted above on the panic after the 2000 election). He and a handful of other recycled Clinton-Gore and New York Democratic political operatives announced a new organization, Americans for Gun Safety (AGS), in October 2000. AGS was underwritten with an enormous infusion of cash from the late billionaire Andrew McKelvey, then CEO of the employment search firm TMP Worldwide. Bennett worked in the Clinton White House, first for Vice President Al Gore, then as Clinton's liaison to state governors.[126] The AGS president, Jonathan Cowan, had been chief of staff to Andrew Cuomo during the latter's tenure as Clinton's secretary of housing and urban development.[127] In 2001 the group was joined by Jim Kessler, a legislative aide to Senator Charles Schumer. Kessler became AGS's director of policy and research.[128]

McKelvey was reported to see "his group falling somewhere in between avid antigun supporters and the National Rifle Association."[129] AGS offered a bounty of $60,000 a year to local gun violence prevention groups who signed up to become instant AGS chapters. Twenty-eight were reported to have taken the bait.[130] The president of one such local group enthused, "Together, we think we're going to dramatically change the debate on gun safety in this country."[131]

AGS certainly did want to change the debate. There would be precious little fact-driven policy, but a surfeit of the kind of political "inoculations" favored by the "centrist" DLC. The golden triangle had come to gun control, carrying a briefcase full of polls. The locals soon found out that they had been sold a pig in a poke. "Within a couple of days, as the state groups began to receive talking points and sample press releases from AGS, they found out what Cowan meant by 'rights': Americans were guaranteed the right to own guns, a position long promulgated by the NRA and opposed by nearly every gun-violence organization in the country." [132]

Citing polling data, AGS's political technicians bulled ahead and began popping up in the news media, proclaiming that there was a "third way" to deal with gun violence "if gun-control proponents and gun-safety advocates would stop fighting long enough to look for common ground." [133] Given the NRA's adamant stance, it may be impossible to overstate the naïveté, or perhaps the cynicism, of this illusory suggestion. "We must declare there are no shades of gray in American freedom," Wayne LaPierre thundered at the NRA's 2002 annual convention. "It's black or white, all or nothing. You're with us or against us." [134]

The recipe for the third way's shade of gray—as attributed to AGS's Cowan and Kessler—was telling. The two urged gun control groups to:

(1) Adopt a new message: respect for gun rights coupled with an insistence on gun responsibility; (2) Back up their rhetoric by "toughening enforcement of current gun laws and passing new laws that crack down on gun crime"; (3) Distance themselves from "traditional strategies that demonize gun owners, call for gun control instead of gun safety, urge a ban on guns, and imply that legal gun ownership is the root cause of gun crime." [135]

Inventing their own revisionist history of the politics of guns, and ignoring or misunderstanding the effect of a greedy industry with a powerful lobby that batters fact-based public policy and shuts down information, the political operatives of AGS defined away the problem of gun violence. The problem was not a matter of torn flesh, spurting blood, shattered bodies, and unconscionable marketing of military weapons by a ruthless industry. To speak of those facts was "demonizing." The problem, in the view of AGS, was nothing but a schoolyard argument between unruly advocates. And that was easy enough to fix. Substance out. Triangulation in. Pabulum like "toughening enforcement" is a page right out of the gun industry and NRA playbook. It ignores the torrent of gun violence by "law-abiding" citizens. So is the blinkered pretense that "legal gun ownership"—in the form of proliferation and militarization—is not a "root cause" of anything more sinister than good times at the SHOT Show. Ditto the mantra of "gun safety" as opposed to "gun control."

None of this reality mattered to third-way acolytes, who failed to get passed any of the federal legislation that they bulldozed into the forefront over the objections of more experienced and knowledgeable gun control groups. What mattered was giving all too many politicians a fig leaf, a plausible way to explain their political indifference to the fate of hundreds of thousands of victims. Within a few years, the vaunted AGS "grass roots" coalition had fallen apart, amid angry recriminations between the founders and their instant chapters. "The activists felt that they had been blindsided and that AGS in general, and Cowan in particular, were being 'a little dictatorial,' as one participant put it," in one contemporary account.[136]

In spite of their dismal failures, the AGS political surgeons declared victory and transplanted their "gun safety" organization as an appendage of a new organization, Third Way. They moved on to other issues. Nominally a think tank but primarily a political workshop, Third Way bills itself as a place that "answers America's challenges with modern ideas aimed at the center."[137] It was blessed at its creation by the third-way pioneer Al From.[138] Matt Bennett told *Roll Call* newspaper in 2005 that he, Cowan, and Kessler had discovered the model for Third Way at AGS while working on gun safety, "a real middle on an issue that had been polarized. We felt like we had a model that worked."[139]

If the third-way model has "worked," it has not diminished the torrent of gun violence in America, caused any uncommonly courageous moderate politicians to shake off the NRA's paralyzing stranglehold, nor resulted in passage of a single important federal law. By obsessing on guns and microtargeting voters in search of a mythical middle ground, the hucksters of the third way have ignored the true significance of the NRA and the coalition to which it is attached—cultural war. As the author and commentator Paul Waldman observed in a fact-based 2012 analysis, gun control has had virtually no effect on the electoral cycles of this war: "The 1994 election was a Republican wave, and as 2006 and 2010 demonstrated, wave elections can happen in a variety of contexts. In 2010, for instance, Republicans won even more seats than they did in 1994—without any significant debate about guns. In fact, the only new laws about guns that took effect during Obama's first two years *expanded* gun rights, allowing people to bring guns to national parks and on Amtrak." [140]

The myth that the NRA is all-powerful and gun control is a "third rail" works in a perverse way—it benefits equally the NRA and the minions of the golden triangle who affect to combat it. The NRA's executives continue to raise huge amounts of cash, pay themselves exceedingly well, and stroll the halls of Congress as if they were ten feet tall. The triangle's pollsters and consultants continue to enjoy lucrative contracts that pay them well. The politicians get to express their sympathies without being expected to take effective action. The losers in this comfortable arrangement are the hundreds of thousands of innocent victims of gun violence who have died or been mutilated with painful injury since the technicians of the golden triangle decided to abandon them.

Thus, even as the political establishment has sidetracked any effective gun control legislation, the gun industry, the NRA, and other elements of the gun lobby continue to barrel through Congress like a midnight express. A vignette from the National Shooting Sports Foundation's website casts light on the gun industry's influence machine. The NSSF sponsors an annual "Fly-In," during which manufacturers and others in the industry descend on Washington to lobby members of Congress. The industry group posted a video on its website encouraging its members to come to its 2012 event and explaining lobbying procedures. "And don't be offended if the person you meet with is a young staffer," Max Sandlin, a retired Texas congressman and NSSF consultant, says in the video. He explains that because the Congress members themselves are quite busy, their staffs often take the actual lobbying meetings. "After the meeting, they are the ones who will carry our water." [141]

These anonymous staff water carriers and their principals continue to do a good, if not widely reported, job for the gun industry. In its report on the 2012 Fly-In, NSSF boasted that "the week began on a high note with the House passage of the Sportsmen's Heritage Act (H.R. 4089), a bill that contains the industry's top priority—the Hunting, Fishing and Recreational Shooting Protection Act (H.R. 1558). Overall, the Fly-In was a great success, and NSSF looks forward to building upon its momentum through the rest of the year." [142] Not everyone in America agreed that passage of the bill was a "high note." Professor Char Miller, an expert in environmental administration, [143] denounced the legislation as "cynically titled," and reported that "it has kicked up a storm of protest with the broad environmental movement, who see it as an ill-disguised assault on the wildlands and the Wilderness Act that . . . early generations fought so hard to protect and secure." [144] Among other things, the bill would boost shooting "sports" into a commanding position in decisions about public land use and prevent regulation of lead shot on public lands, "even though scientists have demonstrated time and again the deleterious impact it has on public health." [145]

For its part, the NRA claims to represent gun owners and frames its ambitious congressional lobbying efforts in terms of defending "gun rights." In fact, the NRA's legislative program is largely driven by the gun industry's business interests. Less regulation, more profits. The Violence Policy Center examined and exposed the financial relationships between the NRA and the gun industry in its 2011 study *Blood Money: How the Gun Industry Bankrolls the NRA*.[146] The report detailed tens of millions of dollars in gun industry support for the NRA and summarized the intimate ties thus:

> The depth and breadth of gun industry financial support for the National Rifle Association makes clear that the self-proclaimed "America's oldest civil rights organization" is, in fact, the gun industry's most high-profile trade association. While the NRA works to portray itself as protecting the "freedoms" of its membership, it is, in fact protecting the gun industry's freedom to manufacture virtually any gun or accessory it sees fit to produce. As NRA Board Member Pete Brownell, owner of Brownells, "the world's largest supplier of firearms accessories and gunsmithing tools," wrote on his website in his successful campaign to join the NRA's board, "Having [NRA] directors who intimately understand and work in leadership positions within the firearms industry ensures the NRA's focus is honed on the overall mission of the organization. These individuals bring a keen sense of the industry and of the bigger fight to the table."
>
> This is a 180-degree turn from the NRA described in *Americans and Their Guns*, an official history of the organization published in 1967 which stated that the NRA "is not affiliated with any manufacturer of arms or ammunition or with any jobber or dealer who sells firearms and ammunition." And today, while in one section of its website the NRA actively courts the financial support of its gun industry "corporate partners," in another—where its industry financial links would heighten valid suspicions, such as in relation to the objectivity and effectiveness of its Eddie Eagle "gun safety" program—the NRA falsely claims that it "is not affiliated with any firearm or

ammunition manufacturers or with any businesses that deal in guns and ammunition." [147]

The saga of Larry Potterfield and the company he founded, MidwayUSA, is an apt parable. The company claims on its website to stock "just about everything for shooting, reloading, gunsmithing and hunting." Potterfield created the "NRA Round-Up" program, which allows buyers to "round up" their purchase to the nearest dollar, with the difference going to the NRA. He has good reason to be grateful to the NRA. Potterfield credits part of his company's success to NRA-backed federal legislation, the Firearms Owners' Protection Act, commonly known as McClure-Volkmer (but called Volkmer-McClure by Potterfield). "By 1987, we were doing about $5 million in business, selling mostly to dealers. The product lines were bulk components and cartridge boxes. The Volkmer-McClure law was enacted in October 1987, which removed the restriction of shipping brass and bullets to FFL holders only. Midway immediately began selling directly to consumers, in addition to selling to dealers." In January 2011 the company announced that for "a second consecutive year" it was serving as "the Official Sponsor of the NRA Annual Meeting and Exhibits" being held in Pittsburgh, Pennsylvania, in spring 2011.[148]

There is no "third way" for the gun industry juggernaut.

The gun lobby's ambitions for the future include enactment of a national law to allow the carrying of concealed handguns anywhere in America (overriding state and local controls); repeal or effective disembowelment of existing federal law severely limiting the ownership of fully automatic machine guns, silencers, and other weapons of war by private persons; and severe dilution of restraints on the export of military-style weapons abroad. The only way for the gun industry is the way of self-enrichment. Like a medieval battering ram, the gun industry continues to hammer at laws and government programs that restrict the sale and possession of guns of any kind in any way.

Brick by brick the walls are coming down. The self-proclaimed best political minds in America have failed to stop or even slow down the gun violence, death, and injury that inevitably stem from the industry's unrestrained marketing binges. If government leaders cower before the altar of the NRA's "great religion," what might work against these evils? That question is addressed in the next chapter.

9

SOLUTIONS WORTHY OF THE NAME

Following a series of shootings, the Seattle City Council discussed the city's response at a public meeting on May 29, 2012, with police officials. At the meeting, Seattle City Council member Tom Rasmussen found nothing new in the police department's proposals to address the violence, observing, "I have some skepticism about whether this will have any effect. We have seen many community vigils, community mobilizations. We've heard about these strategies before. What's going to change?" [1]

The very next day, Seattle was hit by yet another all-American shooting rampage. This mass murder was at a "quirky Seattle hangout," a coffee shop and bar known for its "eclectic music and friendly vibe." [2] The latest murders struck at Seattle's historic association with popular music. Ray Charles played at jazz clubs and made his first recording in Seattle. Jimi Hendrix, a Seattle native, got his start there. Decades later, the grunge era of the 1990s launched Nirvana and other bands. [3] The *New York Times* noted in 2010 that "a growing number of young musicians have been focused on building an autonomous scene, something distinctive and homegrown." One of these young musicians' venues was Café Racer, "distinctly postgrunge, with its scuffed floor and mismatched furniture, its thrift-store paintings on boldly colored walls." [4] The cafe is also the "Official Bad Art Museum of Art (OBAMA)" where one can "gaze in wonder at the astounding paint-by-number and black velvet paintings." [5]

The whimsy ended just before eleven A.M., Wednesday, May 30, 2012, when Ian L. Stawicki, holder of a concealed-carry permit, walked in. Stawicki, forty, had been thrown out of Café Racer previously and banned because of his "loud, bizarre behavior."[6]

This erratic behavior—the hallmark of all too many of America's concealed-carry killers—was familiar to Stawicki's family. His father said Ian had suffered from mental illness for years and his behavior had gotten "exponentially" more erratic. He claimed his son enlisted in the U.S. Army after high school but lasted only about a year before getting an honorable discharge.[7] (An army spokesperson said it had no record of Stawicki's having served.[8]) In any event, the family failed to convince Ian to seek help. Those who knew Stawicki said his life's history was "dotted with clues, including failures, social rejection, episodes of apparent delusions, spasms of violence and a strong interest in guns."[9] None of this stopped Stawicki from getting his "shall issue" concealed-weapons permits from Seattle and Kittitas County.[10] Nor did it prevent him from legally buying three 45 caliber and three 9mm semiautomatic pistols.[11]

The familiar combination of a mentally unstable person legally carrying concealed handguns had its predictable result. Sixty-three seconds after Stawicki—with two 45 caliber pistols in his pockets—walked into Café Racer and was refused service, he had shot four people to death and critically wounded another. Stawicki paused to steal a "bowler style" hat from one of his victims, then left. By 11:30 A.M., he had confronted a businesswoman in a parking lot, shot her to death, and fled in her Mercedes-Benz SUV. He gave "the finger" to bystanders coming to her aid.[12] Police cornered Stawicki at around four P.M. He knelt on the sidewalk and shot himself fatally in the head.[13]

The familiar public ritual commenced. "The city is stunned and seeking to make sense of it," Mayor Mike McGinn said. "I think we have to start by acknowledging the tremendous amount of grief that's out there from the families and friends of the victims."[14]

Yet one of the purposes of this book is to ask the uncomfortable question: How are rituals of community healing, however heartfelt, going to stop the violence with which the gun industry is polluting America? How are makeshift memorials of candles and teddy bears going to stem the flood of militarized killing machines—assault weapons and high-capacity semiautomatic pistols—that abound in every community in America?

The sad but self-evident truth is that the fleeting ritual embrace of public sorrow is not action. At best, these moments of public ritual give the image-hungry media a few seconds of self-conscious sentimentality, and they give policy makers safe platforms to strike "caring" postures. Memorial events are tough-question-free zones. Eventually the cameras leave, the plastic flowers fade, the stuffed toys rot. And in the end, nothing has changed.

At worst, these weepy rituals play into the hands of the gun industry and its lobby. After major shootings, the NRA, the gun industry, and their cohorts suffocate any discussion of effective policies to stop gun violence. They piously argue that "now is the time to mourn." Their self-righteous surrogates pretend that it is disrespectful to discuss gun-violence prevention while families and survivors are grieving—regardless of the fact that it is often fellow victims and survivors from prior attacks who make such demands. No one in his or her right mind would dream of making such a foolish argument in the wake of the crash of a passenger jet. Or after a terrorist attack.

The blizzard of gun violence documented in this book is not a "gun safety" problem. Nor is it a problem of legal versus illegal guns. It is a gun problem. It is the direct and inevitable consequence of the gun industry's cynical marketing, the proliferation of lethal firepower, and the waves of relaxed state laws—concealed carry, shoot first, shoot anywhere, shoot cops, just shoot, shoot, shoot—that the gun industry's handmaiden, the NRA, has inflicted on the country to promote new markets for the industry.

How can it be that Americans tolerate this relentless slaughter, when they have willingly spent trillions of dollars and surrendered their dearest constitutional rights to protect themselves against the comparatively minuscule threat of terrorist attack? One explanation might be that Americans simply don't care about gun violence or its victims—until it strikes them, or their families, or their neighbors, or their co-workers, or the people they worship with, or the artists they create with or listen to. In truth, some clearly do not care. Hypnotized by sepia-tinted fables of "gun rights" and socially impaired by their lack of empathy, they believe that no sacrifice is too great for others to bear so that they can enjoy unbridled access to their deadly toys, their lethal security blankets, and their pretended defense of liberty. The pro-gun writer and advocate Dave Workman, for example, "a loyal foot soldier in the pro-gun publishing and lobbying empire of convicted felon Alan Gottlieb,"[15] uttered an incredibly thick-witted explanation to the local NPR affiliate in Seattle following the Café Racer shooting. Nothing can be done, Workman argued, because the rest of us must respect the choices of gun-toting misfits like Ian Stawicki. "We can't treat him like a child, he's got his own life to live and he can make his own mistakes no matter how horrific those mistakes turn out to be."[16]

But most Americans do care about gun violence. They want change. What they lack first is information about its true dimensions and causes. The media whiteout and the gun industry lockdown of data leave Americans so poorly informed about how common and widespread gun violence is that they are surprised when it strikes them and often write it off to mere chance. They ignore the contradictions inherent in their own observations about the more frequent types of gun violence, such as how the previously law-abiding shooter "seemed like such a nice person, we would never have thought he would do such a thing," or "things like this just don't happen in our community."

From policy makers, the press, and self-appointed experts, we are often presented with statements and plans of action that reinforce common misperceptions about gun violence instead of challenging them. The result is that America lacks a clear national plan of action to significantly reduce gun violence. The essential elements of such a plan are fact-based public health action programs that have been proven effective over decades. "In 1900 the average life expectancy of Americans was 47 years," David Hemenway, director of the Harvard Injury Control Research Center and the Youth Violence Prevention Center, wrote in his 2009 book about the public health approach. "Today it is 78 years. Most of this improvement in health has been due to public health measures rather than medical advances." Hemenway explained that "the concern of public health is to improve the health of societies," and its focus is "not on cure, but on prevention."[17]

Motor vehicle safety—which most Americans now take for granted—is a prime example of fact-based public health action. Between 1966 and 2000, the combined efforts of government and advocacy organizations reduced the rate of motor vehicle death per 100,000 population by 43 percent. This represents a 72 percent decrease in deaths per vehicle miles traveled.[18] And as a direct result of these public health measures, motor vehicle death and injuries continue to decline. In 2010, the number of fatalities in motor vehicle traffic crashes was 32,788—the lowest level since 1949. This drop took place despite a significant increase in the number of miles Americans drove.[19]

Yet as motor vehicle–related deaths have declined, firearm deaths have continued unabated—the direct result of the failure of policy makers to acknowledge and act on this ubiquitous public health problem. In shocking point of fact, gun fatalities exceeded motor vehicle fatalities in ten states in 2009. In that year, as figure 11 shows, gun deaths outpaced motor vehicle deaths in Alaska, Arizona, Colorado, Indiana, Michigan, Nevada, Oregon, Utah, Virginia, and Washington.[20]

What is the difference? It is that firearms are the last consumer product manufactured in the United States that is not subject to federal health and safety regulation. As Hemenway explained in another book, "The time Americans spend using their cars is orders of magnitudes greater than the time spent using their guns. It is probable that per hour of exposure, guns are

Figure 11. Firearm Deaths Exceeded Motor
Vehicle Deaths in Ten States in 2009

State	Gun Deaths	Motor Vehicle Deaths	Gun Death Rate per 100,000	Motor Vehicle Death Rate per 100,000
Alaska	104	84	14.89	12.03
Arizona	856	809	12.98	12.27
Colorado	583	565	11.60	11.24
Indiana	735	715	11.44	11.13
Michigan	1,095	977	10.98	9.80
Nevada	406	255	15.36	9.65
Oregon	417	394	10.90	10.30
Utah	260	256	9.34	9.19
Virginia	836	827	10.61	10.49
Washington	623	580	9.35	8.70

In 2009 there were 31,236 gun deaths nationwide for a rate of 10.19 per 100,000 and 36,361 motor vehicle deaths (both occupant and pedestrian) nationwide for a rate of 11.87 per 100,000 (both totals include data only for the fifty states). WISQARS database, National Center for Injury Prevention and Control, Centers for Disease Control and Prevention.

far more dangerous. Moreover, we have lots of safety regulations concerning the manufacture of motor vehicles; there are virtually no safety regulations for domestic firearms manufacture."[21] Examples of federal agencies and the products for which they are responsible include: Consumer Product Safety Commission (CPSC), household products (except for guns and ammunition); Environmental Protection Agency (EPA), pesticides and toxic chemicals; Food and Drug Administration (FDA), drugs (including tobacco) and medical devices; and the National Highway Traffic Safety Administration (NHTSA), motor vehicles.

Before the advent of the public health approach, the focus in motor vehicle safety was on changing the behavior of the "bad driver" or "the nut behind the wheel," and it had limited results.[22]

The establishment of NHTSA in 1966 marked a distinct change. It was part of a sustained decades-long public health effort to develop and implement a series of injury-prevention initiatives that work and have saved countless lives. These public health initiatives made changes in both vehicle and highway design. Vehicles incorporated such new safety features as better headlights and brakes, head rests, energy-absorbing steering wheels, shatter-resistant windshields, safety belts, and air bags. Roads that vehicles travel have been improved by more effective marking of curves, use of breakaway signs and utility poles, better lighting, barriers separating oncoming traffic lanes, crash cushions at bridge abutments, and guardrails.[23] Experts also cite the increase in the use of seat belts, beginning in the mid-1980s as states enacted belt-use laws, and a reduction in alcohol-impaired driving as Mothers Against Drunk Driving and other organizations changed the public's perception of the problem and laws were enacted to increase the likelihood that intoxicated drivers would be punished. Graduated licensing laws are credited with helping to reduce the number of teen drivers crashing on our nation's roadways.[24]

It is extremely important to note that the creation of NHTSA's comprehensive national data system was a vital part of this success, because it "enabled scientists to determine the main factors affecting road safety and which public policies were and were not effective." [25] Pioneers in vehicle safety "insisted that the injury field be based less on opinion and more on science." [26]

America's failed approach to gun death and injury has been the exact opposite of what has been proven to save lives in hundreds of other fields. Data and information have been shut down. Driven by ideology, triangulation, and flatly misinformed opinion, attention remains focused on "bad people" and exaggerated "rights," not on the greed of the gun industry and on the reckless features of its militarized products—guns that hitherto "good people" use dozens of time a day to kill each other and themselves. The result is that, although more than 90 percent of American households own a car,[27] and fewer than a third of

American households contain a gun,[28] the year-by-year trends of deaths nationwide from these two consumer products are on a trajectory to intersect.

These trends will be encouraged for the worse as the gun industry and the NRA—with the compliant support of many state legislatures—continue to weaken gun control laws in order to hype markets for their deadly products. The reason for the gun industry's frantic efforts is the handwriting that they have seen on the wall. Not only is gun ownership declining in America, it is in free fall among younger cohorts. In the 1970s, approximately 45 percent of respondents under thirty years of age reported that their household owned a gun. Recent surveys have shown that number now to be below 20 percent, a decline of more than half.[29] As one author observed:

> Barring a wholesale return to rural living or a boom in hunting, it seems unlikely that this trend will reverse. Demographic diversity will also likely contribute to a continued decline in gun ownership. White males own guns at higher rates than members of other groups, while gun ownership among African-Americans is lower, and ownership among Latinos and Asians is lower still. Every projection by demographers shows whites declining as a

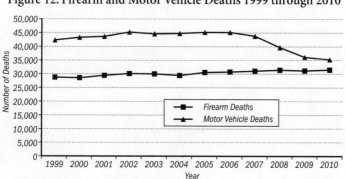

Figure 12. Firearm and Motor Vehicle Deaths 1999 through 2010

proportion of the American population in the next few decades, and Latinos are now the country's largest and fastest-growing minority group. These factors will likely produce a continued, if not accelerated, decline in gun ownership.[30]

But there is no reason to simply wait for demographics to erase the American gun industry. Hundreds of thousands of lives are literally at stake if we do nothing while the gun industry strikes out more and more dangerously, like a wounded rattlesnake in its final throes. There are a number of specific things that can and ought to be done by all Americans who want to see gun violence drastically diminished—and specific groups like activists in all progressive causes, policy makers, the media, foundations, and public health practitioners:

1. Stop accepting excuses from politicians. Americans who care about gun violence need first to take back control of this issue from those politicians who refuse to act forcefully. Politicians who are leaders on gun violence prevention are the exception, not the norm—despite the effects guns have on citizens in every state in the nation. The NRA and the gun industry control this issue because the majority of politicians we elect (and reelect) let them control it. The cries of the victims of gun violence are muffled by poll-driven positions and the comfort of accepted political wisdom of those ensconced in their golden triangle.

The degree to which the gun lobby can control the political debate was starkly illustrated in August 2009 at a White House press conference. During that month, a spate of armed protestors began showing up at presidential events. In Portsmouth, New Hampshire, a man with a gun strapped to his leg stood outside a town hall meeting with a sign reading, "It's time to water the tree of liberty."[31] The reference was to a letter in which Thomas Jefferson wrote, "The tree of liberty must be refreshed from time to time with the blood of patriots and tyrants. It is its natural manure." [32] In Phoenix, Arizona, about a dozen people carrying guns, including one with an AR-15 assault rifle, milled around among protesters outside the convention center, where the president was giving a speech. A spokesman for the Secret Service admitted that incidents of firearms being carried outside presidential events were a "relatively new phenomenon," but insisted that the president's safety was not being jeopardized. [33]

But, one might fairly have asked, what about the safety of other ordinary citizens who aren't carrying guns and don't want to carry guns? What about their rights, and their preferences? What about the intimidation inherent in the open display of guns at political events by people who are, to put it mildly, clearly angry? What will be the effect of this precedent on future presidents—and other public figures? What about the possibility of people showing up with more advanced firepower—such as freely available 50 caliber antiarmor sniper rifles?

When asked about these events, White House Press Secretary Robert Gibbs spoke only to the parochial interests of gun enthusiasts, saying merely that people are entitled to carry weapons outside such events if local laws allow it. "There are laws that govern firearms that are done state or locally," he said. "Those laws don't change when the president comes to your state or locality." [34] But as the commentator E.J. Dionne incisively observed at the time, Gibbs's technical response missed the bigger point. "Gibbs made you think of the old line about the liberal who is so open-minded he can't even take his own side in an argument. What needs to be addressed is not the legal question but the message that the gun-toters are sending." [35]

It was a "teachable moment." But instead of using these events as an opportunity to speak out about "the message that the gun-toters are sending," Gibbs's meek response only validated their threatening actions, further empowering them. Americans must demand that such appeasement of the gun industry and extremist gun enthusiasts end.

2. **Demand an end to the lockdown on gun and gun violence**

data, and insist on the creation of comprehensive databases and open information about guns and gun violence. Chapter 7 demonstrated how the gun industry and its accomplices in Washington have locked down data and information about guns and gun violence. But data and information are essential to the public health approach, to assessing which policies work to reduce death and injury and which do not. It is fundamental to understanding virtually every firearm-related issue—including the effects of concealed-carry and shoot-first laws, the role of assault weapons, traffic in guns abroad, the effects of guns in the home, and more.

Americans, including activists and especially including policy makers, need to understand that the true reason behind this information lockdown is simply and completely protecting the gun industry from accountability for its depredations. The shameful argument that withholding tracing data protects law enforcement officers and the integrity of investigations is plainly fraudulent.

All of the so-called Tiahrt restrictions on crime-gun data should be ended. But much more needs to be done. The federal government should create a comprehensive reporting system—preferably separate from the weak and compromised ATF—that gathers and integrates in one system data about every aspect of firearms and their use in America. Public health analysts, policymakers, and ordinary citizens should be able to find out as much about the trends in gun violence as that which is freely available today about trends in tire blowouts, baby stroller design, tainted foodstuffs, and virtually every item of consumer usage. The industry will argue that such a database would make it possible to compile the wholly imaginary but nonetheless dreaded "national list of gun owners," a supposed prelude to "confiscation." This argument is an extension of paranoia beyond all reason but an excellent fund-raiser for the NRA and others who trade in fear, loathing, and paranoia. If the argument must be taken seriously, it would not be at all difficult to craft a system of data collection and retrieval that would yield the necessary data without including any details of individual ownership.

In the meantime, local activists should aggressively find and pursue sources of data about guns and gun violence in their communities and states, compile it as best they can, and regularly make the information available to the news media in creative reports. These sources include public information such as state Uniform Crime Reports (UCR) data, information from states that participate in the National Violent Death Reporting System (NVDRS) and other statewide information-gathering systems, medical examiners' records, police and court records, legislative hearings, and local government action. This also includes developing personal contacts with people in the community whose work brings them into contact with incidents of gun violence.

3. **Understand that gun violence is not "someone else's" issue.** Gun violence is not an issue just for gun violence prevention activists. Gun violence affects virtually every community—socioeconomic, racial, ethnic—in America, not to mention workplaces, schools, shopping centers, and children's soccer games. Moreover, the gun lobby and gun industry are supported by the agenda of a well-funded, well-organized rightwing coalition. Groups and people who work on the progressive side of issues of domestic violence, school safety, youth violence, and drug abuse, for example, or who work in minority communities should understand that the gun industry, guns, and faux "gun rights" are the ultimate drivers of many of the problems they face. It is their issue too. What is needed is a much grander, better-informed, and better-funded coalition.

Funders—from the largest foundations to the smallest individual donors—and policy makers need to understand that these issues cannot be walled off from each other. For example, guns from the United States empower the criminal organizations in Latin America that produce most of the drugs sold on our streets. Guns empower the organized gangs that sell these drugs at retail in the United States. And guns are often used in the domestic violence that breeds in families and communities shattered by drug abuse.

4. **Learn about guns and the gun industry.** Gun control may be one of the few issues in America in which all opinions, no matter how under- or misinformed, are given equal weight. Few things are as disheartening as listening to a longtime advocate or well-intentioned policy maker talk about guns and the gun industry in a way that makes it clear that she or he has not done the homework. Expounding on assault weapons, for example, without understanding the specific design features that distinguish them from sporting rifles (or fully automatic machine guns) and make them so dangerous does more harm than good.

And yet there is nothing all that complicated about how guns work or how the industry operates. It's not rocket science. Those who want to be involved in this issue should educate themselves about the underlying facts before expounding on solutions. The Violence Policy Center (vpc.org) and other organizations, as well as leading researchers, have posted dozens of monographs online that explain in detail virtually every issue in gun control. These reports and studies contain voluminous notes about the sources on which they are based. They are nothing less than a free university for advocates.

A corollary to this is "know your enemy." Join the National Rifle Association and read their magazines if you plan to become an advocate. Just as most Americans have no idea what the gun industry has turned into, few understand what today's NRA represents. The conspiracy theories and venom that reside between the covers of its activist publication, *America's 1st Freedom*, would leave most Americans torn between laughing and crying. I hope they'd get angry and take action.

5. **Look upstream for gun violence prevention measures.** Once vehicle safety advocates stopped trying to reform people and started looking at the actual designs of vehicles and roads, enormous strides were made in saving lives and preventing injuries. This is precisely what needs to be done to turn around America's gun violence problem. We need to prevent injury be-

fore it happens. To do that, we need to look upstream at the gun industry, its products, and how they are distributed.

Policy makers need, for example, to look at what impact the designs of specific guns have on their use. What, for example, is the effect on death and injury of the proliferation of higher-caliber handguns in smaller sizes? This cannot be divined from the gun industry's or the NRA's self-serving assertions. If the gun industry insists on calling semiautomatic assault rifles "modern sporting rifles," let them. But collect detailed data about make, model, and caliber of guns—their sales and their use in crime and other forms of gun violence. A database that includes all the details of incidents of gun violence—similar to databases on contaminated drugs, automobile crashes, and injuries from defective children's furniture—would yield invaluable information, no matter what label the industry chooses to use in its marketing programs. The gun industry's marketing and distribution programs, coupled with the increasingly lax laws about access to guns, are the equivalent of the badly designed, dangerous, and poorly marked roads before the advent of the vehicle safety public health approach. The crazy-quilt system that currently purports to regulate the manufacture, import (and smuggling) into and out of America, and sale or transfer of guns within America is clearly ineffective. It benefits no one but the gun industry.

6. Learn from successful programs. One of Wayne LaPierre's stock horror stories is that some eggheads in America think that we might learn something about gun control from other nations of the world. He's right. We can learn a lot from the successful experiences of other free and industrialized countries, including those that have sprung from the Anglo-Saxon heritage of which the NRA and the right wing are so protective. Other countries do not suffer the same torrent of needless gun death and injury for the simple reason that neither their citizens nor their leaders will tolerate it.

Moreover, some states in America have succeeded in

implementing reasonable and effective gun control programs. In California, for example, key stakeholders—including the foundation community, the gun violence prevention movement, and sympathetic lawmakers—decided to take on the gun lobby directly after a shocking series of high-profile shootings. They broke the gun lobby's grip on California politics. California is also a good example of how the first round of legislation may not solve a problem, and therefore continued work is necessary. The California assault weapons law was not perfect when it first went into effect, but advocates continued to study how it was working, how the industry was evading it, and what changes were needed to make it effective. In the face of ongoing industry attempts to subvert the law, these efforts continue to this day.

These ideas are intended to suggest taking a different approach to the problem of gun violence—not a third way, not a fourth way, but the right way. America will get the kind of gun violence prevention programs that it deserves only when, and if, the vast, silent majority realizes that strong and effective fact-based policies that significantly reduce gun death and injury are in their interest—and then does something about it.

AFTERWORD

Only weeks after the manuscript for this book was sent to the publisher, Americans voted in what Wayne LaPierre, the NRA's chief executive officer and executive vice president, predicted would be "the most dangerous and decisive election of our lives." He asserted, "This election will decide not only the destiny of our Second Amendment rights, but everything that's *good* and *right* about America."

LaPierre was right. The 2012 election was decisive. Voters all over America decisively rejected the NRA. They decisively rejected its angry worldview. And they decisively rejected all but a forlorn handful of the candidates that the NRA backed. President Barack Obama—whom LaPierre and the NRA political machine vociferously vowed to defeat—was elected to a second term. Mitt Romney's penitent pilgrimage to the NRA's 2012 convention did him no good. In fact, it arguably worked against him, as an example of his alleged tendency to flip-flop on issues.

Beyond Romney, the NRA's endorsement was decisively an electoral kiss of death. In six of the seven Senate races where the NRA spent more than $100,000, its candidate lost. Even though most incumbent House members who ran kept their seats, of those who lost their reelection bids, over two-thirds were endorsed by the NRA, whose paper tiger was once again shown to be a tissue pussycat.

The election of November 6, 2012, cast a historic shadow on the shrinking pool of aging white men who are the core of the NRA and the conservative coalition to which it has attached itself. Americans do not believe that the coalition's obsession with race, ethnicity, guns, and violence defines what is right and good about this country. On the contrary, the election decisively validated the long-term trends cited in this book.

The urgency of the need for change was tragically underscored on December 14, 2012, when a young man named Adam Lanza walked into the Sandy Hook Elementary School in Newtown, Connecticut—home of the National Shooting Sports Foundation—and shot to death twenty first graders and six school employees with a 223 caliber Bushmaster semiautomatic assault rifle. He then used a handgun to kill himself. Lanza had earlier killed his mother, Nancy Lanza, with a 22 caliber rifle.

Horrified by the sheer madness of this slaughter, many expected that the gun industry and its lobby would at last see the need for sensible gun legislation. That hope was dashed—and the intransigence of the gun lobby exposed—on Friday, December 21, when the NRA's leadership emerged in Washington, D.C., after a week of silence. In a defiant broadside, Wayne LaPierre blamed the news media, the film industry, and video games—in short, everything but guns—for causing America's gun violence problem.

The landmark election and the horror of Newtown challenge progressive leaders and policy makers as they have never been challenged before. They must act decisively to address the underlying causes of gun violence in America described in the preceding pages. If they do not, they likely and rightly will be swept aside in favor of new leadership.

This much is certain: the gun industry will dig in as it has always done, and continue to profit from fear and violence—until the very last gun.

January 6, 2013

APPENDIX A:
A WEEK OF REPORTED GUN DEATH
AND INJURY IN AUGUST 2011

The shooting incidents in this appendix are a snapshot of gun death and injury in the United States as reported in the news media during one randomly selected week. This snapshot, however, illustrates only a small fraction of all gun deaths and injuries that actually occurred during that week. This appendix demonstrates that most gun death and injury in the United States is not reported in the news media at all. As a result of this media whiteout, Americans are poorly informed about the extent of gun violence occurring around them every day and everywhere.

These shooting incidents were as many as could be found in U.S. news media during the week of Monday, August 1, 2011, through Sunday, August 7, 2011. They were gathered by extensively searching Google and Nexis. The fifty-two shooting incidents that were found are summarized below. They resulted in seventy gun deaths and twenty-two nonfatal gun injuries.

However, as discussed in chapter 1, there have been an average of 582 gun deaths per week in the United States during the twenty-first century. This is more than eight times the number of deaths that this survey found in news media. Likewise, if this was an average week, 1,319 persons were injured by guns but did not die—almost sixty times as many gun injuries as were reported in the media during the week in question. Nevertheless, these incidents fairly illustrate that the range of gun violence in America goes far beyond the stereotypical, mistaken belief that it happens mostly in the course of other crimes. In fact, as these anecdotes and national data show, routine gun violence in America includes suicide, murder-suicide, rage killings, mass murders, and domestic violence.

Monday, August 1

Probable suicide: Fort Huachuca, Arizona. U.S. Army Sergeant First Class Jose J. Algarin-Colon, thirty-eight, was found dead in his quarters of a gunshot wound. Base officials refused to say whether Algarin committed suicide. However, he had been arrested and escorted back to his quarters by military police the same day for bringing his personal handgun to the base's headquarters.[1]

Tuesday, August 2

Suicide: Lee, New Hampshire. Andrew Hubbard, twenty-seven, killed himself with a shotgun after being involved in a car crash. Neither driver was seriously injured in the head-on collision, but Hubbard grabbed a shotgun out of the back seat of his car, then fatally shot himself behind the premises of a nearby business.[2]

Murder-suicide: Hillsboro, Wisconsin. Joseph C. Satterlee, fifty-five, rammed his wife's car on a street with his own vehicle, climbed into her car, and shot her to death with his .357 Magnum revolver. He then shot himself to death. Satterlee fired a total of eight rounds from his six-shot revolver, pausing once to reload. His wife, Anita K. Satterlee, had filed for divorce on June 20, 2011.[3]

Murder-suicide: Kensington, Maryland. Police officers found the bodies of Margaret F. Jensvold, fifty-four, and her son Ben Barnhard, thirteen, in their residence in a Maryland suburb of Washington, D.C. Investigators concluded that Jensvold, a psychiatrist, had shot her son to death and then killed herself. The son had a number of special needs, and Jensvold was reportedly distressed that the local public school system would not pay for his attendance at a private school.[4]

Wednesday, August 3

Murder-suicide: Deerfield, Ohio. Troy Penn, an eighteen-year-old high school senior, shot and killed his ex-girlfriend, seventeen-year-old Amanda Borsos, with a shotgun in an outside pet exercise area at Four Paws Pet Care and Kennel. He then went home and killed himself with the same gun.[5]

Homicide: Alice, Texas. Mitchell Christopher Soliz, twenty-six, allegedly shot Juan Antonio Sifuentes III, twenty-seven, to death while he was visiting Soliz's home. Sifuentes was the grandson of Juan Antonio Sifuentes, a singer in the Tejano Roots Hall of Fame. Soliz was arrested on suspicion of murder.[6]

Homicide (police legal intervention): Chicago, Illinois. Claude A. Ellis, thirty-five, was shot to death by police after he allegedly attacked two officers, striking one of them in the face and injuring the other. Police had been called to Ellis's home on a domestic violence complaint. Ellis reportedly had five previous felony drug convictions."[7]

Homicide: Richmond, California. Vincent Stephenson Jr., eighteen, was shot and killed in a drive-by shooting while he was standing outside a residence.[8]

Homicide: Phoenix, Arizona. Edgar Sigala, twenty-four, was shot and killed outside a Baskin-Robbins ice-cream shop. His companion, an unidentified twenty-six-year-old woman, was seriously injured. Jose Acuna, twenty-two, was arrested and charged in the shootings.[9]

Unintentional fatal shooting: St. Petersburg, Florida. Wilfredo LaFontaine, fifty, accidentally shot himself to death while simultaneously talking on the phone to his girlfriend and cleaning his handgun. The girlfriend heard a "pop" over the phone and rushed to their apartment, where LaFontaine was found slumped against a door. He explained he had been cleaning his gun. He died later at a hospital.[10]

Homicide: Pensacola, Florida. Elena Rendell, seventeen, allegedly shot and killed her adoptive sister, Christina Sneary, fourteen, with her father's 9mm handgun during an argument between the siblings over a cell phone. Authorities charged Rendell with manslaughter.[11]

Thursday, August 4

Suicide: Jersey City, New Jersey. A twenty-three-year-old man whom police did not publicly identify shot himself in the head with a handgun while sitting in a Cadillac sedan on a public street.[12]

Murder-suicide: Windsor, North Carolina. Frank Cowan, eighty-seven, shot to death his wife, Dorothy Cowan, eighty-six, and then killed himself with the same gun.[13]

Homicide: Staten Island, New York. Shytik Bowman, seventeen, was shot to death in the course of an apparent street robbery. Authorities later charged Stanley Bowens, twenty-one, with the murder, which allegedly happened when Bowman was being robbed of a bracelet worth less than fifty dollars.[14]

Homicide and nonfatal shooting: Pittsburgh, Pennsylvania. Kimberly Wade, forty-five, was shot in the stomach when at least one gunman sprayed her house with bullets. Shortly thereafter, her son, Chris Michaux, nineteen, was shot to death outside a friend's house.[15]

Friday, August 5

Murder-suicide: Santa Clarita, California. Martin Fred Strassner, sixty-four, picked up his in-laws, Leo Moss, ninety-five, and Jean Moss, ninety, from an assisted-living home. He drove them to his own residence, where he parked in the driveway. He shot both of the Mosses to death with a handgun while they were sitting in the car, then turned the gun on himself and committed suicide.[16]

Would-be robber shot with own gun: St. Petersburg, Florida. Almedin Muratovic, twenty-five, attempted an armed robbery of a twenty-five-year-old woman at an automated teller machine. The woman's twenty-nine-year-old boyfriend jumped out of his car and wrestled with Muratovic, who was shot with his own

22 caliber handgun during the struggle. Muratovic was charged with two counts of attempted armed robbery.[17]

Homicide and nonfatal shooting: Detroit, Michigan. Alphonso Thomas, thirty-six, an employee of the Pretty Woman Lounge strip club, was shot to death by an unidentified person who was apparently refused admission to the club, pulled out a handgun, and started shooting. A manager of the club was also shot.[18]

Homicide: Tucson, Arizona. Loran Langston, thirty-four, was shot to death after an altercation with his neighbor Brian Dillon, forty. Dillon claimed he shot Langston in self-defense. No arrest was made pending investigation.[19]

Homicide (mass family murder): Ocala, Florida. James Edward Bannister Sr., thirty-one, allegedly shot to death eight-year-old CorDarrian Hill, six-year-old CorDerica Hill, fifty-two-year-old Bridget Gray, and twenty-seven-year-old Jocalyn Gray. He then set fire to the home. Bannister has been indicted on four counts of first-degree premeditated murder with a firearm and one count of arson of a dwelling.[20]

Homicide, nonfatal shooting: Jacksonville, Florida. Marquis Bing, eighteen, was found shot to death in a car. An unidentified injured woman was also in the car. Police later arrested Clarence Lee Jones, twenty, for the murder. Another suspect, Joseph Donte Patterson, eighteen, was arrested for attempted murder. Patterson allegedly also discharged a firearm in the incident, but his shots did not hit anyone.[21]

Homicide: Los Angeles, California. Marco Antonio Gonzalez, twenty, was shot and killed in his car after a dispute with another driver. Authorities said the dispute appeared to be gang-related.[22]

Unintentional nonfatal shooting: Thonotosassa, Florida. Oscar Thayer Dean, forty-three, was allegedly mishandling a .357 Magnum revolver that he thought was unloaded when he shot his wife in the stomach. When police responded to the emergency call, they observed that the "residence was heavily infested with insects and there was very little food" and concluded that the home was unfit for the couple's six-year-old daughter. Dean was arrested on a charge of child neglect.[23]

Murder-suicide: Farmington Hills, Michigan. Lisa Mazzola, fifty-two, shot and killed her husband, Robert Mazzola, fifty-three, with a handgun, then shot herself to death. The couple were divorcing.[24]

Nonfatal shooting: Buffalo, New York. Darnell Mobley, twenty-four, was shot in the stomach when he ran away from a man with a black revolver who was attempting to hold him up. Mobley was hospitalized and listed in fair condition after the shooting.[25]

Homicide (police legal intervention): Chester, Pennsylvania. Daniel Simms, twenty-one, ran away from a police officer who was attempting to stop him during a routine patrol. When the officer gave chase on foot, Simms pointed a loaded handgun at the officer. The officer fatally shot Simms, and was later cleared of wrongdoing.[26]

Murder, attempted suicide: Englewood, Florida. Frank Olms, sixty-six, shot his wife, Nancy Olms, forty-eight, and then shot himself. Nancy Olms died, but Frank Olms survived and was later charged with first-degree murder.[27]

Suicide: Prospect Heights, Illinois. An unnamed sixteen-year-old boy shot himself to death with his father's 45 caliber pistol.[28]

Saturday, August 6

Nonfatal shooting: Pittsburgh, Pennsylvania. Lataya Anthony, thirty-one, suffered a gunshot wound to the stomach. Ms. Anthony would not cooperate with police, who had no suspect for the shooting.[29]

Homicide, nonfatal shooting: Oakland, California. Lashawna Candies, twenty-five, was killed and her thirty-four-year-old aunt was wounded when they accidentally drove into the middle of a shootout between rival groups.[30]

Murder-suicide: Lincoln, Nebraska. Jerry Crook, fifty-seven, shot and killed Sueann Bedlion, forty-seven, then killed himself with the same gun. Bedlion's twenty-year-old daughter was present and fled the apartment.[31]

Homicide: Bradenton, Florida. Roman Hall, forty-three, was found shot to death outside the backdoor of his residence.[32]

Homicide: Fort Worth, Texas. Larry Lampkin, eighteen, was found dead in a breezeway of the apartment complex in which he lived. He had been shot multiple times. Police later arrested one juvenile and were seeking another for the shooting, which apparently was the result of an argument.[33]

Homicide and nonfatal shooting: Petersburg, Virginia. Corey M. Lewis Jr., sixteen, was shot to death. An unnamed twenty-eight-year-old man was also found shot near by. Police later arrested five suspects, including two juveniles, in connection with the shootings.[34]

Suicide: New Port Richey, Florida. Christos Marangos, thirty, shot himself in the head after exchanging gunfire at his residence with Pasco County sheriff's deputies. Authorities had come to the home to question Marangos, who had a criminal record, about several burglaries. He opened fire when the deputies entered the mobile home.[35]

Homicide: Jersey City, New Jersey. Rakim Priester, twenty-one, was cut down in a hail of more than two dozen bullets. The single bullet that struck Priester out of the many fired at him inflicted a fatal wound. Police later arrested Aziz R. Wright, nineteen, and Donelle L. Golden, twenty-one, in connection with the murder.[36]

Homicide: New Brunswick, New Jersey. Jesse Simons, sixty-one, a hospital worker, was found on a street, mortally wounded by gunshot. He later died in the hospital. No suspects were arrested.[37]

Homicide: Chester, Pennsylvania. After responding to a report of shots fired, police found a thirty-seven-year-old man lying on the ground mortally wounded by gunfire. The man died shortly later. He was not identified.[38]

Nonfatal shooting, homicide of police officer, homicide (police legal intervention): El Cajon and San Diego, California. Dejon

White, twenty-three, approached Martin Hana, twenty-three, who was in his car at an El Cajon In-N-Out Burger. White fired one round with a shotgun, hitting Hana in the face. Hana survived his wounds but required intensive surgery and care. White sped away and shortly afterward pulled up beside a San Diego police car and fired another round through his passenger-side window, killing officer Jeremy Henwood, thirty-six. Investigators tracked White's car to his home address. When they arrived, a shootout ensued, and White was killed by police gunfire. White may have intended so-called suicide by cop.[39]

Sunday, August 7

Homicide, nonfatal shooting: Philadelphia, Pennsylvania. Yavonne Burch, twenty-two, was shot to death, and another woman in her early twenties was injured by gunfire in front of a residence. Authorities later arrested Vincent "Huddy" Leach, twenty-six, in connection with the shootings.[40]

Homicide, nonfatal shooting: Chicago, Illinois. Six-year-old Arianna Gibson was shot dead and two teenagers were wounded when a gunman opened fire through the living room window. Arianna was sleeping on a couch. Authorities believe one of the teenagers was the intended target of the shooter.[41]

Homicide (mass shooting), nonfatal injury, homicide (police intervention): Copley Township, Ohio. Armed with two handguns, Michael Hance, fifty-one, went on a ten-minute rampage through the neighborhood in which he and his girlfriend lived. Hance shot seven people to death and critically wounded his girlfriend. The gunman apparently stalked specific targets, including an eleven-year-old and two teenagers, while allowing others to escape. Hance was shot to death by responding police.[42]

Nonfatal shooting (self-defense): St. Petersburg, Florida. Would-be robber Anthony Lawrence Hauser, seventeen, was shot four times by Raven Smith, thirty-four, when he attempted to hold up Smith's girlfriend in the parking lot of an Applebee's restaurant. Smith had a concealed-carry permit and police ruled the shooting self-defense.[43]

Homicide: Houston, Texas. Salem Saif Al Mazroui and his father, Saif Bin Musallam Al Mazroui, were confronted by two men as they were unloading their vehicle in front of the father's apartment. One of the men opened fire with a pistol when the father and son attempted to flee. The son was fatally injured. He had been visiting his father from the United Arab Emirates. Two suspects were later arrested and charged with capital murder.[44]

Nonfatal shooting: Fort Lauderdale, Florida. James McIvery, seventy-nine, fired two bullets at the ground, one of which struck twelve-year-old Traves Neal in the stomach. McIvery asserted that he did not mean to shoot anyone and merely intended to scare off a group of youths who had been repeatedly pestering him and his disabled daughter.[45]

Attempted murder-suicide: Lake Villa Township, Illinois. After a domestic argument, Gordon D. Olsen, fifty-two, shot his forty-nine-year-old wife in the head and chest, then shot himself. Olsen died. His wife, who was not named in news reports, survived and was expected to make a full recovery from her injuries.[46]

Unintentional nonfatal shooting: Warren, Rhode Island. An unnamed twenty-six-year-old man was shot in the abdomen and buttocks when a firearm accidentally discharged. He recovered. A twenty-four-year-old man was taken into custody on the misdemeanor charge of firing in a compact area.[47]

Homicide, nonfatal shooting: Boston, Massachusetts. Elvis Sanchez, seventeen, and his mother, Elvira Pimentel, forty-three, were shot dead in their home, and another unnamed male was wounded.[48]

Murder-suicide: Buena Park, California. William Schilling, fifty-three, fatally shot his wife, Susan, forty-eight, in the head in the couple's bedroom. He then fatally shot himself in the head. Schilling had recently inherited from his father the 30-06 rifle he used.[49]

Murder-suicide, New Port Richey, Florida. Stephen Michael Searce, fifty-eight, fatally shot to death his wife, Penny Lynn Searce, forty-eight. He then shot himself and died.[50]

Homicide, nonfatal shooting: New Orleans, Louisiana. Jamaal Stewart, twenty-eight, was found shot to death in his vehicle. About an hour later, an unnamed seventeen-year-old boy was shot in the back, thigh, and buttocks while riding his bicycle.[51]

Murder-suicide (family annihilation): Brooklyn Park, Maryland. Kelly Brian Thompson, thirty-three, shot and killed his wife, Nina Thompson, thirty-four, and her fifteen-year-old twin children, Taishawn Pugh and Treshawn Pugh. He fatally shot himself when police arrived.[52]

APPENDIX B:
GLOCK HANDGUNS IN THE NEWS:
MAY 2011–APRIL 2012

The following are representative incidents involving Glock handguns that were reported in U.S. news media between May 1, 2011, and April 30, 2012, based on searches of the Nexis.com database. Because the news media typically underreport such incidents, the following are anecdotal only and should not be regarded as the complete universe nor as a random sample. Given restrictions on the release of more detailed government data, however, news reports often represent the best available source of examples of the use of guns in America. (This appendix includes some incidents that were reported in the news media during the period of the search but which occurred earlier.)

May 9, 2011—DeBary, Florida. Louis Vasquez, twenty-seven, suspicious of his wife, Linda, twenty-two, tracked her down to his mother's home and shot her to death with a 40 caliber Glock 22 pistol. Vasquez, whose mother described him as a real "Mommy's boy" in a 911 call, then committed suicide with the same gun.[1]

May 16, 2011—Gilbert, Arizona. The Maricopa County Attorney's office reported that it would not press charges against Matthew Jon Bohls, twenty-three. On April 9, Bohls shot to death Mitchell Shane Fickes, fifty-six, after an apparent incident of road rage. Bohls told Gilbert police that Fickes got out of his vehicle and threatened him with a 45 caliber Glock handgun. Bohls leaned out of his pickup with his own 9mm Glock pistol, fired, and inflicted fatal wounds on Fickes.[2]

June 13, 2011—Marysville, California. Devin Brendan Parker and Anthony Andrew Oliver were sentenced after pleading guilty to shooting at a car in a gang-related incident on March 9. The judge ordered that the Glock 10mm pistol used in the shooting be destroyed.[3]

June 16, 2011—New Bern, North Carolina. Stan Dale Williams was sentenced to a maximum of twenty-eight years in prison after pleading guilty to the murder of nineteen-year-old Cameron Jamar Gatling in February 2009. Williams shot Gatling with a Glock handgun in a nightclub parking lot after an incident inside the club.[4]

June 28, 2011—Volusia County, Florida. Marcus White, twenty, was arrested and charged with manslaughter after authorities determined that he had lied to them about the circumstances of his unintentional fatal shooting with a 40 caliber Glock pistol of his sleeping father, Douglas White, fifty, on June 7.[5]

July 1, 2011—Miami, Florida. Manuel A. Guarch, twenty-six, a Florida assistant state attorney, discharged his Glock handgun three times inside the parking garage of his condominium building after a night of drinking. Guarch later resigned his post, and his girlfriend, also an assistant state attorney, was demoted for her involvement.[6]

July 5, 2011—Plantation, Florida. Joseph Santy, a Plantation police officer, was off duty, cleaning his police-issued Glock 9mm pistol at his home while listening to his iPod. According to an internal investigation, he "apparently became distracted and failed to remove a round of ammunition from the chamber of the firearm." He pulled the trigger, and shot himself in the abdomen. He survived the shooting and was ordered to undergo further gun training.[7]

July 13, 2011—Dixon, Missouri. Gary Ball, thirty, shot Theron Parlin, thirty-two, seventeen times in the face—emptying a high-capacity magazine—before reloading his 9mm Glock pistol and turning the gun on himself. The incident apparently involved a domestic dispute.[8]

August 1, 2011—Bethlehem, Pennsylvania. Jeffrey Rogers, fifty-eight, a former Bethlehem police officer, filed a lawsuit contending that he was discriminated against when he was suspended and forced to retire on disability after improperly discharging his handgun. According to court papers filed by Rogers, he became woozy while in the police headquarters bathroom on December 31, 2010. His 40 caliber Glock pistol was discharged into the ceiling. In explaining why he failed to report the incident until later in the day, Rogers said that he was disoriented and deafened.[9]

August 5, 2011—Cape Canaveral, Florida. Francis Howard Morrell, a seventy-one-year-old retired dentist, burst into a pet-grooming business and fired a round into the ceiling with his Glock 9mm pistol. He was said to be eccentric and was apparently in a dispute with the business owner. Morrell pointed his pistol at responding police and was shot dead.[10]

September 2, 2011—Jacksonville, North Carolina. Robert Lewis, twenty-nine, a former military policeman, was found guilty of involuntary manslaughter and failure to secure a firearm from a minor. Lewis's three-year-old son, Tyler, shot himself with a Glock 22 pistol left in the home in November 2009. Lewis claimed that he had left the gun on top of a seven-foot-tall home entertainment center, a claim prosecutors disputed. The toddler shot himself in the head with the gun.[11]

October 11, 2011—Helena–West Helena, Arkansas. More than seven hundred law enforcement officers arrested fifty-one people in several small Arkansas Delta towns, the culmination of a major drug-trafficking investigation. A federal indictment in the case said a network of people helped transport drugs, paraphernalia, and weapons, including Glock 40 caliber pistols, AK-47 assault rifles, and AR-15 assault rifles.[12]

October 15, 2011—Gonzales, Louisiana. Celestine Skia, a twenty-two-year-old housekeeper, bought a 40 caliber Glock pistol at Cabela's Sporting Goods for her boyfriend, a federal indictment alleges. The boyfriend is charged in state court with shooting a man to death the same day. Skia, who pleaded not guilty, was also accused of buying a Kel-Tec .223 pistol at a gun show on September 18, 2010, and an assault rifle a year earlier at the same show.[13]

October 27, 2011—Webster, Texas. Blake Powell, twenty-six, was sentenced to eight years in prison after having pled guilty to aggravated assault with a deadly weapon. Powell showed up at a co-worker's home after he was fired for drinking on the job. He then pursued the co-worker in a high-speed chase through a residential neighborhood, firing at least ten rounds from his Glock pistol. "You are kind of like everybody's nightmare about one of those workplace guys that go berserk," Judge Shawna L. Reagin said at Powell's sentencing.[14]

November 4, 2011—Gulfport, Mississippi. A federal judge sentenced Daniel Vashon Cantino, twenty-eight, to more than fifteen years in prison on meth and firearm convictions. Cantino threw a Glock 9mm pistol and 3.5 grams of meth out of his car on the day he was arrested.[15]

November 12, 2011—Lauderhill, Florida. Kristopher Bieger, thirty, a Lauderhill police officer, allegedly emptied his Glock pistol shooting at his ex-girlfriend, Officer Brittny Skinner, thirty-one, while she was sitting in her patrol car. Bieger pleaded not guilty to charges stemming from the incident, which followed Skinner's ending their relationship the week before. The patrol car's trunk, rear driver's side door, and window took most of the shots, although at least one bullet went through the patrol car seat, through Skinner's police uniform, and into her protective vest, police said.[16]

November 13, 2011—Spotsylvania, Virginia. A forty-five-year-old man with a CCW permit died after he accidentally shot himself with his 40 caliber Glock pistol. The man—whom authorities did not identify—was sitting in the front seat of his family's minivan in a shopping center parking lot. He apparently attempted to adjust the pistol he was carrying and inadvertently pulled the trigger. The single bullet struck him in the hip, and he bled to death in a matter of minutes.[17]

November 16, 2011—Mahopac, New York. Michael Boccardi, forty-seven, lay in wait and shot Michael Purdy, fifty-six, to death with a 40 caliber Glock pistol. Both men were separated from their wives. When Boccardi's wife dropped Purdy off at his house after their dinner together, Boccardi came out of his hiding place and fired several shots at Purdy, who was killed by a bullet to the head. Boccardi, a CCW permit holder, then committed suicide with his Glock pistol.[18]

November 24, 2011—Naples, Florida. Police arrested Royce Lee Davis, fifty, after he made "inflammatory" remarks at a family Thanksgiving gathering, dragged a family member outside by the shirt collar, and fired a 40 caliber Glock pistol into the air three times.[19]

December 6, 2011—Jourdanton, Texas. Joe Gonzalez, thirty-one, an instructor at a gym, was shot at work when John Luebano, forty, an employee at the gun shop next door, accidentally fired a 9mm Glock pistol he was unloading. The Bullet Hole gun store and Revolution Athletics are adjacent to each other in the strip mall. The bullet went through a common wall.[20]

December 9, 2011—Weleetka, Oklahoma. Oklahoma law enforcement authorities charged Kevin Sweat, twenty-five, in the June 2008 shooting murder of Taylor Dawn Paschal-Placker, thirteen, and Skyla Jade Whitaker, eleven. The girls were shot multiple times along the side of a rural road near Weleetka. Sweat, who was being held for another murder when the charges were filed, admitted to an investigator that he shot and killed the girls. He called the girls "monsters" and said he "panicked" when they came toward his car, so he grabbed his Glock 40 caliber handgun out of his glove box, shot them both multiple times, then grabbed a 22 caliber gun and shot them again. Sweat was implicated by means of ballistic evidence from the Glock pistol.[21]

December 10, 2011—Phoenix, Arizona. The *Arizona Republic* reported that Daniel Lee Good, forty-two, had been charged with second-degree murder after authorities re-investigated his wife's death in 2008, which had originally been ruled a suicide. Leslie

Good, forty-eight, had been shot in the chest with a 45 caliber Glock pistol.[22]

December 14, 2011—Sevierville, Tennessee. Corporal Chris Huskey, a veteran deputy with the Sevier County Sheriff's Department, was reported to be back at work after completing a firearms refresher course. Huskey was demonstrating a Glock pistol to Deputy Adam Bohanan at a convenience store on November 23 when the weapon discharged, firing a bullet through a computer monitor and the wall of a walk-in freezer, where it lodged in a pack of frozen bologna.[23]

December 16, 2011—Washington, D.C. William N. McCorkle and Andre Clinkscale Jr., both twenty-six, were each sentenced to more than a hundred years in prison on three counts of first-degree murder. The pair shot three men to death at a gas station in May 2008 after an argument. McCorkle was armed with a 9mm Glock pistol equipped with an extended magazine holding at least twenty-nine rounds of ammunition. Clinkscale also had a pistol. The two fired at least thirty-eight shots at the three men, who were hit seventeen times, eleven times, and nine times, respectively, for a total of thirty-seven wounds.[24]

December 25, 2011—Grapevine, Texas. Azizolah "Bob" Yazdanpanah, fifty-six, who was dressed as Santa Claus, shot six family members to death before killing himself. The victims included Yazdanpanah's estranged wife and two children, who lived in the apartment, and three in-laws. The family had been together to celebrate Christmas. Yazdanpanah used both a 40 caliber Glock pistol and a 9mm Smith & Wesson pistol to shoot his victims in the head.[25]

January 2, 2012—Milwaukee, Wisconsin. Raymond Earl Baker, thirty-five, allegedly shot Desiree Marie Harrell, forty-three, to death with a Glock 40 caliber pistol. Harrell was found slumped over the center console of a Buick Regal. She had been shot eight times. Police said Baker confessed to the killing.[26]

January 6, 2012—Evansville, Indiana. Two men were arrested after an early morning shooting inside a bar. The pair were apprehended as they tried to flee in a pickup truck. A loaded Glock pistol was found on the driver, Kem Duerson Jr., thirty-three. Duerson was later charged with dealing cocaine and being a felon in possession of a firearm.[27]

January 10, 2012—Raleigh, North Carolina. Steven Neal Greenoe, thirty-seven, a former U.S. marine, was sentenced to ten years in prison for illegally trafficking dozens of handguns to the United Kingdom, including Glock pistols. Greenoe used his concealed-weapon permit to buy multiple guns at a time at various gun shops in North Carolina. He concealed them in his luggage to transport them to England, where he lived with his British wife. Investigators said the guns were sold to criminal gangs in England. British authorities linked a gun Greenoe purchased to a drive-by shooting in Manchester, England, in February 2011.[28]

January 24, 2012—Cranston, Rhode Island. Steven T. Smith, forty-four, allegedly pulled a Glock 45 caliber pistol out of his desk and threatened to shoot Michael Emerson, forty-six, a former employee who had returned to pick up his welding equipment. Smith was charged with felony assault.[29]

January 31, 2012—Allentown, Pennsylvania. Enrique Manuel Ortiz, twenty-five, was charged with shooting to death Hagos Mezgebo, an Ethiopian refugee and apparent stranger, on January 7, then threatening three women at gunpoint shortly after the shooting. When Ortiz was arrested during a vehicle stop on January 9, police found a 9mm Glock pistol under his seat. Heroin and cocaine were also found in the vehicle, and Ortiz was charged with several drug trafficking–related offenses.[30]

January 31, 2012—Madison, South Dakota. Carl V. Ericsson, seventy-three, allegedly shot to death Norman Johnson, a seventy-two-year-old retired high school English teacher, with a Glock pistol. According to police, Ericsson's motive was a fifty-year grudge he held against Johnson, a high school classmate. Ericsson allegedly knocked on Johnson's door, shot him twice in the face, and walked away, leaving the victim's wife to find the body in the doorway.[31]

February 9, 2012—Portland, Oregon. The families of two women shot to death by an off-duty Clackamas County sheriff's sergeant filed an $8 million wrongful-death lawsuit, claiming that county authorities knew the officer was dangerously unstable and should have intervened. On Feb. 12, 2010, Sergeant Jeffrey A. Grahn confronted his estranged wife, Charlotte, and two of her friends, Victoria Schulmerich and Kathleen Hoffmeister, at the M&M Restaurant & Lounge in Gresham. After arguing with Charlotte Grahn, he grabbed her by her hair, pulled her outside, and shot her in the head with a Glock 40 caliber pistol. He returned to the bar and killed Schulmerich and Hoffmeister with shots to the head. He then went back outside and killed himself.[32]

February 22, 2012—Memphis, Tennessee. Chester Wrushen, thirty-three, and Jamiel Carpenter, thirty-two, admitted to police that they exchanged gunfire in Wrushen's front yard, but each claimed the other fired first. Carpenter's twelve-year-old son was in the car with him, along with a shotgun and a 40 caliber Glock pistol. Both men were arrested and charged with aggravated assault and reckless endangerment.[33]

February 24, 2012—New Haven, Connecticut. The city's Shooting Task Force arrested Gary Williams, twenty-four, who was wanted in a December 17, 2011, shooting in which two men were wounded. Police seized a 40 caliber Glock pistol and a Stag Arms assault rifle from Williams's home. Several 40 caliber shell casings were recovered at the scene of the December shooting.[34]

March 17, 2012—St. Petersburg, Florida. A nine-year-old boy shot his sixteen-year-old cousin in the hand and neck with a 45 caliber Glock pistol he found in the home. The elder child survived the wounds. Police also found an AK-47 assault rifle and an AR-15 assault rifle in the home. The guns, legally owned, were kept under the bed of the injured boy's father.[35]

March 20, 2012—Stamford, Connecticut. A fifty-seven-year-old woman narrowly escaped injury when a bullet fired during a shootout on the street penetrated her apartment. Investigators found a bullet, which had blasted through her air-conditioner frame, under a sheet in her bed. One of the three guns used in the fracas, a 45 caliber Glock, was found in a nearby Dumpster.[36]

April 2, 2012—Petaluma, California. Proceedings began in the first-degree murder trial of Kenneth Doyle Mullennix, fifty-one, charged with firing a single shot from a Glock pistol into the right eye of his wife, Buapha Mullennix, thirty-seven, during an argument in the bedroom of their home in January 2010. Mullennix admitted he shot his wife, with whom he was angry because of an affair she was having. But he claimed she threatened him with the gun, and although he has no specific recollection of shooting her, he contends that the gun must have gone off during a struggle. He was also charged with illegal possession of an SKS semiautomatic assault rifle.[37]

April 9, 2012—Washington, Indiana. Derek Franklin Williams, forty-nine, was sentenced to sixty-five years in prison for the murder of his wife, Kim, on February 4, 2011. Williams shot his wife twice in the head with a 40 caliber Glock pistol, then shot himself under the chin. He survived the injury. The couple's two children were in the home at the time of the shooting.[38]

Apr. 12, 2012—Erie, Pennsylvania. Rachel A. Kozloff, thirty, allegedly shot to death Michael Henry, thirty, with a 9mm Glock pistol she had recently bought. Henry died in his apartment of two gunshot wounds to the torso. Four shell casings were found in the apartment.[39]

April 24, 2012—Port Arthur, Texas. A three-year-old boy was shot by his twenty-two-month-old brother with the family's 9mm Glock pistol in front of their home. The gun had been left on the front seat of the family's truck, and the two children were playing in the front yard.[40]

April 24, 2012—Pompano Beach, Florida. Kenneth Konias Jr., a fugitive, was arrested and surrendered to federal agents the Glock pistol with which he allegedly shot to death his fellow armored-car guard in Pittsburgh, Pennsylvania, on February 28, 2012. Konias had absconded with $2.3 million from the truck.[41]

April 25, 2012—Largo, Florida. James Wolski, thirty-five,

shot to death his forty-year-old wife, Stacie, with a 40 caliber Glock Model 27 in the parking lot of a Walgreens pharmacy, then committed suicide with the gun. The couple left a four-year-old daughter.[42]

April 25, 2012—Milford, New Hampshire. Nathan O'Brien, twenty-three, was arrested and charged with several firearms-related offenses after he allegedly fired a Glock 9mm Model 19 pistol during an altercation with another man, who was not injured.[43]

April 27, 2012—Atlantic City, New Jersey. After police observed nineteen-year-old Khalil Blackwell smoking pot on the steps of a home, they investigated and found two other teenagers and three handguns in the premises, including a 45 caliber Glock pistol. Blackwell was cited for marijuana possession, and the two other teens were charged with illegal gun possession.[44]

NOTES

Introduction: A Reign of Terror

1. David B. Muhlhausen, PhD, and Jena Baker McNeill, *Terror Trends: 40 Years' Data on International and Domestic Terrorism* (Washington, DC: Heritage Foundation, 2011), 1, 9, chart 7. The report states, "The data used in this descriptive analysis by The Heritage Foundation stem from the RAND Database of World-wide Terrorism Incidents (RDWTI). The version of the RDWTI used in this analysis contains information on nearly 38,700 terrorist incidents from across the globe between February 1968 and January 2010" (2).

2. Only one or two terrorist incident databases go back as far as the RAND database, much less back to earlier dates. It is clear from the few that do go back farther, however, that there were relatively few terrorist attacks aimed at the United States before 1969, and the number of Americans killed in those terrorist attacks was a comparative handful. The total would not significantly alter these proportions. See, e.g., Centre for Defence and International Security Studies, "The CDISS Database: Terrorist Incidents 1945 to 2004," www.timripley.co.uk/terrorism; and Infoplease .com, "Terrorist Attacks in the U.S. or Against Americans," www.infoplease.com/ipa/A0001454.html.

3. U.S. Department of State, "Terrorism Deaths, Injuries, Kidnappings of Private U.S. Citizens, 2010," in *Country Reports on Terrorism 2010* (Washington, DC: U.S. Department of State, 2011), 252.

4. U.S. Department of Justice, Federal Bureau of Investigation, "Law Enforcement Officers Feloniously Killed: Type of Weapon, 2001–2010," Table 27 in *Law Enforcement Officers Killed and Assaulted 2010*, www.fbi.gov/about-us/cjis/ucr/leoka/leoka-2010/tables/table27-leok-feloniously-type-of-weapon-01-10.xls.

5. Amy Belasco, *The Cost of Iraq, Afghanistan, and Other Global War on Terror Operations Since 9/11* (Washington, DC: Congressional Research Service, 2011), Summary.

6. John Mueller and Mark G. Stewart, "Does the United States Spend Too Much on Homeland Security?" *Slate*, Sept. 7, 2011, www.slate.com/articles/news_and_politics/politics/2011/09/does_the_united_states_spend_too_much_on_homeland_security.single.html.

7. John Mueller and Mark G. Stewart, *Terror, Security and Money: Balancing the Risks, Benefits, and Costs of Homeland Security* (New York: Oxford University Press, 2011), p. 172.

8. Lisa Riordan Seville, "How Much Is Security Worth?," *Crime Report*, Jan. 23, 2012, www.thecrimereport.org/news/inside-criminal-justice/2012-01-homeland-security-qa.

9. "Perpetual Security State: Post-9/11 Special Powers, Budgets, Agencies Seen Needed Far into Future," *Washington Times*, Sept. 9, 2011 ("When asked last month if the U.S. government could relinquish some of the extraordinary powers or shrink some of the budgets and bureaucracies created to protect Americans since 9/11, Homeland Security Secretary Janet Napolitano gave a one-word response: 'No.'").

10. U.S. Department of Homeland Security, "Secretary Napolitano Announces Fiscal Year 2013 Budget Request," news release, Feb. 13, 2012; U.S. Department of Homeland Security, Overview, Fiscal Year 2010 Budget Request (undated); *The Homeland Security Department's Budget Submission for Fiscal Year 2011, Hearing Before the Committee on Homeland Security and Government Affairs*, 111th Cong. 39ff (2010) (Hon. Janet Napolitano, Secretary, U.S. Department of Homeland Security, "Statement for the Record").

11. Centers for Disease Control and Prevention, "Budget Request Overviews" for FY2012 and FY2013, undated.

12. For a summary of issues the so-called "war on terrorism" has raised, see "The Full Cost of 9/11," *Congressional Quarterly Weekly*, Sept. 3, 2011.

13. Adam Liptak, "Civil Liberties Today," *New York Times*, Sept. 7, 2011.

14. "Remarks by U.S. Attorney General John Ashcroft to the Council on Foreign Relations," Federal News Service, Feb. 10, 2003.

15. The narrative of Airman Santos's actions on November 21 is based on these sources, unless otherwise noted: 50th Space Wing Public Affairs Office, "Officials ID Barricaded Member," news release, Nov. 22, 2011, www.schriever.af.mil/news/story.asp?id=123280946; "Airman in Schriever Standoff Pleaded Guilty to Sex Crime," *Colorado Springs Gazette*, Nov. 22, 2011; "Air Force Investigates Gun After Standoff on Base," Associated Press Online, Nov. 22, 2011; "Gunman at Colorado Air Base Surrenders," Associated Press Online, Nov. 22, 2011.

16. U.S. Air Force, "50th Space Wing," fact sheet, www.schriever.af.mil/library/factsheets/factsheet.asp?id=3909 (accessed Mar. 8, 2012).

17. U.S. Air Force, "50th Security Forces Squadron," fact sheet, www.schriever.af.mil/library/factsheets/factsheet.asp?id=3926 (accessed Nov. 24, 2011).

18. "Airman in Schriever Standoff Pleaded Guilty to Sex Crime." For the particulars of Santos's offense, see "Warrantless Arrest Affidavit" for defendant Nico Cruz Santos, Gilpen County (CO) Sheriff's Office, Case No. 10CR668, Dec. 8, 2010.

19. "Rampage Was the 'Worst Horror Movie,'" *Dallas Morning News*, Nov. 14, 2010. Eleven additional personnel were "injured" in the resulting turmoil, as opposed to having been "wounded" by gunshot. See: U.S. Department of Defense, *Protecting the Force: Lessons from Fort Hood*, Report of the DoD Independent Review (Washington, DC: 2010), 1.

20. U.S. House of Representatives, Committee on Armed Services, *Legislative Text and Joint Explanatory Statement, Public Law 111–383*, Dec. 2010.

21. "Pentagon vs. NRA: Will Gun-Rights Law Raise Risk of Soldier Suicides?" *Christian Science Monitor*, Nov. 4, 2011.

22. Joseph I. Lieberman and Susan M. Collins, *A Ticking Time Bomb: Counterterrorism Lessons from the U.S. Government's Failure to Prevent the Fort Hood Attack: A Special Report* (Washington, DC: U.S. Senate Committee on Homeland Security and Governmental Affairs, 2011), 7.

23. For media examples of these concerns, see "Senate Committee Subpoenas Fort Hood Documents," Associated Press, Apr. 19, 2010; and "Pentagon Report on Fort Hood Details Failures," *New York Times*, Jan. 16, 2010.

24. Although Major Hasan also carried a revolver that day, investigators found that he did not fire it. "Police Recall a Torrent of Bullets," *Austin American-Statesman*, Oct. 21, 2010.

25. Lieberman and Collins, *Ticking Time Bomb*, 15.

26. Ibid., 7.

27. Chairman Joseph I. Lieberman, "Opening Statement," Hearing of the Homeland Security and Governmental Affairs Committee, "Terrorists and Guns: The Nature of the Threat and Proposed Reforms," May 5, 2010.

28. Unless otherwise noted, the details of Major Hasan's purchase and use of his personal handgun are based on the following sources: "Rampage Was 'the Worst Horror Movie' "; "Witness: Man Asked About Gun Capacities," *Austin American-Statesman*, Oct. 22, 2010; "Ft. Hood Suspect Sought Best Gun, Salesman Says," *Los Angeles Times*, Oct. 22, 2010; "Witness: Killer Sought 'High-Tech' Handgun," *Dallas Morning News*, Oct. 22, 2010; "Police Recall a Torrent of Bullets"; "Nurses Recall Carnage at Post," *San Antonio Express-News*, Oct. 20, 2010; "Soldiers Describe Deadly Day," *Dallas Morning News*, Oct. 16, 2010; "Lawyer: Fort Hood Suspect Is Paralyzed," *Virginian-Pilot*, Nov. 23, 2009.

29. "Witness: Man Asked About Gun Capacities."

30. "Ft. Hood Suspect Sought Best Gun, Salesman Says."

31. FN Herstal, "Five-seveN®," www.fnherstal.com/index.php?id=269&back PID=263&productID=66&pid_product=295&pidList=263&categorySelector=5& detail.

32. Ibid.

33. "Ft. Hood Suspect Sought Best Gun, Salesman Says."

34. FN Herstal, "Five-seveN®."

35. "Nurses Recall Carnage at Post."

36. "Soldiers Describe Deadly Day."

37. For a more complete list and greater detail, see Violence Policy Center, "Mass Shootings in the United States Involving High-Capacity Ammunition Magazines," fact sheet, Jan. 2011, www.vpc.org/fact_sht/VPCshootinglist.pdf.

38. U.S. Department of Defense, *Protecting the Force*.

39. Ibid., appendix C, "Summary of Findings and Recommendations," Finding 3.8 and Recommendation 3.8, p. C-7.

40. Office of the Assistant Secretary of Defense (Public Affairs), U.S. Department of Defense, "Interim Fort Hood Recommendations Approved," news release, Apr. 15, 2010.

41. U.S. Secretary of Defense, "Interim Recommendations of the Ft. Hood Follow-on Review," memorandum, Apr. 12, 2010, attachment.

42. "In Defense Spending Bill, a Map Around Congressional Gridlock," *Washington Post*, Jan. 4, 2011.

43 U.S. Secretary of Defense, "Interim Recommendations of the Ft. Hood Follow-on Review."

44. For an exposition of the relationship between the gun industry and the NRA, see Violence Policy Center, *Blood Money: How the Gun Industry Bankrolls the NRA* (Washington, DC: Violence Policy Center, 2011), www.vpc.org/studies/bloodmoney .pdf.

45. For the bill's text, see www.opencongress.org/bill/111-s3388/text.

46. Office of Senator James M. Inhofe, "Inhofe Introduces Gun Bill to Protect Second Amendment Rights of Soldiers, Employees of Department of Defense," news release, May 20, 2010.

47. U.S. House of Representatives, Committee on Armed Services, *Legislative Text and Joint Explanatory Statement, Public Law 111–383*, Dec. 2010, 476.

48. Chris W. Cox, NRA-ILA Executive Director, "Political Report," undated, www .nrapublications.org/index.php/8685/political-report-2.

49. For a detailed discussion of the history and consequence of this trend, see Violence Policy Center, *The Militarization of the U.S. Civilian Firearms Market* (Washington, DC: Violence Policy Center, 2011), www.vpc.org/studies/militarization.pdf.

50. Allan M. Brandt, *The Cigarette Century: The Rise, Fall, and Deadly Persistence of the Product That Defined America* (New York: Basic Books, 2007), 11.

51. Richard Kluger, *Ashes to Ashes: America's Hundred-Year Cigarette War, the Public Health, and the Unabashed Triumph of Philip Morris* (New York: Vintage Books, 1997), 657–58.

52. Brandt, *Cigarette Century*, 440.

53. 15 U.S.C. Sections 7901–3.

54. For a more detailed discussion of the Tiahrt amendments, see Violence Policy Center, *Indicted: Types of Firearms and Methods of Gun Trafficking from the United States to Mexico as Revealed in U.S. Court Documents* (Washington, DC: Violence Policy Center, 2009), 4, www.vpc.org/studies/indicted.pdf.

55. *Terrorists and Guns: The Nature of the Threat and Proposed Reforms, Before the Committee on Homeland Security and Governmental Affairs*, 111th Cong. (May 5, 2010) (statement of Senator Susan M. Collins).

56. Brian Friel, "A New Third Rail," *National Journal*, May 29, 2010.

57. "Issue of Gun Rights Still Holds Sway," *New York Times*, Mar. 15, 2009.

58. "Gun Control Efforts Going Nowhere," *Pittsburgh Post-Gazette*, Apr. 9, 2009.

1. Our Daily Dead: Gun Death and Injury in the United States

1. "Copley Shooter Bought Gun Five Days Before Killing Spree," *Akron Beacon Journal*, Aug. 10, 2011; "Autopsy Notes Hint at Fury with Which Gunman Fired," *Cleveland Plain Dealer*, Aug. 11, 2011.

2. According to the township's website, 13,641 people live in Copley, of whom 86.4 percent are white. The median household income is about $55,000, and only 3.3 percent of the families live below the poverty level. Copley Township,

"Demographics," www.copley.oh.us/about-copley/about-copley/demographics
.html.

3. Kathleen Folkerth, "Police Release Final Report on Copley Shooting," *West Side Leader*, Oct. 13, 2011, http://akron.com/akron-ohio-community-news.asp?aID =13790.

4. Sherri Bevan Walsh, Summit County Prosecuting Attorney, to Chief Michael Mier, Copley Police Department, "Investigation into the Use of Force Involving the Death of Michael Hance," Sept. 20, 2011.

5. Like virtually all U.S. police departments, the Akron Police Department uses a system of numbered codes in radio communications. These are not always uniform. In Akron, a "Code 43" signals a "disturbed person (mental case)." See "Radio Codes and Signals—Ohio," www.bearcat1.com/radiooh.htm.

6. Folkerth, "Police Release Final Report on Copley Shooting"; "Copley Shooter Bought Gun Five Days Before Killing Spree."

7. Marilyn Miller, "Copley Welcomes Back Students Today; Shooting Investigation Continues," *Akron Beacon Journal*, Aug. 25, 2011, www.ohio.com/news/local/copley-welcomes-back-students-today-shooting-investigation-continues-1.231495; "Copley Shooter Bought Gun Five Days Before Killing Spree," *Akron Beacon Journal*, Aug. 10, 2011.

8. Walsh, "Investigation into the Use of Force Involving the Death of Michael Hance." Walsh's letter does not specify what type of "re-loaders" Hance used. There are two kinds of devices used to quickly reload handguns. The "speed-loader" is used to reload all of the chambers of a revolver cylinder at once. Hance could have used this type for his .357 Magnum revolver. A semiautomatic pistol's magazine holds the gun's ammunition, and can be quickly ejected and replaced. Hance could have used this type for his .45 pistol. Walsh's cryptic statement could describe either or both types. For examples of both, see "Magazines & Clips," Cabela's, www.cabelas.com/magazines.shtml.

9. "Police Say Ohio Gunman Practiced at Firing Range," Associated Press State & Local Wire, Aug. 20, 2011.

10. See "Handguns," Hi-Point Firearms, www.hi-pointfirearms.com/handguns/handgun_main.html.

11. "Seal Beach Salon to Reopen After Shooting Spree," Associated Press State & Local Wire, Feb. 3, 2012 ("The wife of a slain salon owner says she plans to reopen the Seal Beach salon where a gunman went on a shooting spree that killed eight people").

12. "Giffords to Attend Vigil Marking One Year Since Shooting Rampage," CNN Wire, Jan. 8, 2012 ("Rep. Gabrielle Giffords will attend events Sunday in Arizona to mark the anniversary of a shooting rampage that left six people dead and the congresswoman with a gunshot wound to the head").

13. "Texas Mass Shooting Strikes Chord in Covina," *San Gabriel Valley Tribune*, Dec. 27, 2011.

14. "IHOP Shooting: Will Police Ever Understand Gunman's Motive?" *Christian Science Monitor*, Sept. 7, 2011 ("As police in Carson City, Nev., seek a motive in the IHOP shooting Tuesday, criminologists say thorough investigations can often turn up the reasons behind mass killings").

15. "Service Seeks Community Healing: 200 Gather to Discuss Mass Murder, Aftermath," *Grand Rapids Press*, July 14, 2011 ("It was the worst mass murder the area has ever seen").

16. For a sardonic editorial comment describing this ritual, see Josh Sugarmann, "Yet Another Mass Shooting," *Washington Post*, Apr. 19, 2009.

17. For example, "Breaking News: Five Dead in Yuma, Arizona, School Shooting," Canwest News Service, June 2, 2011 ("Yuma police say five people have been killed in a shooting that has forced authorities to close schools and the courthouse"). This was actually a case of murder-suicide, not a school shooting. The shooter killed his ex-wife, her lawyer, and three of her friends; wounded another of her friends; and then shot himself to death. "Friend Says Ex-Wife Described Dyess as Controlling, Violent," *Yuma Sun*, June 9, 2011. Another example: "Breaking News: Mass Shooting on Fort Hood, Texas; 7 Dead, 30 Wounded," *Arkansas Tonight*, Nov. 5, 2009 ("At least two shooters have opened fire on Fort Hood near Waco, Texas, leaving seven individuals dead and 30 wounded, Sen. Kay Bailey Hutchison tells MSNBC, citing a general she had spoken with on the post"). There was only one shooter. He was U.S. Army Major Nidal M. Hasan, who shot thirteen victims to death and wounded thirty-two others. "Rampage Was 'the Worst Horror Movie,'" *Dallas Morning News*, Nov. 14, 2010.

18. "32 Dead in Virginia Tech Shootings," *CNN Newsroom*, Apr. 16, 2007.

19. "One Killed, Gunman Apprehended in Florida Shooting: Officials," Agence France-Presse, Nov. 6, 2009.

20. "Atlanta Mayor Back in Front of Spotlight as Shooting Crisis Unfolds," Associated Press State & Local Wire, July 29, 1999.

21. "32 Dead in Virginia Tech Shootings."

22. Ibid.

23. See NRA Political Victory Fund, "NRA-PVF Endorses Randy Forbes for U.S. House of Representatives in Virginia's 4th Congressional District," Oct. 1, 2010, www .nrapvf.org/news-alerts/2010/10/nra-pvf-endorses-randy-forbes-for-us-house-of -representatives-in-virginia%E2%80%99s-4th-congressional-district.aspx.

24. "14 Dead in New York Shooting Rampage," *Campbell Brown: No Bias, No Bull*, CNN, Apr. 3, 2009.

25. "Copley Gunman Hunted Down His Victims, Including Boy, 11," *Cleveland Plain Dealer*, Aug. 9, 2011.

26. "Friend Says Ex-Wife Described Dyess as Controlling, Violent," *Yuma Sun*, June 9, 2011.

27. "Fighter Pilot Murder Mystery; Did Elite Navy Pilot Snap?" *Good Morning America*, ABC, Jan. 5, 2012.

28. "Shooter Targets Former Employer in Orlando Building," *Issues with Jane Velez-Mitchell*, CNN, Nov. 6, 2009.

29. See "Staff Clinical Director," Center for Health Sex, http://centerforhealthy sex.com/about/staff-clinical-director.

30. "Shooter Targets Former Employer in Orlando Building."

31. See "Battle over Anna Nicole Smith's Body," *CNN Newsroom*, CNN, Feb. 23, 2007; "Obama Assassination Threat Plot [*sic*] of Bigger Problem?" *Issues with Jane Velez-Mitchell*, CNN, Oct. 28, 2008; "Remains Found Near Missing Girl's Home,"

Issues with Jane Velez-Mitchell, CNN, Dec. 11, 2008; and "New Jobs Reports Coming," *American Morning*, CNN, Sept. 4, 2009.

32. "Virginia Tech Campus Massacre; The Second Gun; Hospital News Conference on Condition of Virginia Tech Survivors," *CNN Newsroom*, CNN, Apr. 18, 2007.

33. See, e.g., "Cupertino Quarry Massacre 911 Tapes: 'There Are People Dying Right Now. My Supervisor Is Dying,'" *San Jose Mercury News*, Oct. 20, 2011 ("Breathless, the man pleaded with an emergency dispatcher 'Please, please help. They're going to die'"); "911 Tapes from Nev. Shooting Reveal Frantic Scene," Associated Press State & Local Wire, Sept. 7, 2011 ("Dozens of 911 calls made from in and around a Nevada IHOP where a deadly shooting rampage took place detail a frantic scene"); "911 Tapes Released of Calls Made During Shooting Rampage at a Connecticut Beer Distribution Plant Tuesday," NBC News Transcripts, Aug. 5, 2010 (Matt Lauer, co-host: "We're now hearing the chilling 911 calls placed on Tuesday from inside that Connecticut beer distributor where a man went on a shooting spree, killing eight co-workers and then himself").

34. "Shrines Pop Up Across City in Colorful Displays of Caring," *Arizona Daily Star*, Jan. 19, 2011 ("At four impromptu shrines around the Old Pueblo, a mourning community comes bearing flowers, balloons, stuffed animals and votive candles"); "Tape Points Finger in Mass Shooting," Associated Press State & Local Wire, June 11, 2007 ("A makeshift shrine of teddy bears, stuffed bunnies, a dinosaur and candles stood under a tree outside the shooting scene Monday").

35. "14 Dead in New York Shooting Rampage" (pro-gun stalwart Representative J. Randy Forbes of Virginia told CNN after the Virginia Tech massacre that "Virginia is a large family. And you know, we reach out and put our arms around the students that are there, the victims and their families"); "32 Dead in Virginia Tech Shootings."

36. "Texas Mass Shooting Strikes Chord in Covina," *San Gabriel Valley Tribune*, Dec. 27, 2011 (Christmastime mass shootings at homes in Grapevine, Texas, in 2011 and in Covina, California, in 2008); "Thanksgiving Massacre Victim out of Coma: Patrick Knight Was Told That His Wife, Unborn Child Died in Jupiter Attack," *South Florida Sun-Sentinel*, Mar. 10, 2010; "Investigators Confirm Killer ID; Murder-Suicide: Tests Show the Teenage Boy Pulled the Trigger. The Families Had Gathered for a Barbecue," *Riverside (CA) Press Enterprise*, Apr. 1, 2008 (murder of four family members and friends; teenage shooter committed suicide).

37. "Terror in Littleton: The Overview; 15 Bodies Are Removed from School in Colorado," *New York Times*, Apr. 22, 1999 (Columbine High School massacre); "Death Toll 11 Students, 1 Teacher in Nation's recent school shootings," *Arkansas Democrat-Gazette*, Aug. 12, 1998 (survey of school shootings in United States).

38. "Texas Church Shooting Leaves 8 Dead, 7 Hurt; Pipe Bomb Also Used in Ft. Worth Incident; Gunman Kills Himself," *Baltimore Sun*, Sept. 16, 1999.

39. "Amid Mourning, Eerie Details Emerge About Connecticut Shootings: Man Who Killed 8 Went to Work Well Armed," *New York Times*, Aug. 5, 2010 (eight shot to death and shooter committed suicide at Connecticut beer wholesaler).

40. "Recent Violence Puts Stores on Alert: Retailers Prepare for How to React," *USA Today*, Apr. 15, 2011; "Gunman at an Omaha Mall Kills 8 and Himself," *New York Times*, Dec. 6, 2007.

41. "Nurses Recall Carnage at Post," *San Antonio Express-News*, Oct. 20, 2010 (Fort Hood massacre).

42. Dahlia Lithwick, "The Cruelest Month," *Slate*, Apr. 15, 2009.

43. See Violence Policy Center, "Gun Violence," www.vpc.org/gunviolence.htm.

44. "Households by Number of Motor Vehicles: 2010," Research and Innovative Technology Administration, Bureau of Transportation Statistics.

45. For a detailed history of gun ownership in the United States as reported by the General Social Survey conducted by the National Opinion Research Center at the University of Chicago, see Violence Policy Center, *A Shrinking Minority: The Continuing Decline of Gun Ownership in America* (Washington, DC: Violence Policy Center, 2011), www.vpc.org/studies/ownership.pdf.

46. See Violence Policy Center, "Gun Deaths Outpace Motor Vehicle Deaths in 10 States in 2009," May 2012, www.vpc.org/studies/gunsvscars.pdf.

47. Philip J. Cook and Jens Ludwig, "Fact-Free Gun Policy?" *University of Pennsylvania Law Review* 151, no. 4. (Apr. 2003): 1329–40.

48. Matthew Parker, *Panama Fever: The Epic Story of the Building of the Panama Canal*, Kindle ed. (New York: Vintage, 2009), loc. 4759–63.

49. Ibid., loc. 4807–15.

50. See National Shooting Sports Foundation, "About the National Shooting Sports Foundation," www.nssf.org/industry/aboutNSSF.cfm.

51. "The Gun Lobby's Hunting Safety Assessment: Chance of Death Not Included," Media Matters for America, Dec. 6, 2011, http://mediamatters.org/blog/201112060033.

52. See National Shooting Sports Foundation (NSSF), "Modern Sporting Rifle," http://nssf.org/MSR. See also the NSSF YouTube video "The Modern Sporting Rifle," www.youtube.com/watch?v=VbDQUADaIkE.

53. See, e.g., "Traditional Ammunition Campaign," in *A Building Block to History: NSSF 2010*, (Newtown, CT: National Shooting Sports Foundation, 2010), 15; Larry Keane, "Senator Introduces Bill to Protect Traditional Ammunition," National Shooting Sports Foundation blog, Sept. 28, 2010, www.nssfblog.com/senator-introduces-bill-to-protect-traditional-ammunition; and Larry Keane, "EPA Denies Petition to Ban Traditional Ammunition," NSSF blog, Aug. 28, 2010, www.nssfblog.com/epa-denies-petition-to-ban-traditional-ammunition.

54. "State Closes Gouldsboro Gun Range Where Terrorists Trained," *Pocono Record*, May 11, 2010; "6 Men Arrested in a Terror Plot Against Ft. Dix," *New York Times*, May 9, 2007 (plotters of terrorist attack on Fort Dix, NJ, trained at PA gun range); "Security Questions at Shooting Ranges," *New York Times*, Oct. 5, 2003 (members of group that became al Qaeda practiced at New York shooting range).

55. "Police Say Ohio Gunman Practiced at Firing Range," Associated Press State & Local Wire, Aug. 20, 2011; "Ft. Hood Suspect Sought Best Gun, Salesman Says," *Los Angeles Times*, Oct. 22, 2010; "Sirhan's Notes Go Up for Sale: Papers Suggest the Assassin Carefully Calculated His Plan to Kill Robert Kennedy," *Los Angeles Times*, Apr. 8, 2011 (Sirhan Sirhan practiced at shooting range night before he assassinated Senator Robert F. Kennedy); "LAX Shooter Motivated by Personal Woes, Probe Finds," *Los*

Angeles Times, Sept. 5, 2002 (man who shot two to death at El Al counter practiced at shooting range).

56. "Beginning the Next 50 Years: NSSF Remains Dedicated to Ranges and the Shooting Sports," National Shooting Sports Foundation, *Range Report*, Winter 2012, 26.

57. Stephen L. Sanetti, *The National Shooting Sports Foundation: A History 1961 to 2011* (Newtown, CT: National Shooting Sports Foundation, 2011), 7.

58. " 'Ricochet' Goes Behind Scenes of Gun Lobby," National Public Radio, Nov. 15, 2007.

59. Ibid.

60. "Wayne LaPierre Said That Violent Crime in Jurisdictions That Recognize the 'Right to Carry' Is Lower Than in Areas That Prevent It," *St. Petersburg Times*, Feb. 16, 2011.

61. This excerpt is from the NRA's online version of "Obama's Secret Plan to Destroy the Second Amendment by 2016," *America's 1st Freedom*, www.nrapublications .org/index.php/11920/obamas-secret-plan-to-destroy-the-second-amendment-by -2016. A longer and slightly different version appears as the cover story in the February 2012 print edition of *America's 1st Freedom*. The italicized emphasis is in the original.

62. "NRA's Ad Exaggerates Intent of Obama Vote," *Cleveland Plain Dealer*, Oct. 30, 2008 (NRA "ad is misleading because it stretches the truth"); "National Rifle Association Endorses McCain," Associated Press Online, Oct. 9, 2008; "State Target of Gun Lobbyists: Union Claims NRA Tried to Persuade Miners to Criticize Obama During a Filming Last Week," *Charleston Daily Mail*, Sept. 24, 2008 (NRA "announced it is spending $15 million to campaign against Obama." Union leaders say "NRA representatives tried to mislead miners about Sen. Barack Obama's stance on guns and tricked them into criticizing the Illinois senator on camera.").

63. "Focused NRA a Force in U.S. Politics," *Washington Post*, Dec. 15, 2010.

64. Chris W. Cox, NRA-ILA executive director, "Gun Owners Score Wins in Spending Bill," *Political Report*, Jan. 23, 2012, www.nrapublications.org/index.php/ 12330/political-report-22, also published in the February 2012 print edition of the NRA's magazine, *America's 1st Freedom*.

65. "Form Won't Deter Drug Cartels," *USA Today*, Aug. 9, 2011.

66. "Why do you look at the speck of sawdust in your brother's eye and pay no attention to the plank in your own eye? How can you say to your brother, 'Let me take the speck out of your eye,' when all the time there is a plank in your own eye? You hypocrite, first take the plank out of your own eye, and then you will see clearly to remove the speck from your brother's eye." Matthew 7:3–5, The Holy Bible, New International Version, 1984, http://niv.scripturetext.com/matthew/7.htm.

67. Massachusetts Historical Society, "Adams Quotations," www.masshist.org/ adams/quotes.cfm.

68. E.G. Krug et al., "Firearm-Related Deaths in the United States and 35 Other High- and Upper-Middle-Income Countries," *International Journal of Epidemiology* 27 (1998): 214, 218–19.

69. E.G. Richardson and David Hemenway, "Homicide, Suicide, and Unintentional Firearm Fatality: Comparing the United States with Other High-Income Countries, 2003," *Journal of Trauma, Injury, Infection, and Critical Care* 70, no. 1 (Jan. 2011): 238, 241.

70. David Hemenway, *Private Guns, Public Health* (Ann Arbor: University of Michigan Press, 2006), 1.

71. "Army Releases ID of Ariz. Soldier Who Died on Base," Associated Press State & Local Wire, Aug. 4, 2011.

72. Clynton Namuo, "Driver Shoots Self After Head-on Crash," *New Hampshire Union-Leader*, Aug. 3, 2011, www.unionleader.com/article/20110803/NEWS07/708 039962; "Police: Lee Crash May Have Been Suicide Attempt," Associated Press State & Local Wire, Aug. 4, 2011.

73. Matt Johnson, "Satterlee Was 'On a Mission' When He Murdered Wife, Committed Suicide," *Vernon County Broadcaster*, Aug. 3, 2011, http://lacrossetribune.com/vernonbroadcaster/news/local/article_12a4aee0-be23-11e0-a3ab-001cc4c03286.html; "Sheriff's Deputy Was Told of Murder-Suicide Plan," *Wisconsin State Journal*, Aug. 4, 2011.

74. "Md. Mom Who Killed Son Agonized over School Costs," Associated Press, Aug. 8, 2011; "Md. Doctor Kills Son, Self," *Washington Post*, Aug. 4, 2011.

75. See Violence Policy Center, "Gun Violence," www.vpc.org/gunviolence.htm.

76. Anne Leland and Mari-Jana "M-J" Oboroceanu, "U.S. Active Duty Military Deaths, 1980 Through 2008, Part II, Cause of Death," Table 5 in *American War and Military Operations Casualties: Lists and Statistics* (Washington, DC: Congressional Research Service, 2010), 8.

77. "Pentagon vs. NRA: Will Gun-Rights Law Raise Risk of Soldier Suicides?" *Christian Science Monitor*, Nov. 4, 2011.

78. Matthew Miller and David Hemenway, "Guns and Suicide in the United States," *New England Journal of Medicine*, Sept. 4, 2008, 990.

79. Elspeth Cameron Ritchie, "The Third Rail: Guns and Suicide in the Army," Battleland blog, *Time*, June 15, 2011, http://battleland.blogs.time.com/2011/06/15/the-third-rail-guns-and-suicide-in-the-army/#ixzz1fOXOemVJ.

80. Dr. Margaret C. Harrell and Nancy Berglass, *Losing the Battle: The Challenge of Military Suicide* (Washington, DC: Center for a New American Security, 2011), 6.

81. Ritchie, "Third Rail."

82. Data on gun deaths and injuries in this report is from the WISQARS database of the U.S. Centers for Disease Control and Prevention, National Center for Injury Prevention and Control.

83. While injury estimates for the years 2009 (66,769) and 2010 (73,505) are available, it is impossible to assess the significance of this information without complete gun death data. Unfortunately, there is usually a two- to three-year lag on the release of firearm-related fatality numbers, and therefore 2008 was the latest year for which complete data was available at time of analysis.

84. Leland and Oboroceanu, "U.S. Active Duty Military Deaths, 1980 Through 2008, Part I, Total Military Personnel," Table 4 in *American War and Military Operations Casualties*, 7.

85. Leland and Oboroceanu, "U.S. Active Duty Military Deaths, 1980 Through 2008, Part II, Cause of Death," 8.

86. Anthony R. Harris et al., "Murder and Medicine: The Lethality of Criminal Assault 1960–1999," *Homicide Studies* 6, no. 2 (May 2002): 128–66, 130.

87. "Medical Advances Help Keep Murder Rate Down," *Dayton Daily News*, Apr. 24, 2011.

88. "Survival Soars for Victims of Violence: Rapid Transport, New Technology and Advances in Surgical Protocol Have Helped More Survive," *Birmingham News*, May 25, 2008.

89. "Survival Rate Up for Gun Victims: Doctor's Report Is a Mixed Bag," *Boston Globe*, May 18, 2006.

90. Federico C. Vinas, "Penetrating Head Trauma," *Medscape Reference—Drugs, Diseases & Procedures*, http://emedicine.medscape.com/article/247664-overview.

91. National Spinal Cord Injury Statistical Center, "Spinal Cord Injury Facts and Figures at a Glance, February 2011," www.nscisc.uab.edu.

92. For a detailed discussion of this trend, see Violence Policy Center, *The Militarization of the U.S. Civilian Firearms Market* (Washington, DC: Violence Policy Center, 2011), www.vpc.org/studies/militarization.pdf.

93. "Critical Care: Shock Trauma Confuses Data on Killing Rate," *Washington Times*, May 11, 2003.

94. Harris et al., "Murder and Medicine," 157.

2. Supreme Nonsense and Deadly Myths

1. The day before, Wesley Neal Higdon, a twenty-five-year-old press-machine operator at a plastics plant in Henderson, Kentucky, went on a rampage with a 45 caliber handgun, shot five co-workers to death, seriously wounded another, and then committed suicide with his gun. "Angry Worker Kills 5, Himself in Henderson," *Louisville Courier-Journal*, June 26, 2008.

2. "Radio Missing, Man Shoots into the Air," *Corpus Christi Caller-Times*, June 27, 2008.

3. "2 Slain in City; Boy Killed by Car," *Cleveland Plain Dealer*, June 28, 2008.

4. "Violence Between Repo Men, Car Owners on the Rise," *Birmingham Times*, Mar. 5, 2009; "Man Shot Dead in Fracas over Repossessed Car," Associated Press State & Local Wire, June 27, 2008.

5. "Police: Shootings a Result of Suicide Attempt," *Muskegon Chronicle*, June 27, 2008.

6. "Elgin Man Formally Charged in Shooting," *Chicago Daily Herald*, June 29, 2008.

7. "Teen Accidentally Shoots Friend in the Arm," *Tampa Tribune*, June 27, 2008.

8. "Daughter was Abuse Victim, Mom Says," *Harrisburg Patriot News*, June 28, 2008; "Couple Found Shot, Dead Inside Apartment," *Harrisburg Patriot News*, June 27, 2008.

9. "Killer's Brother Held in Threat; Guns Seized After Wife Goes to Police," *Hartford Courant*, June 27, 2008; "A Push to Tighten Security: Lawyer Wounded in

Shooting Joins Call for Increased Safety Measures in Courts," *Hartford Courant*, Feb. 7, 2007.

10. "Man Who Allegedly Killed His Wife at YMCA Was Under Court Restraint," *Newark Star-Ledger*, June 28, 2008; "Woman Killed in Apparent Domestic Dispute at Y," *Bergen Record*, June 27, 2008.

11. "Woman Held for Shooting at Crowd," *Connecticut Post Online*, June 27, 2008.

12. "Broward Girl, 3, Recovering from Gun Shot to Leg," *Miami Herald*, June 29, 2008; "Girl, 3, Wounded in Gunfire," *Miami Herald*, June 28, 2008.

13. "3 Teens in Jail After Shooting and Car Chase," *Rock Hill* (SC) *Herald*, June 28, 2008.

14. "Deputies Investigate Shooting of Girl, 5, by Younger Brother," *Arkansas Democrat-Gazette*, July 1, 2008.

15. "7 Wounded in Night's Gunfire: Police Have Made an Arrest in One of the Three Shootings Thursday," *Omaha World-Herald*, June 27, 2008.

16. "Two City Shootings, One a Homicide: Crimes Took Place Only Minutes Apart, but Were Not Related, Police Say," *Hartford Courant*, June 28, 2008.

17. "3 Found Dead, Including Woman Who Held Police at Bay for Hours," *Arizona Daily Star*, June 28, 2008.

18. "Couple's Death Ruled Murder-Suicide," *Hattiesburg American*, July 1, 2008.

19. See, e.g., "Supreme Court Strikes Down D.C. Gun Ban; Antiwar MoveOn .org Ad Uses Baby," *Glenn Beck*, CNN, June 26, 2008 ("In one of the most anticipated decisions in recent memory . . ."); "Gun Ruling: History at the Court," *ABC World News with Charles Gibson*, June 26, 2008 ("Today, for the first time ever, the Supreme Court defined those words"); and "What's Next After Supreme Court's Gun Decision?" McClatchy-Tribune News Service, June 26, 2008 ("The Supreme Court's landmark decision Thursday striking down the District of Columbia's gun ban will have wide-ranging legal, political and public safety consequences").

20. *District of Columbia v. Heller*, 554 U.S. 570 (2008).

21. A search of the Nexis.com news database using the words "Supreme Court" and "Heller" for the dates June 26–27, 2008, returned 501 citations. Copies of the search request and the resulting number are in the files of the Violence Policy Center in Washington, DC.

22. Facts about the Supreme Court's architecture in this section are from "The Court Building." www.supremecourt.gov/about/courtbuilding.aspx.

23. "Justices List Their Assets; Wide Range of Wealth," *New York Times*, June 7, 2008; "Supreme Court Justices Report Travel, Income for 2006: Most Are Millionaires," Associated Press Financial Wire, June 8, 2007. For more detailed information, the Justices' annual financial reports back to 2004 can be accessed through an Opensecrets.org link to the personal financial disclosure database of the Center for Responsive Politics at www.opensecrets.org/news/2011/02/supreme-court-justices -personal-finances.html. According to this database, the net worth of each of the members of the Court reported in 2010 was as follows. Chief Justice John Roberts: $2,575,040 to $6,205,000; Justice Samuel A. Alito: $1,035,021 to $3,030,000; Justice Stephen Breyer: $3,480,058 to $8,035,000; Justice Ruth Bader Ginsburg: $2,365,013 to $5,030,000;

Justice Elena Kagan: $1,115,019 to $2,645,000; Justice Anthony Kennedy: $315,003 to $665,000; Justice Antonin Scalia: $1,380,022 to $3,210,000; Justice Sonia Sotomayor: $1,420,005 to $3,245,000; Justice Clarence Thomas: $515,003 to $1,125,000.

24. An audio file of Scalia's announcement and reading of a summary of the decision can be downloaded from the website of the Oyez Project at Chicago-Kent College of Law, www.oyez.org/cases/2000-2009/2007/2007_07_290.

25. For example, "Hartford-born scholar and dictionary-maker Noah Webster warned in 1799 that quarantine was a foolish and wrong-headed health policy. Most diseases, he believed, were of local origin, caused by filthy streets and rotting garbage that created a dangerous miasma (atmosphere) that could threaten every person. . . . In 1793, during the yellow fever epidemic, pious Philadelphians warned that epidemics came to those who had sinned or had allowed their fellow citizens to wallow in sin, and they demanded that the mayor close the city's theaters, whose irreligious plays had created widespread moral corruption." Yale professor Naomi Rogers, "Virulent Ideas: Fear of Epidemic Creates Ineffective Strategies, Misplaced Blame; Fear of Flu," *Hartford Courant*, May 3, 2009. "Colonial America's leaders deemed bathing impure, since it promoted nudity, which could only lead to promiscuity. Laws in Pennsylvania and Virginia either banned or limited bathing. For a time in Philadelphia, anyone who bathed more than once a month faced jail. . . . 'People always talk about the good old days, before pesticides and pollution,' says [epidemiology professor V.W.] Greene. 'But in the good old days of Europe and the United States, people lived in filth, with human and animal fecal matter all around. The rivers were filthy. Clothing was infested with vermin.' Disease ran rampant." "Cleanliness Has Only Recently Become a Virtue," *Smithsonian*, Feb. 1, 1991.

26. "Wilkinson and Posner, "Dissenting: Two Conservative Judges Challenge Justice Scalia," *Weekly Standard*, Dec. 15, 2008.

27. *District of Columbia v. Heller*, 554 U.S. 570 (2008), 635.

28. Audio file downloaded from the Oyez Project at Chicago-Kent College of Law, www.oyez.org/cases/2000-2009/2007/2007_07_290.

29. "A Santorum Barrage in the Culture Wars," *Washington Post*, Feb. 27, 2012.

30. Richard A. Posner, "In Defense of Looseness," *New Republic*, Aug. 27, 2008.

31. *District of Columbia v. Heller*, 554 U.S. 570 (2008), 629.

32. "Justice Scalia was emphatic that the right to possess a gun is not absolute." Posner, "In Defense of Looseness." Thus, Scalia wrote in *Heller*, "nothing in our opinion should be taken to cast doubt on longstanding prohibitions on the possession of firearms by felons and the mentally ill, or laws forbidding the carrying of firearms in sensitive places such as schools and government buildings, or laws imposing conditions and qualifications on the commercial sale of arms. . . . We identify these presumptively lawful regulatory measures only as examples; our list does not purport to be exhaustive . . . we also recognize another important limitation on the right to keep and carry arms. *Miller* said, as we have explained, that the sorts of weapons protected were those 'in common use at the time.' . . . We think that limitation is fairly supported by the historical tradition of prohibiting the carrying of 'dangerous and unusual weapons.'" *District of Columbia v. Heller*, 554 U.S. 570 (2008), 627–28.

33. See: http://blackslawdictionary.org/ipse-dixit.

34. Allen Rostron, "Protecting Gun Rights and Improving Gun Control After District of Columbia v. Heller," *Lewis & Clark Law Review* 13, no. 2 (summer 2009): 383, 387–88.

35. Adam Liptak, "In Re Scalia the Outspoken v. Scalia the Reserved," *New York Times*, May 2, 2004.

36. "Joyce Lee Malcolm, Professor of Legal History," curriculum vitae downloaded from George Mason University School of Law website, www.law.gmu.edu/faculty/directory/fulltime/malcolm_joyce.

37. "About Bentley University," www.bentley.edu/about/about-bentley-univer sity.

38. Antonin Scalia, *A Matter of Interpretation: Federal Courts and the Law* (Princeton, NJ: Princeton University Press, 1997), 136–37, n13.

39. Carl T. Bogus, "The History and Politics of Second Amendment Scholarship: A Primer," *Chicago-Kent Law Review* 76, no. 1 (2000): 3, 11.

40. "Justices' Ruling on Guns Elicits Rebuke, from the Right," *New York Times*, Oct. 21, 2008.

41. See "Jeffrey Toobin," CNN, www.cnn.com/CNN/anchors_reporters/toobin .jeffrey.html.

42. Jeffrey Toobin, "Name That Source; Why Are the Courts Leaning on Journalists?" *New Yorker*, Jan. 16, 2006.

43. "In Brief," *Richmond Times Dispatch*, Jan. 30, 2006.

44. Adam J. White, "Wilkinson and Posner, Dissenting: Two Conservative Judges Challenge Justice Scalia," *Weekly Standard*, Dec. 15, 2008.

45. Ibid.

46. Margaret Talbot, "Supreme Confidence; The Jurisprudence of Justice Antonin Scalia," *New Yorker*, Mar. 28, 2005.

47. J. Harvie Wilkinson III, "Of Guns, Abortions, and the Unraveling Rule of Law," *Virginia Law Review* 95, no. 2 (Apr. 2009).

48. *Roe v. Wade*, 410 U.S. 113 (1973).

49. Wilkinson, "Of Guns, Abortions, and the Unraveling Rule of Law.".

50. Posner, "In Defense of Looseness."

51. Ibid.

52. Ibid.

53. Ibid.

54. Damon W. Root, "Conservatives v. Libertarians: The Debate over Judicial Activism Divides Former Allies," *Reason*, July 1, 2010.

55. Scalia, *Matter of Interpretation*, 136–37, n13 (emphasis in original).

56. "Supreme Court Justice Champions Hunting at Wild Turkey Event," Associated Press State & Local Wire, Feb. 26, 2006; "Scalia Champions Hunting and Conservation," *Nashville Tennessean*, Feb. 26, 2006.

57. Antonin Scalia, "Financial Disclosure Report for Calendar Year 2006," 4.

58. "Oral Arguments in McDonald v. Chicago Second Amendment Case Eyewitness Report," AmmoLand.com, Mar. 3, 2010.

59. " 'There's a Whole Lot of Luck Involved,' " *Washington Post*, Apr. 10, 2008; Talbot, "Supreme Confidence."

60. Diana Rupp, "Dispatch from Germany," *Sports Afield* ("I was fascinated to learn that this respected jurist is a die-hard turkey hunter!"). This 2006 article (which is not more specifically dated) was downloaded on June 25, 2008, from the *Sports Afield* website, www.sportsafield.com/DianaRupplWA.htm. That specific link no longer works at this writing; however, a hard copy of the article is in the files of the Violence Policy Center in Washington, DC.

61. Jim Shea, "What's Up When Scalia's Social and Judicial Calendars Mix?" *Saint Paul Pioneer Press*, Mar. 5, 2004; "Buds of a Feather: By Blasting Away at Ducks, Joe Robinson Wonders, Did Cheney and Scalia also Super Glue Their Psyches into One Wild, Symbiotic Soul?" *Los Angeles Times*, Mar. 2, 2004; "Scalia Took Trip Set Up by Lawyer in Two Cases; Kansas Visit in 2001 Came Within Weeks of the Supreme Court Hearing Arguments," *Los Angeles Times*, Feb. 27, 2004 ("Supreme Court Justice Antonin Scalia was the guest of a Kansas law school two years ago and went pheasant hunting on a trip arranged by the school's dean, all within weeks of hearing two cases in which the dean was a lead attorney. . . . 'When a case is on the docket before a judge, the coziness of meeting privately with a lawyer is questionable,' said Chicago lawyer Robert P. Cummins, who headed an Illinois board on judicial ethics. 'It would seem the better part of judgment to avoid those situations.' "); "Commentary; Old MacDonald Had a Judge . . . , " *Los Angeles Times*, Feb. 17, 2004.

62. See, e.g., "Supreme Court's Credibility Problem," *Virginian-Pilot*, Dec. 5, 2011 ("More recently . . . [Justice Clarence] Thomas and Scalia were featured guests at a Federalist Society dinner sponsored by, among others, the law firm that will argue against the health care law, a trade group opposed to the law and the pharmaceutical giant Pfizer Inc., which has a major stake in the case. The dinner was held on the very day the Supreme Court decided to hear the lawsuit against the Affordable Care Act."); "Law Group Seeks Ethics Code for Supreme Court," *Washington Post*, Feb. 24, 2011 ("Thomas and Scalia have been criticized by a public interest group for attending private political meetings sponsored in January 2007 and 2008 by David and Charles Koch, conservative billionaires who made large contributions during last year's election and have financially backed the tea party movement"); Jonathan Turley, "The Price of Scalia's Political Stardom," *Washington Post*, Jan. 23, 2011 ("The Bachmann event takes this posturing to a new level. Scalia will be directly advising new lawmakers who came to Congress on a mission to remake government in a more conservative image. Many of them made pledges to repeal health-care reform, restrict immigration and investigate the president—pledges based on constitutional interpretations that might end up before the court. At best, Scalia's appearance can be viewed as a pep talk. At worst, it smacks of a political alliance."); "The Over-the-Top Justice," *New York Times*, Apr. 2, 2006 ("[S]peaking on March 8 at a university in Switzerland, he dismissed as 'crazy' the notion that military detainees are entitled to a 'full jury trial,' and the idea that the Geneva Conventions apply to those held at Guantánamo Bay, Cuba. In the process, Justice Scalia seemed to prejudge key issues in a momentous case involving the rights of Gitmo detainees. That should have caused him to recuse himself. . . ."); "Justice and Junkets," *New York Times*, Jan. 27, 2006 ("Justice Scalia was apparently unchastened by the criticism of his 2004 duck-hunting excursion with Vice President Dick Cheney, one of that term's most prominent Supreme Court

litigants. Last September, he skipped the swearing-in of Chief Justice John Roberts Jr. because of another ethically dubious trip, this time to the posh Ritz-Carlton at the Beaver Creek ski resort in Colorado."); and "How Scalia Faced Ethics Issue: Though a Past Consultant, He Sat on AT&T Case," *Washington Post*, June 22, 1986 ("Monroe H. Freedman, former dean of the Hofstra Law School and a longtime legal activist and commentator on legal ethics . . . called Scalia's participation an act of 'serious misjudgment' ").

63. Liptak, "In Re Scalia the Outspoken v. Scalia the Reserved" ("Justice Abe Fortas resigned in an ethics scandal in 1969, and Justice William O. Douglas's unorthodox private life and public statements led Gerald R. Ford, then the House minority leader, to call for his impeachment in 1970").

64. Josh Sugarmann, "Gun Industry 'Ambassador' Antonin Scalia to Hear Gun Law Case," *Huffington Post*, Mar. 1, 2010, www.huffingtonpost.com/josh-sugarmann/gun-industry-ambassador-a_b_481182.html. According to WFSA, each of its "ambassadors" is given the silver reproduction. "Torben Espensen," www.wfsa.net/amb_01.html.

65. "The World Forum Sport Shooting Ambassador Award," www.wfsa.net/award.html.

66. "Global Sport Shooting Group Honors Scalia," *New Gun Week*, Apr. 10, 2007.

67. "The Knox Update form [*sic*] the Firearms Coalition: The History of the Gun Rights War," *Shotgun News*, June 1, 2011.

68. "Personal Story: Interview with Alan Gottlieb and Lisa Lange," Fox News Network, *The O' Reilly Factor*, Fox News, Mar. 7, 2002.

69. "Jolly Greed Giant," *The Oregonian*, Aug. 16, 1992.

70. "Gun Advocate Trains Sights on I-676: Disarming Personality Conceals Steely Resolve of National Figure," *Spokesman Review*, Sept. 28, 1997.

71. "Jolly Greed Giant."

72. Rick Anderson, "Barack & Load; Alan Gottlieb's Challenge to a Gun Ban in the President's Adopted Hometown Has Made It All the Way to the Supreme Court, and Fattened the Ex-con's Wallet in the Process," *Seattle Weekly*, Nov. 11, 2009.

73. Ibid.; Steve Bailey, "A.K.A. Gunnut," *Boston Globe*, Aug. 10, 2007.

74. See Antonin Scalia, "Financial Disclosure Report for Calendar Year 2007," sec. V, "Gifts," 5. It is possible that the gift was not reported because its value was inconsequential. That cannot be known without a more detailed description of the gift than is available on the public record. The average price of silver in 2007 was $13.3836 per ounce. Source: Goldmasters Gold Coins & Precious Metals, http://goldmastersusa.com/silver_historical_prices.asp.

75. For examples, see James Oberg, "Soviet Space Propaganda: Doctored Cosmonaut Photos," *Wired*, Apr. 12, 2011, www.wired.com/wiredscience/2011/04/soviet-space-propaganda.

76. " 'Fantasy' Website Helps Students Learn About Supreme Court," CNN.com, Nov. 23, 2010.

77. "Gun Chic: Out Among the Firearms Experts at the Fairfax Rod & Gun Club," *Daily Standard*, Apr. 23, 2002; "How to Win Your Very Own Glock 9mm," *Newsweek* Web Exclusive, May 14, 2001.

78. "High Court to Consider Pledge in Schools; Scalia Recuses Himself from California Case," *Washington Post*, Oct. 15, 2003.

79. Dave Kopel, "Conservative Activists Key to DC Handgun Decision," *Human Events Online*, June 27, 2008.

80. Anderson, "Barack & Load."

81. Dorie E. Apollonio and Lisa A. Bero, "The Creation of Industry Front Groups: The Tobacco Industry and 'Get Government off Our Back,'" *American Journal of Public Health*, Mar. 2007.

82. Bailey, "A.K.A. Gunnut."

83. "Raging Bitch Beer Ban Spurs Flying Dog Brewery to Sue Michigan Liquor Control Commission on First Amendment Grounds," *Business Wire*, Mar. 28, 2011.

84. "The New Terminators: The Anti-Indian Movement Resurfaces," *Native Americas*, Sept. 30, 2000.

85. "Influence Game: Leaks Show Group's Climate Efforts," Associated Press Financial Wire, Feb. 16, 2012.

86. See Violence Policy Center, *Joe Camel with Feathers: How the NRA with Gun and Tobacco Industry Dollars Uses Its Eddie Eagle Program to Market Guns to Kids* (Washington, DC: Violence Policy Center, 1997), www.vpc.org/studies/eddiecon.htm.

87. Naomi Oreskes and Erik M. Conway, *Merchants of Doubt: How a Handful of Scientists Obscure the Truth on Issues from Tobacco Smoke to Global Warming* (New York: Bloomsbury Press, 2010), 236.

88. Ibid., 217.

89. Brief *Amicus Curiae* of The Heartland Institute in Support of Petitioners, *McDonald v. City of Chicago*, Docket No. 08-1521, Supreme Court of the United States, p. 2; "Gun Rights," Heartland Institute, http://news.heartland.org/ideas/gun-rights ("In this case, Otis McDonald and the other Petitioners seek the right to possess handguns within their homes for the purpose of self-defense. They need handguns.").

90. "Agenda: 2011 Emerging Issues Forum," http://eif.heartland.org/?page_id=39.

91. "Policy Documents," Heartland Institute, http://heartland.org/policy-documents/heartlander-july-2002.

92. See, e.g., "The U.S. Is on a Suicide Watch," AmmoLand.com, Jan. 18, 2012 ("Conservative think tanks like The Heritage Foundation, the Cato Institute, The Heartland Institute, the Competitive Enterprise Institute, and others have spelled out programs that can and will save America . . ."); "Charlton Heston, Meet Joe Camel," *Washington Post*, May 4, 1999 ("The free-market Heartland Institute, arguing against gun control . . .").

93. Lee Fang, "Memo: Health Insurance, Banking, Oil Industries Met with Koch, Chamber, Glenn Beck to Plot 2010 Election," *Think Progress*, Oct. 20, 2010, http://think progress.org/politics/2010/10/20/124642/beck-koch-chamber-meeting/?mobile=nc.

94. "Advocacy Group Says Justices May Have Conflict in Campaign Finance Cases," *New York Times*, Jan. 20, 2011.

95. Brad Friedman, "Exclusive Audio: Inside the Koch Brothers' Secret Seminar: A Close-up View of the Oil Billionaires' Dark-Money Fundraiser and 2012

Strategy Session," *Mother Jones*, Sept. 6, 2011, http://motherjones.com/politics/2011/09/exclusive-audio-koch-brothers-seminar-tapes.

96. "Beck Claims 'This Game Is for Keeps' with 'the Left', Asks Listeners to 'Pray for Protection,' " Media Matters, Sept. 8, 2009, http://mediamatters.org/mmtv/200909080010 (from the Sept. 8 edition of Premiere Radio Networks' *Glenn Beck Program*).

97. "Beck Repeats Call for Prayers, Claims, 'You Can Shoot Me in the Head . . . but There Will Be 10 Others That Line Up,' " Media Matters, Sept. 08, 2009, http://mediamatters.org/mmtv/200909080013 (from the Sept. 8 edition of Premiere Radio Networks' *Glenn Beck Program*). "You can try to put the lid on this group of people, but you will never silence us. You will never—you can shoot me in the head, you can shoot the next guy in the head, but there will be 10 others that line up. And it may not happen today, it may not happen next week, but freedom will be restored in this land."

98. Fang, "Memo: Health Insurance, Banking, Oil Industries Met."

99. Petition for Declaratory Judgment, *Koch v. Washburn*, Johnson County, Kansas District Court, Case No. 12CV01749, filed Mar. 1, 2012.

100. "Policy Group Caught in Rift over Direction," *New York Times*, Mar. 6, 2012.

101. "Supreme Court Strikes Down D.C. Gun Ban; Antiwar MoveOn.org Ad Uses Baby," *Glenn Beck*, CNN, June 26, 2008.

102. "Naples Man Behind Major Supreme Court Decision Plays as Hard as He Works," *Naples Daily News*, June 27, 2008.

103. "For Young Area Lawyer, the Supreme Compliment," *Washington Post*, Mar. 18, 2008.

104. "Lawyer Who Wiped Out D.C. Ban Says It's About Liberties, Not Guns," *Washington Post*, Mar. 18, 2007.

105. "Heller Attorneys Awarded $1.1M in Fees, One-Third of Their Request," The BLT blog, *Legal Times*, Dec. 29, 2011, http://legaltimes.typepad.com/blt/2011/12/heller-attorneys-awarded-11m-in-fees-one-third-of-their-request.html.

106. "Robert A. Levy, Chairman," Cato Institute, www.cato.org/people/robert-levy.

107. "Robert A. Levy, Legal Briefs," Cato Institute, www.cato.org/people/pub_list.php?auth_id=225&pub_list=5.

108. "Lawyer Who Wiped Out D.C. Ban Says It's About Liberties, Not Guns."

109. "Staff, Clark Neily, Senior Attorney," Institute for Justice, www.ij.org/index.php?option=com_content&task=view&id=607&Itemid=165; Cato Institute, "Robert A. Levy, Chairman."

110. "For Young Area Lawyer, the Supreme Compliment," *Washington Post*, Mar. 18, 2008.

111. "Lawyer Who Wiped Out D.C. Ban Says It's About Liberties, Not Guns."

112. "Commentary: Scalia, Writing Expert Team Up to Offer Practice Pointers, Stress Self-Preparation," *North Carolina Lawyers Weekly*, June 9, 2008; Liptak, "In Re Scalia the Outspoken v. Scalia the Reserved"; "Acerbic Scalia Hurls Barbs from the Bench," Associated Press, July 3, 1994.

113. *United States v. Miller*, 307 U.S. 174 (1939).

114. Bogus, "History and Politics of Second Amendment Scholarship," 3, 4.

115. Ibid., 3, 4–5.

116. Robert J. Spitzer, "Lost and Found: Researching the Second Amendment," *Chicago-Kent Law Review* 76, no. 1 (2000): 349, 376.

117. Bogus, "History and Politics of Second Amendment Scholarship," 3, 14.

118. "Good Day for the Bill of Rights," Cato@Liberty blog, June 27, 2008.

119. Posner, "In Defense of Looseness."

120. Anderson, "Barack & Load."

121. Violence Policy Center, "National Rifle Association Receives Millions of Dollars from Gun Industry 'Corporate Partners,' New VPC Report Reveals," news release, Apr. 13, 2011, www.vpc.org/press/1104blood.htm.

122. Law Center to Prevent Gun Violence, "Post-Heller Litigation Summary," Aug. 1, 2012, http://smartgunlaws.org/post-heller-litigation-summary.

123. "Portion of Md. Gun Law Ruled Too Broad," *Washington Post*, Mar. 6, 2012.

124. David Hemenway, *Private Guns, Public Health* (Ann Arbor: University of Michigan Press, 2006), 61–62.

125. "Shooting from the Lip: Justice Scalia's New Book on Judging Is Brilliant but Acerbic," *ABA Journal*, Jan. 1997.

126. For a detailed discussion, see Violence Policy Center, *Unintended Consequences: Pro-Handgun Experts Prove That Handguns Are a Dangerous Choice for Self-Defense* (Washington, DC: Violence Policy Center, 2001).

127. Arthur L. Kellermann, "Do Guns Matter?" *Western Journal of Medicine* 161 (Dec. 1994): 614.

128. Arthur L. Kellermann, Dawna S. Fuqua-Whitley, Tomoko R. Sampson, and Walter Lindenmann, "Public Opinion About Guns in the Home," *Injury Prevention*, Sept. 2000, 189–94.

129. Lisa Hepburn, Matthew Miller, Deborah Azrael, and David Hemenway, "The US Gun Stock: Results from the 2004 National Firearms Survey," *Injury Prevention* 13 (2007):15–19.

130. Violence Policy Center, *A Shrinking Minority: The Continuing Decline of Gun Ownership in America* (Washington, DC: Violence Policy Center, 2011), www.vpc.org/studies/ownership.pdf.

131. Hepburn et al., "US Gun Stock."

132. Ibid.

133. Anderson, "Barack & Load."

134. Duane Thomas, *The Truth About Handguns: Exploding the Myths, Hype, and Misinformation* (Boulder, CO: Paladin Press, 1997), 45.

135. Chris Bird, *The Concealed Handgun Manual: How to Choose, Carry, and Shoot a Gun in Self Defense* (San Antonio: Privateer Publications, 1998), 40.

3. Women and Children Last

1. "Pistol-Packing Soccer Dad Gives Tearful Apology," *Muskegon Chronicle*, Aug. 17, 2010.

2. "Soccer Dad Pleads No Contest to Gun Charge: Judge Commits to Capping Sentence to 30 Days for Felony Conviction," *Grand Rapids Press*, July 9, 2010.

3. "Asst. Coach Pulls Gun on Soccer Dad: Coach Was Arrested for Felonious Assault," WOOD-TV (Grand Rapids, MI), May 28, 2010, www.woodtv.com/dpp/news/local/muskegon_county/assistant-coach-pulls-gun-on-soccer-dad.

4. "Soccer Dad Pleads No Contest to Gun Charge."

5. "Pistol-Packing Soccer Dad Gives Tearful Apology."

6. "Militia on the Move: Group Training in Manistee National Forest to 'Help Our Citizens,'" *Muskegon Chronicle*, June 25, 2011.

7. "Our Story," Fruitport Township website, www.fruitporttownship-mi.gov/visitors/25-the-township/20-our-story.html.

8. "Pistol-Packing Soccer Dad Gives Tearful Apology."

9. Result of search to "Verify a License/Registration" for James Ian Sherrill, Michigan Department of Licensing and Regulatory Affairs website, Mar. 4, 2012, in files of Violence Policy Center, Washington, DC.

10. "Nothing to Conceal Here," *Muskegon Chronicle*, June 26, 2011.

11. "'Soccer Dad' Waives His Preliminary Exam," *Muskegon Chronicle*, June 9, 2010.

12. "One Handgun Connects Humphrey's Past to His Future," *Janesville Gazette*, May 8, 2011.

13. "Pistol-Packing Soccer Dad Gives Tearful Apology."

14. "Defusing Parents at Games," *Newsday*, Oct. 11, 2007.

15. Brooke de Lench, "Misbehaving Youth Sports Parents Too Common," June 23, 2008, www.momsteam.com/successful-parenting/game-day/sideline-behavior/misbehaving-youth-sports-parents-too-common.

16. "Lubbock Sports Officials Cry Foul over Parents' Abusive Behavior at Youth Games," *Lubbock Avalanche-Journal*, Oct. 26, 2008.

17. "Man Guilty of Aiming Rifle During Practice," *Roanoke Times*, Dec. 6, 2003; "Police: Roanoke County Man Aimed Rifle at Kids' Soccer Team," *Roanoke Times*, Sept. 13, 2003.

18. "Man Pulls Gun at Game, Now Charged with Assault," Oct. 20, 2008, KCBD (Lubbock, TX), www.kcbd.com/Global/story.asp?S=9209796&nav=menu69_2_12.

19. "Grand Jury No Bills Man Who Pulled Gun at Soccer Match," KCBD (Lubbock, TX), Nov. 24, 2008, www.kcbd.com/story/9408464/grand-jury-no-bills-man-who-pulled-gun-at-soccer-match?clienttype=printable.

20. "Parent Cleared in Peewee-Game Fight," *Philadelphia Inquirer*, Apr. 18, 2007; "Gun at Pee-Wee Football: Sad Lesson," *Philadelphia Inquirer*, Oct. 24, 2006.

21. E-mail communications with Tennessee Department of Public Safety, in files of Violence Policy Center, Washington, DC; "Gun Permit Suspended After Incident at Ball Game," Associated Press State & Local Wire, June 15, 2010; "Dad in Alleged Row Out on Bond: Accused of Pulling Gun on Son's Coach," *Memphis Commercial Appeal*, June 12, 2010; "Police Look for Armed, Mad Dad: Man Allegedly Pulls Gun on Coach over Son's Play," *Memphis Commercial Appeal*, June 10, 2010.

22. "Police: Roanoke County Man Aimed Rifle at Kids' Soccer Team," *Roanoke Times*, Sept. 13, 2003.

23. "Guns in Parks and Kids' Sports," *Memphis Commercial Appeal*, June 14, 2010.

24. "County Gun Laws Stiffened in Split Decision," *Jefferson* (NC) *Post*, Feb. 9, 2012.

25. For detailed accounts of the confusion, see "Seaford Pharmacy Shootings: DA's Confidential Memo Details Druggist's First-hand Report of Fatal Confrontation," *Newsday*, Feb. 9, 2012; and "Memo Offers New Account of ATF Agent's NY Shooting," Associated Press, Feb. 9, 2012.

26. "CHL Holder Fired Shot That Killed Store Clerk," MyFoxHouston.com, May 30, 2012, www.myfoxhouston.com/story/18661869/chl.

27. "Gun Bans Fall, Raising Applause, Concerns; Restrictions at Places Such as Parks Yield to a State Law That Allows Firearms. Nationwide, Advocates Welcome New Rights, Opponents Worry About Safety," *Harrisburg Patriot News*, May 14, 2010.

28. "Victory for Concealed Carry in Forsyth County, NC," AmmoLand.com, Feb. 16, 2012.

29. See generally Violence Policy Center, *When Men Murder Women: An Analysis of 2009 Homicide Data—Females Murdered by Males in Single Victim/Single Offender Incidents* (Washington, DC: Violence Policy Center, 2011), www.vpc.org/studies/wmmw2011.pdf.

30. Leonard J. Paulozzi et al., "Surveillance for Homicide Among Intimate Partners—United States, 1981–1998," *Morbidity and Mortality Weekly Report (MMWR) Surveillance Summaries* 50 (Oct. 12, 2001): 1–16.

31. In 2009, justifiable homicides involving women killing men occurred in: California (1), Indiana (1), Louisiana (4), Maryland (1), Michigan (2), Mississippi (1), North Carolina (1), Oklahoma (2), Oregon (2), South Carolina (1), Tennessee (1), Texas (3), and Virginia (1). In 2009, justifiable homicides involving women killing men with a firearm occurred in: Louisiana (1), Michigan (2), Mississippi (1), Oklahoma (2), Oregon (2), South Carolina (1), Tennessee (1), Texas (2), and Virginia (1). Of these, handguns were used in: Louisiana (1), Michigan (2), Mississippi (1), Oklahoma (1), Oregon (2), South Carolina (1), Texas (1), and Virginia (1). Violence Policy Center, *When Men Murder Women*.

32. Shannon Catalano, "National Crime Victimization Survey: Victimization During Household Burglary," Special Report, Sept. 2010, U.S. Department of Justice, Office of Justice Programs, Bureau of Justice Statistics, fig. 1, "Number and Percent of Household Burglaries, 2003–2007," 1.

33. Ibid., table 17, "Victim-Offender Relationship in Violent Household Burglary, 2003–2007," 9.

34. "Long Guns Short Yardage: Advances in Bullet Technology Make the .223 an Excellent Choice for Home Defense," *Guns & Ammo*, Mar. 1, 2012.

35. Some accounts state that Hain was the mother of four children. The discrepancy is apparently that she was stepmother to one child in addition to her own three children. See "Gun-Toting Woman Divides Community," *Philadelphia Inquirer*, Dec. 12, 2008.

36. "Daughter Was Abuse Victim, Mom Says," *Harrisburg Patriot News*, June 28, 2008.

37. "Pistol-Packin' Soccer Mama Brings On Heat," *Lebanon Daily News*, Sept. 24, 2008.

38. "Glock 26," Glock, www.glock.com/english/glock26.htm.

39. See Lebanon County, PA, website, www.lebcounty.org/Pages/default.aspx.

40. "Gun-Toting Woman Divides Community."

41. Ibid.

42. Ibid.

43. "Police-Fire Digest," *Lancaster New Era*, Apr. 20, 2006.

44. "Gun Carrier Sues for $1 Million: Woman Claims Permit Revocation Violated Constitutional Rights," *Harrisburg Patriot News*, Nov. 25, 2008.

45. "Gun-Toting Woman Divides Community."

46. Ibid.

47. "Pistol-Packin' Soccer Mama Brings On Heat."

48. Ibid.

49. "Gun-Toting Woman Divides Community."

50. "Pistol-Packin' Soccer Mama Brings On Heat."

51. "Gun Carrier Sues for $1 Million"; "Guns at a Kids' Game: Judge Wisely Points Out Difference Between Legality, Sensibility," *Harrisburg Patriot News*, Oct. 18, 2008.

52. "New Life to Aging Murder Tops List," *Lebanon Daily News*, Dec. 27, 2008.

53. "Gun-Toting Mom Gets Permit Back," *Lebanon Daily News*, Oct. 14, 2008.

54. Ibid.

55. "I Am Happy Being a Gun Owner," *Harrisburg Patriot News*, Dec. 27, 2008.

56. "Soccer Parents Wince at Prospect of Guns at Games," *Harrisburg Patriot News*, Oct. 18, 2008.

57. Ibid.

58. "I Am Happy Being a Gun Owner" ("There is no doubt Hain aroused a storm of controversy—making headlines locally and nationally. Whenever *The Patriot-News* published a story about Hain on PennLive.com, dozens, sometimes hundreds, of readers weighed in."); "Gun-Toting Mum," *The Advertiser* (Adelaide, Australia), Nov. 26, 2008.

59. "Gun Carrier Sues for $1 Million."

60. Ibid.

61. "Matthew B. Weisberg Esq.," Weisbarg Law, P.C., www.ppwlaw.com/Bio/MatthewWeisberg.asp; "Gun Carrier Sues for $1 Million."

62. "Gun Carrier Sues for $1 Million."

63. "I Am Happy Being a Gun Owner."

64. Ibid.

65. "Gun-Toting Woman Divides Community."

66. "Pistol-Packin' Soccer Mom Shot Dead in Lebanon," *Lebanon Daily News*, Oct. 8, 2009.

67. "Gun-Toting Soccer Mom, Husband Shot Dead," *Philadelphia Inquirer*, Oct. 9, 2009; "Lebanon Soccer Mom Shot by Husband While Chatting on Webcam," *Lebanon Daily News*, Oct. 9, 2009; Hain v. DeLeo, 2010 U.S. Dist. Lexis 116393, U.S. District Court for the Middle District of Pennsylvania, Nov. 2, 2010.

68. "Gun-Toting Soccer Mom, Husband Shot Dead."

69. Ibid.

70. "Pistol-Packin' Soccer Mom Shot Dead in Lebanon."

71. "Lebanon Soccer Mom Shot by Husband While Chatting on Webcam."

72. "Pistol-Packin' Soccer Mom Shot Dead in Lebanon."

73. Ibid.

74. "Lebanon Soccer Mom Shot by Husband While Chatting on Webcam."

75. Ibid.

76. "Gun-Toting Soccer Mom, Husband Shot Dead."

77. Josh Sugarmann, "Beyond the Easy Irony of Murdered Gun Advocate Meleanie Hain," *Huffington Post*, Oct. 9, 2009, www.huffingtonpost.com/josh-sugarmann/beyond-the-easy-irony-of_b_315731.html.

78. "Gun-Toting Mother's Lawsuit Dismissed," *Harrisburg Patriot News*, Nov. 4, 2010; *Hain v. DeLeo*, 2010 U.S. Dist. Lexis 116393, U.S. District Court for the Middle District of Pennsylvania, Nov. 2, 2010.

79. See, e.g., "Meleanie Hain (shefearsnothing) Memorial Dinner: March 26, 2011," Pennsylvania Firearm Owners Association forum, http://forum.pafoa.org/general-114/127586-meleanie-hain-shefearsnothing-memorial-dinner.html; "Meleanie Hain Memorial Shoot—Nov. 1st," Pennsylvania Firearm Owners Association forum, http://forum.pafoa.org/general-2/74983-meleanie-hain-memorial-shoot-nov-1st-nepa.html; and "Meleanie Hain Memorial Shoot 11/01/09," Maryland Shooters forum, www.mdshooters.com/showthread.php?t=26203.

80. Garen Wintemute et al., "Increased Risk of Intimate Partner Homicide Among California Women Who Purchased Handguns," *Annals of Emergency Medicine* 41, no. 2 (2003): 282.

81. Douglas Wiebe, "Homicide and Suicide Risks Associated with Firearms in the Home: A National Case-Control Study," *Annals of Emergency Medicine* 41, no. 6 (2003): 775.

82. K.M. Grassel et al., "Association Between Handgun Purchase and Mortality from Firearm Injury," *Injury Prevention* 9 (2003): 50.

83. Violence Policy Center, *When Men Murder Women*.

84. The following discussion is based on extracts from Violence Policy Center, *American Roulette: Murder-Suicide in the United States*, 3d ed. (Washington, DC: Violence Policy Center, 2008), www.vpc.org/studies/amroul2008.pdf.

85. "Man Kills Woman and Self at Plant: Longtime Employees Were Common-Law Couple, Police Say," *Harrisburg Patriot News*, May 13, 2005.

86. "Motive Still Unclear in Recent Shootings," *Harrisburg Patriot News*, Feb. 17, 2010.

87. "Man in Custody After Deadly Jackson Township Shooting," *Lebanon Daily News*, Feb. 11, 2011.

88. "Suicides Up by 1 in 2011," *Lebanon Daily News*, Feb. 3, 2012; "Coroner Reports on 2010 Deaths," *Lebanon Daily News*, Feb. 27, 2011; "Coroner: County Suicides Up in 2008," *Lebanon Daily News*, Jan. 23, 2009; "Report Profiles '07 Coroner Cases," *Lebanon Daily News*, Feb. 1, 2008.

89. "Marketing to Women: Six Ways to Increase Your Sales," *Shooting Industry*, Nov. 1, 2009.

90. Kevin Reese, "Women Hit the Woods: NRA's Eight-Day Women's Wilderness

Escape Is a Camp Like None Other," National Shooting Sports Foundation, www
.nssf.org/events/featurette/0711-2.cfm.

91. "Men vs. Women in Competitive Shooting," AmmoLand.com, Feb. 29, 2012.

92. "Annual Report for the Fiscal Year Ended Dec. 31, 2011," Freedom Group,
Inc.

93. See "NRA Women's Programs," NRA, www.nrahq.org/women/index.asp.

94. Reese, "Women Hit the Woods."

95. "Stocking Beyond Guns; Arms and the Woman," *Shooting Industry*, Nov. 1,
2011; "The Real Deal with Pink," *Shooting Industry*, Sept. 1, 2011.

96. "Final Civilian Rankings for the Palmetto GLOCK Girl Shootout Held at the
B.E.L.T. Training in Reevesville, SC," www.gssfonline.com/results/2011/2011rsc.pdf.

97. "GLOCK Sport Shooting Foundation Announces First Ever Ladies-Only
Match," AmmoLand.com, May 23, 2011.

98. See, e.g., "Between the Lines," *Hernando Today*, Aug. 30, 2011. (In Brooksville,
Florida, the Hernando Sportsman's Club "is inviting women for a 'Ladies Day' all-day
event running from 9 a.m. to 5 p.m. at the gun range on Oct. 29. The event serves as
an introduction to rifles, shotguns and pistols for women only and will help facilitate
exposure of shooting sports to women . . . all firearms and ammo will be supplied for
the women attending the event.")

99. "Marketing to Women: Six Ways to Increase Your Sales," *Shooting Industry*,
Nov. 1, 2009.

100. Ibid.

101. See www.gungoddess.com.

102. "Host a Camp Wild Girls Hunting Party and Profit," *Shooting Industry*, July 1,
2010.

103. Advertisement in *Shotgun News*, June 1, 2012, 4.

104. Ibid., 47.

105. There is no direct link, but the calendars can be found by clicking on the button labeled CALENDARS on the company's website, http://eaacorp.com.

106. Violence Policy Center, *A Shrinking Minority: The Continuing Decline of Gun
Ownership in America* (Washington, DC: Violence Policy Center, 2011), www.vpc
.org/studies/ownership.pdf.

107. "Men vs. Women in Competitive Shooting."

108. Families Afield website, www.familiesafield.org.

109. For a detailed discussion of the problem from the industry point of view, see
Families Afield, *Revised Youth Hunting Report*, research compiled by Silvertip Pro-
ductions, Southwick Associates, and U.S. Sportsmen's Alliance, National Shooting
Sports Foundation, and National Wild Turkey Federation, available at www.nwtf
.org/images/Youth_Hunting_Report.pdf.

110. "Hunting for Young Bucks: Attracting Young Hunters Vital as Overall Number of Hunters Declines in Michigan," *Jackson Citizen Patriot*, Oct. 28, 2007.

111. U.S. Sportsman Alliance, *Revised Youth Hunting Report*, 13.

112. Ibid., 7.

113. "Deputies Investigate Shooting of Girl, 5, by Younger Brother," *Arkansas
Democrat-Gazette*, July 1, 2008.

114. "3-Year-Old Kills Self with Gun in Car in Wash.," Associated Press Online, Mar. 14, 2012.

115. "Counseling, Not Jail, for Boy, 9: Plea Deal in Shooting at Bremerton School—Girl, 8, Remains in Serious Condition," *Seattle Times*, Mar. 7, 2012; "Prosecutors Don't Want to Lock Up Boy Responsible for Bremerton Shooting," KCPQ/KMYQ-TV, Feb. 25, 2012.

116. Sugarmann, "Beyond the Easy Irony of Murdered Gun Advocate Meleanie Hain."

117. "Daughter of Marysville Officer Identified: Died from Gunshot Wound to Torso," KCPQ/KMYQ-TV, Mar. 12, 2012; "Wash. Officer's Daughter Shot Dead by Sibling," Associated Press State & Local Wire, Mar. 12, 2012.

118. "The Life & Death of 'Princess': Emilee Randall Led an Idyllic Life, but a Gun-Centered Culture Helped Cut It Short," *The Columbian*, Feb. 16, 2003.

119. Mathew Miller, Deborah Azrael, and David Hemenway, "Firearm Availability and Unintentional Firearm Deaths, Suicide, and Homicide Among 5–14 Year Olds," *Journal of Trauma Injury, Infection, and Critical Care* 52 (2002): 272.

120. Ibid., 273.

121. "Prosecutors Don't Want to Lock Up Boy Responsible for Bremerton Shooting," KCPQ/KMYQ-TV, Feb. 25, 2012.

122. Miller, Azrael, and Hemenway, "Firearm Availability," 267.

4. Two Tales of a City

1. See www.distancebetweencities.net/lebanon_pa_and_murfreesboro_tn.

2. "Geographic Center of Tennessee," Historical Marker Database, http://www.hmdb.org/marker.asp?marker=26067.

3. The following are examples. In March 2011, Nith Sim shot to death her husband, Daniel Sim, in La Vergne, not far from Murfreesboro. He was sleeping in the bedroom. She then killed herself. Nith Sim apparently tried to use one handgun, but it jammed, so she used another. Both of the couple's two children, ages two months and five years, were in the bedroom at the time of the shooting. Daniel Sim's mother was in another room inside the house. "LPD: Woman Shoots Husband, Self," *Murfreesboro Daily News Journal*, Mar. 26, 2011. In November 2009, a Rutherford Country grand jury indicted William Jones on a charge of first-degree premeditated murder. Jones had reported his wife, Lashawn Anna Jones, missing the month before. Police allege he shot his wife to death and dumped her body in a wooded area. "Grand Jury Indicts Man for Wife's Murder," *Murfreesboro Daily News Journal*, Nov. 11, 2009. In Murfreesboro, neighbors expressed "shock and disbelief" when informed of the murder-suicide of eighty-year-old Robert "Bob" Givens and his seventy-eight-year-old wife, Dot, in May 2008. Police did not reveal who shot whom or what type of gun was used. "She was a really sweet lady and always waving and conversing," a neighbor said. "They were always around the house and went out in the yard together. They were a good old American couple." "Apparent Murder-Suicide Shocks Neighbors," *Murfreesboro Daily News Journal*, May 24, 2008. Two months earlier, a Rutherford County man, Royce Mitchell Markam, shot to death his

estranged wife, Joyce Anne, in the driveway of her home. He then went into the house and shot to death James Edward Hollowell. Markam returned to the driveway and shot himself to death. He used a 30 caliber rifle, according to police. "Three Dead in Murder-Suicide," *Murfreesboro Daily News Journal*, Mar. 3, 2008. Several days before that, a man "distraught" by personal troubles shot himself when he was stopped by police in La Vergne. He was last reported to have been on life support. "Briefly: Man Who Shot Self on Life Support," *Murfreesboro Daily News Journal*, Mar. 1, 2008. In February 2008, Michael Vance was arrested and charged with shooting to death his wife, Suzanne Vance. Suzanne was seeking to finalize their divorce at the time Vance is accused of murdering her. Seeking a restraining order, she had written in a court document, "He has told me that if I left, he would kill me." According to police accounts, Vance tried unsuccessfully to commit suicide after he shot his wife, and then led police on a high-speed chase. He was later indicted on a charge of first-degree murder. "Murfreesboro Man Indicted in Killing of Wife," *Murfreesboro Daily News Journal*, Feb. 15, 2010; "Estranged Husband Charged in Wife's Death," *Murfreesboro Daily News Journal*, Feb. 29, 2008. In August 2006, Joe Rizzo shot and killed his wife, Sue, at a veterinary office where she worked, then turned the gun on himself. "He fired a shot as she was entering the hallway," the Murfreesboro police report stated. "She dropped, and he stood over her firing more shots. The suspect stepped into the hall and one more shot was fired." "Murfreesboro Police Investigating Possible Murder-Suicide," Associated Press State & Local Wire, Aug. 31, 2006.

4. David Hemenway, *While We Were Sleeping: Success Stories in Injury and Violence Prevention* (Berkeley: University of California Press 2009), 159.

5. Tennessee Suicide Prevention Network, *Status of Suicide in Tennessee 2012* (Nashville: Tennessee Suicide Prevention Network, 2012), 9, http://tspn.org/wp-content/uploads/SOST122.pdf.

6. Ibid., 16. Matthew Miller and David Hemenway, "Guns and Suicide in the United States," *New England Journal of Medicine*, Sept. 4, 2008, 990 ("The association between guns in the home and the risk of suicide is due entirely to a large increase in the risk of suicide by firearm that is not counterbalanced by a reduced risk of non-firearm suicide").

7. "Amber Glen Subdivision in Murfreesboro TN," Exit Realty of the South, www.smyrna.exitrealtyofthesouth.com/blog/Amber+Glen+Subdivision+in+Mur freesboro+TN; "Murfreesboro Tennessee Real Estate Subdivisions," Bob Parks Realty, www.bobparks.com/murfreesboro-tennessee-subdivisions.html.

8. See "Cason Lane Academy: About This School," Education.com, www.educa tion.com/schoolfinder/us/tennessee/murfreesboro/cason-lane-academy/#students -and-teachers. The Cason Lane Academy's 2008 first grade can be seen on a YouTube video of the school's Veteran Day program: www.youtube.com/watch?v=6yYliqjZSU 8&feature=related.

9. "Murfreesboro Shooting Adds to Suburb's Spiral of Fear," *Nashville Tennessean*, Feb. 22, 2012; "Several Key Details of Cason Lane Shooting Discussed in Juvenile Court Tuesday," *Murfreesboro Daily News Journal*, Feb. 21, 2012.

10. Ibid.

11. "Murfreesboro Shooting Adds to Suburb's Spiral of Fear."

12. "Dr. Robert Sanders, Crusader," *Nashville Tennessean*, Jan. 20, 2006.

13. Robert S. Sanders Jr., *Dr. Seat Belt: The Life of Robert S. Sanders, M.D., Pioneer in Child Passenger Safety* (Murfreesboro, TN: Armstrong Valley, 2010), 27–46, 54, 74–75, 78–79.

14. Deborah Wagnon and Christian Hidalgo, *Images of America: Murfreesboro* (Charleston, SC: Arcadia, 2007), 57.

15. Sanders, *Dr. Seat Belt*, 85.

16. Ibid., 45.

17. Ibid., 85.

18. Ibid., 85–87.

19. Anne Teigen and Melissa Savage, "Most Precious Cargo," *State Legislatures*, Mar. 2008.

20. Sanders, *Dr. Seat Belt*, 88–90.

21. Teigen and Savage, "Most Precious Cargo"; Sanders, *Dr. Seat Belt*, 94–96.

22. "Results Praised in States Requiring Auto Safety Devices for Children," *New York Times*, Nov. 28, 1982.

23. "Who's Who at WPLA: Trooper Jim Foster," RadioYears, www.radioyears.com/wpla/details.cfm?id=969.

24. "House Rejects 72-Hour Cooling-Off Period for Handguns," Associated Press, Jan. 28, 1982.

25. Michael D. Decker, Mary Jane Dewey, Robert H. Hutcheson Jr., and William Schaffner, "The Use and Efficacy of Child Restraint Devices: The Tennessee Experience, 1982 and 1983," *Journal of the American Medical Association* 252 (Nov. 9, 1984): 2573.

26. Ibid., 2572–73.

27. Ibid., 2574.

28. Ibid.

29. Hemenway, *While We Were Sleeping*, 159.

30. Decker et al., "Use and Efficacy of Child Restraint Devices," 2575.

31. Puneet Narang, Anubha Paladugu, Sainath Reddy Manda, William Smock, Cynthia Gosnay, and Steven Lippmann, "Do Guns Provide Safety? At What Cost?" *Southern Medical Journal* 103, no. 2 (Feb. 2010): 152.

32. Ibid.

33. Sanders, *Dr. Seat Belt*, 93.

34. U.S. Department of Transportation, National Highway Traffic Safety Administration, "Traffic Safety Facts 2009 Data: Occupant Protection," 4.

35. "Barrett's 30th Anniversary," Barrett, http://barrett.net/about.

36. "Gunmaker Is Surviving Fight Against .50-Caliber," *Nashville Tennessean*, Jan. 9, 2005.

37. "AP Centerpiece: Small-Time Tinkering Leads to Big-Time Guns, Sales by Tennessee Company," Associated Press, Nov. 25, 2005.

38. Ibid.

39. Ibid.

40. "Ronnie's Inspiration," Barrett blog, Sept. 28, 2011, http://blog.barrett.net/?p=288.

41. The ammunition that 50 caliber sniper rifles fire today was originally developed during the First World War as both an antitank and machine-gun round. Developments in tank armor soon made tanks generally impervious to 50 caliber rounds, but according to the Marine Corps and other authorities, the 50 caliber can still blast through more lightly armored vehicles, such as armored personnel carriers, and thus clearly through armored limousines. It is not true, nor has the Violence Policy Center ever claimed, that a 50 caliber round can penetrate the armor of a modern tank, despite occasional erroneous reports to that effect. What is true is that the 50 caliber can force tank crews to "button up," and well-placed shots could destroy or degrade certain external equipment and vision blocks on some tanks. Violence Policy Center, *Voting from the Rooftops: How the Gun Industry Armed Osama bin Laden, Other Foreign and Domestic Terrorists, and Common Criminals with 50 Caliber Sniper Rifles* (Washington, DC: Violence Policy Center 2001), 12, www.vpc.org/graphics/rooftop.pdf.

42. "Ma Deuce Still Going Strong," *Defense Industry Daily*, Mar. 5, 2012, www.defenseindustrydaily.com/ma-deuce-still-going-strong-03539.

43. U.S. Army, "Small Arms—Crew-Served Weapons," in *2012 US Army Weapon Systems Handbook*, 292, available from Federation of American Scientists, www.fas.org/man/dod-101/sys/land/wsh2012/index.html.

44. U.S. Patent No. 4,677,897, "Anti-Armor Gun," issued to Ronnie G. Barrett on July 7, 1987.

45. "The Big Gun: Controversy over the 50-Caliber Rifle," *60 Minutes*, CBS, Jan. 9, 2005.

46. "AP Centerpiece: Small-Time Tinkering Leads to Big-Time Guns, Sales by Tennessee Company," Associated Press, Nov. 25, 2005.

47. Barrett Firearms, "Ronnie Barrett, President and Founder of Barrett Firearms, Named as an Ernst and Young Entrepreneur of the Year for 2006," news release, July 5, 2006.

48. Robert H. Boatman, *Living with the Big .50: The Shooter's Guide to the World's Most Powerful Rifle* (Boulder, CO: Paladin Press, 2004), 6, 9.

49. Ibid., 6.

50. "Barrett's Shorty: The M82CQ Carbine," *Tactical Response*, Jan.–Feb. 2007.

51. "Army Approves Full Fielding of M-107 Sniper Rifle," Army News Service, Mar. 31, 2005, www4.army.mil/ocpa (accessed Apr. 1, 2005).

52. See the following reports, all of which are available on the Violence Policy Center's website, www.vpc.org: *Clear and Present Danger: National Security Experts Warn About the Danger of Unrestricted Sales of 50 Caliber Anti-Armor Sniper Rifles to Civilians* (July 2005); *The Threat Posed to Helicopters by 50 Caliber Anti-Armor Sniper Rifles* (Aug. 2004); *Really Big Guns: Even Bigger Lies* (Mar. 2004); *"Just Like Bird Hunting"—the Threat to Civil Aviation from 50 Caliber Sniper Rifles* (Jan. 2003); *Sitting Ducks—The Threat to the Chemical and Refinery Industry from 50 Caliber Sniper Rifles* (Aug. 2002); *The U.S. Gun Industry and Others Unknown—Evidence Debunking the Gun Industry's Claim That Osama bin Laden Got His 50 Caliber Sniper Rifles from the U.S. Afghan-Aid Program* (Feb. 2002); *Voting from the Rooftops: How the Gun Industry Armed Osama bin Laden, Other Foreign and Domestic Terrorists, and Common*

Criminals with 50 Caliber Sniper Rifles (Oct. 2001); *One Shot, One Kill: Civilian Sales of Military Sniper Rifles* (May 1999).

53. "The Football," GlobalSecurity.org, www.globalsecurity.org/wmd/systems/nuclear-football.htm (accessed Apr. 11, 2005).

54. Don A. Edwards, "Large Caliber Sniper Threat to U.S. National Command Authority Figures," Research Report Submitted to Faculty, National War College, Washington, DC, 1985, 20.

55. Ibid., 22–23.

56. James Bonomo et al., *Stealing the Sword: Limiting Terrorist Use of Advanced Conventional Weapons* (Santa Monica, CA: RAND Corporation, 2007), 64.

57. Ibid., 39.

58. Ibid.

59. Ibid., 39–40.

60. Ibid., 75.

61. Ibid., 76.

62. "No Recession for Firearms Industry," *New York Times*, Jan. 13, 1992.

63. Violence Policy Center, *Voting from the Rooftops: How the Gun Industry Armed Osama bin Laden, Other Foreign and Domestic Terrorists, and Common Criminals with 50 Caliber Sniper Rifles* (Washington, DC: Violence Policy Center, 2001), 35, www.vpc.org/graphics/rooftop.pdf.

64. Violence Policy Center, *Clear and Present Danger: National Security Experts Warn About the Danger of Unrestricted Sales of 50 Caliber Anti-Armor Sniper Rifles to Civilians* (Washington, DC: Violence Policy Center, 2005), 11, www.vpc.org/studies/50danger.pdf.

65. Two VPC monographs document the bin Laden transaction and the rebuttal of Barrett's story in great detail. See *The U.S. Gun Industry and Others Unknown—Evidence Debunking the Gun Industry's Claim That Osama bin Laden Got His 50 Caliber Sniper Rifles from the U.S. Afghan-Aid Program* (Washington, DC: Violence Policy Center, 2002), www.vpc.org/graphics/snipercia.pdf; and *Voting from the Rooftops*.

66. "Gunmaker Is Surviving Fight Against .50-Caliber," *Nashville Tennessean*, Jan. 9, 2005.

67. "What Did You Do in the War, Charlie?" *Dallas Morning News*, June 15, 2003.

68. "Charlie Wilson's Death Touches Murfreesboro," *Murfreesboro Post*, Feb. 14, 2010, www.murfreesboropost.com/charlie-wilson-s-death-touches-murfreesboro-cms-21921.

69. Violence Policy Center, *Voting from the Rooftops*, 28, fn q.

70. "Church Leader Fans Fires of Fear," *The Oregonian*, Dec. 10, 1989.

71. "Arms Seized in Spokane Snare IRA Suspect in Miami," *The Oregonian*, Jan. 19, 1990.

72. Violence Policy Center, *Voting from the Rooftops*, 30.

73. See Violence Policy Center, "Criminal Use of the 50 Caliber Sniper Rifle," www.vpc.org/snipercrime.htm.

74. Violence Policy Center, *Voting from the Rooftops*, 34.

75. Violence Policy Center, *Clear and Present Danger*, 10–11.

76. Office of Special Investigations, U.S. General Accounting Office, "Briefing

Paper: Criminal Activity Associated with .50 Caliber Semiautomatic Rifles," No. GAO/OSI-99-15R, presented to representatives of the U.S. House Committee on Government Reform, July 15, 1999, 3.

77. Copies of the court documents from which this data was extracted are in the files of the Violence Policy Center in Washington, DC.

78. Colby Goodman and Michel Marizco, "U.S. Firearms Trafficking to Mexico: New Data and Insights Illuminate Key Trends and Challenges," Working Paper Series on U.S.-Mexico Security Cooperation, Woodrow Wilson International Center for Scholars: Mexico Institute and the University of San Diego Trans-Border Institute, Sept. 2010, 171–72.

79. Violence Policy Center, "Vast Majority of Mexican Crime Guns Originate in U.S., New ATF Trace Data Reveals," news release, Apr. 26, 2012, www.vpc.org/press/1204atf.htm.

80. Goodman and Marizco, "U.S. Firearms Trafficking to Mexico," 167–68.

81. Ibid., 172–73.

82. For TCO operations in Africa and their use of Africa as a conduit to Europe, see, e.g., "Statement of Michele M. Leonhart, Administrator, Drug Enforcement Administration, U.S. Department of Justice, Before the House Committee on the Judiciary, Subcommittee on Crime, Terrorism, and Homeland Security, June 20, 2012," *CQ Congressional Testimony*, June 20, 2012; Alex Pena, "DEA: Mexican Drug Cartels Reach Further Across Africa," Voice of America, June 15, 2012, www.voanews.com/content/illegal-drugs-cartels-africa-mexico/1211572.html.

83. National Drug Intelligence Center, *National Drug Threat Assessment 2011* (Washington, DC: U.S. Department of Justice, 2011), 7.

84. Ibid., 11.

85. National Drug Intelligence Center, *The Economic Impact of Illicit Drug Use on American Society* (Washington, DC: U.S. Department of Justice, 2011), xi.

86. National Gang Intelligence Center, *2011 National Gang Threat Assessment: Emerging Trends* (Washington, DC: Federal Bureau of Investigation, 2011), 26.

87. Ibid., 43.

88. Ibid., 46.

89. "100 Gang Members ID'd Locally," *Murfreesboro Post*, Aug. 19, 2007.

90. "Indictments Show Gangs' Spread in Middle TN," *Nashville Tennessean*, Oct. 28, 2009; "Nine Charged in '07 Violence," *Murfreesboro Daily News Journal*, Oct. 28, 2009.

91. "Police Intensify Crackdown on Gang Activity," *Nashville Tennessean*, Jan. 27, 2012.

92. "The Big Gun; Controversy over the .50-Caliber Rifle," *60 Minutes*, CBS News Transcripts, Jan. 9, 2005.

93. Ibid.

94. U.S. Bureau of Alcohol, Tobacco, and Firearms (now U.S. Bureau of Alcohol, Tobacco, Firearms, and Explosives), "Firearms and Explosives Application Inspection Summary," for applicant Ronnie Gene Barrett, Jan. 20, 1984.

95. "Gunmaker Is Surviving Fight Against .50-caliber," *Nashville Tennessean*, Jan. 9, 2005.

96. Ibid.

97. Ibid.

98. David Hemenway, *Private Guns, Public Health* (Ann Arbor: University of Michigan Press, 2006), 1–3.

99. Jonathan Berr, "Gun Sales Go Soft as Economy Improves, Fears Subside," *Daily Finance*, Apr. 14, 2010, www.dailyfinance.com/story/company-news/gun-sales -go-soft-as-economy-improves-fearssubside/19437972.

100. Frank Hobbs and Nicole Stoops, *Demographic Trends in the 20th Century* (Washington, DC: U.S. Census Bureau, 2002), appendix A, table 1, "Total Population for the United States, Regions, and States: 1900 to 2000."

101. National Shooting Sports Foundation, "Small-Arms Production in the United States," in *Industry Intelligence Reports* (Newtown, CT: National Shooting Sports Foundation, 2007), 2, table, "25 Years Small-Arms Production (1980–2005)."

102. "Industry Hanging onto a Single Category," *Shooting Wire*, Dec. 17, 2008, www .shootingwire.com/archived/2008-12-17_sw.html.

103. "Man Accidently Shoots Wife," *Murfreesboro Daily News Journal*, Mar. 2, 2009.

104. Jeff Woods, "Oops! Handgun Permit Holder Shoots His Wife While Watching Cher on TV," *Nashville Scene*, www.nashvillescene.com/pitw/archives/2009/03/04/ oops-handgun-permit-holder-shoots-his-wife-while-watching-cher-on-tv.

5. The Third Wave: Beyond the Gunshine State

1. For a summary of Florida's national influence toward relaxation of gun laws, see "Florida: Fertile Ground for Pro-Gun Laws," *Miami Herald*, Mar. 27, 2012.

2. " 'Gunshine State': How NRA Attained Dominance in Florida," *Palm Beach Post*, Apr. 7, 2012 (Florida's "reputation as the 'Gunshine State' is rooted in politics, culture and the seemingly irresistible force of Marion Hammer"); Daniel Ruth, "More Madness in Gun-Happy Florida," *St. Petersburg Times*, op-ed, Jan. 21, 2011 ("But this is Florida, the Gunshine State, where barely conscious yahoos can arm themselves right up to the drool"); "Firearms Issue: Concealed Weapons Law Is Riddled with Flaws—Some Potentially Fatal," *South Florida Sun-Sentinel*, editorial, Feb. 1, 2007 ("Such is life in the 'Gun shine State' ").

3. "How Did Florida Get Its Nickname, the Sunshine State?" MyFlorida.com, Aug. 7, 2002, http://myflorida.custhelp.com/app/answers/detail/a_id/695/~/how-did -florida-get-its-nickname,-the-sunshine-state%3F.

4. "About NRA-ILA," NRA Institute for Legislative Action, www.nraila.org/ about-nra-ila.aspx.

5. Hammer won the "Roy Rogers Man of the Year" Award in 1985. "Marion P. Hammer," Winning Team, http://nrawinningteam.com/hammer.html.

6. "Pistol-Packin' Populace: Florida Up in Arms; Gun Sales Soar Under the State's New Liberalized Law," *Washington Post*, Oct. 22, 1987.

7. "Marion P. Hammer."

8. Text accompanying "Unified Sportsmen of Florida Membership Application," downloaded from www.scgaa.org/usf.pdf. According to the National Rifle

Association, "Ms. Marion Hammer, Executive Director of Unified Sportsmen of Florida, did business with the NRA in the amount of $122,000 for 2011." National Rifle Association of America, "Report of the Secretary to the Annual Meeting of Members," Apr. 14, 2012 (in the files of the Violence Policy Center).

9. See, e.g., "Marion Hammer," *St. Petersburg Times*, Aug. 11, 1996 ("The new president of the National Rifle Association glances up at several aides holding two-way radios, and growls, 'If one of those things squawks during my best sound bite, I'll kill you' "); and "Leader as Hard as Nails Is Taking Reins at N.R.A.," *New York Times*, Apr. 14, 1996 ("Instead of getting rid of all firearms to end the seething national debate over gun control, she wonders out loud, why not just 'get rid of all liberals?' ").

10. "Pistol-Packin' Populace."

11. One gun control activist in Florida, Joe Shutt, concluded exactly that in 1987. "The citizens of Florida got exactly what they deserved," he said. "Outgunned," *Miami Herald*, Sept. 27, 1987.

12. For an editorial summary of ALEC's role in state gun legislation, see Paul Krugman, "Lobbyists, Guns and Money," *New York Times*, Mar. 26, 2012.

13. See "National FOP President: Reject SB 1!!!" Fraternal Order of Police, Grand Lodge, www.fop.net/servlet/display/news_article?id=4515&XSL=xsl_pages/public_news_individual.xsl&nocache=8133486.

14. "Insanity Defense," 2011 Florida Statutes, sec. 775.027.

15. "Cop Killer Gets Death," *Tampa Bay Times*, Feb. 11, 2012.

16. "Man Held in Shooting Was Officer," *Tampa Tribune*, Aug. 21, 2009.

17. "Records Detail Slaying of Tampa Officer," *Tampa Tribune*, Dec. 9, 2009.

18. "Family Describes Delgado's Delusions," *St. Petersburg Times*, Nov. 10, 2011; "Fear Gripped Murder Suspect," *St. Petersburg Times*, Oct. 25, 2011.

19. "Family Describes Delgado's Delusions."

20. "Records Detail Slaying of Tampa Officer."

21. "Man Held in Shooting Was Officer."

22. "Doctor: Fears Drove Delgado," *St. Petersburg Times*, Nov. 11, 2011; "Records Detail Slaying of Tampa Officer."

23. "Accused Cop Killer's Life Revealed," 10connects.com, Dec. 8, 2009.

24. "Accused Police Killer: Who Is He?" 10connects.com, Aug. 21, 2009.

25. "Officer Was on His Back When Shot," *St. Petersburg Times*, Sept. 1, 2009; "Affidavit for Search Warrant," Sixth Judicial Circuit, Pinellas County, FL, filed Aug. 20, 2009, by Detective Salvatore J. Augeri, Tampa Police Department, and Detective Keith Johnson, Pinellas County Sheriff's Office.

26. "Guns Plus, Spring Lake, NC," NC Gun Owners forum, www.ncgunowners.com/forum/showthread.php?tid=477.

27. "Outfitting the Modern Sporting Rifle," *Shooting Industry*, Mar. 1, 2012.

28. "Officer Was on His Back When Shot"; "Police: Tampa Cop-Killing Suspect Is Ex-Officer," Associated Press State & Local Wire, Aug. 20, 2009.

29. See, e.g., "Officer Was on His Back When Shot."

30. See B. Gil Horman, "Kel-Tec PLR-16 5.56/.223 Semi-Automatic Pistol," *American Rifleman*, Mar. 1, 2012, www.americanrifleman.org/articles/kel-tec-plr-16-review.

31. "Family Describes Delgado's Delusions."

32. "Accused Cop Killer's Life Revealed."

33. "Fear Gripped Murder Suspect."

34. "Trial Begun in Officer's Killing," *St. Petersburg Times*, Nov. 5, 2011; "Dead Officer, Ranting Suspect," *St. Petersburg Times*, Dec. 9, 2009.

35. "Dead Officer, Ranting Suspect"; "Records Detail Slaying of Tampa Officer."

36. "Records Detail Slaying of Tampa Officer."

37. "Trial Begun in Officer's Killing"; "Records Detail Slaying of Tampa Officer"; "Officer Was on His Back When Shot."

38. "Records Detail Slaying of Tampa Officer."

39. "Officer Was on His Back When Shot."

40. "Prosecutor, Defender Lay Out Cases in Delgado Murder Trial," *Tampa Bay Times*, Nov. 5, 2011.

41. "Doctor: Fears Drove Delgado."

42. For a more detailed discussion, see Violence Policy Center, *Concealed Carry: The Criminal's Companion* (Washington, DC: Violence Policy Center, 1995).

43. "Outgunned."

44. Ibid.

45. Ibid.

46. Ibid.

47. Ibid.

48. "Counties, Cities Remove Their Gun Laws: Change in State Law," *South Florida Sun-Sentinel*, Aug. 7, 2011; "Update: Three Gun Bills Pass Senate," *Tallahassee Democrat*, Apr. 28, 2011.

49. "Counties, Cities Remove Their Gun Laws."

50. The new law decreed in relevant part, "Except as expressly provided by the State Constitution or general law, the Legislature hereby declares that it is occupying the whole field of regulation of firearms and ammunition, including the purchase, sale, transfer, taxation, manufacture, ownership, possession, storage, and transportation thereof, to the exclusion of all existing and future county, city, town, or municipal ordinances or any administrative regulations or rules adopted by local or state government relating thereto. Any such existing ordinances, rules, or regulations are hereby declared null and void." 2011 Florida Statutes, sec. 790.33, "Field of regulation of firearms and ammunition preempted."

51. "Counties, Cities Remove Their Gun Laws."

52. "Update: Three Gun Bills Pass Senate."

53. 2011 Florida Statutes, sec. 790.06, "License to carry concealed weapon or firearm."

54. "Pistol-Packin' Populace."

55. Ibid.

56. See "Executive Summary," in Violence Policy Center, *Concealed Carry*.

57. Violence Policy Center, "Concealed Carry Killers," Mar. 22, 2012, www.vpc .org/ccwkillers.htm.

58. These figures are regularly updated by the Violence Policy Center's Concealed Carry Killers project. The latest totals can be found at www.vpc.org/ccwkillers.htm.

59. See, e.g., "A Night Inside South Florida's Gang Wars," CBS Miami, May 7, 2012, http://miami.cbslocal.com/2012/05/07/a-night-inside-south-floridas-gang-wars.

60. "Pistol-Packin' Populace."

61. "Tinier, Deadlier Pocket Pistols Are in Vogue," *Wall Street Journal*, Sept. 12, 1996. For a recent assessment of this market, see Violence Policy Center, *"Never Walk Alone"—How Concealed Carry Laws Boost Gun Industry Sales* (Washington, DC: Violence Policy Center, 2012), www.vpc.org/studies/ccwnra.pdf.

62. "Industry Suffers Sales Slump, Manufacturer Sued, Hearings Support Gun Rights," *Shooting Industry*, May 1, 1995.

63. "The Defensive Handguns Your Customers Will Be Looking for in 1996," *Shooting Industry*, Mar. 1, 1996.

64. "Hot-Selling Handguns: Customers Are Still Buying! From Palm-Size Self-Defense Pistols, to Massive Hunting Revolvers, Dealers Are Making Sales!" *Shooting Industry*, Sept. 1, 2002.

65. "Self-Defense Profits! Increase Your Sales with a Product Checklist and a Solid Game Plan!" *Shooting Industry*, May 1, 2004.

66. "The Defensive Handguns Your Customers Will Be Looking for in 1996."

67. "Where's the Money? Handgun Accessories: Accessories Are Important to a Gun Dealer's Overall Profit!" *Shooting Industry*, Feb. 1, 2003.

68. "A Handful of Extras to Boost Your Handgun Sales," *Shooting Industry*, Feb. 1, 1994.

69. "Tactical Gear and Gun Clothing," *Shooting Industry*, Aug. 1, 2003.

70. "Preparing for Your Winter Gun Sales," *Shooting Industry*, July 1, 2006.

71. "Spring Handgun Marketing," *Shooting Industry*, June 1, 1996.

72. "Self-Defense Is Big Business," *Shooting Industry*, May 1, 2000.

73. "Pistol-Packin' Populace."

74. Florida Department of Agriculture and Consumer Services, Division of Licensing, "Number of Licensees by Type as of: 08/31/2012," Statistical Reports, Total Active Licensees Reports, available from http://licgweb.doacs.state.fl.us/news/reports.html.

75. "Taurus Today: The Bull Is Loose!: With a Whole New Center of Semiautomatics, the 'Revolver Company' from Brazil Has Quietly Reinvented Itself with a New Focus on Self-Defense Pistols Loaded with Features and Quality," *American Handgunner*, May 1, 2002.

76. Ibid.

77. "Taurus Edges Smith & Wesson for Manufacturer of the Year Award," PR Newswire, May 25, 2000.

78. "Taurus Today: The Bull Is Loose!"

79. "At Every Traffic Stop, Police Face the Prospect of Death," *Washington Post*, Nov. 22, 2010.

80. Steven Jansen and M. Elaine Nugent-Borakove, *Expansions to the Castle Doctrine: Implications for Policy and Practice*, National District Attorneys Association, undated report of a March 2007 symposium convened by the American Prosecutors Research Institute, 3.

81. Ibid., 5.

82. "Benjamin N. Cardozo," Historical Society of the Courts of the State of New York, www.courts.state.ny.us/history/cardozo.htm.

83. *People v. Tomlins*, 213 N.Y. 240 (1914), 243.

84. "Whaddayaknow," *Chicago Tribune*, Sept. 14, 1997.

85. *People v. Tomlins*, 213 N.Y. 240 (1914), 245.

86. "What Are My Legal Rights to Use Force If Attacked?" *Miami Herald*, Sept. 20, 2004.

87. "A Note from the Commissioner," Florida Department of Agriculture and Consumer Services, Division of Licensing, http://licgweb.doacs.state.fl.us/weapons/about.html.

88. "Gun Bill Could Mean: Shoot First, Ask Later," *Palm Beach Post*, Mar. 23, 2005.

89. See, e.g., "Deadly Force Bill Passes House: Next Stop for Measure Is Governor's Office," *Tallahassee Democrat*, Apr. 1, 2005 ("Rep. Dennis Baxley, the Ocala Republican sponsoring the bill . . . could not point to a case where a lawful gun owner shot someone in self-defense and was incarcerated").

90. Jansen and Nugent-Borakove, *Expansions to the Castle Doctrine*, 5–6.

91. "Gun Bill Could Mean: Shoot First, Ask Later."

92. "Self-Defense Bill Gets Early Senate OK; Legislative Session 2005," *Lakeland Ledger*, Mar. 23, 2005.

93. "Gun Bill Could Mean: Shoot First, Ask Later."

94. "15 States Expand Right to Shoot in Self-Defense," *New York Times*, Aug. 7, 2006.

95. "Gun Bill Could Mean: Shoot First, Ask Later."

96. "Florida Democrats Support Pro-Gun Law," Cox News Service, Apr. 5, 2005.

97. "Deadly Force Bill Moving on a Fast Track," *Palm Beach Post*, Mar. 24, 2005.

98. "Wild West Redux: 'Castle Doctrine' Law Opens Way to Shootouts," *Bradenton Herald*, Apr. 21, 2005.

99. "GOP State Representatives Stand Firm on Deadly-Force Bill," *Palm Beach Post*, Apr. 1, 2005.

100. "Self Defense Sells! Outfit Your Customers for Personal Protection!" *Shooting Industry*, June 1, 2005.

101. "Fla. Gun Law to Expand Leeway for Self-Defense; NRA to Promote Idea in Other States," *Washington Post*, Apr. 26, 2005.

102. "Florida Expands Right to Use Deadly Force in Self-Defense," *New York Times*, Apr. 27, 2005.

103. "Group: Think Tank Holds Legislative Sway," *Daily Press* (Newport News, VA) *Daily Press*, Mar. 18, 2012.

104. "Justifiable Killings Up as Self-Defense Is Redefined," *Washington Post*, Apr. 8, 2012; Center for Media and Democracy and Common Cause, "Connecting the Dots Between ALEC, Wal-Mart, the NRA, and the Florida Law Cited by Some to Immunize Trayvon Martin's Killer," Mar. 23, 2012.

105. "Napolitano OKs Eased Self-Defense: Burden of Proof in Killings Shifts to Prosecutors," *Arizona Daily Star*, Apr. 25, 2006.

106. "Self-Defense Unleashed! No Season on Sales, No Limit on Profits!" *Shooting Industry*, Feb. 1, 2007.

107. "Justifiable Killings Up as Self-Defense Is Redefined."

108. "Force Measure Goes Too Far," *South Florida Sun-Sentinel*, Apr. 7, 2005.

109. "Justifiable Killings Up as Self-Defense Is Redefined."

110. "Florida Expands Right to Use Deadly Force in Self-Defense," *New York Times*, Apr. 27, 2005.

111. "A Right Goes Wrong: Man's Killer Is Protected by Alabama Law," *Winston-Salem Journal*, Dec. 21, 2008; "U. Central Florida Valencia Student Enters Wrong Home, Shot," *University Wire*, Oct. 13, 2008.

112. "Justifiable Killings Up as Self-Defense Is Redefined."

113. "Now Everyone in Florida Can Play Dirty Harry," *Lexington Herald Leader*, May 15, 2005.

114. "Two Men Charged in Killing Declared Immune," *Tallahassee Democrat*, May 18, 2010.

115. "Fatal Shootings Test Limits of New Self-Defense Law in Texas," *New York Times*, Dec. 13, 2007.

116. "What Is Known, What Isn't About Trayvon Martin's Death," *Miami Herald*, Mar. 31, 2012.

117. "Evidence to Arrest Gunman Lacking, Sanford Police Say," *Orlando Sentinel*, Mar. 13, 2012.

118. "Scott Names Special Prosecutor to Investigate Trayvon Martin Shooting," *Tallahassee Democrat*, Mar. 23, 2012.

119. "Senator Forms Stand-Ground Panel: Democrat Chris Smith Says the Governor Is Taking Too Long to Convene a Task Force on the Gun Law," *Palm Beach Post*, Apr. 4, 2012.

120. "Justice Dept., FBI to Probe Black Teen's Death," *Washington Post*, Mar. 20, 2012.

121. "Trayvon Martin Shooter George Zimmerman Charged with Second-Degree Murder, Turns Himself In," *Miami Herald*, Apr. 11, 2012.

122. Ibid.

123. "Text of Probable-Cause Affidavit," *Orlando Sentinel*, Apr. 13, 2012.

124. "Trayvon Martin Shooter George Zimmerman Charged with Second-Degree Murder."

125. " 'Stand Your Ground' Hearing Sought," *South Florida Sun-Sentinel*, Aug. 10, 2012.

126. "Outcry Over Gun Law: Teen's Death Spurs Calls to Review Statute," *Palm Beach Post*, Mar. 21, 2012.

127. "Charges Reveal 'Stand Your Ground' Law's Flaws," *Orlando Sentinel*, Apr. 13, 2012.

128. See "About," *New American*, http://thenewamerican.com/about ("*The New American* . . . is published by American Opinion Publishing, a wholly owned subsidiary of The John Birch Society").

129. "Gun Rights on Trial," *New American*, Sept. 1, 2008.

130. *Barnes v. Indiana*, Indiana Supreme Court, May 12, 2011, 2.

131. Ibid., 4.

132. Ibid., 4–5.

133. Jacob Sullum, a writer for the libertarian *Reason* magazine, wrote that "the justices were eager to repudiate a straightforward extension of self-defense that struck them as an outmoded impediment to law enforcement." "Home Is No Castle When Cops Barge In," *Chicago Sun-Times*, May 25, 2011. Thomas R. Eddlem wrote in the right-wing magazine *The New American*, "The consequences of the *Barnes* decision, if citizens indeed have 'no right to reasonably resist unlawful entry by police officers,' are indeed frightening. If a policeman enters a man's house to rob him or rape his wife or daughter, under this decision, a citizen cannot legally resist him. Thomas R. Eddlem, "Indiana Supreme Court Says Citizens Can't Resist Rogue Police," *New American*, May 16, 2011, www.thenewamerican.com/usnews/constitution/item/7959-indiana-supreme-court-says-citizens-cant-resist-rogue-police.

134. "Young Vows to Fight Indiana Supreme Court Ruling on Police Entry; Will Author Legislation to Clarify Indiana law," PlusNews, May 18, 2011.

135. "Unlawful Entry Bill Has One Foot in the Door: House Approves Measure That Homeowners Could Stop Police," *Evansville Courier & Press*, Mar. 2, 2012.

136. "Ind. Lawmakers Weigh Home Entry Police Ruling," Associated Press State & Local Wire, Aug. 25, 2011.

137. "Unlawful Entry Bill Has One Foot in the Door."

138. "Indiana Police Groups Object over Right to Resist," Associated Press State & Local Wire, Feb. 23, 2012.

139. "Governor Signs Bill on Residents Resisting Police," Associated Press State & Local Wire, Mar. 21, 2012.

140. State of Indiana, "Protecting Those That Serve and Protect Us," news release, Mar. 20, 2012.

6. As Close as You Can Get Without Enlisting

1. "It Just Gives Me the Creeps to Be Here," *Denver Post*, Aug. 1, 2012; "Midnight Massacre, Aurora Theater Shooting: 'Our Hearts Are Broken,'" *Denver Post*, July 21, 2012.

2. "Midnight Massacre, Aurora Theater Shooting."

3. See "S.W.A.T., Special Weapons and Tactics," Los Angeles Police Department, www.lapdonline.org/inside_the_lapd/content_basic_view/848.

4. "'Controlled Detonation' Successful at Holmes' Home, Police Say," *Anderson Independent-Mail*, July 21, 2012.

5. Ibid.; "'It Almost Seemed like Fun to Him': 12 Dead, 59 Injured in Aurora, Colorado, Theater Shooting," *Fort Collins Coloradoan*, July 20, 2012.

6. "A Day of Tears and Twists in Colorado," *Washington Post*, July 23, 2012; "Gun's Magazine Shaped the Pace of Colorado Theater Massacre," *Los Angeles Times*, July 22, 2012, www.latimes.com/news/nation/nationnow/la-na-nn-theater-shooting-magazine-20120722,0,4212661.story; "Midnight Massacre, Aurora Theater Shooting."

7. "'It Almost Seemed like Fun to Him.'"

8. "Midnight Massacre, Aurora Theater Shooting."

9. "Interview with General Wesley Clark," *Crossfire*, CNN, June 25, 2003.

10. The catalog text is reproduced in Violence Policy Center, *The Militarization of the U.S. Civilian Firearms Market* (Washington, DC: Violence Policy Center, 2011), 11, www.vpc.org/studies/militarization.pdf. "Special Operations Forces (SOF) are elite military units with special training and equipment that can infiltrate into hostile territory through land, sea, or air to conduct a variety of operations, many of them classified. SOF personnel undergo rigorous selection and lengthy specialized training. The U.S. Special Operations Command (USSOCOM) oversees the training, doctrine, and equipping of all U.S. SOF units." Andrew Feickert, *U.S. Special Operations Forces (SOF): Background and Issues for Congress*, (Washington, DC: Congressional Research Service, 2012), 1.

11. The image is reproduced in Violence Policy Center, *The Militarization of the U.S. Civilian Firearms Market* (Washington, DC: Violence Policy Center, 2011), 19, www.vpc.org/studies/militarization.pdf.

12. Ibid., 5.

13. Ibid.

14. Ibid., 15; Tom Diaz, *Making a Killing: The Business of Guns in America* (New York: The New Press, 1999), 81–82.

15. Violence Policy Center, *Militarization of the U.S. Civilian Firearms Market*, 16; Diaz, *Making a Killing*, 77–78.

16. *Glock Annual 11* (New York: Harris Publications), inside cover. The publication is also known as *Glock Autopistols 2011*. The two are evidently the same, and are produced for and distributed by Glock—one directly distributed by the gun maker, the other through newsstand sales. See "What Is the 'Glock Autopistols' Magazine?" www.glockfaq.com/content.aspx?ckey=Glock_FAQ_General_Glock_Info#annual.

17. Violence Policy Center, *Understanding the Smith & Wesson M&P15 Semiautomatic Assault Rifle Used in the Aurora, Colorado, Mass Murder* (Washington, DC: Violence Policy Center, 2012), 2, www.vpc.org/studies/M&P15.pdf.

18. Ibid., 3.

19. Freedom Group, Inc., Annual Report for the Fiscal Year Ended December 31, 2011, 2.

20. Freedom Group, Quarterly Report for the Quarterly Period Ended June 30, 2012, 21.

21. Ibid.

22. Ibid., 22.

23. Freedom Group, Annual Report for the Fiscal Year Ended December 31, 2011, 11.

24. Freedom Group, Quarterly Report for the Quarterly Period Ended June 30, 2012, 6.

25. Ibid., 22.

26. "What Will You Do When the Zombies Come?" *Shotgun News*, July 20, 2012.

27. "Outbreak Omega 5 Sets Attendance Record & Breaks New Ground," AmmoLand.com, June 26, 2012.

28. "Capturing Success in 2012: Dealers Reveal Tactics for the New Business Year," *Shooting Industry*, Jan. 1, 2012.

29. "What Will You Do When the Zombies Come?"

30. Violence Policy Center, "New VPC On-Line Resource—*Cross-Border Gun Trafficking*—Uses Federal Court Documents to Detail Types of Firearms Favored, Methods Used, by Illegal Trans-Border Gun Traffickers," news release, July 11, 2012, www.vpc.org/press/1207indict.htm.

31. Violence Policy Center, *Target: Law Enforcement—Assault Weapons in the News, March 1, 2005–February 28, 2007* (Washington, DC: Violence Policy Center, 2010), www.vpc.org/studies/targetle.pdf.

32. "Stanton Heights," PittsburghCityLiving.com, http://pittsburghcityliving.com/neighborhoodProfile.php?neighborhood=Stanton%20Heights.

33. "Gunman Kills 3 Police Officers in Pittsburgh," *New York Times*, Apr. 5, 2009; "Stanton Heights."

34. "Slain Officer's Wife Thought He Was Safe in Stanton Heights Shootout," *Pittsburgh Tribune-Review*, Apr. 16, 2009; "Gunman Kills 3 Police Officers in Pittsburgh."

35. "Map of Pittsburgh Police Zones," www.pittsburghpa.gov/police/zones.htm.

36. "Poplawski Bought Guns Through Shop in Wilkinsburg," *Pittsburgh Post-Gazette*, Apr. 7, 2009.

37. Posted on Pennsylvania Firearms Owners Association website, Jan. 26, 2008; Anti-Defamation League, *Richard Poplawski Selected On-Line Postings, 2007–2009, Compiled by the Anti-Defamation League* (New York: Anti-Defamation League, 2009), 38, www.adl.org/extremism/Richard-Poplawski-Comments-Categorized.pdf.

38. "Poplawski Trial: Penalty Phase Day 1," *Pittsburgh Tribune-Review*, June 29, 2011.

39. Bill Morlin, "Racist Pittsburgh Triple Cop-Killer Gets Death," Hatewatch blog, Southern Poverty Law Center, June 29, 2011, www.splcenter.org/blog/2011/06/29/racist-pittsburgh-triple-cop-killer-gets-death.

40. "Poplawski Trial: Penalty Phase Day 1"; Morlin, "Racist Pittsburgh Triple Cop-Killer Gets Death."

41. "GED Definition," City College of San Francisco, www.cscsf.edu/NEW/en/student-services/matriculation_services/ged_center/ged_definition.html.

42. "Defense Rests in Penalty Phase of Pa. Cop Killings," Associated Press State & Local Wire, June 28, 2011.

43. Morlin, "Racist Pittsburgh Triple Cop-Killer Gets Death"; "Poplawski's Vest Barred Cop Bullets, DA Says," *Pittsburgh Tribune-Review*, June 23, 2011.

44. Morlin, "Racist Pittsburgh Triple Cop-Killer Gets Death"; "Who Is Richard Poplawski? A Portrait of Contrasts Emerges from Those Who Knew Officers' Accused Killer," *Pittsburgh Post-Gazette*, Apr. 12, 2009.

45. "Who Is Richard Poplawski?"

46. " 'Truly a Tragic and Very Sorrowful Day': Deadly Ambush Claims the Lives of 3 City Police Officers," *Pittsburgh Post-Gazette*, Apr. 5, 2009.

47. "SWAT Officers Feared Ambush After Poplawski Surrendered," *Pittsburgh Tribune- Review*, June 21, 2011.

48. "Poplawski Browsed Web Just Before Shooting," *Pittsburgh Tribune-Review*, June 24, 2011. "Created by former Alabama Klan boss and long-time white supremacist Don Black in 1995, Stormfront was the first major hate site on the Internet. Claiming more than 130,000 registered members (though far fewer remain active), the site has been a very popular online forum for white nationalists and other racial extremists." Southern Poverty Law Center, "Stormfront," www.splcenter.org/get-informed/intelligence-files/groups/stormfront.

49. "Poplawski's Murderous Roots Started Early: Trial Revealed Terrible Upbringing," *Pittsburgh Tribune-Review*, July 3, 2011. For a complete compendium of Polawski's Internet postings, see Anti-Defamation League, *Richard Poplawski Selected On-Line Postings, 2007–2009*.

50. "Who Is Richard Poplawski?"

51. "Poplawski's Murderous Roots Started Early."

52. "Suspected Killer Poplawski's Weapons Cache May Have Been Legal," *Pittsburgh Tribune-Review*, Apr. 7, 2009.

53. Martin Luther King Jr., "I Have a Dream," American Rhetoric, www.americanrhetoric.com/speeches/mlkihaveadream.htm.

54. Posted on Pennsylvania Firearms Owners Association website, Dec. 29, 2007, in Anti-Defamation League, *Richard Poplawski Selected On-Line Postings*, 37.

55. Posted on Pennsylvania Firearms Owners Association website, Nov. 24, 2007, in Anti-Defamation League, *Richard Poplawski Selected On-Line Postings*, 36.

56. "Alleged Cop-Killer Poplawski's 'Hit List' Surfaces," *Pittsburgh Tribune-Review*, Jan. 23, 2010.

57. "Poplawski's Murderous Roots Started Early."

58. "I've seen it. He showed it to me. He said 'Eddie, get one of these,'" Perkovic told a newspaper reporter. "Poplawski Bought Guns Through Shop in Wilkinsburg," *Pittsburgh Post-Gazette*, Apr. 7, 2009. Perkovic later pleaded guilty to charges of reckless endangerment and two DUI charges and was sentenced to six month's probation. "Lawrenceville Rifle Incident Nets 6 Months' Probation," *Pittsburgh Tribune-Review*, Mar. 10, 2010. He was arrested after an incident in which he argued with his girlfriend while holding a rifle and told her, "More cops should of died. I'm gonna go out and shoot more cops." "Alleged Cop-Killer Poplawski's 'Hit List' Surfaces."

59. Posted on Pennsylvania Firearms Owners Association website, Nov. 10, 2008, in Anti-Defamation League, *Richard Poplawski Selected On-Line Postings*, 39 ("I recently purchased some body armor from a friend").

60. "Poplawski's Vest Barred Cop Bullets, DA Says."

61. Posted on LetsGoPens website, Dec. 3, 2008, in Anti-Defamation League, *Richard Poplawski Selected On-Line Postings*, 40.

62. "Wilkinsburg Gun Shop Tied to 2000 Rampage Sold Arms to Poplawski," *Pittsburgh Tribune-Review*, Apr. 8, 2009; "Poplawski Bought Guns Through Shop in Wilkinsburg."

63. "Putting the Pieces Together: Clinton to Comment on Tragedy in Address," *Pittsburgh Post-Gazette*, Mar. 4, 2000.

64. "Weapon Used in Shootings Bought Legally: Store in Wilkinsburg Sold Gun

in 1982," *Pittsburgh Post-Gazette*, Mar. 3, 2000; "Wilkinsburg Gun Shop Tied to 2000 Rampage Sold Arms to Poplawski."

65. Posted on Stormfront website, in Anti-Defamation League, *Richard Poplawski Selected On-Line Postings*, 41. Right-wing conspiracy enthusiasts often use the acronyms SHTF (shit hits the fan) and TEOTWAWKI (the end of the world as we know it). Anti-Defamation League, "Extremism in the News: Richard Poplawski, the Making of a Lone Wolf," Apr. 8, 2009. www.adl.org/learn/extremism_in_the_news/ White_Supremacy/poplawski%20report.htm.

66. " 'Truly a Tragic and Very Sorrowful Day.' "

67. "Prosecution Rests: Jury Expected to Begin Deliberations Saturday Night," *Pittsburgh Tribune-Review*, June 24, 2011.

68. "Gun Guide Goes to 911 Operators: Procedures Changed in Wake of Shootings," *Pittsburgh Post-Gazette*, Apr. 9, 2009.

69. " 'Truly a Tragic and Very Sorrowful Day.' "

70. "Slain Officer's Wife Thought He Was Safe in Stanton Heights Shootout." Time and distance obtained by Google map search.

71. "911 Call Set Battle Plan in Motion: Accused Killer Put Bulletproof Vest On and Armed Himself," *Pittsburgh Post-Gazette*, June 25, 2011; "Prosecution Rests."

72. "Details of Stanton Heights Police Shootings Emerge in Filings," *Pittsburgh Tribune-Review*, Apr. 5, 2009.

73. "Prosecution Rests."

74. "911 Call Set Battle Plan in Motion."

75. Ibid.

76. "Details of Stanton Heights Police Shootings Emerge in Filings."

77. "911 Call Set Battle Plan in Motion; " 'A Day of Cowards and of Heroes': Prosecutors Present Graphic Evidence of 2009 Shooting Deaths of 3 Pittsburgh Police Officers," *Pittsburgh Post-Gazette*, June 21, 2011.

78. "Poplawski Trial Evidence Reveals a Bloody Scene: 900-Plus Rounds Found After Shootout," *Pittsburgh Post-Gazette*, June 23, 2011.

79. Ibid.; "Poplawski's Vest Barred Cop Bullets, DA Says."

80. "911 Call Set Battle Plan in Motion"; "Prosecution Rests"; "Medical Examiner: Kelly Shot Before Exiting His Vehicle," *Pittsburgh Tribune-Review*, June 20, 2011.

81. " 'A Day of Cowards and of Heroes' "; "Slain Officer's Wife Thought He Was Safe in Stanton Heights Shootout."

82. "911 Call Set Battle Plan in Motion."

83. "Medical Examiner: Kelly Shot Before Exiting His Vehicle."

84. "Poplawski's Vest Barred Cop Bullets, DA Says."

85. " 'A Day of Cowards and of Heroes.' "

86. "SWAT Officers Feared Ambush After Poplawski Surrendered."

87. " 'A Day of Cowards and of Heroes.' "

88. "Talks Key to Poplawski's Arrest: 'You Know, I'm a Good Kid, Officer.'— Richard Poplawski in His Surrender Call," *Pittsburgh Post-Gazette*, June 22, 2011.

89. Ibid.

90. "911 Call Set Battle Plan in Motion."

91. "SWAT Officers Feared Ambush After Poplawski Surrendered."

92. Ibid.

93. Ibid.

94. "85- to 190-Year Term Added for Poplawski: 'Let Him Recede into Distant Memory,' Prosecutor Urges at Sentencing for Convicted Police Killer," *Pittsburgh Post-Gazette*, Sept. 7, 2011.

95. For detailed discussions of the history of semiautomatic assault weapons, their marketing by the gun industry, and their impact in the United States, see the following reports, all of which are available on the Violence Policy Center's website, www.vpc.org: Violence Policy Center, *The Militarization of the U.S. Civilian Firearms Market* (June 2011); Violence Policy Center, *Target: Law Enforcement—Assault Weapons in the News, March 1, 2005–February 28, 2007* (Feb. 2010); and Violence Policy Center, *Bullet Hoses: Semiautomatic Assault Weapons—What Are They? What's So Bad About Them?* (May 2003).

96. A considerable amount of energy is expended in distinguishing between clips and magazines as ammunition-holding devices, as the NRA itself points out in the following sections from its online glossary of gun-related terms. Purists insist that the word *magazine* can be applied only to a self-contained spring-loaded metal box into which ammunition is loaded. The box may be an integral part of the gun or a free-standing box that is inserted into the gun. The purists restrict the term *clip* to devices, often metal strips but not spring-loaded boxes, to which ammunition is attached. The ammunition from these devices is stripped off the device and into the gun by a variety of means. The NRA's glossary seems not to endorse this orthodoxy. Thus, "Clip. A device for holding a group of cartridges. Semantic wars have been fought over the word, with some insisting it is not a synonym for 'detachable magazine.' For 80 years, however, it has been so used by manufacturers and the military. There is no argument that it can also mean a separate device for holding and transferring a group of cartridges to a fixed or detachable magazine or as a device inserted with cartridges into the mechanism of a firearm becoming, in effect, part of that mechanism." By comparison, "Magazine. A spring-loaded container for cartridges that may be an integral part of the gun's mechanism or may be detachable. Detachable magazines for the same gun may be offered by the gun's manufacturer or other manufacturers with various capacities. A gun with a five-shot detachable magazine, for instance, may be fitted with a magazine holding 10, 20, or 50 or more rounds. Box magazines are most commonly located under the receiver with the cartridges stacked vertically. Tube or tubular magazines run through the stock or under the barrel with the cartridges lying horizontally. Drum magazines hold their cartridges in a circular mode. A magazine can also mean a secure storage place for ammunition or explosives." "Glossary," NRA Institute for Legislative Action, http://nraila.org/glossary.aspx.

97. Chuck Taylor, *The Fighting Rifle: A Complete Study of the Rifle in Combat* (Boulder, CO: Paladin Press, 1984), 5.

98. Duncan Long, *The Terrifying Three: Uzi, Ingram, and Intratec Weapons Families* (Boulder, CO: Paladin Press, 1989), 104.

99. "W. Memphis Police to Carry Semiautomatic Rifles," *Memphis Commercial Appeal*, June 29, 2010.

100. Duncan Long, *Assault Pistols, Rifles and Submachine Guns* (Boulder, CO: Paladin Press, 1986), 1.

101. See "How Effective Is Automatic Fire?" *American Rifleman*, May 1980, 30.

102. Long, *Terrifying Three*, 11.

103. See, e.g., "Calico M-100 Rifle," *American Rifleman*, Jan. 1987, 60, 61 ("the full 100 rounds were sent downrange in 14 seconds by one flicker-fingered tester").

104. Ian Hogg, *Jane's Guns Recognition Guide* (Glasgow: HarperCollins, 2000), 302.

105. Taylor, *Fighting Rifle*, 4.

106. "History and Evolution of the M-16," *West Point Parents Club of Georgia Newsletter* 13 (Mar. 1999): 8.

107. Joe Poyer, *The M16/AR15 Rifle: A Shooter's and Collector's Guide* (Tustin, CA: North Cape, 2000), 13.

108. "Widening the Funnel," *Shooting Wire*, Sept. 30, 2009, www.shootingwire.com/archived/2009-09-30_sw.html.

109. For detailed discussions of the history of semiautomatic assault weapons, their marketing by the gun industry, and their impact in the United States, see Violence Policy Center, *Militarization of the U.S. Civilian Firearms Market*; Violence Policy Center, *Target: Law Enforcement*; and Violence Policy Center, *Bullet Hoses*.

110. "Nation Seeing Rise in Killings," *Augusta Chronicle*, May 16, 2012; "Even as Violent Crime Falls, Killing of Officers Rises," *New York Times*, Apr. 9, 2012.

111. "Nation Seeing Rise in Killings."

112. "Slain West Memphis Officers' Autopsies Released," *Arkansas Democrat-Gazette*, Aug. 27, 2010.

113. "Anti-System Father, His Son Killed Officers: Ohioan Denied the Validity of Banks, U.S. Government," *Arkansas Democrat-Gazette*, May 22, 2010.

114. "Contempt for the Law; the 'Sovereign Citizen' Movement, Blamed for the Deaths of Six Police, Is Now on the FBI's Radar," *Los Angeles Times*, Feb. 24, 2012. "This is a movement that has absolutely exploded," Mark Potok, a senior fellow at the Southern Poverty Law Center, told the *Los Angeles Times*. According to the center, more than a hundred thousand Americans have aligned themselves with the sovereign citizens movement.

115. "'Outgunned': Chief Says Officers' Pistols No Match for Heavily Armed Teenager," *Memphis Commercial Appeal*, May 26, 2010.

116. "Suspects Tied to Violent Group: Trail of Guns, Warrants Spans Several States Before LaPlace," *New Orleans Times-Picayune*, Aug. 18, 2012; "Two Deputies Are Shot and Killed in a Louisiana Ambush," *New York Times*, Aug. 17, 2012.

117. "7 Arrested in Probe of La. Deputy Shootings," Associated Press Online, Aug. 18, 2012.

118. "Suspects Tied to Violent Group."

119. "DA to Seek Death Penalty in Slaying of Penn Hills Officer," *Pittsburgh Post-Gazette*, Jan. 20, 2010; "Confession Details Events Leading to Police Officer's Killing," *Pittsburgh Post-Gazette*, Dec. 19, 2009; "Parolee Held in Cop's Death: Suspect in Penn Hills Killings Could Have Served Time Until February," *Pittsburgh Post-Gazette*,

Dec. 8, 2009; "Officer Responding to Pa. Home Disturbance Killed," *News Journal* (Wilmington, DE), Dec. 7, 2009.

120. For a more detailed discussion of the illusory effects of the 1994 ban, see Violence Policy Center, *Illinois—Land of Post-Ban Assault Weapons* (Washington, DC: Violence Policy Center, 2004), www.vpc.org/graphics/IllinoisAWstudy.pdf.

121. See, e.g., "Assault Rifles—Dirt Cheap . . . and Legal!" *New York Times*, May 24, 1998.

122. For a detailed discussion of the industry's ability to evade the 1994 law, see Violence Policy Center, *United States of Assault Weapons: Gunmakers Evading the Federal Assault Weapons Ban* (Washington, DC: Violence Policy Center, 2004), www.vpc.org/studies/USofAW.htm.

123. "Gold Star for DoubleStar," *Shooting Wire*, July 15, 2009, www.shootingwire.com/archived/2009-07-15_sw.html.

124. "New Products, New Political Twists," *Shooting Wire*, Oct. 15, 2008, www.shootingwire.com/archived/2008-10-15_sw.html.

125. "S&W Showing New and Announced Products," *Shooting Wire*, Aug. 19, 2009, www.shootingwire.com/archived/2009-08-19_sw.html.

126. "NSSF Announces Media Resources on 'Assault Weapons,'" *Shooting Wire*, Nov. 29, 2009, www.shootingwire.com/archived/2008-11-24_sw.html.

127. "Rebranding is the creation of a new name, term, symbol, design or a combination of them for an established brand with the intention of developing a differentiated (new) position in the mind of stakeholders and competitors." "Rebranding," Wikipedia, http://en.wikipedia.org/wiki/Rebranding.

128. "Ruger's Mini-14 Tactical Rifle," *Gun World*, Aug. 2010, p. 58.

129. Ibid.

130. "AR Pistols: The Hugely Popular Rifle Platform Makes a Pretty Cool Handgun as Well," *Handguns*, June–July 2011. One notable AR-15 pistol owner was the Boston mobster and FBI informant Whitey Bulger. In a July 2012 *Boston Herald* column on Bulger's guns, Howie Carr offered this characterization of Bulger's assault pistol by a "gun-loving friend" called Larry the Loner: "Good for bank jobs, small massacres and going out in a hail of bullets if you're also planning on taking out a few guys along with you." See "Old-Fashioned Piece-Nik," *Boston Herald*, July 1, 2012.

131. In files of Violence Policy Center, downloaded July 16, 2012.

132. "Century Arms' Draco AK 7.62 PDW," *Tactical Weapons*, Mar. 2011.

133. A Violence Policy Center website, Cross-Border Gun Trafficking: An Ongoing Analysis of the Types of Firearms Illegally Trafficked from the United States to Mexico and Other Latin American and Caribbean Countries as Revealed in U.S. Court Documents, contains indictments and other documents related to federal gun-trafficking prosecutions filed since 2006, primarily in the southwest United States. The site is available in both English (www.vpc.org/indicted.htm) and Spanish (www.vpc.org/indictedesp.htm). The website's data and legal documents offer a unique view of the weapons favored by Mexican traffickers not revealed in the trace statistics compiled by the Bureau of Alcohol, Tobacco, Firearms and Explosives (ATF)—the make and model of guns favored by traffickers and the methods by which they obtain such weapons. (While the site's findings offer a snapshot of the

types of firearms preferred by cross-border gun traffickers, the findings should not be viewed in any way as offering an estimate of the overall numbers of guns attempted to be trafficked from the United States into other countries.)

134. "SAS Gets Handgun That Can Shoot Through Walls," *Sunday Times* (London), July 7, 1996.

135. Dan Shea, "Military Small Arms Update: FN's FiveseveN System," *American Rifleman*, Nov.–Dec. 1999, p. 51.

136. Charles E. Petty, "FN Five-seveN," *American Handgunner*, Jan.–Feb. 2000, p. 54.

7. Top Secret: America's Guns

1. "18 Rounds in 5 Seconds: How Glock Became 'America's Gun,'" *Las Vegas Sun*, Jan. 17, 2012.

2. "Bio: Paul M. Barrett," *Bloomberg Businessweek*, www.businessweek.com/authors/1989-paul-m-barrett.

3. Paul M. Barrett, *Glock: The Rise of America's Gun* (New York: Crown, 2012).

4. See, e.g., excerpts from reviews on Amazon: "*Glock* is a riveting tale with masterful pacing and meticulous research. Paul Barrett knows his subject intimately, and it shows. . . . It's a must-read for anyone with an interest in handguns or the firearm industry or even American pop culture." (Cameron Hopkins, editor in chief, *Combat Tactics* magazine; *American Rifleman's* Industry Insider blog.) "With his customary insight and crystal-clear style, Paul Barrett has told the story of how a simple toolmaker from Austria came to be the dominant force in the manufacture and sale of pistols in the United States. . . . *Glock* is not at all just for the gun enthusiast. This book is for anyone concerned about the level of gun violence in America, and that should be all of us." (Richard Aborn, president, Citizens Crime Commission of New York City; former president, Handgun Control, Inc.) See www.amazon.com/Glock-The-Rise-Americas-Gun/dp/0307719936.

5. "Glock Targeted the Gun World," *Atlanta Journal-Constitution*, Jan. 29, 2012.

6. Examples of Internet marketing of Glock high-capacity magazines include the following: Glockstore.com offers "High Capacity Glock Factory Magazines," including "Super Hi-Capacity Magazines: Glock Factory 33 Rd 9mm / 22 Rd 40," http://glockstore.com/pgroup_descrip/3_Mags+&+Extensions/7272_High+Capacity+Glock+Factory+Magazines. Botachtactical.com also offers magazines, www.botachtactical.com/glockmagazines.html.

7. "Our Man at ATF," *Shooting Industry*, Jan. 2006, 97.

8. "NSSF Launches National Retailer Organization," *Shooting Industry*, Dec. 1, 2000.

9. "NAFR Retailer University Goes on the Road," *Shooting Industry*, May 1, 2002.

10. "The Shooting, Hunting, Outdoor Trade Show and Conference: The Industry Returns to Las Vegas as Manufacturers Unveil Hot New Products and Dealers Sharpen Their Business Skills!" *Shooting Industry*, Dec. 1, 2003.

11. See, e.g., Richard Feldman, *Ricochet: Confessions of a Gun Lobbyist* (Hoboken, NJ: Wiley, 2007).

12. Barrett, *Glock*, 260.

13. Bureau of Alcohol, Tobacco, Firearms and Explosives, Office of Strategic Intelligence and Information, "Mexico: Calendar Years 2007–2011 (as of Mar. 12, 2012)."

14. Ibid.

15. Ibid.

16. "Founded in 1976 as a nonprofit organization, the Police Executive Research Forum (PERF) is a police research organization and a provider of management services, technical assistance, and executive-level education to support law enforcement agencies. PERF helps to improve the delivery of police services through the exercise of strong national leadership; public debate of police and criminal justice issues; and research and policy development." See "About PERF," Police Executive Research Forum website, www.policeforum.org/about-us.

17. Police Executive Research Forum, "Gun Violence in America: One Week, Six Cities, and the Implications," Apr. 26, 2012, http://policeforum.org/library/crime/PERFPresentationonGunViolence.pdf.

18. The Michigan concealed-handgun-permit deaths reported by VPC consisted of five pending criminal homicides (including the murder of a law enforcement officer), four criminal homicide convictions, and twenty-nine suicides. Violence Policy Center, "Michigan Reports 38 Deaths, Including the Murder of a Law Enforcement Officer—VPC Concealed Carry Killers April Update," news release, May 1, 2012, www.vpc.org/press/1204ccw.htm.

19. Violence Policy Center, "Michigan Reports 38 Deaths."

20. According to the Congressional Research Service, "For FY2004 and every fiscal year thereafter, Congress has required ATF to include the following disclaimers in any published firearms trace reports: (a) Tracing studies conducted by the Bureau of Alcohol, Tobacco, Firearms and Explosives are released without adequate disclaimers regarding the limitations of the data; (b) The Bureau of Alcohol, Tobacco, Firearms and Explosives shall include in all such data releases, language similar to the following that would make clear that trace data cannot be used to draw broad conclusions about firearms-related crime: (1) Firearm traces are designed to assist law enforcement authorities in conducting investigations by tracking the sale and possession of specific firearms. Law enforcement agencies may request firearms traces for any reason, and those reasons are not necessarily reported to the Federal Government. Not all firearms used in crime are traced and not all firearms traced are used in crime. (2) Firearms selected for tracing are not chosen for purposes of determining which types, makes or models of firearms are used for illicit purposes. The firearms selected do not constitute a random sample and should not be considered representative of the larger universe of all firearms used by criminals, or any subset of that universe. Firearms are normally traced to the first retail seller, and sources reported for firearms traced do not necessarily represent the sources or methods by which firearms in general are acquired for use in crime." William J. Krouse, *Report for Congress:*

Gun Control Legislation (Washington, DC: Congressional Research Service, 2012), 28, n98.

21. Angela Jacqueline Tang, *Note: Taking Aim at Tiahrt, William & Mary Law Review* 50 (Apr. 2009): 1787, 1798.

22. Jay Dickey and Mark Rosenberg, " 'Senseless' Is Not Studying Gun Violence," *Washington Post*, July 29, 2012.

23. "N.R.A. Takes Aim at Study of Guns as Public Health Risk," *New York Times*, Aug. 26, 1995.

24. "In America: More N.R.A. Mischief," *New York Times*, July 5, 1996.

25. "Sway of N.R.A. Blocks Studies, Scientists Say," *New York Times*, Jan. 26, 2011.

26. Dickey and Rosenberg, " 'Senseless' Is Not Studying Gun Violence."

27. "18 Rounds in 5 Seconds: How Glock Became 'America's Gun,' " *Las Vegas Sun*, Jan. 17, 2012.

28. "Lawmen Uncover Clues in Girls' Killings: Counselors Will Be Available for Students Today," *Oklahoma City Oklahoman*, June 10, 2008.

29. "Weapon Info Is Clue," *Tulsa World*, June 12, 2008.

30. Ibid.

31. "Girls' Shooting Deaths Rattle Rural Oklahoma Town," CNN.com, June 10, 2008.

32. "Two Girls Found Slain Were Shot 13 Times," *Tulsa World*, Aug. 9, 2008.

33. "High Profile, High Pressure for Police," *Oklahoma City Oklahoman*, June 12, 2008.

34. "Weapon Info Is Clue."

35. Ibid.

36. Affidavit of Oklahoma State Bureau of Investigation agent Kurt Titsworth, filed in support of a criminal information, Okfuskee County District Court, *State of Oklahoma vs. Kevin Joe Sweat*, Case No. CF-2011-126, Dec. 9, 2011, 1–2.

37. Nebraska State Patrol, "Firearms," in *Crime Laboratory Manual*, https://statepatrol.nebraska.gov/crimelaboratorymanual.aspx. Marks on fired bullets (as opposed to shell casings) can also be examined. The barrels of modern guns have spiral impressions called *rifling*, which impart stabilizing spin to the projectile. "The raised portions of the rifling are known as lands and the recessed portions are known as grooves. When a weapon is fired, these lands and grooves cut into the bullet. . . . The impressions of lands and grooves remain on the bullet after it has been fired. Since rifling characteristics can differ from one firearm manufacturer to another, forensic firearm examiners can determine the type of weapon that fired a particular bullet by examining the impressions of the lands and grooves on the bullet. They examine the width, the number, and the direction of the twist of the lands and grooves. For example, a 9mm pistol made by one company might have a barrel with 6 lands and grooves that twist to the right and another company's 9mm might have 6 that twist to the left. In addition, the width of the lands and grooves may differ. Because each barrel will have imperfections left by the manufacturing process that will leave unique marks on a bullet, firearm examiners can determine whether a bullet recovered from a crime scene or victim was fired from a weapon

taken from a suspect. Georgia Bureau of Investigation, Division of Forensic Sciences, "Firearms Analysis, Basics of Firearms Comparisons," http://dch.georgia.gov/00/article/0,2086,75166109_75730713_81669662,00.html.

38. Affidavit of Oklahoma State Bureau of Investigation agent Kurt Titsworth, 1–2.

39. "The .40 at 20: Guns Magazine's 55th Anniversary Year Coincides with the 20th for the .40 Smith & Wesson Cartridge," *Guns Magazine*, Jan. 1, 2010.

40. For a more complete discussion of the rise of Glock in America, its aggressive tactics for selling to law enforcement, and its long-range strategy of reaching the civilian market through its sales to law enforcement, see Tom Diaz, *Making a Killing: The Business of Guns in America* (New York: The New Press, 1999).

41. "Holstering Heightened Firepower: Target Practice Provides Feel for New Weapon," *Atlanta Journal-Constitution*, Oct. 4, 2004. Terminal ballistics, also known as wound ballistics, is "the study of how a projectile behaves when it hits its target and transfers its kinetic energy to the target. The bullet's design, as well as its impact velocity, plays a huge role in how the energy is transferred." See "Terminal Ballistics," Hornady Manufacturing, www.hornady.com/ballistics-resource/terminal.

42. "Man Sought for Questioning as 2 Girls Buried," *Oklahoma City Oklahoman*, June 14, 2008.

43. "OSBI: No DNA Evidence Discovered," Associated Press State & Local Wire, June 8, 2009; "Man Sought for Questioning as 2 Girls Buried."

44. "OSBI Cuts Officers on Weleetka Killings," *Tulsa World*, Sept. 13, 2008.

45. Affidavit of Oklahoma State Bureau of Investigation agent Kurt Titsworth, 2.

46. "Murder Charges Filed in Weleetka Girls' Slayings," *Tulsa World*, Dec. 9, 2011,

47. Affidavit of Oklahoma State Bureau of Investigation agent Kurt Titsworth, 1–2.

48. Ibid., 2.

49. Ibid., 2.

50. Ibid., 3.

51. "Police Weapon Traced to Killings: Glock, Once City-Owned, Used to Kill Two Okla. Girls," *Baltimore Sun*, Dec. 18, 2011.

52. Affidavit of Oklahoma State Bureau of Investigation agent Kurt Titsworth, 2–3.

53. "Agents Use New Tools to Trace Handguns," Associated Press Online, July 14, 2007.

54. Ibid.

55. "After Gun Industry Pressure, Veil Was Draped over Tracing Data," *Washington Post*, Oct. 24, 2010.

56. "Firearms Measure Surprises Some in GOP," *Washington Post*, July 21, 2003.

57. *City of Chicago v. Department of Treasury*, 287 F.3d 628, 631 (7th Cir. 2002).

58. Colin Miller, "Lawyers, Guns, and Money: Why the Tiahrt Amendment's Ban on the Admissibility of ATF Trace Data in State Court Actions Violates the Commerce Clause and the Tenth Amendment," *Utah Law Review* 2010, no. 665 (2010): 665, 677.

59. Federal Judicial Center, "Bauer, William Joseph," in *Biographical Directory of Federal Judges*, www.fjc.gov/public/home.nsf/hisj.

60. *City of Chicago v. Department of Treasury*, 287 F.3d 628, 634 (7th Cir. 2002). Tiahrt and the NRA claimed that the lawsuits compromised eighteen ATF investigations. But ATF associate chief counsel Barry Orlow told the *Washington Post* that none was compromised. "After Gun Industry Pressure, Veil Was Draped over Tracing Data."

61. *City of Chicago v. Department of Treasury*.

62. Ibid.

63. See "Foreign Intelligence and Counterintelligence Records System," U.S. Department of Justice, www.justice.gov/nsd/foia/mis/ficrs.htm.

64. See, e.g., letter from Ronald Weich, Assistant Attorney General, U.S. Department of Justice to the Honorable Joseph R. Biden Jr., President, U.S. Senate, dated Apr. 30, 2012.

65. Angela Jacqueline Tang, "Note: Taking Aim at Tiahrt," *William & Mary Law Review* 50 (Apr. 2009): 1787, 1821.

66. "Police Union Lobbyist Has Influence in Gun Debate, Beyond," *Washington Post*, Dec. 15, 2010.

67. Compare National Fraternal Order of Police directory, www.fop.net/contact/index.shtml#Admin, and First Quarter 2011 Lobbying Report of Jim Pasco and Associates, filed under the Lobbying Disclosure Act of 1995.

68. "Philip Morris Is Client of Police Lobbyist Fighting Tobacco Bill," *USA Today*, May 12, 1998.

69. Ibid.

70. "Big Tobacco Quietly Tries to Grow Grass Roots: Industry's Sophisticated Lobbying Tactics Strike Some Critics as Deceptive," *Washington Post*, May 16, 1998; "Philip Morris Is Client of Police Lobbyist Fighting Tobacco Bill."

71. "Police Union Lobbyist Has Influence in Gun Debate, Beyond."

72. Ibid.

73. Chuck Canterbury, "Don't Buy Claims About Tiahrt Gun Amendment," *Wichita Eagle*, Apr. 24, 2007.

74. Chris W. Cox, NRA-ILA executive director, "Political Report: One on One with Chuck Canterbury, National President, Fraternal Order Of Police," www.nra publications.org/index.php/10217/political-report-16.

75. "Lawmakers Ask Feds to Share Info on Gun Trace Data That Could Help Find the Source of Guns," Associated Press, May 2, 2007.

76. "Police Union Lobbyist Has Influence in Gun Debate, Beyond."

77. See "Jim Pasco," CornerStone Associates, www.cornerstone-associates.org/biographies.html#jim_pasco.

78. See "Capabilities," CornerStone Associates, www.cornerstone-associates.org/capabilities.html.

79. See "Our Clients," CornerStone Associates, www.cornerstone-associates.org/clients.html.

80. "Endorsements: U.S. Senate and House, Kansas Governor," *Wichita Eagle*, July 25, 2010.

81. Miller, "Lawyers, Guns, and Money," 665, 681–82. See also "After Gun Industry Pressure, Veil Was Draped over Tracing Data."

8. Paper Tiger

1. Richard Lacayo, "Under Fire," *Time Magazine*, Jan. 29, 1990. A version dated June 24, 2001, is available at www.time.com/time/magazine/article/0,9171,153695,00 .html.

2. Josh Sugarmann, *NRA: Money, Firepower & Fear* (Washington, DC: Violence Policy Center, 2010), 14–15.

3. "Former Gov. Mitt Romney, R-Mass., Presidential Candidate, Delivers Remarks at the National Rifle Association Annual Meeting Celebration of American Values Leadership Forum," CQ Transcriptions, Apr. 13, 2012. The speech can be watched at "Mitt Romney at 2012 NRA Annual Meeting," YouTube, www.youtube .com/watch?v=J1qz_IPNOz0.

4. "Dem-Backed Crime Bill Has Romney's Support," *Boston Herald*, May 29, 1994.

5. "Romney Cries Foul, Dares Kennedy to Debate Him," *Boston Herald*, June 2, 1994.

6. "Herald Panel Grills Romney on Crime," *Boston Herald*, Aug. 1, 1994.

7. "Mitt Rejects Right-Wing Aid," *Boston Herald*, Sept. 23, 1994.

8. "Massachusetts to Enforce Strict Gun Safety Laws," *New York Times*, Apr. 3, 2000.

9. "Area Gun Lovers Mad at Romney," *The Republican*, July 10, 2003.

10. "Bay State Enacts Assault Weapons Ban," *Boston Globe*, July 2, 2004.

11. "Massachusetts Governor Shares Election Views," *Hannity & Colmes*, Fox News, Aug. 4, 2004.

12. The VPC defined states with "strong" gun laws as those that add significant state regulation in addition to federal law, such as restricting access to particularly hazardous types of firearms (for example, assault weapons), setting minimum safety standards for firearms and/or requiring a permit to purchase a firearm, and restrictive laws governing the open and concealed carrying of firearms in public. States with "weak" gun laws were defined as those that add little or nothing to federal restrictions and have permissive laws governing the open or concealed carrying of firearms in public. Violence Policy Center, "Massachusetts Has Lowest Gun Death Rate in Nation," news release, Apr. 23, 2012, www.vpc.org/press/1204death.htm.

13. Violence Policy Center, "Massachusetts Has Lowest Gun Death Rate in Nation."

14. "In farming, sheep dipping is a chemical bath given to sheep to rid them of bugs or disease or to clean their wool before shearing. In CIA terminology, sheep dipping means disguising the identity of an agent by placing him within a legitimate organization. This establishes clean credentials that can later be used to penetrate adversary groups or organizations. Similar to the real sheep, the agent is cleaned up so that nobody knows where he's been, kind of like money laundering." See "11 Terms

Used by Spies," HowStuffWorks, http://people.howstuffworks.com/11-terms-used
-by-spies.htm.

15. "Romney Assures Gun Rights Group of His Fealty," *New York Times*, Apr.
14, 2012; "Mitt Romney Announces Support of Conservationist Rob Keck," Targeted
News Service, Feb. 21, 2012.

16. Ibid.

17. "Former Gov. Mitt Romney, R-Mass., Presidential Candidate, Delivers Remarks at the National Rifle Association Annual Meeting Celebration of American
Values Leadership Forum."

18. Ibid.

19. James William Gibson, *Warrior Dreams: Violence and Manhood in Post-Vietnam America* (New York: Hill & Wang, 1994).

20. Ibid., 11.

21. The Free Congress Foundation was a pioneer in marshaling funds from the
ultra-wealthy and in coordinating the strategy of the far right's culture war against
the perceived excesses of liberalism. "FCF is also widely credited as one of the pioneer
organizations of political action through organized coalition. Before the foundation's
creation, established conservative leaders and institutions often acted individually in
accordance with their beliefs. FCF introduced conservatives to the 'coalition model,'
which trained them to coordinate—and time—their efforts with conservative members of Congress, journalists, think tanks and grassroots groups. This would ensure
that initiatives had broad-based coordinated support." See "History," www.freecon
gress.org/about/history. The late Paul Weyrich, who founded both the Heritage
Foundation and the Free Congress Foundation with the help of the beer magnate
Joseph Coors, was credited in a 1998 article surveying the right-wing landscape with
laying the foundation of the "new conservative labyrinth." This labyrinth "includes
dozens of national and regional think tanks (Heritage, American Enterprise, Free
Congress Research and Education, Cato, Hudson, Hoover, Manhattan, and so on),
legal centers (Institute for Justice, Washington Legal Foundation, and the Pacific, Atlantic, New England, and Southeastern Legal Foundations), magazines (*American
Spectator*, *Weekly Standard*), journals (*Public Interest*, *National Interest*), and an extensive communications and marketing capacity." Karen M. Paget, "Lessons of Right-Wing Philanthropy," *American Prospect*, Sept.–Oct. 1998.

22. Speech by National Rifle Association First Vice President Charlton Heston,
delivered at the Free Congress Foundation's 20th Anniversary Gala, Dec. 7, 1997,
available at www.vpc.org/nrainfo/speech.html.

23. For a detailed discussion of the NRA's alignment with the right-wing's
"movement conservatives," see Violence Prevention Campaign, *From the Gun War to
the Culture War: How the NRA Has Become the Pillar of the Right* (Washington, DC:
Violence Policy Center, 2002), www.vpc.org/graphics/gunwar.pdf.

24. "Call to Arms," *Washington Post*, Aug. 6, 2000.

25. Gibson, *Warrior Dreams*, 11–12.

26. Southern Poverty Law Center, "T.J. Ready," Intelligence Files, www.spl
center.org/get-informed/intelligence-files/profiles/jt-ready. "Ready was well known

as a friend of Russell Pearce, former president of the Arizona Senate, sponsor of the state's draconian anti-immigrant law, known as S.B. 1070. The two were photographed and videotaped together at a 2007 rally. When confronted by a reporter at the time, Pearce claimed he hardly knew Ready. But, in fact, as the *Phoenix New Times* reported, Pearce was part of a small group that had celebrated Ready's baptism into the Church of Jesus Christ of Latter-day Saints in 2003 or 2004. And when Ready was running for the Mesa City Council in 2006, Pearce called him a 'true patriot' in a video supporting his candidacy, according to *New Times*. The newspaper also reported that Ready described Pearce as a 'father figure' who had groomed him for a possible run for the Arizona state legislature."

27. "Police Believe Neo-Nazi Killed 4, Himself in Ariz.," *Salt Lake Tribune*, May 5, 2012.

28. Ibid.

29. Speech by National Rifle Association First Vice President Charlton Heston.

30. "Former Gov. Mitt Romney, R-Mass., Presidential Candidate, Delivers Remarks at the National Rifle Association Annual Meeting Celebration of American Values Leadership Forum."

31. Violence Policy Center, *Lessons Unlearned: The Gun Lobby and the Siren Song of Anti-Government Rhetoric* (Washington, DC: Violence Policy Center, 2010), 8, www.vpc.org/studies/lessonsunlearned.pdf.

32. "Call to Arms."

33. Becky Bowers, "In Context: Ted Nugent Saying If Obama Wins, 'I Will Either Be Dead or in Jail,'" PolitiFact, Apr. 19, 2012, www.politifact.com/truth-o-meter/article/2012/apr/19/context-ted-nugent-saying-if-obama-wins-i-will-be.

34. "Romney Goes on Offensive on Guns at NRA Gathering; Likely GOP Nominee: Obama Waiting for Second Term to Act," *Baltimore Sun*, Apr. 14, 2012.

35. "Biography—William J. Clinton," William J. Clinton Presidential Library and Museum, www.clintonlibrary.gov/_previous/bios-WJC.htm.

36. *NRA Action* (periodical of the NRA Institute for Legislative Action), Sept. 1992, www.saf.org/pub/rkba/wais/data_files/aphrodite/nraction0992 (accessed June 20, 2003); "Call to Arms"; brief item, Associated Press, Oct. 15, 1982.

37. "At Election Time, Political Mouths Open," Associated Press, Oct. 25, 1982; brief item, Associated Press, Oct. 15, 1982.

38. *NRA Action*, Sept. 1992.

39. "Call to Arms"; *NRA Action*, Sept. 1992.

40. "The NRA works with gun owners and lawmakers to enact preemption laws in the few states that still permit local ordinances more restrictive than state law. To ensure uniform firearm laws throughout your state and to guarantee equal rights for all, support statewide firearms preemption." National Rifle Association, "Firearms Preemption Laws," NRA-ILA Fact Sheet, Dec. 16, 2006, www.nraila.org/news-issues/fact-sheets/2006/firearms-preemption-laws.aspx. Clinton alluded to the NRA campaign in 1991, saying the issue wasn't one of gun control, but local government control, and was being pressed by the NRA. "They have a chart up on the wall in their Washington office with a check after the states that pass this," he said. "Showdown

Brews as Clinton, NRA Duel over Gun Bill," *Memphis Commercial Appeal*, Feb. 2, 1991.

41. "Clinton Vetoes Bill to Ban Local Laws on Gun Control," *Memphis Commercial Appeal*, Mar. 30, 1991.

42. *NRA Action*, Sept. 1992.

43. "Clinton Looking into System to Check Histories of Gun Buyers," *Arkansas Democrat-Gazette*, May 14, 1991.

44. For an overview of the rise and regulation of semiautomatic assault weapons, see Tom Diaz, *Making a Killing: The Business of Guns in America* (New York: The New Press, 1999), 120–34.

45. "Clinton Vetoes Firearms Bill: He Calls It 'Unwise Encroachment' on Local Governments," *Arkansas Democrat-Gazette*, Mar. 22, 1989.

46. "Governors Want More Road Money," *Arkansas Democrat-Gazette*, Feb. 6, 1991.

47. "Schaefer Lobbies Governors for U.S. Ban on Assault Weapons," *Washington Post*, Aug. 17, 1991.

48. Ibid.

49. See, e.g., "Assault Weapons Ban OKd—by the Narrowest of Margins; House Vote Is Stunning Victory for Clinton," *San Francisco Chronicle*, May 6, 1994; and "Brandishing a Loaded Symbol: Clinton Uses Police Officer's Death to Push Assault Weapon Ban," *Washington Post*, May 3, 1994.

50. "The Great Gun Divide," *National Journal*, July 22, 2000.

51. Paul Waldman, "The Myth of NRA Dominance Part I: The NRA's Ineffective Spending," *Think Progress*, Feb. 9, 2012, http://thinkprogress.org/justice/2012/02/09/421893/the-myth-of-nra-dominance-part-i-the-nras-ineffective-spending.

52. Christopher Kenny, Michael McBurnett, and David Bordua, "The Impact of Political Interests in the 1994 and 1996 Congressional Elections: The Role of the National Rifle Association," *British Journal of Political Science* 34 (2004): 331–44. "This article would not have been possible without the co-operation of Tanya Metaksa, former Director of the NRA's Institute for Legislative Affairs [*sic*], and Paul Blackman, research director for the NRA. Ms. Metaksa made available the data on ratings, endorsements and membership numbers used in the analyses. The authors accept responsibility for interpretations made with these data" (331fn).

53. Ibid., 332.

54. Waldman, "Myth of NRA Dominance Part I."

55. Ibid.

56. Kenny, McBurnett, and Bordua, "Impact of Political Interests," 344.

57. See "Swimming with Sharks," Indiana Public Media, http://indianapublicmedia.org/amomentofscience/swimming-with-sharks ("If remoras could talk, they would calmly explain something called commensalism—a relationship where one species benefits from proximity to the other without harming or helping the other species. In this case, remoras benefit from riding on sharks without doing the sharks any harm").

58. Waldman, "Myth of NRA Dominance Part I."

59. Tom Rosenstiel, "Political Polling and the New Media Culture: A Case of More Being Less," *Public Opinion Quarterly* 69, no. 5 (special issue 2005): 699, 706.

60. See, e.g., Christopher Preble, "Ike Reconsidered: How Conservatives Ignored, and Liberals Misconstrued, Eisenhower's Warnings About Military Spending," *Washington Monthly*, Mar. 1, 2011 ("Whereas the Keynesians thought this a useful by-product of a large national security state, Eisenhower viewed it as a threat to the Republic. Later scholars would call it the Iron Triangle."); and Shane Harris, "Own the Sky," *Washingtonian*, Nov. 2010 ("The Air Force would get its planes. Members of Congress would score a win for their constituencies and American industry. And Boeing would be saved. The three points in the 'iron triangle' of the defense business were all satisfied.").

61. Lawrence R. Jacobs and Robert Y. Shapiro, "Polling Politics, Media, and Election Campaigns," *Public Opinion Quarterly* 69, no. 5 (special issue 2005): 640. The "golden triangle" business is lucrative. A 1996 article in the *Chicago Tribune*, for example, detailed how Bill Clinton's "unpaid" political consultant Dick Morris, the pollsters Penn & Schoen, and the media firm of Squier Knapp & Ochs carved up commissions of $4.25 million from just one year's worth of "media buys." Morris's share was an estimated $1.5 million. This amount did not include fees for other services, nor did it include more commissions from later media buys. "Clinton's 'Unpaid' Political Whiz Is Really a Gun for Hire," *Chicago Tribune*, Aug. 25, 1996.

62. Rosenstiel, "Political Polling and the New Media Culture," 701.

63. Ibid., 701–3.

64. Ibid., 707.

65. Andrew Kohut, "But What Do the Polls Show?" Pew Research Center, Oct. 14, 2009, http://pewresearch.org/pubs/1379/polling-history-influence-policymaking -politics.

66. "Most of Fiske's Whitewater Legal Staff Won't Serve Under Starr," *Washington Post*, Aug. 31, 1994; "Fiske Ousted in Whitewater Case: Move Is Surprise," *Los Angeles Times*, Aug. 6, 1994.

67. "Democrats Glum About Prospects as Elections Near," *New York Times*, Sept. 4, 1994.

68. "Shooting in the Dark," *National Journal*, Feb. 12, 1994.

69. "Experts Doubt Effectiveness of Crime Bill," *New York Times*, Sept. 14, 1994.

70. "Prevention Plans Seen as 'Mush,'" *The Oregonian*, Aug. 16, 1994.

71. "'Pork' Attacked by GOP Predates Current Debate," *Washington Post*, Aug. 18, 1994.

72. Peter J. Boyer, "Whip Cracker," *New Yorker*, Sept. 5, 1994, 38–39.

73. "Crime Bill Fails on a House Vote, Stunning Clinton," *New York Times*, Aug. 12, 1994.

74. See "About the Committee on Rules," U.S. House of Representatives, www .rules.house.gov/singlepages.aspx?NewsID=1&RSBD=4.

75. "When the resolution comes to the floor, members who oppose the bill in any form may seek to defeat the rule, to prevent its consideration. Defeat of the rule effectively returns it (and the issue of scheduling the underlying bill) to the Rules

Committee." Charles J. Finocchiaro and David W. Rohde, "War for the Floor: Partisan Theory and Agenda Control in the U.S. House of Representatives," *Legislative Studies Quarterly* 33, no. 1 (Feb. 2008).

76. "Crime Bill Fails on a House Vote, Stunning Clinton."

77. "A President Staggering," *New York Times*, Aug. 12, 1994.

78. See, e.g., "Decision in the Senate: The Overview; Crime Bill Approved, 61–38, but Senate Is Going Home Without Acting on Health," *New York Times*, Aug. 26, 1994 ("Senator Joseph R. Biden Jr., the Delaware Democrat who is the author of the bill and is chairman of the Judiciary Committee, said Mr. Clinton's insistence on keeping its ban on 19 types of assault weapons 'was the ultimate leverage Joe Biden and George Mitchell had' in keeping the bill and that provision alive.").

79. " 'Pork' Attacked by GOP Predates Current Debate," *Washington Post*, Aug. 18, 1994.

80. "Crime Bill Fails on a House Vote, Stunning Clinton."

81. Boyer, "Whip Cracker," 39.

82. Ibid., 39–40.

83. "Playing on the Public Pique: Consultant Taps Voter Anger to Help GOP," *Washington Post*, Oct. 27, 1994.

84. "Decision in the Senate."

85. "Crime Bill Is Signed with Flourish: With Few Republicans at Ceremony, Clinton Urges More Cooperation," *Washington Post*, Sept. 14, 1994.

86. Ibid.

87. "GOP Offers a 'Contract' to Revive Reagan Years," *Washington Post*, Sept. 28, 1994.

88. "Playing on the Public Pique."

89. "Republican Contract with America," U.S. House of Representatives, in the files of the Violence Policy Center.

90. See "Taking Back Our Streets Act," U.S. House of Representatives, in the files of the Violence Policy Center.

91. "NRA's Answer to Gun Control: An Arsenal of TV Ads," *USA Today*, Nov. 3, 1994.

92. "Gun Control Backers Are Tuesday's Targets: NRA Shelling Out Big Bucks Across U.S.," *Washington Post*, Nov. 7, 1994.

93. See Violence Prevention Campaign, *From the Gun War to the Culture War*.

94. "A Historic Republican Triumph: GOP Captures Congress; Party Controls Both Houses for First Time Since '50s," *Washington Post*, Nov. 9, 1994.

95. "Tide of Anger Sweeps Out Foley: Speaker Personified Congress in a Year Voters Resented Capitol Hill," *Washington Post*, Nov. 10, 1994.

96. "Clinton Assumes Some Blame," United Press International, Nov. 9, 1994.

97. "Republican Gains and Obligations," *New York Times*, Nov. 9, 1994.

98. Ibid.

99. "Voters Tell Why They Switched," *Boston Globe*, Nov. 14, 1994.

100. "The Harder They Fall: Tom Foley So Busy Speaking He Couldn't Hear the Message," *Seattle Post-Intelligencer*, Nov. 13, 1994.

101. "Tide of Anger Sweeps Out Foley."

102. "House Republicans Target Crime-Prevention Programs Turnabout: GOP Expected to Go After Billions as Part of 'Contract,' " *San Jose Mercury News*, Nov. 26, 1994 ("Some conservatives and the National Rifle Association have called on the new Congress to repeal two gun-control measures enacted in the last year—the crime bill's ban on assault weapons and the Brady law's five-day wait for the purchase of a handgun—but that's not likely").

103. "Republicans Earn NRA's Ire over Assault Weapons: Overturning Ban Isn't a Priority," *Washington Times*, Jan. 19, 1995.

104. "Weapon Ban Repeal Slips off Calendar," *Cleveland Plain Dealer*, July 19, 1995.

105. "Second Amendment Blues: The NRA Under the Gun," *Weekly Standard*, Oct. 23, 1995.

106. "A Conversation with President Clinton," *Cleveland Plain Dealer*, Jan. 14, 1995.

107. "Gun Lobby Shot Down Democrats in Congress," *Cleveland Plain Dealer*, Jan. 14, 1995.

108. Ibid.

109. Rosenstiel, "Political Polling and the New Media Culture," 701.

110. "Terror in Littleton: The President; Clinton's New Gun Proposals Include Charging Parents of Children Who Commit Gun Crimes," *New York Times*, Apr. 27, 1999 ("Even Senator Tom Daschle of South Dakota, the Democratic leader, threw cold water today on a focus on guns. 'I'm not sure that gun legislation is what we need,' he told reporters.").

111. "Clinton's Shots at NRA Off Target," *Cleveland Plain Dealer*, Jan. 29, 1995. See also "Stuart Rothenberg," *Rothenberg Political Report*, http://rothenbergpolitical report.com/contributors/stuart-rothenberg.

112. "Clinton's Shots at NRA Off Target."

113. "Roger Stone on Political Scandals, Birthers, and What It's Like to Work for Richard Nixon," Stone Zone, May 22, 2012, http://stonezone.com/article.php?id=498.

114. "Clinton's Shots at NRA Off Target."

115. "Political Notebook: Kerrey Returns NRA's Fire; Romney Cashes In at 'Home,' " Associated Press, Oct. 24, 1994.

116. Paul Waldman, "The Myth of NRA Dominance Part III: Two Elections the NRA Did Not Win," *Think Progress*, Feb. 22, 2012, http://thinkprogress.org/justice/2012/02/22/430560/the-myth-of-nra-dominance-part-iii-two-elections-the-nra-did-not-win.

117. "Clinton, Playing the Early Bird, Is Lining Up Campaign-Style Ads," *New York Times*, June 24, 1995.

118. Ibid.

119. "Clinton's 'Unpaid' Political Whiz Is Really a Gun for Hire."

120. "Mutual Mistrust, Competing Goals for Clinton and Congressional Dems," Associated Press, Oct. 26, 1995.

121. "Beyond the Clinton Presidency," *New Republic*, Sept. 16–23, 1996.

122. "Why Democrats Dumped Gun Control," *Salon*, Apr. 18, 2007.

123. Celinda Lake, "Attention Democrats: It Wasn't Gun Stance That Lost Votes," *Charleston Gazette*, June 8, 2003.

124. Waldman, "Myth of NRA Dominance Part III."

125. Jules Witcover, "Bullets and Ballots," *Baltimore Sun*, May 16, 2003.

126. "Matt Bennett," Third Way, www.thirdway.org/staff/3.

127. "Jonathan Cowan," Third Way www.thirdway.org/staff/2.

128. "Jim Kessler," Third Way, www.thirdway.org/staff/5.

129. "Monster.com Owner Joins in Gun Control Battle," Associated Press State & Local Wire, Oct. 1, 2000. "I'm a parent not a politician. I'm fed up with the lack of common sense in this debate, and I know many other Americans feel the same way," McKelvey, a former board member of the Brady Organization, said in an AGS press release announcing the new organization. "I believe deeply that if we present the American people with the unbiased facts about this problem, they will help lead us to the most sensible solutions." "New National Centrist Organization, Americans for Gun Safety, Seeks to Re-shape Gun Debate by Emphasizing Gun Rights and Responsibilities: Group Commits Significant Support for Colorado and Oregon Campaigns to Close 'Gun Show Loophole,' Millions More for National Education on Gun Violence; Launches with Chapters in Twenty-Eight States," *PR Newswire*, Oct. 3, 2000.

130. "Monster.com Owner Joins in Gun Control Battle."

131. "New National Centrist Organization, Americans for Gun Safety."

132. Nicholas Confessore, "Control Freaks: Americans for Gun Safety Set Out to Give Gun Control a Shot in the Arm; Instead, They May Give It a Shot to the Head," *American Prospect*, Apr. 2002.

133. "A Way to Win Back Southern Democrats on the Gun Issue," *St. Petersburg Times*, May 5, 2002.

134. "NRA Takes Credit for Bush's Win: Democrats Sen. Miller Agrees," Associated Press State & Local Wire, Apr. 29, 2002.

135. "A Way to Win Back Southern Democrats on the Gun Issue."

136. Confessore, "Control Freaks."

137. "About Us," Third Way, www.thirdway.org/about_us.

138. "In Search of the Third Way: The Centrist Democratic Universe Just Got a Little More Crowded," *Roll Call*, May 2, 2005.

139. Ibid.

140. Waldman, "Myth of NRA Dominance Part III."

141. "2012 NSSF Congressional Fly-In Invitation," National Shooting Sports Foundation video, www.nssf.org/GovRel/FlyInVideo.cfm.

142. "Industry Leaders Meet with U.S. Senators, Representatives," National Shooting Sports Foundation, www.nssf.org/bulletpoints/view.cfm?Iyr=2012&b ISSUE=042312.HTM.

143. Miller is, among other things, director of the Environmental Analysis program and is the W.M. Keck Professor of Environmental Analysis at Pomona College in California, http://ea.pomona.edu/faculty/char-miller.

144. Char Miller, "The U.S. Senate Should Shoot Down the Sportsmen's Heritage Act—Now!" *Back Forty*, June 13, 2012, www.kcet.org/updaily/the_back_forty/

commentary/golden-green/the-senate-should-shoot-down-the-sportsmens-heritage
-act.html.

145. Ibid. For a detailed discussion of the environmental consequences of lead ammunition, see Violence Policy Center, *Poisonous Pastime: The Health Risks of Shooting Ranges and Lead to Children, Families and the Environment* (Washington, DC: Violence Policy Center, 2001), www.vpc.org/graphics/poison.pdf.

146. Violence Policy Center, *Blood Money: How the Gun Industry Bankrolls the NRA* (Washington, DC: Violence Policy Center, 2011), www.vpc.org/studies/blood money.pdf.

147. Ibid., 4–5.

148. Ibid., 8–10.

9. Solutions Worthy of the Name

1. "Cops: Guns, Not Gangs, Are Issue; Police Outline Plans to Quell Violence—Council Skeptic: 'What's Going to Change?' " *Seattle Times*, May 30, 2012.

2. "Day of Horror, Grief in a Shaken City: Gunman Kills Five, Fatally Shoots Self as Police Close In—Family Cites Mental Illness: 'We Could See This Coming,' " *Seattle Times*, May 31, 2012.

3. "A Brief History of Seattle Music," Seattle's Big Blog, Aug. 25, 2010, http://blog.seattlepi.com/thebigblog/2010/08/25/a-brief-history-of-seattle-music.

4. "Alt-Rock Hub, Purring with Jazz," *New York Times*, Aug. 29, 2010.

5. See "Cocktails and Bad Art at Seattle's Official Bad Art Museum of Art," Obscura Day, http://obscuraday.com/events/seattles-official-bad-art-museum-of-art.

6. "Police Laud 'Hero' in Seattle Shootings," Associated Press Online, June 1, 2012; "Day of Horror, Grief in a Shaken City."

7. "Police Laud 'Hero' in Seattle Shootings."

8. "A Life Full of Rage, a Shocking Final Act; Gunman's Father: 'We Let Him Down . . . We Let a Lot of Other People Down . . . , ' " *Seattle Times*, June 1, 2012.

9. Ibid.

10. Ibid.

11. "Police Release Details, 911 Calls of Café Racer and First Hill Killings, May 31, 2012," CHS Capitol Hill Seattle Blog, www.capitolhillseattle.com/2012/05/31/police-release-details-of-cafe-racer-and-first-hill-killings.

12. "Day of Horror, Grief in a Shaken City"; Casey McNerthney and Scott Gutierrez, "Police: Seattle Shootings Were Like an Execution; Suspect Gave the Finger to People Helping Woman Near Town Hall," Seattlepi.com, May 31, 2012, www.seattlepi.com/local/article/Police-Seattle-shootings-were-like-an-execution-3599900.php#ixzz1wfyCu8RU.

13. "Day of Horror, Grief in a Shaken City."

14. "Police Laud 'Hero' in Seattle Shootings."

15. "Josh Sugarmann, "Seattle Mass Shooting Latest by a Concealed Handgun Permit Holder," *Political Machine*, June 1, 2012.

16. Ibid.

17. David Hemenway, *While We Were Sleeping: Success Stories in Injury and Violence Prevention* (Berkeley: University of California Press 2009), 1.

18. David A. Sleet et al., "Traffic Safety in the Context of Public Health and Medicine," AAA Foundation for Traffic Safety (2007).

19. National Highway Traffic Safety Administration, "Traffic Fatalities in 2010 Drop to Lowest Level in Recorded History," news release, Apr. 1, 2011.

20. See Violence Policy Center, "Gun Deaths Outpace Motor Vehicle Deaths in 10 States in 2009," May 2012, www.vpc.org/studies/gunsvscars.pdf.

21. David Hemenway, *Private Guns, Public Health* (Ann Arbor: University of Michigan Press, 2004), 182.

22. Hemenway, *While We Were Sleeping*, 23.

23. "Motor-Vehicle Safety: A 20th Century Public Health Achievement," *Journal of the American Medical Association* 281, no. 22 (June 9, 1999): 2080–82.

24. "50 Years of Progress: Where Do We Go from Here?" presentation by Adrian K. Lund, president, Insurance Institute for Highway Safety at Edmund's Safety Conference: Truly Safe? May 24, 2011.

25. Hemenway, *While We Were Sleeping*, 9.

26. Ibid., 23.

27. Research and Innovative Technology Administration, "Households by Number of Motor Vehicles: 2010," Bureau of Transportation Statistics.

28. For a detailed history of gun ownership in the United States as reported by the General Social Survey conducted by the National Opinion Research Center at the University of Chicago, see Violence Policy Center, *A Shrinking Minority: The Continuing Decline of Gun Ownership in America* (Washington, DC: Violence Policy Center, 2011), www.vpc.org/studies/ownership.pdf.

29. Paul Waldman, "The Myth of NRA Dominance Part IV: The Declining Role of Guns in American Society," *Think Progress*, Mar. 1, 2012, http://thinkprogress.org/justice/2012/03/01/435437/the-myth-of-nra-dominance-part-iv-the-declining-role-of-guns-in-american-society.

30. Ibid.

31. "White House Backs Right to Arms Outside Obama Events: But Some Fear Health Talks Will Spark Violence," *Washington Post*, Aug. 19, 2009.

32. "The Tree of Liberty . . . (Quotation)," Monticello, www.monticello.org/site/jefferson/tree-liberty-quotation.

33. "White House Backs Right to Arms Outside Obama Events; But Some Fear Health Talks Will Spark Violence," *Washington Post*, Aug. 19, 2009; "Man Carrying Assault Weapon Attends Obama Protest," Associated Press Online, Aug. 18, 2009.

34. "White House Backs Right to Arms Outside Obama Events."

35. E.J. Dionne, "The Politics of the Jackboot," *Charleston Gazette*, Aug. 22, 2009.

Appendix A: A Week of Reported Gun Death and Injury in August 2011

1. "Army Releases ID of Ariz. Soldier Who Died on Base," Associated Press State & Local Wire, Aug. 4, 2011.

2. Clynton Namuo, "Driver Shoots Self After Head-on Crash," *New Hampshire Union Leader*, Aug. 3, 2011, www.unionleader.com/article/20110803/NEWS07/708039962; "Police: Lee Crash May Have Been Suicide Attempt," Associated Press State & Local Wire, Aug. 4, 2011.

3. Matt Johnson, "Satterlee Was 'On a Mission' When He Murdered Wife, Committed Suicide," *Vernon County Broadcaster*, Aug. 3, 2011, http://lacrossetribune.com/vernonbroadcaster/news/local/article_12a4aee0-be23-11e0-a3ab-001cc4c03286.html; "Sheriff's Deputy Was Told of Murder-Suicide Plan," *Wisconsin State Journal*, Aug. 4, 2011.

4. "Md. Mom Who Killed Son Agonized over School Costs," Associated Press, Aug. 8, 2011; "Md. Doctor Kills Son, Self," *Washington Post*, Aug. 4, 2011.

5. "Teens Dead in Apparent Murder-Suicide," *Cincinnati Enquirer*, Aug. 4, 2011; "Letter to Whites Raises Ruckus: Hate Group Targets Area of Black-White Homicide-Suicide," *Dayton Daily News*, Aug. 10, 2011.

6. "Alice Shooting Leaves One Dead, One Arrested: Altercation at Home Led to Homicide," *Corpus Christi Caller-Times*, Aug. 4, 2011; "The Grandson of a Famous Tejano Singer Shot and Killed," KIII News, www.kiiitv.com/story/15205673/the-grandson-of-a-famous-tejano-singer-shot-and-killed.

7. "Police Shoot, Kill Alleged Attacker," *Chicago Sun-Times*, Aug. 4, 2011; William Lee, "Man Killed by Police Was Frequent Target of Protective Orders," *Chicago Tribune*, Aug. 4, 2011, http://articles.chicagotribune.com/2011-08-04/news/chi-man-killed-by-police-frequent-subject-of-protective-orders-20110804_1_protective-orders-ellis-female-officer.

8. "Drive-by Victim IDd as Man, 18," *San Francisco Chronicle*, Aug. 5, 2011.

9. "Man Arrested in Connection with Phoenix Shooting," Associated Press State & Local Wire, Aug. 5, 2011; "Shooting Outside Phoenix Baskin Robbins Turns Fatal," Aug. 4, 2011, MyFoxPhoenix.com, in the files of the Violence Policy Center.

10. "Man Fatally Shoots Himself While Cleaning Gun," Associated Press State & Local Wire, Aug. 4, 2011; "Man Shoots, Kills Self While on Phone," *St. Petersburg Times*, Aug. 5, 2011.

11. "Shooting Suspect Remains in Jail," *Pensacola News Journal*, Sept. 29, 2011; "Sister Shot, Killed over Cellphone, Deputies Say," *Pensacola News Journal*, Aug. 5, 2011.

12. "Gun Suicide by Man, 23, Draws Crowd to Caddy," *Jersey Journal*, Aug. 6, 2011.

13. "Elderly Couple Found Dead in Murder-Suicide," *Charlotte Observer*, Aug. 7, 2011; "Elderly Couple Dead After Murder-Suicide," WCTI12.com, Aug. 4, 2011.

14. "Bronx Man Charged in Island Slaying," *Staten Island Advance*, Aug. 19, 2011; "Cops See Robbery Motive in Mariners Harbor Slay," *Staten Island Advance*, Aug. 6, 2011.

15. "Man, 19, Dead After Shooting in Perry South: Mother Shot Earlier, in Serious Condition," *Pittsburgh Post-Gazette*, Aug. 6, 2011; "Tragedy Again Hits Family in North Side," *Pittsburgh Tribune Review*, Aug. 6, 2011.

16. "Suicide Note Hints at Fear of Old Age," *Daily News of Los Angeles*, Aug. 10,

2011; "Sheriff's Officials Name Murder-Suicide Victims," *Daily News of Los Angeles*, Aug. 7, 2011.

17. "Man Shot with His Own Gun Is Charged," *St. Petersburg Times*, Aug. 7, 2011; "Fla. Man Wrestles Gun from ATM Robber," Associated Press State & Local Wire, Aug. 6, 2011.

18. "1 Killed, 1 Hurt in Shooting at Detroit Strip Club," Associated Press State & Local Wire, Aug. 5, 2011; "One Dead After Detroit Strip Club Shooting," CBS-Detroit.com, Aug. 5, 2011, http://detroit.cbslocal.com/2011/08/05/one-dead-after-detroit-strip-club-shooting.

19. "Man Dead After Squabble Between Tucson Neighbors," Associated Press State & Local Wire, Aug. 7, 2011; Pima Country Sheriff's Department, "Shooting-Update," news release, Aug. 6, 2011.

20. "State to Seek Death Penalty Against Ocala Man," Associated Press State & Local Wire, Nov. 16, 2011.

21. "Arrests Made in Labelle Street Shooting," *US State News*, Sept. 7, 2011; "1 Arrested in Eureka Death," *Florida Times-Union*, Sept. 8, 2011.

22. "California Briefing/Los Angeles; Motorist Is Fatally Shot," *Los Angeles Times*, Aug. 7, 2011.

23. Hillsborough County Sheriff's Office, "Deputies Respond to Shooting in Thonotosassa," news release, Aug. 5, 2011.

24. "Farmington Hills Woman Kills Husband, Then Herself," *Detroit Free Press*, Aug. 7, 2011; "Wife Kills Husband, Fatally Shoots Herself," Associated Press State & Local Wire, Aug. 7, 2011.

25. "Police & Courts: Man Shot in Stomach Is Listed in Fair Condition," *Buffalo News*, Aug. 7, 2011.

26. "DA Clears Pa. Officer in Fatal Shooting of Man, 21," Associated Press State & Local Wire, Dec. 22, 2011; "Officer Kills Fleeing Pedestrian," *Harrisburg Patriot News*, Aug. 7, 2011.

27. "Man Charged with Murder in Wife's Death," *St. Petersburg Times*, Aug. 8, 2011.

28. "Missing Prospect Heights Teen Found Dead," *Chicago Tribune*, Aug. 8, 2011.

29. "Woman Identified as Shooting Victim," *Pittsburgh Post-Gazette*, Aug. 8, 2011.

30. "Antioch Mother Killed, Aunt Wounded After Getting Caught in East Oakland Shootout," *San Jose Mercury News*, Aug. 6, 2011.

31. "Police ID Neb. Man Who Shot, Killed Woman and Self," Associated Press State & Local Wire, Aug. 8, 2011.

32. "Bradenton Slaying May Be Drug-Related," *Bradenton Herald*, Aug. 7, 2011.

33. "15-Year-Old Arrested in Slaying in West Fort Worth," *Fort Worth Star-Telegram*, Aug. 12, 2011; "Teen Shot and Killed at Fort Worth Apartment Complex," *Fort Worth Star-Telegram*, Aug. 7, 2011.

34. "5 Arrested in Teen's Death," *Petersburg Progress-Index*, Aug. 8, 2011; "Investigation Continues into Shooting That Killed Petersburg Teen, Injured Prince George Man," *Petersburg Progress-Index*, Aug. 15, 2011.

35. "Man in Standoff Killed Himself, Report Says," *Tampa Tribune*, Aug. 19, 2011; "Man Killed by SWAT Team Id'd," *St. Petersburg Times*, Aug. 8, 2011.

36. "19-Year-Old Second Suspect in Murder of Jersey City Man Turns Self in to Police," *Jersey Journal*, Aug. 10, 2011; "Shot Dead in the Back," *Jersey Journal*, Aug. 8, 2011.

37. "Police Investigating Shooting of Hospital Worker," *New Brunswick Courier*, Aug. 8, 2011; "Authorities: NJ Hospital Worker Shot to Death," Associated Press State & Local Wire, Aug. 7, 2011.

38. "Chester Police Investigate Man Found Shot to Death on Street," *Harrisburg Patriot News*, Aug. 8, 2011.

39. "San Diego Officer Dies: Suspect Left Suicide Note," Associated Press, Aug. 8, 2011; "Shooting Victim Is Improving, but Faces Months in Hospital," *San Diego Union-Tribune*, Aug. 10, 2011.

40. "Daily News' 'Wanted' Column Helps Nab Suspects," *Philadelphia Daily News*, Nov. 29, 2011; "Reward Offered for Suspect in Port Richmond Slaying," *Northeast Times Star*, Aug. 23, 2011, www.bsmphilly.com/northeast-times/3602-reward-offered-for-suspect-in-port-richmond-slaying.html; "2 Women Struck—1 Dead—in Daylight Shooting," *Philadelphia Daily News*, Aug. 8, 2011.

41. "Person of Interest Questioned in Fatal Shooting of 6-Year-Old Englewood Girl," *Chicago Sun-Times*, Aug. 9, 2011; "Child's Slaying Rattles Block: 6-Year-Old Girl Shot Dead After Summer Party Was Getting Ready to Start First Grade on Monday," *Chicago Tribune*, Aug. 8, 2011.

42. "Autopsy Notes Hint at Fury with Which Gunman Fired," *Cleveland Plain Dealer*, Aug. 11, 2011; "Copley Gunman Hunted Down His Victims, Including Boy, 11: He Let 5 Others Hiding with Child Leave Unharmed," *Cleveland Plain Dealer*, Aug. 9, 2011.

43. "Armed Victim Stops Attack," *St. Petersburg Times*, Aug. 9, 2011.

44. "Second Update: Second Suspect Arrested, Charged in Fatal Shooting at 8181 El Mundo," *States News Service*, Aug. 15, 2011; "Father and Son Attacked by Robbers in Houston," *Gulf News* (United Arab Emirates), Aug. 9, 2011.

45. "Man, 79, Receives Pretrial Release," *South Florida Sun-Sentinel*, Aug. 25, 2011; "79-Year-Old Charged in Shooting of Boy, 12," *South Florida Sun-Sentinel*, Aug. 9, 2011.

46. "Shooting Victim Expected to Recover," *Chicago Daily Herald*, Aug. 10, 2011; "Coroner: Shooting an Apparent Murder-Suicide Attempt," *Chicago Daily Herald*, Aug. 9, 2011.

47. "RI Man Injured in Accidental Shooting," Associated Press State & Local Wire, Aug. 8, 2011; Sara Bagwell, "Warren Police Log: Barton Street Shooting Victim Recovers, Five Arrested Last Week," *Bristol-Warren Patch*, Aug. 17, 2011, http://bristol-warren.patch.com/articles/warren-police-log-barton-street-shooting-victim-recovers-five-arrested-last-week.

48. "Teen, Mother Were Slain After a Grand Jury Date: Link to Previous Killing Investigated," *Boston Globe*, Aug. 19, 2011; "Woman, Teen Shot to Death in Roslindale: Residents Lament Surge of Violence," *Boston Globe*, Aug. 8, 2011.

49. "Couple Died from Gunshots to Head," *Orange County Register*, Aug. 12,

2011; "Buena Park Deaths a Murder-Suicide Case, According to Police," *Orange County Register*, Aug. 8, 2011.

50. "Dead Couple Had Rift," *Tampa Tribune*, Aug. 10, 2011; "Deaths Called Murder-Suicide," *St. Petersburg Times*, Aug. 9, 2011.

51. "Hollygrove Beset by 2 Shootings, One Fatal: 17-Year-Old Hit While Riding His Bicycle," *New Orleans Times-Picayune*, Aug. 9, 2011.

52. "Police: 4 Killed in Md Home in Murder-Suicide," Associated Press State & Local Wire, Aug. 8, 2011; "Four Dead in Anne Arundel Co. in Apparent Murder-Suicide: Two Adults, Two Teens Found Sunday in Brooklyn Park, Police Investigating," *Baltimore Sun*, Aug. 8, 2011.

Appendix B: Glock Handguns in the News: May 2011–April 2012

1. "Shooter in Murder-Suicide Reportedly Jealous," *Daytona Beach News Journal*, May 11, 2011; Susan Jacobson, "Cops: Man Who Killed Wife, Then Himself, Threatened to Shoot Her 2 Days Before," *Orlando Sentinel*, May 10, 2011, http://articles.orlandosentinel.com/2011-05-10/news/os-murder-suicide-domestic-violence-20110510_1_domestic-violence-linda-vasquez-louis-vasquez.

2. "No Charges Coming in Fatal Shooting near SanTan Village," *Arizona Republic*, May 21, 2011.

3. "Two Sentenced in Marysville Gang Shooting," *Marysville Appeal-Democrat*, June 14, 2011.

4. "Williams Enters Guilty Plea, Sentenced to 28 Years in Prison," *New Bern Sun Journal*, June 16, 2011.

5. "Son, 20, Charged in Father's Shooting," *Daytona Beach News Journal*, June 29, 2011.

6. "Miami-Dade Prosecutor Resigns After Brickell Key Shooting Incident: Police," *Miami Herald*, July 13, 2011.

7. "Brief: Plantation Cop Who Shot Himself to Receive Weapons Training," *South Florida Sun-Sentinel*, Sept. 10, 2011.

8. "Springs Man Killed in Apparent Murder-Suicide," *Colorado Springs Gazette*, July 14, 2011.

9. "Ex-Cop Claims Victim of Bias: Former Bethlehem Officer Was Suspended When Gun Discharged," *Eastern Express Times*, Aug. 3, 2011.

10. "Retired Dentist's Violent Death Leaves Unanswered Questions," *Florida Today*, Oct. 9, 2011; "Sheriff: Deputies Had No Choice but to Shoot Cape Canaveral Gunman," *Florida Today*, Aug. 6, 2011.

11. "Lewis Found Guilty of Manslaughter," *Jacksonville Daily News*, Sept. 2, 2011.

12. "Drug Raid in Delta Nabs 51: U.S. Says 4 Police Officers, Ex-sheriff Deputy Arrested," *Arkansas Democrat-Gazette*, Oct. 12, 2011.

13. "Woman Tied to Hankton Case Pleads Not Guilty: Feds Charge Her with Gun Purchases," *New Orleans Times-Picayune*, Nov. 18, 2011; "Women Play Backup Roles in Hankton Drama: Housekeeper Accused of Buying Guns for Revenge Killing Suspect," *New Orleans Times-Picayune*, Nov. 17, 2011.

14. "Trapped by a Man with a Gun and a Grudge: Co-worker Went Berserk After He Was Fired for Showing Up Drunk," *Houston Chronicle*, Oct. 28, 2011.

15. "Gang Member Gets Prison in Meth, Gun Case," *Biloxi Sun Herald*, Nov. 5, 2011.

16. "Bieger Pleads Not Guilty to Attempted Murder in Shooting of Fellow Lauderhill Cop," *South Florida Sun-Sentinel*, Dec. 22, 2011.

17. "Man Killed by His Own Concealed Weapon: He Was Trying to Adjust Gun, for Which He Had Permit," *Richmond Times Dispatch*, Nov. 18, 2011.

18. "NY Man Kills Man Who Dined with His Estranged Wife," Associated Press State & Local Wire, Nov. 17, 2011; "Friends' Murder-Suicide Shootings Stun Mahopac," LoHud.com, Nov. 17, 2011, www.lohud.com/article/20111118/NEWS04/111180334/Mahopac-Carmel-murder-suicide.

19. "Thanksgiving Get-Together Ends with Attack, Gun Shots, Authorities Say," *Naples Daily News*, Nov. 25, 2011.

20. "News Roundup," *San Antonio Express-News*, Dec. 8, 2011.

21. "Man Charged in '08 Killings of Two Girls Near Weleetka," *Oklahoma City Oklahoman*, Dec. 10, 2011.

22. "Man Charged with Murder in Wife's '08 Goodyear Death," *Arizona Republic*, Dec. 10, 2011.

23. "Maine Shipyard Gets a Load of Black Widow Spiders," *Lewiston Morning Tribune*, Dec. 14, 2011.

24. "Two District Men Sentenced to More Than 100 Years in Prison for Triple Homicide in Trinidad Area of Northeast Washington," Targeted News Service, Dec. 16, 2011; "2 District Men Convicted of 1st-Degree Murder While Armed in Triple Homicide in Trinidad Area of Northeast Washington," Federal News Service, Oct. 12, 2011.

25. "Mourners Gather to Honor Grapevine Shooting Victims," *Fort Worth Star-Telegram*, Dec. 29, 2011; "Christmas Massacre Was Premeditated: Police." NBC 5 Dallas–Fort Worth, Dec. 28, 2011, www.nbcdfw.com/news/local/Christmas-Massacre-Was-Premeditated-Police-136270438.html.

26. Bruce Vielmetti, "Man Is Charged in Slaying of Woman Found in Car," *Milwaukee Journal-Sentinel*, JSOnline, Jan. 6, 2012, http://m.jsonline.com/newswatch/136839548.htm.

27. Mark Wilson, "Extra Charge Filed Following Arrests in Shooting at Fast Eddy's," *Evansville Courier & Press*, Jan. 11, 2012, www.courierpress.com/news/2012/jan/11/no-headline–ev_shootingcharges; "Pair Charged After Shooting," *Evansville Courier & Press*, Jan. 7, 2012.

28. "Ex-Marine Gets 10-Year Sentence," *Raleigh News & Observer*, Jan. 11, 2012; and "Sentencing Memorandum," filed Jan. 03, 2012, in *United States v. Stephen Neal Greenoe*, U.S. District Court for the Eastern District of North Carolina, Western Division, Docket No. 5:10-cr-277-h.

29. "Police Digest: Boss Allegedly Pulls Gun on Worker Who Quit," *Providence Journal*, Feb. 8, 2012.

30. "Cops: Alleged Killer Waved Gun at Others: Enrique Manuel Ortiz Charged with Jan. 7 Shooting in Allentown," *Eastern Express Times*, Feb. 1, 2012.

31. "50-Year Grudge Led to Killing, Police Say," *Sioux Falls Argus Leader*, Feb. 3, 2012.

32. "Families of Women Killed by Sergeant Sue County," *The Oregonian*, Feb. 10, 2012.

33. "Police Report," *Memphis Commercial Appeal*, Feb. 24, 2012.

34. "New Haven Shooting Task Force Makes 1st Arrest," *New Haven Register*, Feb. 27, 2012.

35. "Dad Owned Gun Used in Shooting," *Tampa Bay Times*, Mar. 20, 2012.

36. "Stray Bullet Misses Woman's Head," *Stamford Advocate*, Mar. 22, 2012.

37. "Petaluma Man Charged in Wife's Killing Says She Threatened His Life," *Santa Rosa Press Democrat*, Apr. 24, 2012; "Trial Begins for Petaluma Man Charged in Wife's Killing," *Santa Rosa Press Democrat*, Apr. 2, 2012; Paul Payne, "Weapons Charge Added in Murder Case Against Husband," *Press Democrat*, Jan. 12, 2010, www.petaluma360.com/article/20100112/community/100119851.

38. "Williams Sentenced to 65 Years," *Washington Times-Herald*, Apr. 9, 2012; "Williams' Son: 'She Loved Me . . . with All Her Heart,'" *Washington Times-Herald*, Mar. 7, 2012.

39. "Where Is Gun Used in East Erie Homicide?" *Erie Times-News*, Apr. 26, 2012.

40. "Update: PA Shooting Leaves Child in Stable Condition," *Port Arthur News*, Apr. 25, 2012.

41. "Tip to City Police Came Monday from Woman's Boyfriend," *Pittsburgh Post-Gazette*, Apr. 25, 2012.

42. "Girl, 4, Is Left Alone by Murder-Suicide," *Tampa Bay Times*, Apr. 27, 2012.

43. "Wilton Man Charged with Firing Handgun During Argument," *Manchester Union Leader*, Apr. 27, 2012.

44. "Atlantic City Teen Smoking Pot Leads to Arrests and Recovery of Three Guns," *Press of Atlantic City*, Apr. 27, 2012.

CELEBRATING INDEPENDENT PUBLISHING

Thank you for reading this book published by The New Press. The New Press is a nonprofit, public interest publisher. New Press books and authors play a crucial role in sparking conversations about the key political and social issues of our day.

We hope you enjoyed this book and that you will stay in touch with The New Press. Here are a few ways to stay up to date with our books, events, and the issues we cover:

- Sign up at www.thenewpress.com/subscribe to receive updates on New Press authors and issues and to be notified about local events
- Like us on Facebook: www.facebook.com/newpressbooks
- Follow us on Twitter: www.twitter.com/thenewpress

Please consider buying New Press books for yourself; for friends and family; or to donate to schools, libraries, community centers, prison libraries, and other organizations involved with the issues our authors write about.

The New Press is a 501(c)(3) nonprofit organization. You can also support our work with a tax-deductible gift by visiting www.thenewpress.com/donate.